D1518203

DIVIDED LENSES

DIVIDED LENSES

Screen Memories of War in East Asia

Edited by Michael Berry and Chiho Sawada

University of Hawai'i Press

Honolulu

Publication of this book was made possible in part by a
subvention from the Walter H. Shorenstein Asia-Pacific Research
Center at Stanford University.

21 20 19 18 17 16   6 5 4 3 2 1

Library of Congress Cataloging-in-Publication Data

Divided lenses : screen memories of war in East Asia / Edited by
Michael Berry and Chiho Sawada.
pages cm
Includes bibliographical references and index.
ISBN 978-0-8248-5151-4 (cloth : alk. paper)   1. World War,
1939–1945—Motion pictures and the war.   2. Motion
pictures—East Asia—History—20th century.   3. Motion
pictures—Political aspects—East Asia—History—
20th century.   I. Berry, Michael, editor.
II. Sawada, Chiho, editor.
D743.23.D58 2016
791.43′658405425—dc23
2015025353

Contents

Acknowledgments

This volume evolved out of a conference and film festival organized by Chiho Sawada and Daniel C. Sneider at the Walter H. Shorenstein Asia-Pacific Research Center (Shorenstein APARC) at Stanford University during 2008–2009. This book is part of a multiyear Shorenstein APARC research project, Divided Memories and Reconciliation, that has explored the legacies of twentieth-century wars in East Asia by investigating the role of textbooks, then cinema and various forms of popular culture, and finally perspectives from elite opinion makers in China, Japan, South Korea, and the United States. The first volume in this series—*History Textbooks and the Wars in Asia: Divided Memories,* edited by Gi-Wook Shin and Daniel Sneider of Stanford University—was published in 2011. Other volumes include *Confronting Memories of World War II: European and Asian Legacies*, edited by Daniel Chirot, Gi-Wook Shin, and Daniel Sneider, and a forthcoming volume on elite opinion and wartime memory, co-authored by Gi-Wook Shin and Daniel Sneider. *Divided Lenses* marks the extension of the project that collectively revisits this period of war in East Asia from a variety of perspectives and approaches. The project has enjoyed the generous support of the Northeast Asia History of Foundation (NEAHF) of South Korea, the United States–Japan Foundation, and the Taiwan Democracy Foundation. In particular, we thank Yongdeok Kim, then president of NEAHF, and David Janes, director of foundation grants of the United States–Japan Foundation.

Many people have helped us guide *Divided Lenses* to completion and publication. Gi-Wook Shin and Daniel C. Sneider provided invaluable counsel throughout the entire process, and their talented staff members at Shorenstein APARC—especially Debbie Warren—offered indispensible administrative and logistical support for the conference and film festival. Furthermore, we are grateful to Clint Eastwood, who opened the conference with a thought-provoking dialogue with Robert Toplin, and to Barbara Bundy, founding executive director of the Center for the Pacific Rim at the University of San Francisco and former president of Dominican University, who hosted a preparatory workshop for this book project. Thanks are also due to Kyung Hyun Kim, Ban Wang, Scott Bukatman, Alisa Jones, and Jenny Lau for their contributions to the original conference and to Tony Williams for his support. Pamela Kelley of the University of Hawai'i Press and the external readers all provided valuable suggestions along the way, for which we are deeply indebted. We extend special thanks to all the contributors for their patience and responsiveness throughout the editorial process. Last but certainly not least, the editors acknowledge the loving support of our families.

M.B. & C.S.

Introduction
Divided Lenses

Michael Berry

The twentieth century was an era that witnessed massive social, political, and economic changes throughout East Asia. From imperialist expansions to dynastic contractions, civil wars to internal purges, and socialist revolutions to capitalist reinventions, the century opened with Japan and Korea struggling with the impact of Japanese imperialism, China on the verge of dynastic crisis, and Japan continuing its Meiji-era expansionism and development. By the early twenty-first century, though Korea is now divided with continued tensions between North and South, and conflicts linger between China and Japan regarding the Senkaku/Diaoyu Islands, East Asia has in many ways emerged as an economic powerhouse on the global stage with many predicting this to be the "East Asian century."[1] However, even as we move further into this new global era of unprecedented pan-Asian collaboration, in which national economies are increasingly intervolved with international investments and national identities are increasingly shaped by pop culture and global trends, the shadow of the past is still haunting. While Hong Kong gangster films, Japanese anime, Korean television dramas, and Chinese martial arts films freely cross cultural, linguistic, and national boundaries, hinting at a new integrated pan-Asian cultural space operating according to a logic not dictated by traditional national boundaries, historical scars remain difficult to heal. When thinking back to the inter-Asian conflicts that occurred throughout the twentieth century, the roughly two-decade period from 1931 to 1953 stands out in terms of the complex series of wars, battles, and protracted struggles that played out in East Asia.

This period encompassed conflicts such as the Second Sino-Japanese War (aka the Chinese War of Resistance) (1937–1945), the Pacific War (1941–1945), the Chinese Civil War (1945–1949), and the Korean War (1950–1953) as well as seminal events such as the Mukden Incident (1931), the Rape of Nanjing (1937–1938), the attack on Pearl Harbor (1941), the Battle of Iwo Jima (1945), and the bombings of Hiroshima and Nagasaki (1945). These make the two-decade span particularly important in terms of the lasting impact of the events on East Asia and the world. Decades later, these events, as translated into history, memory, propaganda, or sometimes dogmatic keywords, exert incredible power as Japan, China, Taiwan, and North and South Korea continue to navigate their side of complex intertwined paths and a shared historical burden. This volume attempts to explore these two decades of war in Asia by examining how the conflicts of 1931–1953 have been imagined, framed, and revisited using the lens of screen culture. Film, television, and other forms of visual culture have played a pervasive role in the way in which these conflicts have been remembered, commemorated, and reconstructed for later generations living in the shadow of these events. After all, the twentieth century was a time not only of the genesis of a new breed of technologically advanced modern warfare (which, in many cases, led to new forms of morally blind atrocities) but also of the exponential spread and reproduction of new visual technologies—photography, film, television, video games, and the Internet—all of which would have a profound impact on how wars are captured, remembered, recreated, and, in some cases, waged. At the same time, we should not forget Paul Virilio's lessons about the intertwined and mutually dependent relationship between war and representation. For Virilio, "the deadly harmony that always establishes itself between the functions of eye and weapon" includes not only the theatrical and cinematic aspects of war[2] but also the ways in which film can be transformed into a propagandistic arm of war itself. While much has been written about war and representation and, indeed, for many the notion of "film as representation" looms large in the realm of war films, we should also consider the alternative possibilities when it comes to war films: film as weapon, film as propaganda, film as resistance, film as testimony, film as experiment, and film as entertainment. The war film in East Asia comprises these and many other forms, and as we watch these celluloid and digital vestiges (or acts?) of violence, we should never forget to question the complex artistic, industrial, economic, and political forces behind these images.

In recent years, an increasing number of works have been published on how war trauma from this period has been recontextualized in popular film culture, especially studies highlighting national cinemas. In Japanese cinema and war studies, monographs on this period include Peter B. High's *The Imperial Screen: Japanese Film Culture in the Fifteen Years' War, 1931–1945* (2003) and Jerome F. Shapiro's *Atomic Bomb Cinema: The Apocalyptic Imagination on Film* (2002); in Chinese studies, scholars like Ban Wang have explored trauma in Chinese cinema,[3] often as related to the Second Sino-Japanese War, though, a full-length study of China's War of Resistance cinema has yet to appear in English;[4] Korean cinema scholars as well have likewise failed to publish a volume dedicated to Korean War cinema, although scholars like Suk-Young Kim have examined the intersection of film, theater, and performance in light of the Korean War and the ensuing national division, and Kyung Hyun Kim has examined South Korean cinema in light of the North Korean Other.[5] Scholarship on Hollywood cinema depicting this period is, by comparison, robust, with numerous filmographies and guides as well as many monograph-length studies on topics ranging from Hollywood's cultural construction of "defeated Japan" to "Orientalism and war."[6] But while the collective body of literature on this topic continues to grow, comparative studies remain few—notable exceptions being recent publications such as *Chinese and Japanese Films of the Second World War*.[7] To date, no single work has appeared that attempts to assemble perspectives of this period from the different, and often contesting, national cinemas involved—China, Japan, Korea, Taiwan, and the United States. The aim of *Divided Lenses: Screen Memories of War in East Asia* is to bring together scholars from different backgrounds, experts in their respective fields, to collectively explore the myriad ways in which this tumultuous historical period is manifested in film and other forms of visual culture. How cinema has attempted to come to terms with history can be greatly affected if not determined by artistic strategies and national policies. However, due to the primacy the image has taken on and the ways in which photographic images (even recreated and staged ones) can be used to persuade audiences and "authenticate" history, cinema wields a special power in contemporary culture. When different critical voices are collected, what emerges is not a unified view but a set of unique, disparate, and, in some cases, irreconcilable perspectives that illustrate the diversity and complex nature of not only the history represented but also the strategies employed to approach that history. It is our belief that only through these "divided lenses" can we even begin to understand the fractured and convoluted ways in which historical narrative shifts across different regions and generations and to unravel the cultural meaning of these perspectives.

In keeping with this approach, the editors have adopted a strategy that favors inclusiveness in terms of the time periods, regions, and media covered. Although the historical period at the core of this book is from 1931—with the Mukden Incident, which marked the beginning of Japanese aggression in China—to the end of the Korean War in 1953, our scope is not just visual representations produced during that period but subsequent attempts to revisit the events of that period. Only through this wider historical lens can we begin to see the myriad ways in which historical memory and cultural commemoration can be transformed in light of shifting political, economic, and historical changes. *Divided Lenses* comprises chapters by scholars of Japanese, Chinese, and Korean cinema, which are the regions most directly involved, however, we also include chapters on American perspectives, primarily through Hollywood films. This decision was made for several reasons: first, the key role of the United States in many of the conflicts discussed, particularly the Korean War and the Pacific War; second, the looming influence of Hollywood in the production of hundreds of big-budget war films. Hollywood has played a crucial part in the way in which this era has been viewed and serves as an essential counterpoint for the other national cinemas discussed in this volume. Finally, although feature-length war films are the central focus of most of the chapters, this volume embraces a broader notion of "screen culture," including television, documentaries, the Internet, and video games. Although these disparate categories each have their own unique historical and practical background, theoretical approaches, audiences, and methods of consumption, along with cinema, they have collectively helped to shape the emergence of a common visual culture and set of "screen memories" of an unforgettable period in East Asian history.

The book is divided into two parts: Part I, on "Screen Histories of War in East Asia," and Part II, on "Reading War Trauma." The five chapters in Part I take a broad historical approach, delineating how different regions and national cinema traditions have viewed various aspects of military conflict in East Asia. While firmly rooted in cinema history, these chapters also help contextualize the case studies offered in Part II. Many of these chapters provide historical introductions that should be suitable for students and scholars interested in how different regions' film industries have approached war films from this period and which recurrent themes and genres have dominated. At the same time, many of these chapters also focus on particularly important titles.

In Chapter 1, "War, History, and Remembrance in Chinese Cinema," Yingjin Zhang provides a general overview of the evolution and development of the war film genre in Chinese-language cinema from the Nationalist era (1911–1949) to the present, with examples drawn primarily from mainland China but also from Taiwan and Hong Kong. Zhang not only describes different modes and subgenres in war films but also examines opposing trends, from pacifist films to war hero films, from propaganda to entertainment, and even a discussion of directors whose work embodies the shift "from dissent to consent," such as Wu Ziniu and Feng Xiaoning. Along the way, Zhang frames his chapter by revisiting Jay Winter's notion of "collective remembrance" vis-à-vis the war film in China.

Although China's eight-year War of Resistance against Japan did not officially begin until 1937, most film scholars in China date the origins of War of Resistance cinema to 1931, shortly after the Mukden Incident, which marked the beginning of hostilities between China and Japan. This point deserves to be emphasized because the 1930s also correspond to the golden age of early Chinese cinema, and many of the great film masterpieces of this era are deeply tied to the war effort ideologically. In addition to classic war films, countless other Chinese-language titles from this period—*Little Toys* (*Xiao wanyi*, 1933), *The Highway* (*Dalu*, 1935), *Crossroads* (*Shizi jietou*, 1937), and *Street Angel* (*Malu tianshi*, 1937)—are all informed by deep anti-Japanese sentiment related to the resistance movement. Even a film like Fei Mu's *Blood on Wolf Mountain* (*Langshan diexueji*, 1936), which told of a rustic village besieged by wolf attacks, was widely interpreted as a scathing allegory about Japan's intrusion into China, just as his later masterpiece *Spring in a Small Town* (*Xiaocheng zhi chun*, 1948) is often read as a meditation on postwar pathos. After 1949, resistance war films continued to be a robust part of Mao Zedong's "Red Cinema" and even a cornerstone work of Fifth-Generation films in the 1980s, Zhang Yimou's explosive debut *Red Sorghum* (*Hong gaoliang*, 1987), used the Second Sino-Japanese War as a backdrop. Today, the war continues to serve as inspiration for countless films as well as an increasingly long roster of television miniseries.

From Zhang's sweeping overview, we move on to Wenchi Lin's discussion of the war film as it is manifested in Taiwan. Chapter 2, "Of Female Spies and National Heroes: A Brief History of Anti-Japanese Films in Taiwan from the 1950s to the 1970s," begins with a comprehensive introduction to the history of anti-Japanese cinema in Taiwan from 1949, when Japanese colonial rule over Taiwan ended, until the 1960s. Because of shared cold war political interests (pro-American, anti-communist stance) in Taiwan and Japan and the fact that all three major film studios in Taiwan at the time were state sponsored, there was a curious lack of films willing to address the complex role that Taiwan played during the Pacific War. But Lin excavates some of the overlooked cinematic examples of Taiwanese war films from this period, from early documentary films to a now-lost 1957 film about the Musha Incident, a violent uprising led by Taiwanese aboriginal tribes against the Japanese in 1930. Lin shows that the way in which the Second Sino-Japanese War eventually found its way back into mainstream films came about somewhat surreptitiously via the genre of popular 007-style spy thrillers. Eventually, further shifts in Taiwan's political environment led to a more robust attempt to commemorate the war—as a means of building patriotic sentiment—through a series of big-budget state-sponsored war films centering on famous battles and illustrious generals.

While the Chinese terms for the body of Taiwan films examined often fall under the umbrella of "anti-Japanese war films" (*kangri zhanzheng dianying/duiri kangzhan dianying*), Lin argues that this is often a misnomer. Although the films examined are set against the Second Sino-Japanese War, "Japan's ambition of invasion and inhuman cruelty are not portrayed or condemned," leaving very little in the films that is ideologically "anti-Japanese." The Japanese and the war simply serve as convenient plot devices and backdrops for genre thrillers and spy films, whose central goal is entertainment. Lin even suggests that later nationalistic war films like *The Everlasting Glory* (*Yinglie qianqui*, 1974) and *Eight Hundred Heroes* (*Babai zhuangshi*, 1975) also follow a similar formula of downplaying actual anti-Japanese sentiment. Lin proposes instead the alternate and more neutral term "resistance war films" (*kangzhan dianying*) to categorize this body of films.[8] But even more interesting is the set of larger questions that Lin's probe opens up. When facing taxological questions of cinematic form and genre, what actually makes a war film a war film? How do we differentiate "war films" and other genre pictures that simply use war as a backdrop for another story? Do we hold these different forms to the same artistic and ethical standards? Are entertainment-based productions (like female spy thrillers) somehow exempt from the ideological and moral scrutiny to which other "serious" films are held up? These questions resonate with later chapters by Wong and

Berry on other cinematic touchstones of the Sino-Japanese War concerning "comfort women" and the Nanjing Massacre.

Whereas the Taiwan war film (along with the general trend of the entire local film industry) has been in a state of decline since the 1980s, that has certainly not been the case with South Korea. In South Korea, the war film has emerged as one of the most dominant commercial types of multiplex blockbusters. In Chapter 3, "The 'Division Blockbuster' in South Korea: The Evolution of Cinematic Representations of War and Division," Hyangjin Lee presents a snapshot of three distinct periods in the history of South Korean cinema. Beginning with an overview of state censorship and the burgeoning democracy movement in the 1980s, Lee goes on to discuss "nationalism in the arena of cultural consumption" during the increasingly globalized 1990s, before finally tackling the innovation of a new mode of war films that she describes as a "division blockbuster." With the Korean War and the subsequent national division between North and South Korea emerging as the predominant focus, theme, and often obsession of these films, the traumatic memory of the war continues to fuel a rich variety of commercial genre forms, from mainstream war films (*Taegukgi: The Brotherhood of War*) and spy thrillers (*Shiri, The Secret Reunion*) to horror films (*The Guard Post*).

In Chapter 4, "Under the Flag of the Rising Sun: Imagining the Pacific War in the Japanese Cinema," David Desser offers an impressive survey of Japanese variations on the "World War II combat film" genre, spanning from the 1930s to the first decade of the twenty-first century, with close readings focused on war-themed films of the 1950s and 1960s: notably, *Harp of Burma* (*Biruma no tategoto*, 1956), *Fires on the Plain* (*Nobi*, 1959), *The Human Condition* trilogy (*Ningen no jōken*, 1959–61), *Hoodlum Soldier* (*Heitai yakuza*, 1965), and *Red Angel* (*Akai tenshi*, 1966). Even among these essentially antiwar works, Desser discerns a duality or tension between representations of Japan as perpetrator and Japan as victim. To further explore this tension and the question of how postwar Japanese cinema has grappled, or not, with larger public debates over Japan's war responsibility, the second half of his chapter scrutinizes cinematic representations of four recurring icons that have generated a great deal of debate: comfort women, the Nanjing Massacre, Yasukuni shrine, and the atom bomb. As Desser navigates this rich body of films, which alternately depict the war, allegorize the war, and deal with the traumatic aftereffects of war, the tendency toward "victim consciousness" often seems to weigh just as heavily as the "burden of history." Between revisionist discourses of denial, Japan's own narratives about wartime (and postwar) suffering, and the narrative urge to extract lofty humanistic lessons from Japanese wartime aggression, Japanese films about the war continue to elicit controversy both within Japan and in the countries that once suffered as involuntary parts of its "co-prosperity sphere."

While Desser's chapter is devoted to Japanese feature films about the war, in Chapter 5, Kyu Hyun Kim extends this narrative by examining an alternative page in Japanese popular visual representation of war—manga and anime. Over the course of the past three decades, manga and anime have emerged as two of Japan's leading modes of entertainment and among their most popular cultural exports, but how have these media navigated the often-perilous terrain of war memory? That is the question that Kim takes up in his chapter, "Japanese Manga and Anime on the Asia-Pacific War Experience." Kim provides a rich overview of the diverse array of themes, genres, and styles through which the Second Sino-Japanese War and the Pacific War have been reimagined in the sometimes-interconnected worlds of manga and anime. Beginning with brief historical introduction to the history of representation in this area, the chapter goes on to provide overviews of the work of Mizuki Shigeru, Matsumoto Leiji, Tezuka Osamu, Yamagami Tatsuhiko, and Kobayashi Yoshinori, highlighting a startling diversity in themes, genres, and ideologies when it comes to Japanese manga/anime artists attempt to reconfigure one of the most violent, traumatic, and, for some, shameful pages in modern history using a style of representation that is sometimes thought of as juvenile, lowbrow, and escapist. Kim is able to convincingly demonstrate just how keenly engaged artists were in attempting to use science fiction, avant-garde techniques, allegory, realism, and comedy to make serious contributions to the subject of war memory in pop culture.

While Hollywood has its own robust catalog of war films set in East Asia, such as *Across the Pacific* (1942), *Lady from Chungking* (1942), *Dragon Seed* (1944), and *Cease Fire* (1953), in Chapter 6, Robert Brent Toplin examines the myriad ways in which the conflicts in East Asia fundamentally reshaped the onscreen portrayal of Asian characters in films about the war, and beyond. In "Continuity and Change in Hollywood's Representations of American-Asian Relations in War and Peace," Toplin examines Japanese, Chinese, and, to a lesser extent, Korean characters in American films from the 1930s to the 2000s to reveal a "pattern of flexibility and quick adjustments" corresponding primarily but not exclusively to geopolitical shifts.

While filmgoers from 1937 to 1939 could hardly have failed to notice the urbane and brilliant detective Mr. Moto, played by Peter Lorre, fighting crime (usually in partnership with an American ex-serviceman) in exotic locales in no less than eight films during those years, within months of the attack on Pearl Harbor, films like *Little Tokyo, U.S.A.* (1942), would portray Japanese-Americans in California plotting sabotage. Following the Pacific War and the U.S. Occupation of Japan (1945–1952), the image of Japanese characters would be renegotiated yet again—this time primarily through a domesticated, feminized guise, as in *Japanese War Bride* (1952), *Teahouse of the August Moon* (1956), and *Sayonara* (1957). Similarly, Toplin traces shifting characterizations of Chinese characters. During much of the 1930s and 1940s, Hollywood portrayed them as hearty hard-working people who eked out a living in an unforgiving land; after the "loss of China" in 1949 and the outbreak of the Korean War in 1950, they suddenly became tyrannical communists, who heartlessly massacred their enemies and were hell-bent on destroying the Free World.

Lurking behind these representations is the pervasive impact the war years had on Hollywood's representation and continued revision of Asian characters and Asian-Americans. Throughout all these shifts, Toplin wryly observes, "American moviemakers and their audiences rather easily abandoned old prejudices and adopted new ones." While much of the chapter discusses "positive" and "negative" ways in which Asian characters were portrayed before and after World War II, the chapter also opens the door for further critical engagement with questions such as the complex racial politics at work in Hollywood's casting of Caucasian actors in many leading Asian roles and Hollywood's widespread objectification of Asian women as docile, sexualized objects to be conquered by Caucasian leading men. While Topin argues that these postwar films highlighting romances between Asian and white characters can be seen as a reversal of Hollywood's wartime demonization of Japanese characters, the ways in which U.S. wartime military prowess over Asia is replaced by U.S. postwar sexual prowess over Asian women can also be read not so much as a reversal as a further display of Hollywood's power to drive viewers' perspectives on war and sexuality, not to mention the long-term effects of Hollywood's skewed representation of Asian characters—both of which continue to haunt Hollywood's relationship with East Asia.

Part II homes in on more specific issues in the politics, aesthetics, and ethics of historical representation in film. In Chapter 7, Lily Wong confronts the dark historical legacy of the comfort woman through the unlikely lens of Hong Kong and mainland Chinese exploitation cinema and television miniseries. While the comfort women issue has become a hotbed for social movements in China, Japan, Korea, Taiwan, and elsewhere that protesters demand justice through apologies and reparations, one of the more unexpected responses has been a series of Chinese-language films that frame historical violence as soft-core titillation. In her chapter, "Oscillating Histories: Representations of Comfort Women from *Bamboo House of Dolls* to *Imperial Comfort Women*," Wong navigates the often murky ethical waters and complex sexual politics surrounding such productions as the Shaw Brothers' *Bamboo House of Dolls* (*Nü jizhongying*, 1972) and the television miniseries *Imperial Comfort Women* (*Diguo junji*, 1995).

Another unexpected page in the history of visual presentations of the Second Sino-Japanese War is unearthed in Chapter 8, "Shooting the Enemy: Photographic Attachment in *The Children of Huang Shi* and *Scarlet Rose*," by Michael Berry. Although a series of feature-length films has appeared in China about the Nanjing Massacre, Berry highlights the role of photography as a tool within this genre as a means of both chronicling and providing witness to historical atrocities. Eventually his discussion turns from feature film to television, offering an extended analysis of the genre-crossing 2007 television miniseries *Scarlet Rose: The Goddesses of Jinling* (*Xuese meigui: Jinling nüshen*). Through his discussion of *Scarlet Rose*, Berry describes not only a transition from realism and melodrama to a more diverse and genre-crossing mode of representation but also a shift from tropes of passive victimization and historical testimony to a new phase of "history making" in Nanjing Massacre cinema and television.

Picking up where David Desser left off in Part I, Aaron Gerow offers a new twist on what is being remembered or forgotten in war-themed Japanese films. In Chapter 9, "War and Nationalism in Recent Japanese Cinema: *Yamato*, Kamikaze, Trauma, and Forgetting the Postwar," Gerow situates his reading of *Yamato* (*Otokotachi no Yamato*, 2005)—a blockbuster film about the last days of the famed battleship—within the "Shōwa 30s [1955–1964] *boomu*" or cultural revival, which by its peak in the mid-2000s had produced an outpouring of nostalgic and sanitized narratives of the early postwar period. Then, engaging the concept of "trauma cinema," Gerow suggests that Yamato and recent kamikaze films represent wartime suffering in ways that not only elide issues of Japan's war responsibility but also "divert the audience's attention from what, for the majority of the audience, born after the war ended, might be the greater trauma: the postwar era" and its turbulent history of economic upheaval, protests against U.S. military bases, and other social tensions.

The final chapters of *Divided Lenses* push the project into new media by examining war through an array of popular and screen cultures, including television and video games. As technology and new media evolve, so do the means through which we represent and imagine war transform, but how have these new forms of digital history and game-based approaches, in which one stalks the battlefield and shoots the enemy in virtual space, changed our relationship with lived history? In Chapter 10, "The Promise and Limits of 'Pop Culture Diplomacy' in East Asia: Contexts-Texts-Reception," Chiho Sawada explores the complex interactions between transnational flows of pop culture and the process of achieving "thick reconciliation" in the Asia-Pacific region. With special attention to Japanese-Korean relations, Sawada provides a contextualized overview of cultural exchanges since the late 1990s. Exploring the transformation of Korean-Japanese relations and the corresponding rise in regional cooperation with respect to cultural production and distribution, the chapter proceeds not only to analyze the polysemous and therefore often problematic content of "historical" film, television, and video but also to grapple with tricky questions about media effects and reception. While the post–cold war acceleration and diversification of cultural flows in the Asia-Pacific region have opened new possibilities for mutual understanding and forgiveness, it must be said that "pop culture diplomacy," though attractive, remains an elusive goal. While Sawada's discussion touches upon a wide array of pop culture texts that have circulated between Japan and Korea since the 1990s—from *Winter Sonata* (*Kyŏul yŏn'ga*, 2002) and the Korean Wave to the co-production *2009 Lost Memories* (2009)—it is only too clear that these cultural currents are still influenced (and often strained) by the shadow of colonialism and wartime memory.

We conclude with another form of screen culture—the video game, a widely popular form whose worldwide revenue surpassed that of the film industry in 2008 yet remains largely overlooked in serious academic studies. A startling number of video games produced in the United States and Asia take the various military conflicts of 1931–1953 as their setting, allowing players to vicariously "experience" war using a television, computer monitor, personal gaming device, or cellphone. In Chapter 11, "History and Its Alternatives: War Games as Social Form," Eric Hayot begins with prophecy and speculative fiction, which he defines as "histories of the future" from the early twentieth century that projected an impending world conflict before moving to the present moment's fascination with Internet and computer-based "war games." The chapter outlines three categories of historical fiction, "history of the future," "history of the past/historical fiction," and "alternative history," which Hayot examines in both fiction and different forms of video games. Along the way, he explores the inherent challenges posed to those engaging in critical studies of video-game representations of the Pacific War due to the very nature of a medium in which "form absolutely dominates content." The ensuing discussion of how formal structures of different types of video games (FPS, MMORPG, etc.) dictate content provides an eye-opening glimpse of the fundamentally different ways in which video games are designed and function vis-à-vis other representational media. At the same time, Hayot's argument also prods us to rethink how the filmic and television portrayals discussed in earlier chapters may, albeit to a lesser degree, also be partially dictated by generic conventions and structural norms silently woven in local film industries' respective narrative traditions.

Part of the aim of this volume is to provide a diverse array of critical and historical entry points for reflecting on two decades of violent conflicts that would go on to leave an indelible historical scar and play a crucial role in shaping the political, economic, and cultural trajectories of all the countries involved in the future. Given the complexity of the subject matter, this volume does not pretend to be comprehensive in scope, instead, we offer a rich panorama of a few examples of cultural texts that have tried to recreate, subvert, or question this period of war in East Asia through an assemblage of strategies that range from propaganda and pedagogy to soft-core pornography. Absent are topics ranging from the important role of documentary cinema and the often-overlooked wartime film productions under the Japanese puppet regime in "Manchukuo" to a more nuanced examination of North Korean war cinema, but it is our hope that the critical entry points this volume offers will inspire further exploration of other facets of this important subject. It is our hope that through these case studies, we will be able to highlight some of the key questions explored directly by the films and other texts examined as well as the many other questions their production and distribution (sometimes unknowingly) raise. From the ethics of representation and historical revisionism to the place these cultural texts play in contemporary East Asian political and economic relations, the texts navigate difficult territory and, while time has long left those historical moments behind, the cultural terrain continues to transform and shift.

Throughout the "fractured and convoluted" cinematic history that emerges through this volume, certain trends come to the fore. Side-by-side readings of these different regional cinematic approaches to war reveal not only the shifts and trends unique to each national cinema tradition but also larger trends and countertrends and cinematic dialogues between different countries. Some of the "dialogues" include direct call-and-response films, as one might describe the revisionist Nanjing Massacre films that Desser covers in his chapter, while other dialogues involve subtler tweaks to long-standing cinematic formulas in response to shifting geopolitical alliances. Within this cinema of war in East Asia, and through these "divided lenses," recurrent motifs that seem to haunt these films include the imbrication between entertainment and propaganda, the popcorn blockbuster and nationalistic sentiment, and the bottom line and the burden of history. While many local film industries highlighted in this volume (including those in China, South Korea, North Korea, and Taiwan) relied heavily upon state subsidies and sponsorships throughout the cold war period of the 1950s–1980s, in the past several decades these industries have one by one faced privatization (with the notable exception of the one in North Korea).[9] While one might anticipate this means that the war film as a genre has been unfettered from the nationalistic and propagandistic elements that were once a mainstay, this has not always been the case. Certain long-standing tropes in each national cinema's war film tradition—from Japanese cinema's "victimhood consciousness" to China's lingering "anti-Japanese complex"—continue to loom large. However, one salient change that has come with this shift away from state-sponsored war cinema has been the increasing reliance on sensationalized, "crowd-pleasing" spectacles to reframe the war. The combination of lingering tropes from ideologically infused cold war–era films, combined with new market forces and entertainment imperatives, seems to be the underlying force in this new breed of East Asia war cinema.

At the time of this writing, even a cursory survey of recent developments in the film industries in the respective countries studied in this volume reveals the lingering shadows of war. In 2007, one of the most commercially and critically successful films of the year in China was Feng Xiaogang's big-budget war film *Assembly* (*Jijie hao*), which offers a powerful reexamination of the Korean War. In 2009, Lu Chuan's *The City of Life and Death* (*Nanjing! Nanjing!*) revisited the Nanjing Massacre and, in the process, elicited a firestorm of controversy. And continuing the cinematic excavation of this brutal historical massacre, the single most anticipated film in China in

2011 was Zhang Yimou's *The Flowers of War* (*Jinling shisanchai*), an epic war film also set during the Nanjing Massacre that stars Christian Bale. And this does not include the inundation of popular primetime Chinese television miniseries portraying the Chinese Civil War, the Sino-Japanese War, and the Korean War or the recent rise of the new feature-film genre of "resistance war comedies" (*kangri gaoxiao dianying*), a form unthinkable a generation ago but now quite popular thanks to films like *Put Your Hands Up* (*Juqi shoulai*, 2003) and *Lay Down Your Arms If You Want to Live* (*Jiao-qiang busha*, 2007).

Although the Taiwan film industry has eschewed big-budget war films over the past two decades, Wei Te-sheng's long-awaited two-part epic *Warriors of the Rainbow: Seediq Bale* (*Saideke balai,* 2011) chronicles the 1930 Musha Incident involving aboriginal Taiwanese tribes and the Japanese. The film's recreation of this long overlooked and understudied indigenous insurrection and its tragic suppression by the Japanese colonial machine has broken box-office records in Taiwan and become a veritable cultural phenomenon that, for some, functions as a social barometer of Taiwanese nationalism. Likewise, in Korean cinema, this historical period, particularly the Korean War era, weigh heavily in the cinematic imagination. While not examined in detail in the chapters here, the Korean War was also a central theme in numerous North Korean films, culminating with such classic works as *Wŏlmi Island* (*Wŏlmi-do,* 1982) in the 1980s. And although in recent years North Korea has turned away from war films (due in part to the prohibitively large budgets required), in South Korea the war remains one of the most popular and profitable subjects in film. One of the biggest South Korean box-office hits of 2010 was Lee Jae-han's *Into the Fire* (*P'ohwa sokŭro*), which not only portrayed the historical Battle of P'ohang-dong but also served as a cinematic commemoration of the sixtieth anniversary of the battle. *Into the Fire* is but one example of a much larger urge to revisit the war in film, which also includes such local blockbusters as *Taegukgi: The Brotherhood of War* (*T'aegŭkki hwinallimyŏ,* 2004), which boasted record sales of 11.74 million tickets.

Although Japan's role as aggressor during the war years and ongoing controversies over issues such as war reparations, apologies to victims, and leadership tributes to war dead at national shrines (for more on these topics, see Chapter 4), one might suspect the Japanese film industry of shying away from cinematic attempts to revisit the war, but that has not been entirely the case. Films like Tetsuo Shinohara's *Battle under Orion* (*Manatsu no*

Orion, 2009), which explores the war memories of a former soldier through his relationship with a schoolgirl, and *Oba: The Last Samurai* (*Taiheiyō no kiseki: fokkusu to yobareta otoko,* 2011), which depicts a Japanese captain who finds himself directing the remaining soldiers during the famous battle of Saipan, attest to the staying power of the war in Japanese cinema. And while these types of rather straightforward historical narratives have prevailed, in recent years the Japanese film industry has also produced a robust "what if" genre that attempts to completely reimagine the war and its aftermath. Examples include the 2003 anime feature film *The Place Promised in Our Early Days* (*Kumo no mukō, yakusoku no basho*), which imagines an alternate version of Japan that has been divided into two separate states in the wake of World War II occupied respectively by the United States and the Soviet Union. Other examples include *Lorelei: The Witch of the Pacific Ocean* (*Rōrerei,* 2005), which explores the "what if" scenario of the Japanese military's efforts to prevent "the third atom bomb" from being dropped on Tokyo. While such portrayals reveal a rich landscape of creative energy and cinematic imagination not seen in other regions, at the same time, they also run the risk of working in concert with revisionist stances on history and reducing actual widespread historical atrocities to escapist mass entertainment. Nevertheless, it remains a curious fact that the primary aggressor in the Pacific War has emerged as the most unbridled and imaginative when it comes to reimagining the war years.

When dealing with this historical period, Hollywood cinema has traditionally given more attention to events in the European theater, however, recent films like Bill Guttentag and Dan Sturman's feature-length documentary *Nanking* (2007), Clint Eastwood's cinematic pair *Flags of Our Fathers* (2006) and *Letters from Iwo Jima* (2006), and even *Gran Torino* (2008), which can be read as a posttraumatic exploration of the legacy of the Korean War, indicate Hollywood's continuing fascination and ongoing renegotiation with this period of history. In 2005, Rob Marshall directed an $85 million adaptation of Arthur Golden's *Memoirs of a Geisha.* And while the film's plot is set, in part, against the events of World War II, the extraordinary controversy that the film generated in China seemed to have much less to do with how the film navigated the war than with the fact that Chinese actors (Michelle Yeoh, Gong Li, and, especially, Zhang Ziyi) were portraying Japanese geisha, with special outrage reserved for Zhang for the scenes in which she has sexual relations with the general (played by the Japanese actor Ken Watanabe). The controversy surrounding the film was generally explained in the media as being directly related to traumatic memories of the Nanjing Massacre and comfort women in China.[10] In Peter Webber's 2013 film *Emperor,* Hollywood provided a fictional reevaluation of General Douglas MacArthur's (portrayed by Tommy Lee Jones) investigation into the Japanese emperor's role during World War II with an all-star cast. At the same time, Hollywood continues to play an important role in the cinematic imagination of this period in the other regions discussed, not only as an aesthetic and narrative model but as a way in which co-productions and Hollywood-Asia collaborations continue to affect war films. Some examples include Zhang's casting of Bale in *Flowers of War,* the casting of Hollywood actors (Daniel Baldwin, Treat Williams, Sean McGowen) in Hideyuki Hirayama's *Oba: The Last Samurai,* which was also adapted from original source material by Don Jones,[11] all of which attest to Hollywood's mediating role in East Asian film productions focused on war memory.

All these years later, not only do the events of 1931–1953 continue to be a focal point for the film industries of multiple countries but these films have increasingly become one of the primary battlegrounds for the fight over historical memory. As the actual events recede in time, these films, television series, and video games become the means through which younger generations can vicariously "experience" or, at least, "imagine" history. *Divided Lenses* attempts to open a new space for comparative studies and intercultural dialogue by not only revisiting this disturbing page in history but also juxtaposing the often radically divergent means through which historical memory is manifested in popular culture.

Notes

1   Thanks to Suk-Young Kim and Michael Emmerich for their input and responses to queries regarding Korean and Japanese cinema. Special thanks to my co-editor Chiho Sawada for his feedback and contributions to this introduction.
2   Paul Virilio, *War and Cinema* (New York: Verso, 1986), 69.
3   Ban Wang, *Illuminations from the Past: Trauma, Memory, and History in Modern China* (Stanford, CA: Stanford University Press, 2004); other relevant studies include, Michael Berry, *A History of Pain: Trauma in Modern Chinese Literature and Film* (New York: Columbia University Press, 2008).
4   Such studies have appeared in Chinese, such as Tian Benxiang and Shi Bogong, *Kangzhan dianying* (War of Resistance films) (Kaifeng: Henan daxue chubanshe, 2005).

5   Suk-Young Kim, *DMZ Crossing: Performing Emotional Citizenship along the Korean Border* (New York: Columbia University Press, 2014); idem, *Illusive Utopia: Theater, Film, and Everyday Performance in North Korea* (Ann Arbor: University of Michigan Press, 2010); Kyung Hyun Kim, *Virtual Hallyu: Korean Cinema of the Global Era* (Durham, NC: Duke University Press, 2011).

6   Paul W. Edwards, *A Guide to Films on the Korean War* (Westport, CT: Greenwood, 1997); Robert J. Lentz, *Korean War Filmography: 91 English Languages Features through 2000* (Jefferson, NC: McFarland, 2008); Hiroshi Kitamura, *Screening Enlightenment: Hollywood and the Cultural Reconstruction of Defeated Japan* (Ithaca, NY: Cornell University Press, 2010); Tarak Barkawi and Keith Stanski, *Orientalism and War* (New York: Columbia University Press, 2013).

7   King-fai Tam, Timothy Y. Tsu, and Sandra Wilson, ed., *Chinese and Japanese Films of the Second World War* (London: Routledge, 2014).

8   One complication of the term *kangzhan dianying* is that, in addition to referring literally to "resistance war films," it is also a common abbreviated form of *Kangri zhanzheng dianying* (lit., Resist Japan war films), which suggests the same anti-Japanese sentiments as *duiri kangzhan dianying.*

9   While the Chinese film industry has also undergone radical privatization since the 1990s, many of the new "private" film production companies are still owned or controlled by state-run enterprises.

10   Among the numerous articles covering this controversy, see David Gritten, "Memoirs of a Very Controversial Geisha," *The Telegraph*, December 2, 2005. In addition to controversy in China, some Japanese audiences and critics also resented the fact that all the leading Japanese female roles were portrayed by Chinese actors.

11   Other examples include the recently announced $100 million Korean-Hollywood coproduction *1950* to be directed by Rob Cohen. See *The Hollywood Reporter* coverage of the production deal at http://www.hollywoodreporter.com/news/rob-cohen-direct-korean-war-216693/.

PART I

SCREEN HISTORIES OF WAR IN EAST ASIA

CHAPTER 1

War, History, and Remembrance in Chinese Cinema

Yingjin Zhang

To privilege "remembrance" is to insist on specifying agency, on answering the question who remembers, when, where, and how? And on being aware of the transience of remembrance, so dependent on the frailties and commitments of the men and women who take the time and effort to engage in it.

Jay Winter, *Remembering War*

Film, Witness, History

As in many national cinemas, the war film has been a mainstay in Chinese cinema. Given China's tumultuous history of civil wars and foreign invasion in the first half of the twentieth century, the prominence of war in Chinese films is comprehensible. However, the impact of Chinese war films on the formation of collective memory—often sanctioned by the nation-state—has been more often assumed than investigated. This chapter follows Jay Winter's recommendation that we "shift from the term 'memory' to the term 'remembrance' as a strategy to avoid the trivialization of the term 'memory' through inclusion of any and every facet of our contact with the past, personal or collective" and to rethink "the notion of memory as unstable, plastic, synthetic, and repeatedly reshaped."[1] In light of this new conceptualization, the war film constitutes a public arena of remembrance in which contending parties—from rival nation-states to rivals within a nation-state and generations of artists and audiences—produce, exhibit, and receive war images and narratives in their respective efforts to reshape history and memory and to reassert their agency and subjectivities in drastically different sociopolitical environments. To borrow Winter's concept of "collective remembrance," I contend that the war film "points to time and place and above all, to evidence, to traces enabling us to understand what groups of people try to do when they act in public to conjure up the past."[2] War films thus function as acts of remembrance that leave deep marks on collective memory, regardless of whether they conform to official history. Winter's emphasis on remembrance reminds us to delve into the intricate ways in which private memories and remembrances on the screen corroborate, challenge, or subvert collective memory, thereby rendering the latter unstable and open to modification and reconstruction.

With an emphasis on Chinese cinematic treatments of conflicts in the Asia-Pacific region as exercises in remembrance, this chapter pays particular attention to the question, as Winter puts it, of "who remembers, when, where, and how." Indeed, in view of a consistent lack of interest in the war film,[3] this chapter also aims to fill a gap in English-language scholarship by providing an overview of Chinese war films over the past century, identifying prevailing modes and paradigms, and analyzing alternative tactics and images. Once we start looking beneath the surface of state-sanctioned collective memory of Chinese nationalism and communist heroism, we can see that subtle, sometimes subversive acts of remembrance have all along been staged or referenced in Chinese war films, thus generating an intricate dynamic involving public and private histories, memories, and remembrances.

To begin with one example: the imbrication of war, history, and remembrance is dramatized to a shocking extent in the final scene of *Devils at the Doorstep* (*Guizi laile*, 2000). In the closing days of World War II, Ma Dasan (portrayed by Jiang Wen) treats with kindness a Japanese soldier and a Chinese interpreter forced into his care by the communist guerrillas, and he eventually returns them to the Japanese troops stationed near his village in exchange for sacks of grain. However, he is devastated after he returns home to find his fellow villagers massacred and the entire village set on fire by the Japanese on the day of Japan's surrender. In an act of revenge, Ma sneaks into the prisoner of war (POW) camp and stabs a few Japanese, but he is arrested and sentenced to die in a public execution. What is ironic is that a crippled Chinese Nationalist army officer orders the Japanese POW whose life Ma has saved to carry out the beheading. With unrivaled professional precision, the POW swings his sword, and the camera assumes the point of view of Ma's head, which rolls on the ground, as the screen is splattered with red.[4] Even more unsettling is that, after his head is shown on the ground, Ma's eyes wink at the camera, as if to signal not only the irrationality of this unexpected aftermath of the war victory but also of the "frailty" and "transience" of private remembrance.[5]

Shot in black and white until the final sequence, *Devils at the Doorstep* acknowledges the major political forces in wartime history—the United States, the Chinese Nationalists, and the Japanese. However, the Chinese communists are conspicuous by their absence. The only time when a communist representative appears is at the beginning of the film when he is masked and remains mostly off-screen in darkness, pointing a pistol and then a bayonet at Ma's face and ordering him to take care of the POW wrapped in a large sack. This unexpected moment of political intrusion is contrasted with its prior scene, in which Ma and his girlfriend are secretly engaged in passionate lovemaking. Symbolically, this act of political intrusion into a private space serves as a reminder not so much of the patriotic duty of Chinese villagers as of the brutal coercion (carried out with the pistol and the bayonet pointed at Ma's face) resorted to in times of war. The official memory of heroic resistance and the private remembrance of humble survival by innocent villagers vis-à-vis political forces are at odds in this film, which is narrated from the perspective of an unlikely witness. As layers of official, collective, and private memories are interwoven into the film, a crucial question emerges as to whose history is being displayed in *Devils at the Doorstep.*

In recent years, various notions of memory, witness, and testimony have been problematized in literary and film criticism as much as in historical study in what is commonly known as a period of a memory boom.[6] For instance, Yomi Braester articulates a concept of "witness against history," in which the myth of official history is challenged, if not dismantled, when a witness refuses to speak on behalf of the teleological history. "Witness for history," he writes, "is evident in the words of those—party ideologues and social critics alike—who have spoken in the name of 'history' to evoke a sense of events as tangible and purpose-driven"; on the contrary, "witness against history" refers to cases in which "writing is divorced from 'history' (understood as the sign of reality, progress, and national destiny)" and where "authors challenge their own capacity to bear witness," ultimately leading to a situation in which *"bearing witness against history perforce becomes bearing witness against testimony itself."*[7]

To return to *Devils at the Doorstep,* we now recognize that the director, Jiang Wen (b. 1963), has created an improbable scene of bearing witness in which testimony itself is discounted precisely at the moment when it is staged. Ma Dasan thus represents a "witness against history" not just because he is in diametric opposition to the textbook history of spontaneous Chinese nationalism but also because he does not pretend to know the meaning of patriotism and heroism or the significance of his own place in the war. Ma's decapitation, therefore, is an unlikely testimony of martyrdom—in the sense not so much of "sacrificing one's life for a just cause" as of "displaying one's agonizing pain and suffering in public."[8] In the latter sense, Ma has become a martyr in spite of himself, an anguished "witness" par excellence who is physically reduced to a chopped-off head and who is allowed no place to live in the grand history of China's wartime resistance. Nonetheless, the unsettling final shot implies that, even though Ma's private remembrance is violently erased and his testimony discounted by history, his winking eye points to a placeless (and therefore haunting) memory outside the purview of official history. In this subtle way, *Devils at the Doorstep* succeeds in bearing witness to a haunting cinematic act of private remembrance, because it is unforgettable as well as placeless.

The War Film: Cycles, Modes, Paradigms

For people familiar with the war film in China, the dominance of official history and collective memory on screen are all too obvious. In terms of large-scale warfare, Chinese cinema covers (1) the War of Resistance against Japan in 1937–1945 (hereafter "War of Resistance"), which created widespread devastation;[9] (2) the Civil War between the communists and the Nationalists in 1945–1949, which concluded with the former's victory and the latter's retreat to Taiwan; and (3) the Korean War, in which the Chinese volunteer army fought side by side with North Korea against South Korea and the U.S.-led United Nations troops in 1950–1953. In terms of political interpretation, the communists shared with the Nationalists (during their rule of the mainland before 1949 and in Taiwan from the 1950s to the 1990s) a sustained effort at glorifying Chinese heroic resistance and denouncing Japanese wartime atrocities. However, the Nationalists became the archenemy when the communists established the People's Republic of China in 1949 and its own state-owned studios started to produce war films in large quantities in order to legitimatize their rule and indoctrinate audiences.[10] The Korean War provided the communists with another stage for propagating their ideology of anti-imperialism and self-reliance, although in recent decades films exclusively addressing this war would become increasingly less numerous.

As a genre, the war film refers to "films about the waging of war in the twentieth century," in which "scenes of combat are a requisite ingredient and these are dramatically central."[11] In current scholarship, the war film has been subdivided into various interrelated cycles, such as the combat film, the home-front drama, and sometimes the antiwar film.[12] The broader definition of a war film, inclusive of the home-front drama, is adopted by Huangfu Yichuan in the first book-length history of Chinese war film. Huangfu notices a peculiar absence of war films in early Chinese cinema, which he attributes in part to insufficient technical capability and financial constraints in China's cottage film industry at the time. A few films from the 1920s reference military battles among China's regional warlords, but typically in these films, the experience of the war remained in the background, and a strong "pacifist" (*feizhan*), if not "antiwar" (*fanzhan*), sentiment from this silent period disappeared beginning in the 1930s.[13]

Huangfu delineates four high points in the production of Chinese war films in the twentieth century, creating four major cinematic modes. First, the mode of "outcry" (*nuhou*) emerged in the late 1930s and continued through the early 1940s, and war films in this mode aimed to mobilize the Chinese population during the War of Resistance, although most of these films are considered rather simplistic in depicting heroes and criticizing cowards. Second, the mode of "eulogy" (*ouge*) prevailed in films from 1950 to 1966, which glorify the communist victory and demand that audiences remember the past and work selflessly for socialism. Third, the mode of "reflection" (*fansi*) lasted from the late 1970s to the mid-1980s, and films in this mode reexamine the complicated relationship between war and humanity, delve into psychological realms, and introduce stylistic innovations. Fourth, the mode of "entertainment" (*yule*) was introduced in the 1990s as a result of the dual pressure of official ideology and market reforms; films in this mode borrow from commercial filmmaking and succeed in making leitmotif films (*zhuxuanlü*) entertaining.[14]

Huangfu's delineation is geopolitically limited because the outcry mode actually started first in the early 1930s in Hong Kong, where patriotic films were produced by commercial studios, instead of Shanghai because it was subject to restrictions by the Nationalist government and authorities in the foreign concession, both of whom were eager to maintain peaceful relations with Japan at the time, even after it occupied Manchuria in 1931.[15] To a great extent, Hong Kong productions such as *The Critical Moment* (*Zuihou guantou,* 1937) helped articulate the rising patriotic sentiments there and on the mainland. At the outset of the War of Resistance, the Nationalist Party–owned studios were also active in producing war films, and the Nationalist troops' courageous defense of Shanghai in August 1937 became the subject of *Eight Hundred Heroic Soldiers* (*Babai zhuangshi,* 1938), one of the earliest full-scale combat films in China. The popular memory of this battle is so persistent that, thirty-eight years later, the Nationalist government in Taiwan produced a remake with the same Chinese title, *Eight Hundred Heroes* (*Babai zhuangshi,* 1975), which would win awards for the year's best film and best actress (Brigitte Lin; Lin Qingxia, b. 1954) at the 1976 Asia Film Festival. Twelve years later, Lin worked with the director Ting Shan-si (Ding Shanxi, b. 1936) again in a Hong Kong remake, *Flag of Honor* (*Qi zheng piaopiao,* 1987). Lin's rising star power parallels the transition from the eulogy mode to the entertainment mode (as delineated by Huangfu) but outside mainland China.[16]

As suggested in the title *Eight Hundred Heroic Soldiers,* most Chinese cinematic treatments of the War of Resistance promoted heroism and martyrdom in times of national crisis. The trend continued through the postwar period in the late 1940s, when home-front dramas dominated the screen, with tear-jerking tales of extended family separations, traumatic refugee experiences, and the precarious living conditions under Japanese occupation.[17] During the 1950s to the 1970s, Chinese war films were dominated by what I have elsewhere described as the "paradigms of nationalism, patriotism, and heroism."[18] Not surprisingly, the Chinese word for "hero" (*yingxiong*) is prominently featured in several films from the 1950s: both *Heroes from Lüliang Mountains* (*Lüliang yingxiong,* 1950) and *New Story of Heroic Sons and Daughters* (*Xin ernü yingxiong zhuan,* 1950) dramatize Chinese villagers' resistance against Japanese invaders under communist leadership. The obsession with on-screen heroism persisted to the mid-1960s, when *Heroic Sons and Daughters* (*Yingxiong ernü,* 1964), adapted from a story by Ba Jin (1904–2005), includes an incredible episode during the Korean War in which a single Chinese soldier, Wang Cheng, defends his fallen comrades' position by blowing himself up with an explosive amid a large group of terrified U.S. troops. The heroic screen image of Wang Cheng—made memorable by his self-sacrificing request to the communist army headquarters, "Aim the artillery shelling at me" (*xiangwo kaipao*)—was anticipated by other war films eulogizing the martyrdom of real-life heroes. *Zhao Yiman* (*Zhao Yiman*, 1950), which presents a communist woman who withstands several rounds of torture at the hands of the Japanese and then dies without compromising her integrity, and *Dong Cunrui* (*Dong Cunrui*, 1955), in which the titular character blows himself up with an explosive under a Nationalist army field blockhouse, are among a growing number of propaganda films that projected larger-than-life models of heroism for Chinese viewers to re-member and emulate.

War films made after 1949 could be further divided into two subcat-egories, communist hagiography and military strategy. *Daughters of China* (*Zhonghua ernü*, 1949), which glorifies eight female resistance fighters in Northeast China who drown themselves in the Mudan River rather than letting themselves be captured by the Japanese, joined war films such as *Zhao Yiman* and *Dong Cunrui* in a long list of historical figures enshrined in com-munist screen hagiography. As for military strategy, *From Victory to Victory* (*Nanzheng beizhan*, 1952) restaged major battles from the Civil War and paved the way for other exciting combat films to come. Large-scale fighting and intricate military strategy would produce a "thriller cycle" (*jingxian yangshi*), which includes *Capture Mount Hua by Stratagem* (*Zhiqu Huashan*, 1953) and *Reconnaissance across the Yangtze* (*Dujiang zhenchaji*, 1954), re-spectively showcasing picturesque mountain peaks and river torrents as a backdrop for military combat. Twenty years later, when Chinese feature film production resumed after a hiatus in the early chaotic years of the Cultural Revolution in the early 1970s, *Reconnaissance across the Yangtze* (*Dujiang zhenchaji*, 1974) and *From Victory to Victory* (*Nanzheng beizhan*, 1974) were two prominent remakes of war films, judged politically safe by studios and artists at a time when ultraleftist ideology reigned.

Similarly, *Guerrillas on the Plain* (*Pingyuan youjidui*, 1974) is another rare remake approved in the early 1970s, but this film belongs to the cycle of "folk legends" (*chuanqi yangshi*) popular during the 1950s,[19] which in-clude *Guerrillas on the Plain* (*Pingyuan youjidui*, 1955) and *Guerrillas along the Railroad* (*Tiedao youjidui*, 1956). The elements of folk culture are also discernible in two war films produced for military education: *Landmine Warfare* (*Dilei zhan*, 1962) and *Tunnel Warfare* (*Didao zhan*, 1965). Their repeated showings nationwide—frequently in open-air settings—throughout the Cultural Revolution (1966–1976) gained legendary status for both of them while having tremendous impact on children's minds. Indeed, the communist regime recruited children to actively participate in watching war films. *Letter with Feather* (*Jimao xin*, 1954) and *Zhang Ga, a Boy Soldier* (*Xiaobing Zhang Ga*, 1963) present legendary child heroes who outsmart Japanese enemies and seek pleasure in military fighting as they are initiated into the communist revolution.

Evidently, Chinese war films have engaged in something similar to what James Chapman perceives as "war as adventure" in Hollywood productions. Chapman finds "the pleasure culture of war" evident in all societies where children play at being soldiers and collecting war toys; the war film, therefore, "is a vehicle through which ruling elites set out to indoctrinate the masses with the mentality necessary for the perpetuation of the warfare state."[20] In China, such cinematic perpetuations of the state of warfare have lasted for decades and have yielded a collective memory in which communist heroes—real as well as fictional—have become household names. Producing and exhibiting war films thus function as rituals of collective remembrance strictly controlled and widely propagated by the party-state. It was not until the mid-1980s that images of disquiet and dissent began to emerge in Chinese films.

Collective Memory Revisited: Humanity, Brutality, Transnationality

Against the backdrop of cultural reflection in the 1980s, which represents Chinese intellectuals' efforts at collective remembrance of the presocialist and socialist pasts to explore what might have gone wrong during the socialist revolution, Chinese cinema started to present alternatives to the still-dominant paradigms of nationalism, patriotism, and heroism. A general trend was to integrate human qualities (*renxing*) into otherwise one-dimensional, almost abstract figures of heroism, and this would lead to scenarios in which even top communist leaders (e.g., Mao Zedong, Zhou Enlai, and Deng Xiaoping), albeit still stereotypes, are now increasingly allowed emotional moments and humorous dialogue.[21] Another noticeable development was that, contrary to the 1950s, when heterosexual romance was either absent or disguised in war films, after 1976 such romances would become a dramatic centerpiece in home-front dramas like *The Call of the Front* (*Guixin sijian*, 1978).[22]

Yet collective memory of official communist history is only modified or dressed up by the elements of humanity suggested above, along with a more tolerant historical view according to which the Nationalist army's decisive contribution to the War of Resistance is acknowledged in combat films such as *The Battle of Tai'erzhuang* (*Xuezhan Tai'erzhuang*, 1987). A fundamental challenge emerged only when a new generation of directors sought to view war and revolution from an entirely new perspective. Armed with a transcendent view of humanity and disquieting images of brutality, in the mid- to late 1980s "the Fifth Generation directors looked forward to salvation: not only their own salvation, but also the salvation of memory, history, nation, and subsistence."[23] Here, the Fifth Generation refers to the first group of directors who graduated from the Beijing Film Academy after the Cultural Revolution in the early 1980s and who were committed to experimental filmmaking that would distinguish them from their predecessors in the socialist era.

No doubt, early Fifth-Generation films like *One and Eight* (*Yige he bage*, 1984) and *Red Sorghum* (*Hong gaoliang*, 1987), both featuring brutal images of war and violence, indicated a new direction—cinematic realism. Let us take a closer look at *Evening Bell* (*Wanzhong*, 1988), an exceptional war film intended symbolically to "bury wars" and to signify "the burial and termination of a tragic but heroic era."[24] An outspoken director, Wu Ziniu (b. 1952) did not hide his voice of dissent when he asserted in a 1988 interview: "We cannot forever stay with the heroism of the past decades, promoting the national spirit and endorsing the invincibility of the Communist Party and its armies. . . . We have too many such films. Can't we do something different? Can't we represent war from a higher angle?"[25] As I have demonstrated elsewhere, *Evening Bell* is precisely such a "different" war film aspiring to a "higher angle," namely that of humanity transcending any geopolitical nationalism.[26] A small team of communist soldiers is dispatched to bury their fallen comrades, but they encounter a group of Japanese troops who have hidden in a cave without any knowledge of Japan's surrender and who have cannibalized Chinese laborers during a prolonged period of hunger. Despite their outrage, the communist soldiers decide to leave food for the Japanese and take them as POWs instead of killing them in revenge.

The reference to cannibalism in *Evening Bell* reminds us of the recurrent images of brutality, especially decapitation, in Wu's other war films.[27] More than serving as a witness against history (as in *Devils at the Doorstep*), Wu might have intended scenes of decapitation in his unconventional war films to substantiate a vision of history as barbarism and catastrophe: "There is no document of civilization which is not at the same time a document of barbarism."[28] The subversive equation of civilization with barbarism destabilizes the fundamental grounding of heroism in times of war, and the line between victims and victimizers is purposefully blurred so that both appear to be the equally helpless victims of war from a "higher" view of humanity that transcends the military, racial, and national conflicts. In *Evening Bell,* the idea of Japanese soldiers as victims of war is unmistakably present in the sequence before the credits, in which a group suicide is committed, with raging blazes and machine-gun firing. Such extraordinary sympathy for the Japanese accounts for the months of difficulty that *Evening Bell* had in struggling to gain censorship approval in China.[29]

With its fresh but disquieting images of brutality, *Evening Bell* certainly qualifies as an antiwar film, and a similar antiwar message is conveyed in *The Dove Tree* (*Gezi shu,* 1985), a rare war film that addresses the sensitive topic of the Sino-Vietnamese border war in the late 1970s. The film expresses sympathy for the Vietnamese, who had been allies of the Chinese in the Vietnam War but had unexpectedly become staunch enemies due to changing power configurations within the communist bloc.[30] Its antiwar message is symbolized by the dove in the title (a symbol intertextually linked to the courier pigeon in the pre-credit sequence of *Evening Bell*) and evidenced by a scene in which a Chinese soldier, who has just spared a Vietnamese mother carrying a child on her back, is killed by her in return. Because of this antiwar sentiment, *The Dove Tree* is banned in China along with another war film set in the time of the same border war, *In Their Prime* (*Tamen zheng nianqing,* 1986). Both *The Dove Tree* and *In Their Prime* foreground the disillusionment with war among Chinese soldiers, and the absence of a morally justifiable victory or even a clear sense of the war's purpose turns these two films into isolated acts of individual remembrances, which cannot help functioning as suppressed testimonies against official history. The communist authorities are arguably afraid that, if released publicly, antiwar films like these would undermine the widespread myth of heroism and martyrdom that communist filmmaking has spent decades constructing, in such popular war films as *Shanggan Ridge* (*Shangganling,* 1956), set during the Korean War, and *Garlands at the Foot of the Mountain* (*Gaoshan xiade huahuan,* 1984), also set during the Sino-Vietnamese border war.[31]

Historically, an antiwar voice was heard in Chinese cinema as early as the mid-1920s. *Spring Dream* (*Chungui mengli ren,* 1925) and *God of Peace* (*Heping zhi shen,* 1926), both directed by Hou Yao (1903–1942), expressed the artist's belief that contemporary chaos in China had been caused in part by armed conflicts among regional warlords.[32] The brutality of war was similarly depicted in *Military Prize* (*Zhangong,* 1925), in which two soldiers return home crippled, one losing his left arm and the other a hand and a foot. In a point-of-view shot, a medal awarded to one soldier transforms into a skeleton before the eyes of his girlfriend, who asks him: "Is this your military prize?"[33] Assuming the primacy of human values over the military prize, this question represents an early example of antiwar—or at least pacifist—ideals in Chinese film history, and the persistent absence of antiwar messages for the subsequent half-century makes its reemergence after the mid-1980s all the more striking.

In the mid-1990s, nonetheless, Wu Ziniu revised his antiwar position and repackaged his pacifist ideas in *Nanjing 1937* (*Nanjing datusha*, 1995), which concerns the Nanjing Massacre in 1937, in which over 300,000 Chinese lost their lives and which remains the worst national trauma of the anti-Japanese War of Resistance and a politically sensitive subject in Sino-Japanese relations. As are typical in most other recent films on the Nanjing Massacre, fictional as well as documentary,[34] Wu offers an impassioned denunciation of Japanese wartime atrocities and an acknowledgment of a dozen foreigners' valiant efforts to protect Chinese refugees. But he also includes the perspective of a Chinese-Japanese couple, each bringing a child from a previous marriage, in his film. As a collective remembrance of the Chinese wartime experience, the film surprises the viewer by having the first words spoken in Japanese. Rieko, the pregnant Japanese wife, asks her husband, Chengxian, a Chinese medical doctor from Shanghai, whether Nanjing is safe from the imminent Japanese attack. Chengxian answers in the affirmative, but the viewer already knows the fate of Nanjing in December 1937, and the film shows in excruciating detail the Japanese attack on the city, their indiscriminate slaughter of Chinese soldiers and civilians, their brutal rape of women, and killing of old men and babies. One source of dramatic tension is created by the mixed marriage, as it intensifies Japanese brutality—as exemplified by Rieko's desperate scream in Japanese when her teenage daughter is about to be raped by a Japanese solider—and exposes the utter senselessness of war—as Rieko's use of Japanese within the International Safety Zone created by foreign missionaries prompts a mob of Chinese refugees to hunt her down. Consistent with his transnational vision of humanity, Wu includes multiple languages and nationalities in the film—Chinese, English, Japanese, and German—to foreground the irrationality and inhumanity of a war that was carried out with its all-too-rational observation of binary demarcations such as China versus Japan, friend versus enemy, and compassion versus efficiency.

Nevertheless, given its melodramatic plot involving the mixed couple, *Nanjing 1937* does not transcend the binary divides in war, as *Evening Bell* and *The Dove Tree* had done previously. In fact, despite his alleged view of transcendent humanity, Wu's emphasis on the Chinese perspective in *Nanjing 1937*, which is shared by the foreigners sympathetic to the Chinese plight, is fundamentally in line with official Chinese history this time around;[35] This may have laid the groundwork for Wu's acceptance of mainstream ideology in his two subsequent patriotic films. The *National Anthem* (*Guoge,* 1999) glorifies the underground communists in Shanghai during the 1930s, and *Hero Zheng Chenggong* (*Yingxiong Zheng Chenggong,* 2000) celebrates a "national hero" (*minzu yingxiong*) who recovered Taiwan from Dutch rule in 1661. Constructed as "a monument to the national spirit, to the Chinese nation, and outstanding Chinese people," The *National Anthem* is intended "to tell the audience that they must love their nation, otherwise, they would have no individual existence at all."[36] Wu's statement, which privileges the nation over the individual, sharply contrasts with what he said in 1988, quoted earlier, which maintain an absolute distinction from the mainstream. Thus moving "from dissent to consent" within a decade, Wu has readjusted his previously revisionist position on war and history and has resolutely moved away from private remembrance and toward collective memory.[37]

Wu is not alone in modifying positions with regard to war films. To a large extent, Feng Xiaoning (b. 1954) shares Wu's aesthetic of visual violence and establishes his own reputation as an experimental war film director with *The Meridian of War* (*Zhanzheng ziwu xian,* 1990), in which twelve children lose their lives to save one nameless injured communist soldier. Like Wu's early films, *The Meridian of War* is packed with brutal war scenes and subtly questions the disregard for human lives in the dominant discourse of heroism in Chinese war films. Yet, in an effort to move toward "entertaining war films," Feng subsequently incorporated cross-ethnic and transnational relationships in his war trilogy set in three picturesque areas: Tibetan grasslands and snow-covered peaks, mountains along the Yellow River, and forests in the Great Xing'an Range between Northeast China and the Russian Far East. In *Red River Valley* (*Honghe gu,* 1997), a young Chinese woman (Ning Jing) caught in a love triangle between a Tibetan herdsman and a Tibetan prince joins forces with patriotic Tibetans in resisting the British invasion of Tibet in the early 1900s. The film ends with Jones, a British man sympathetic to Tibetan culture, gazing at the distant sacred snow peak, which bears witness to war atrocities that were depicted in the film. The

Western perspective is also offered in *Grief Over the Yellow River* (*Huanghe juelian,* 1999), in which Irving, an aging American ex-pilot, narrates and recounts in flashbacks the emergency landing of his reconnaissance aircraft near the Great Wall and his rescue by heroic Chinese villagers and soldiers during World War II. Irving falls in love with an "angelic" Chinese army nurse, An Jie (portrayed by Ning Jing), who in the end sacrifices her life so that Irving can escape the Japanese by swimming across the Yellow River.[38] In *Purple Sunset* (*Ziri,* 2001), Feng Xiaoning has worked out a different triangle, this time a male Chinese labor camp survivor, a female Russian soldier, and a Japanese schoolgirl recruited to fight in the final days of World War II. Speaking in Chinese, Russian, and Japanese, the three characters gradually transcend their differences and develop trust as they journey across forests, hills, and swamps. The tragedy occurs at the end, when the Japanese girl, who has finally turned pacifist, dies when she is rushing to announce Japan's surrender and is shot by a Japanese army officer who is killing Japanese civilians unwilling to take part in a planned group suicide.

As happens at the end of *Evening Bell,* the beautiful sunset captured repeatedly in *Purple Sunset* symbolizes the human aspiration for peace and dignity that transcends national boundaries. However, like Wu Ziniu in leitmotif films such as *The National Anthem* and *Hero Zheng Chenggong,*[39] Feng returns to ethnic nationalism in *Gada Meilin* (*Gada Meilin,* 2002), an epic film spiced up with romance that dramatizes the Mongolians' tragic-heroic resistance against foreign invasion. As reflected in the career trajectories of Wu and Feng, by the early 2000s, Chinese war films seem to have come full circle and returned to the mainstream paradigms of nationalism, patriotism, and heroism.

Conclusion: Remembrance, Recognition, Respect

In a larger framework of contemporary Chinese cinema, going "from dissent to consent" is not unique to Wu Ziniu or Feng Xiaoning, for a similar career trajectory characterizes many Chinese directors in the twenty-first century, although they may work in different film genres.[40] Feng Xiaogang (b. 1959) reinvented himself in the late 1990s, transforming from a social satirist mired in censorship problems to the most popular commercial director, sought after by cash-rich producers. He gradually abandoned his trademark urban comedy "new year's pictures" or "holiday films" (*hesuipian*) and explored other genres, such as the thriller, historical drama, and the war film.[41] During the 2007 holiday season, Feng surprised the Chinese film world with a war film, *Assembly* (*Jijie hao,* 2007), which projected brutal images of war at a time of year when people would otherwise expect light-hearted entertainment.

Hailed as the Chinese equivalent to *Saving Private Ryan* (1998) and set in a period stretching from the Civil War to the Korean War and the ensuing decades, *Assembly* adopts all three typical approaches to a war film: "war as spectacle," "war as tragedy," and "war as adventure."[42] First, as spectacle, *Assembly* is rich with audiovisual assaults on the audience and achieves an unusual sense of realism about war using high-tech artifice. The initial urban street fights and the subsequent battle to defend a military position at all costs create a feel approximating that of a Hollywood blockbuster war film and convinced many viewers that the Chinese war film had finally come of age in terms of technical sophistication.[43] Second, as tragedy, *Assembly* does not shy away from the causalities of war. By showing realistic scenes, such as when a communist officer is blown to pieces by a bomb and forty-seven soldiers give their lives so that their main troops can retreat unharmed, the film poses a persistent question as to the meaning of human sacrifice. Gu Zidi, the leader and only survivor of his platoon, finds it not just tragic but unjust that all his fallen comrades are classified as "missing in action" rather than "martyrs" and that they have not received proper recognition from the authorities. Third, as adventure, *Assembly* follows the typical war narrative of a "man on a mission,"[44] but this time the "mission" is less one on the battlefield than one from the postwar peace, when Gu's one-man intervention eventually succeeds in setting the historical record straight by revealing concrete evidence to prove that his comrades all died in action. Gu's unlikely tragic-heroic adventure on behalf of unofficial or not-yet-official history solicits the audience's identification with him and translates his private remembrance into a public memory of—indeed, a popular homage to—a different kind of individual heroism.[45]

A war film with a compelling narrative, emotional acting, and powerful images, *Assembly* was immediately greeted with widespread critical and popular acclaim and earned RMB 260 million (around $42 million USD) at the domestic box office in 2007.[46] Although a few recent television drama series may have rekindled audience interest in war and military genres,[47] scholars were quick to celebrate Feng's war film as a sure sign of the maturity of Chinese commercial blockbusters, a successful blend between blockbuster films and mainstream ideology and a monument dedicated to tens of thousands of ordinary soldiers.[48] Sure enough, because of the film's popularity, Gu Zidi's private remembrance is shared by enthusiastic audiences and scholars, although it is still not part of the collective memory authorized by the state. What is at stake in the film is less the value of human life than official recognition of individual honor: it is the loss of identity and belonging of his fallen comrades in official history that motivates Gu's one-man mission to seek recognition for them and to restore an honorable place for his otherwise nameless soldiers, and through his heroic efforts he receives overdue respect, and his name is added to a new roster of Chinese screen war heroes.

As mentioned in the introduction to this chapter, Gu Zidi is fundamentally different from Ma Dasan in *Devils at the Doorstep*. Politically unaffiliated, Ma is at best an exceptional Chinese villager whose private remembrance of the War of Resistance falls outside mainstream narratives and is categorically dismissed by official history. On the contrary, Gu is politically affiliated with the communist cause, albeit misunderstood and marginalized because of his eccentric behavior, but his private remembrance is never meant to challenge the legitimacy of the communist system; instead it aims to humanize it by helping it recognize its nameless fallen heroes. The success of *Assembly* arises as much from its ultimate conformity with official ideology as from its sensitive treatment of personal sacrifice and honor. The fictional account of Gu's success, nonetheless, only intensifies the film's function of providing relief and consolation to a viewing public obsessed with widespread injustice and inequality off screen. Like *Devils at the Doorstep*, *Assembly* serves as a haunting reminder that private remembrance often departs significantly from official history, in which victory is celebrated in carnival-like fashion at the expense of those who have fallen and in which the viewer is discouraged from posing the critical question as to who remembers, when, where, and how. It is through such critical questioning that we can arrive at a better understanding of war, history, and remembrance in Chinese cinema.

Notes

1   Jay Winter, *Remembering War: The Great War between Memory and History in the Twentieth Century* (New Haven, CT: Yale University Press, 2006), 3–4.

2   Ibid., 5.

3   Zhang Yingjin and Zhiwei Xiao, *Encyclopedia of Chinese Film* (London: Routledge, 1998), 355–356.

4   Jerome Silbergeld, *Body in Question: Image and Illusion in Two Chinese Films by Director Jiang Wen* (Princeton, NJ: P.Y. and Kinmay W. Tang Center for East Asian Art, Princeton University, 2008), 105–130.

5 On the "frailty" and "transience" of private remembrance, see Winter, *Remembering War*.

6 On the memory boom, see ibid.; and Ban Wang, *Illuminations from the Past: Trauma, Memory, and History in Modern China* (Stanford, CA: Stanford University Press, 2004).

7 Yomi Braester, *Witness against History: Literature, Film, and Public Discourse in Twentieth-Century China* (Stanford, CA: Stanford University Press, 2003), ix–x.

8 Zhang Yingjin, "Zhao Dan: Spectrality of Martyrdom and Stardom," *Journal of Chinese Cinemas* 2, no. 2 (2008): 108.

9 Zhou Zhengbao and Zhang Dong, "Zhanzheng pian yu Zhongguo kangzhan ticai gushi pian" (War films and Chinese features films dealing with the anti-Japanese war), *Wenyi yanjiu* (Studies in Literature and Art) 5 (1995).

10 Large state-run studios (e.g., Beijing, Changchun, and Shanghai) were given annual quotas for war film productions from the early 1950s onward, but the August First Studio was established in 1952 to specialize in the production of war or military-themed films.

11 Steve Neale, *Genre and Hollywood* (London: Routledge, 2000), 125.

12 James Chapman, *War and Film* (London: Reaktion, 2008), 7–16.

13 Huangfu Yichuan, *Zhongguo zhanzheng dianying shi* (History of Chinese war films) (Beijing: Zhongguo dianying chubanshe, 2005), 20–26.

14 Ibid., 266. Five other separate modes are differentiated in war films of the socialist period: (1) joining, (2) growing, (3) liberating, (4) playing, and (5) new narration in an international context. The first three modes concern the protagonist's character development in relation to individual and historical situations, while the last two involves points of view and narrative strategies. See Qu Liping, "Zhanzhengpian xushi moshi jiqi yanbian" (Transformation of narrative patterns in war films), in *Zhongguo dianying zhuanye shi yanjiu: dianying wenhua juan* (Studies in the history of Chinese cinema: The volume on film culture), ed. Yang Yuanying (Beijing: Zhongguo dianying chubanshe, 2006).

15 For instance, *Life Line* (*Shengming xian*, 1935) was directed by the U.S.-educated Moon Kwan (Guan Wenqing, 1896–1995) and produced by Grandview (Daguan), a company relocated from San Francisco to Hong Kong in 1935.

16 *Qi zheng piaopiao*, the Chinese title of the Hong Kong remake *Flag of Honor*, is also the title of the allegedly first patriotic song to emerge prior to the War of Resistance, which became popular when it was featured as a theme song in a Shanghai film, *Return My Land* (*Huangwo shanhe*, 1934). See Zhang Junxiang and Cheng Jihua, ed., *Zhongguo dianying da cidian* (Encyclopedia of Chinese cinema) (Shanghai: Shanghai cishu chubanshe, 1995), 746.

17 The best example of such a home-front drama is *Spring River Flows East*
(*Yijiang chunshui xiangdong liu,* 1947), which broke the Chinese box-office
record. For the prewar and wartime periods, see Zhang Yingjin, *Chinese
National Cinema* (London: Routledge, 2004), 13–95; for postwar productions,
see Paul G. Pickowicz, "Victory as Defeat: Postwar Visualizations of China's
War of Resistance," in *Becoming Chinese: Passages to Modernity and Beyond,*
ed. Wen-hsin Yeh (Berkeley: University of California Press, 2000).

18 Zhang Yingjin, *Screening China: Critical Interventions, Cinematic
Reconfigurations, and the Transnational Imaginary in Contemporary Chinese
Cinema* (Ann Arbor: Center for Chinese Studies, University of Michigan,
2002), 182–185.

19 Huangfu, *Zhongguo zhanzheng dianying shi,* 119.

20 Chapman, *War and Film,* 185.

21 Hong Junhao, "The Evolution of China's War Movie in Five Decades:
Factors Contributing to Changes, Limits, and Implications," *Asian Cinema*
10, no. 1 (1998).

22 One example of the repressed romance is *War and Love* (*Zhanhuo zhong de
qingchun,* Wang Yan, 1959), in which a cross-dressing woman solider has to
leave the army once her gender identity is discovered following an injury. An
exception to the absence of romance in the socialist period is *Story of Liubao
Village* (*Liubao de gushi,* 1957), where romance takes center stage, albeit only
to be put aside so that the couple involved can concentrate their energies on
the revolutionary cause in separate realms.

23 Dai Jinhua, *Dianying lilun yu piping shouce* (Handbook on film theory and
criticism) (Beijing: Kexue jishu wenxian chubanshe, 1993), 44.

24 Ibid., 44.

25 Liu Weihong, "Yu Wu Ziniu tan Wu Ziniu" (An interview with Wu Ziniu),
Dangdai dianying, no. 4 (1988): 112.

26 Zhang Yingjin, "*Evening Bell:* Wu Ziniu's Visions of History, War and
Humanity," in *Chinese Films in Focus: 25 New Takes,* ed. Chris Berry
(London: British Film Institute, 2003).

27 Other than those mentioned in the text, Wu Ziniu's war films include *Joyous
Heroes* (*Huanle yingxiong,* 1988), *Between Life and Death* (*Yingyang jie,* 1988),
and *The Big Mill* (*Da mofang,* 1990), all of which feature disturbing images of
communist characters who, far from being "joyous" and "heroic," suffer from
miserable conditions in life and death. See Zhang, *Screening China,* 178–179.

28 Walter Benjamin, *Illuminations: Essays and Reflections,* ed. Hannah Arendt
and trans. Harry Zohn (New York: Schocken, 1969), 256.

29 Zhang, "*Evening Bell,*" 84–85.

30 The official term for this largely unprepared and unpopular war, subsequently
rarely mentioned in public, is paradoxically "Zhong-yue bianjie ziwei fanji

zhan" (Sino-Vietnamese border self-defense offensive war). The war had as much to do with deteriorating Sino-Soviet relations as with Sino-Vietnamese relations.

31 Like *In Their Prime, Shanggan Ridge* elaborates the difficulties Chinese soldiers encounter in keeping their military position based in a cave, but unlike *In Their Prime,* where soldiers suffer from claustrophobia and hysteria in a cave, in *Shanggan Ridge* their former counterparts endure hardships with enthusiasm and patriotic pride, including singing a theme song that would become popular off screen for decades to come. Perhaps the only released film on the Sino-Vietnamese border war, *Garlands at the Foot of the Mountain,* justifies itself in terms of Chinese nationalism and communist martyrdom.

32 Zhongguo dianying ziliaoguan (China Film Archive), ed., *Zhongguo wusheng dianying juben* (Screenplays of Chinese silent films) (Beijing: Zhongguo dianying chubanshe, 1996), 1:278.

33 Ibid., 257.

34 Apart from Wu Ziniu's film, recent fictional dramatizations of the Nanjing Massacre include *Massacre in Nanjing (Tucheng xuezheng,* 1987); *Black Sun (Hei taiyang,* 1995), a Hong Kong production; *May and August (Wuyue Bayue,* 2002), a Chinese–Hong Kong coproduction narrated from the children's perspective; *Qixia Temple 1937 (Qixia si,* 2005), a story about patriotic Buddhist monks outside Nanjing; *Tokyo Tribunal (Dongjing shenpan,* 2006), a leitmotif film; *The Children of Huangshi* (Roger Spottiswoode, 2008), a coproduction of Australia, China, and Germany; *City of Life and Death (Nanjing! Nanjing!,* 2009), a war disaster film; and *Flowers of the War* (2011), a blockbuster film featuring Christian Bale. In addition to a Chinese documentary film, *Nanjing Massacre* (1982), and other Chinese television productions, recent foreign documentaries include *Rape of Nanjing* (2006), a U.S. production; *Nanjing* (2007), another U.S. release that won the Humanitarian Award at the Hong Kong Film Festival and the Documentary Film Editing Award at the Sundance Film Festival, both in 2007; and *Iris Chang: The Rape of Nanjing* (2007), a Canadian television production, which won the Special Jury's Award at the Guangzhou International Documentary Film Festival in December 2007.

35 Wu's alignment with official textbook history is seen as a major problem in *Nanjing 1937,* which is said to have resulted in the film's lack of true emotions and distinct vision and its largely propagandist tone and ineffective presentation.

36 Wu Ziniu, "Pai *Guoge* de chuzhong" (My original intentions in shooting *The National Anthem*), *Dangdai dianying* 5 (1999): 5–6.

37 Zhang, "*Evening Bell*," 86–87. Wu has since worked mostly as a director of television drama series, such as the thirty-one-episode *Grain Storage* (*Tianxia liangcang*, 2002).

38 Zhang, *Screening China*, 197–201.

39 Ibid., 191–201.

40 Another key figure who renounced his earlier position of "bankable dissent" is Zhang Yuan (b. 1963), who was considered an "outlaw" director and a leading figure of the early Sixth Generation in the early 1990s but who has accepted to work within the state system since 1999. See Zhang Yingjin, *Cinema, Space, and Polylocality in a Globalizing China* (Honolulu: University of Hawai'i, 2009).

41 Zhang Rui, *The Cinema of Feng Xiaogang: Commercialization and Censorship in Chinese Cinema after 1989* (Hong Kong: Hong Kong University Press, 2008).

42 Chapman, *War and Film.*

43 The Hollywood feeling is in part attributed to the work of a South Korean special effects team, which helped produce a successful Korean blockbuster, *Taegukki: Brotherhood of War* (*T'aegŭkki hwinallimyŏ*, 2004). See Jia Leilei, "Shijian dianying: *Jijie hao*" (*Assembly:* An event film), *Dangdai dianying* (Contemporary cinema) 3 (2008): 6.

44 Chapman, *War and Film*, 204.

45 Gu Zidi's success is "unlikely" because, as Feng Xiaogang acknowledged in a post-screening discussion at the University of Southern California in April 2008, the real-life prototype of Gu Zidi died without achieving his mission of getting official recognition for his fallen comrades. Feng admitted to having considered this ending of failure, but his scriptwriter Liu Heng objected on the ground that the audience would demand a happy ending. See Rao Shuguang, "*Jijie hao* zai sikao" (Thoughts on *Assembly*), *Dangdai dianying* 3 (2008): 20.

46 In this case, *Assembly* is comparable to the 2007 top box office in China set by a Hollywood blockbuster import, *Transformers* (2007), which raked in RMB 280 million (around $45 million). See Jia, "Shijian dianying," 5.

47 Recent public interest in war-related genres is evident in the popularity of the thirty-episode television drama series *Soldiers* (*Shibing tuji*, 2007), directed by Kang Honglei, who would lead the same team to create another successful series, the forty-three-episode *My Commander and My Regiment* (*Wode tuanzhan wode tuan*, 2009).

48 Jia, "Shijian dianying," 4–7.

CHAPTER 2

Of Female Spies and National Heroes
A Brief History of Anti-Japanese Films in Taiwan from the 1950s to the 1970s

Wenchi Lin

Japan's invasion of China on September 18, 1931, and the war between the two countries brought fourteen years of tremendous hardship and pain to the Chinese people, who had already been suffering from the aftereffects of the Republican revolution and conflict among warlords. During the period of the "War of Resistance," numerous documentaries, such as *The Marco Polo Bridge Incident* (*Lugouqiao shibian*, 1937) and *Recapturing Tai'erzhuan* (*Kefu Tai'erzhuang*, 1939), depicted Japan's military atrocities. Both documentaries highlighted memorable battles during the first year of the war, but an even more robust cinematic record was captured in the many fiction films about the war. According to scholar Wang Chaoguang, the "China Motion Picture Studio and Central Film Studio made nineteen fiction films between 1938 and 1949, almost all directly dealing with the Anti-Japanese War. . . . These films preserve the history of the Chinese people's brave and resolute resistance against the invading enemy."[1] Before it fell to the Japanese in 1941, Hong Kong had produced more patriotic films set during wartime than the mainland. As the anti-Japanese war escalated, many filmmakers and actors escaped to Hong Kong and boosted its film industry. The Hong Kong–based film scholar Yu Muyun claims that:

> Hong Kong made more than seventy anti-Japanese patriotic films (several times more than China did). It became a trend of Hong Kong cinema

in the 1930s. Those films not only fortified nationalist beliefs among Chinese citizens, domestically and abroad, but also taught a heartfelt lesson to film workers in Hong Kong, that is, one should never work for the Japanese when ruled by them.[2]

According to the film critic Liang Liang, as many as twenty-five out of the eighty-five films made in Hong Kong in 1937 were patriotic films, calling on people to fight Japan in defense of China.[3]

The anti-Japanese war ended when Japan surrendered unconditionally to the Allies in 1945. But before China had time to recover from eight years of devastation, a full-scale civil war between the Nationalist (Guomindang, GMD) and communist forces broke out. In Wang's estimation, of the 150 fiction films made during the postwar period between 1945 and 1949, about 30 were on anti-Japanese themes, and he divides these films into two major categories, spy thrillers and social dramas.[4] Among them were two successful films: *Spy Number One* (*Tianzi diyihao,* 1946), an entertaining spy thriller based on a theatrical play, and *Spring River Flows East* (*Yijiang chunshui xiangdong liu,* 1947), an epic film depicting the hardships ordinary people endured during the war and the injustices of postwar society under the Nationalist government. In the mid-1960s, both films were remade in Taiwan. *Spy Number One* even created a genre of its own and began a revival of anti-Japanese films.

In 1949, the Nationalist government fled to Taiwan, founding the Republic of China (ROC), and on the mainland the Chinese Communist Party established the People's Republic of China (PRC). For the next fifteen years, while the PRC continued to produce anti-Japanese films focused on guerrilla battles and intelligence activities—including many popular works such as *Daughters of China* (*Zhonghua ernü,* 1949), *Guerrillas on the Plain* (*Pingyuan youjidui,* 1955), *The Eternal Wave* (*Yong bu xiaoshi de dianpo,* 1958), and *Zhang Ga, a Boy Soldier* (*Xiaobing Zhang Ga,* 1963)—the Nationalist government in Taiwan found no strong motivation for making films about the war. The three state-owned studios in Taiwan—the Central Motion Picture Corporation (CMPC), the China Motion Picture Studio, and the Agricultural Education Studio—made only two films with anti-Japanese themes in the 1950s. The first is *The Assault* (*Xuezhan,* 1958), a coproduction of the Gaohe Film Company and the General Political Department of the Ministry of National Defense, which was in charge of the China Motion Picture Studio. The film presents realistic battle scenes of a squad on the front lines without a clear indication of when and where the battle took place. The story was so little known that an introduction by a military officer had to be added to verbally celebrate the bravery of the soldiers and the anti-Japanese spirit, which was invoked to emphasize the importance of anti-communism. The second one is *The Slut and the Saint* (*Dangfu yu shengnü,* 1959) made by the CMPC. It depicts the early revolt against Japan by the Taiwanese after Taiwan was ceded to Japan in 1895. In the film, a patriotic girl who helps local insurgents conceals her actions by living with a man, for which she is labeled a slut, and is later accused of murder. She commits suicide as means of protesting the unfair accusations against her, and her good name is finally restored after Taiwan's colonial era under Japanese control ended in 1945.

During the war, the Nationalists, particularly their leader, Chiang Kai-shek, were accused of focusing on combating the communists, whom they feared were taking advantage of the conflict with Japan to build up their own military capability, rather than on defeating Japan. Shi Bogong has pointed out that anti-Japanese films made between 1937 and 1945 seldom portray images of the Japanese invaders or Chinese military officials due to what was perceived as Chiang's compromising attitude toward Japan.[5] After 1945, Chiang needed Japan's help in the civil war against the communists and in protecting Taiwan, and thus the Nationalist government in Taiwan had very practical political reasons for not encouraging anti-Japanese sentiment. In 1949 he even secretly invited Japanese military advisors to return to Taiwan to form the Japanese Military Assistance Advisory Group, the "White Group" (Baituan), which played a key role in the training of the Nationalist army in Taiwan. Thus, the three state-sponsored studios refrained from portraying anti-Japanese sentiments on the screen. At the same time, as Shiu Ruei-mei (Xu Ruimei) argues, after fifty years of colonization under the Japanese the Nationalist government was also keen on restoring a Chinese identity to the people on the island.[6]

It was not until the mid-1960s that state-owned studios began to make films about the anti-Japanese war. In 1963, Taiwan Film Studio (Taiwansheng dianying shezhi chang) made *The Fighting Acrobats* (*Dihou zhuangshi xie*) for audiences to "admire those brave anti-Japanese deeds." Directed by the actor-director Wang Yin, the film depicts a family of acrobat performers that is helping the government to destroy a Japanese arsenal. A year later, the CMPC made *An Unseen Triggerman* (*Leibao fengyun,* Li Jia, 1965), which tells the story of a militia formed by a local clan in Henan Province. After the death of its commander, the militia splits into two factions (led respectively by the son and the nephew of the commander), which are on the verge of having a major fallout because of subversive activities organized by an ambitious bandit. The two factions reunite and ward off the bandit and his military gang thanks to the efforts of a young Nationalist army officer. Both films use a family story to tell a war story and emphasize the importance of unity, appealing to the audience's desire for unification in a new state. But these titles released by state-run studios were in the minority, as most anti-Japanese films made in Taiwan in the 1950s and 1960s were produced by local film companies.

Film critic Huang Ren laments:

> There must have been plenty of stories to be told about the Taiwanese's resistance against Japan during the colonial period. But among the roughly 1,000 titles promoting local culture, less than 10 percent were anti-Japanese films. Though there might be other reasons, I believe [this lack of enthusiasm] was mainly a result of the government's policy not to encourage, support, nor produce any such film. It was indeed the worst mistake made by the government.[7]

The Taiwanese apparently had very different anti-Japanese tales to tell. It was only a year after the first film using Taiwan dialect had been made in 1956 that He Jiming directed the first anti-Japanese film in Taiwan: *Bloodshed on the Green Mountains (Qingshan bixue,* 1957). The film is a realistic representation of the Musha (Wushe) Incident of 1930, the last major uprising against colonial Japan by the indigenous Seediq tribe led by the tribal chief Mona Rudao. In the incident, the Seediq aborigines fought bravely against the Japanese soldiers equipped with modern weaponry and eventually drove them to resort to using poison gas to end the revolt. He learned about this story while working among the aborigines and decided to turn it into a film after his newly founded film company had made money on an earlier popular hit. This film, like many other films in Taiwan dialect, unfortunately has been lost, and only descriptions of the content and a few stills remain to indicate what the film was like. It was clearly very difficult to shoot in the mountains, and He did not receive military support for the extensive battle scenes, even though that was often customary for big-budget patriotic war films. The script won first prize at the first Taiwan Dialect Film Festival. The following year, He made *Bloody Battle of Ta-pa-ni (Xuezhan jiaobanian,*

1958), which recounts an armed revolt against the Japanese in 1915 by Han Taiwanese (i.e., descendants of those who had migrated from the mainland) led by Yu Qingfang, in what became known as the Ta-pa-ni incident. The patriotic theme of this film won it the only award a film in Taiwan dialect has ever received from the Ministry of Education, though it did not prevent He's film studio from going out of business in 1961. Huang Ren describes the failure of He's studio as not only "a great loss to Taiwanese cinema but a loss to Taiwanese culture as well."[8] Three other films about Taiwanese revolts against colonial Japan came out in the mid-1960s: *Heroes on the Island* (*Taiwan yinglie zhuan*, 1965), *Legend of Bagua Mountain* (*Baguashan chuanqi*, 1965), and *Turbulence at Musha* (*Wushe fengyun*, 1965). These were historical films with apparently greater commercial intentions than He Jiming's two previous efforts. Although the three later films have all been lost, too, their quality was doubtful at best, as indicated by the fact that He did not find *Turbulence at Musha* "realistic enough" and Qiu Jinlong complained that the aboriginal characters looked like Native American Indians.[9]

In addition to films about historical revolts, Taiwan's local film companies made about ten films between the 1950s and the 1960s depicting traumatic experiences during World War II of the islanders under colonialism. Some of them told sad stories of lost loved ones and broken families caused by the conscription of young Taiwanese men into the Japanese army, such as *Night Fragrance* (*Yelaixiang*, 1957), *Farewell My Love* (*Songjun xin mianmian*, 1965), and *Love You Until Death* (*Ai ni dao si*, 1967). Other films portray the hardships Taiwanese draftees had to endure in the war as well as their patriotic acts of sabotage and revolt, such as *Songs of Southern Island* (*Hun duan nanhai*, 1958) and *Return from the Hainan Island* (*Hainandao zhanhou guilai*, 1958). And still others depict the sad experiences of families divided by the war as well as the reunions with lost loved ones after 1949, when the Nationalist government moved to Taiwan. Films in this genre include *Waiting for You Year after Year* (*Deng ni yinian guo yinian*, 1964) and *Tarzan and the Treasure* (*Taishan yu baozang*, 1965).

It is a great pity that most of these films no longer exist, for collectively they provide a powerful counterweight to the colonial propaganda film *Sayon's Bell* (*Sayon no kane*, 1943). Directed by Hiroshi Shimizu and starring the Japanese actress Yoshiko Yamaguchi (aka Li Xianglan) as a Taiwanese aboriginal young woman, this joint production of the Japanese colonial government in Taiwan, the Manchu Film Association, and the Shochiku

Company was meant to inspire patriotism among the aborigines to join the Takasago Volunteers to help the Japanese fight the war in the South Pacific. The film was based on an incident in which a young girl named Sayon was accidentally drowned in a river while carrying the luggage of a drafted Japanese police officer on his way to report for duty. A series of propaganda campaigns by the Japanese government portrayed her as a brave and loyal colonial young woman sacrificing her life for the Japanese emperor. A memorial bell engraved with the words "The bell of Sayon, a patriotic girl" was dedicated to her.[10] In the words of Zuo Yi'en, this manufactured "cultural myth" transformed an innocent Taiwanese aboriginal young woman into a model imperial subject for all Taiwanese to follow.[11] The film not only stresses that going to war for Japan is the greatest honor an aboriginal young man can ever enjoy but adds a romantic element by portraying Sayon as a girl who wants her love interest to become a soldier for the emperor. According to the writer Chen Kehua, the film was so popular that many young aborigines were inspired by it to join up as Takasago Volunteers.

Films such as *Farewell My Love,* one of the few films still available, reveal the traumatic experiences of the Taiwanese during the war. Despite a toned-down depiction of racial clashes between the Taiwanese and the Japanese (to comply with government censorship standards), the film still conveys a strong anticolonial sentiment by having the male Taiwanese protagonist, an elementary school teacher, and his friend stare back at a Japanese military official who had slapped him for no good reason at the beginning of the film. They decide to take action in order to teach the Japanese official a lesson by throwing stones at his window that night. They are caught, jailed, and eventually sent to the South Pacific, leaving the protagonist's girlfriend, pregnant with his child, to endure the hardship of separation. Several years go by and, convinced that her lover was killed in the war, the girl reluctantly agrees to marry another man for the sake of her child. Although the film ends with a happy reunion, with the protagonist returning home just in time to stop the wedding, the film still reveals the pain and sadness of many Taiwanese who suffered under Japanese colonial rule. When the director Xin Qi was interviewed about his abandoned film project *A Man Who Lost His Fatherland* (*Meiyou zuguo de ren*), which he deeply regretted not having enough money to make in the 1950s, he said that it was this sadness of life under colonialism that he wished to express: "As Taiwanese, we must leave something to posterity. After the long years of colonial rule by a foreign people, we must express the sadness accumulated in our hearts."[12] Only a handful of films were made that depict the colonial experience of Taiwan, and most of them have been lost.

The Sino-Japanese War Spy Thriller

While relatively few films exploring Taiwan's colonial history under Japan were made between the 1950s and the early 1960s due to the government's policy of befriending Japan, a surge of Taiwanese spy films about the anti-Japanese war began to appear in 1964 thanks to the popularity of *Dr. No* (1962) and subsequent James Bond films, which whet Taiwanese audience's appetites for local spy thrillers. The producer/director Zhang Ying and his wife, the actress Bai Hong, quickly came up with the idea of remaking *Spy Number One* as a local version of a spy film. The film substitutes the typical background of a James Bond film, the cold war, with the anti-Japanese war in China. Bai played agent Li Cuiying, Spy No. 1, who, in order to fulfill her mission, gives up her lover, Zhou Lingyun (portrayed by Ke Junxiong), to marry a Shanghai-based government minister who is a traitor to China working for the Japanese. Her job proves even more difficult when, three years later, Lingyun, who had also become an agent (Spy No. 53), strolls into her house. Not knowing her true identity, Lingyun still resents what she had done to him and accepts advances from his young cousin, despite his lingering feelings for Cuiying. This romantic drama is interwoven with a thrilling plot rich with the twists and turns of the spy genre as well as strong comic performances from minor characters. Despite its hodgepodge of seemingly incompatible film elements, the film was an immediate success, and a sequel was made the same year, followed by three more in the next two years.

Other filmmakers did not wait long to capitalize on this new interest in spy thrillers (*jiandie pian*). According to a filmography of Taiwanese cinema compiled by Xue Huiling and Wu Junhui, at least thirty spy-genre films were released in the 1960s.[13] Most of the films have been lost, but, based on extant materials we can estimate that no less than half these titles used the War of Resistance against Japan as their historical background. Films set during the War of Resistance still available today include *Female Agent No. 7* (*Di qi hao nüjiandie*, 1964), *Secret Agent Queen* (*Tewu nüjiandie wang*, 1965), *Golden Chicken Heart* (*Jinjixin*, 1965), *Spy Red Rose* (*Jiandie hongmeiguei*, 1966), *Agent Peony* (*Qingbaoyuan baimudan*, 1966), and *Red Rose, Real and False* (*Zhenjia hongmeiguei*, 1966). These films were made in Taiwanese but are also available dubbed in Mandarin to maximize the potential viewership. Unfortunately, like many other Taiwanese films of this period, they were shot and edited hastily in order to make a quick profit while spy thrillers were still in vogue. These and far too many similar films were churned out over a relatively short period. The popularity of the genre did not last long, and by 1968 the Sino-Japanese War "Taiwanese spy film" was already passé.

The titles of these Taiwanese spy films demonstrate that they were not prompted by anti-Japanese sentiment, which was no more than a pretext. Rather, they focus on the female agents and intelligence activities in a genre combining the thriller and comedy. Although some films, such as *Spy Number One,* include documentary footage of Japanese air raids and Chinese refugees, these images are inserted to provide background, not to evoke memories of the war in China. The Japanese agents and military officers, as well as Han traitors (*hanjian*), in these films are simplistic and flat characters, who are almost always lecherous yet impotent. The entertaining attraction of these spy films lies in the clever tricks that the female Chinese agents pull off against their Japanese counterparts. Bai Hong's many identities in disguise in the *Spy Number One* series are one such example. The earnest but clumsy lead male agent—also the male lead in the film—whom the female agent secretly has to protect, is in comparison quite dull. Although some films try to display high-tech gadgets and modern inventions, such as X-ray guns and automatic sliding doors in the style of the Bond movies, others still adopt the conventions of traditional martial arts films, such as portraying the female agent incognito in black garb with flying daggers as her weapon of choice. It is also not uncommon for the films to display partial female nudity, often in the form of a dance performance in the plot, to provide additional appeal. The free adaptation and borrowing of elements from Bond movies point to the vitality of the budding Taiwanese film industry in the 1960s. But the cavalier handling of anti-Japanese history testifies to the government's postwar policy toward Japan to "manufacture Taiwan as a friendly country," as Shiu Ruei-Mei convincingly argues.[14]

As entertainment, these Taiwanese spy thrillers construct an imaginary world of China/Taiwan. In this world, the nation is perfunctory, and virtually no attention is paid to lofty issues such as "national loyalty." This is in sharp opposition to postwar Hong Kong's anti-Japanese films, such as *Flower Street* (*Huajie,* 1950), which deals with the serious social and ethical dimensions of the war.[15] In these Taiwanese films, however, despite recurrent plots based on covert missions, undercover Chinese agents never have to address questions regarding their national loyalty. The demarcation between loyal Chinese, evil Japanese, and sneaky Chinese traitors is drawn all too clearly, with no moral ambiguity between characters on each side. Ironically, in several of these anti-Japanese narratives, it is often the Chinese agents' recognition of one another that helps move the plot along. Take, for instance, in *Female Agent No. 7,* one of the first films in this genre, the male lead agent disguises himself as the president of the Shanghai Sino-Japanese Friendship Society to frequent the headquarters of the Japanese secret service. Over the course of the film, he realizes that not only was the captain of the detective unit in the Japanese secret service a mole but that she was the daughter of the director of the secret service, who also turns out to be the mysterious Chinese spy in black: Agent No. 7.

While these scenes of recognition between different Chinese agents are entertaining because they are thrilling moments that are common in spy films, they also reveal a subtle and inadvertent expression of Taiwan's unique postcolonial situation. The drama of a "Chinese" having difficulty in telling whether other Chinese are on the Chinese side or the Japanese side may have provided the Taiwanese audience, whose national identity was still problematic in the eyes of the Nationalist government and in their own minds, with a kind of pleasure of mimicry, as Homi Bhabha describes it.[16] A scene in *Female Agent No. 7* demonstrates this very well. In the film, when the Japanese agent Kawashima Yoshiko tries to sniff out all the Chinese undercover agents working in the secret service, she rounds up the suspects and puts them in jail. Then she asks the captain to surprise them by calling out "Attention!" in Mandarin. Two workers instantly respond by standing stiffly still—they were, of course, the Chinese agents, who both later commit suicide after being interrogated. The joke could only work in a film like this, in which all Japanese and mainland Chinese characters are played by Taiwanese actors speaking Taiwan dialect. In this context, Mandarin was introduced as the official language of Taiwan by the Nationalist government, and it was the only "foreign" language, despite the fact that the film was set in Shanghai. The scene not only revealed the foreignness of the official language and turned it into a metaphor for the Nationalist government in general, but it also served as a form of mimicry that made fun of the Taiwanese people's obedience-by-coercion under the Nationalists. The film's excessively patriotic ending, which adopted the national anthem for its soundtrack with a shot of the national flag flying, can be read as a symptom of the film's uneasiness about its own ideological indiscretions and challenges to the Nationalists' hegemony.

In the end, the genre of the anti-Japanese spy thriller survived the short-lived Taiwanese spy films after 1968, but in a new form. The sensationally successful example of the Mandarin spy film by the Hong Kong director Li Hanxiang, *Storm over the Yangtze River* (*Yangzijiang fengyun*), in 1969 began a second wave of anti-Japanese spy films. Unlike Taiwanese spy films, which were made by local film companies for the purpose of making a quick profit, the production of *Storm over the Yangtze River* was a carefully planned project helmed by the general manager of the China Motion Picture Studio, Mei Chang-ling, who later became the president of the CMPC. Unhappy that the domestic market was dominated by three film genres—Huangmei opera films (*Huangmeidiao yingpian*), Qiong Yao romance films (*Qiong Yao aiqing wenyipian*), and martial arts films (*wuxia pian*)—he decided to "make a film filled with the nationalist spirit, capable of lifting the people's morale and stimulating patriotism" (China Motion Picture Studio 5). He asked the scriptwriter Zhang Yongxiang to create film adaptations of two novels, *Bridge of Death* (*Siqiao*) and *Secret Agent Yangtze River No. 2* (*Changjiang er hao*), which were based on historical novels by Zou Lang,[17] and invited Li Hanxiang to direct the films. The adaptation of *Bridge of Death* was released under the title *Storm over the Yangtze River* (*Yangzijiang fengyun*) in 1969. The film had a star-studded cast, with the leading actors of the day Peter Yang (Yang Qun), Ke Junxiong, Li Lihua, Zhang Meiyao, Ou Wei, and Sun Yue. The film depicted a battle that took place in Jianli County, Hubei Province, during the War of Resistance and the intense interactions between secret agents of the Nationalist government, the CCP, and the Japanese army. Wang Fan (portrayed by Yang Qun) is a double agent, who, on the surface, works for the Japanese secret service. Unable to reveal his true identity as an undercover Nationalist agent, not only is he forced to endure threats and humiliation at the hands of his compatriots but he also has to be disgraced with respect to his family and endure rejection by his own son. He later discovers that his associate, the Widow Zhuo (portrayed by Li Lihua), is another undercover agent, whose true identity is as the commander of a guerrilla brigade. Together they help the director of the Nationalist county intelligence agency to persuade the division commander of the Japanese puppet army to defect, ultimately leading to the defeat of the Japanese army on the outskirts of the county. At the end of the film, Wang's true identity is finally revealed and his honor is publicly restored, and the film ends with a tear-jerking reunion between father and son.

Compared with previous Taiwan spy films, *Storm over the Yangtze River* is a much higher-quality production in almost all aspects. Being the first film in Taiwan to show grand-scale battle scenes of the War of Resistance also helped boost audience interest. Many viewers were moved by the film's displays of patriotism, especially those exhibited by the character Wang Fan. As one audience member at the time put it, "Wang Fan was just an ordinary person in the distant countryside of a province. The sacred mission of the nation and patriotism called forth a noble spirit from this small character to sacrifice for the great cause [of the nation]."[18] The film was the single most profitable title in Taiwan the year of its release.[19] Critics in general also applauded this film, which was the first film shot in Taiwan by the director Li Hanxiang. The veteran film critic Huang Ren, for instance, praised the film's achievement in "convincingly portraying the people's passionate nationalist spirit as well as the underground agents' willingness to sacrifice for the better good in a well-told narrative," as opposed to the Taiwanese spy films, which "were mostly imitations of foreign science fantasy films without a speck of historical truth."[20] Under Li Hanxiang's direction, the actors performed the roles vividly and demonstrated a psychological depth not found in earlier Taiwanese spy films. The film went on to win three major acting awards at the Seventh Golden Horse Festival in Taiwan (1969), including one for Li Lihua for the best performance by an actress, Peter Yang for the best performance by an actor, and Sun Yue for the best performance in a supporting role.

The success of *Storm over the Yangtze River* ushered in a second wave of spy films in Taiwan, mostly in the style of spy war films (*jiandie zhanzhengpian*). According to a report in *Qingnian zhanshi bao* (Youth Soldier Daily) on August 15, 1969, seven spy war films were already in preproduction then—namely *Galloping Horses on Central China* (*Yuema zhongyuan*), *Storm over the Han River* (*Hanjiang fengyun*), *Secret Agent Yangtze River No. 1* (*Changjiang yihao*), *Widow Zhuo* (*Zhuo guafu*), *The Battle of Yalu River* (*Yalujiang zhizhan*), *Mother Son Agents* (*Zimu jiandiewang*), and other similar stories and scripts were being prepared. It estimated that at least ten spy war films would begin production by the end of the year.[21] A few veteran directors of Taiwanese spy films also jumped on the bandwagon. *Secret Agent Yangtze River No. 1* (1970), for instance, was directed by Liang Zhefu, who had made *Spy Red Rose* and *Red Rose, Real and False*. The film was also based on a novel by Zou Lang and featured the same cast playing the same characters. It depicted the Japanese army's attempts to assassinate Wang Fan and the Widow Zhuo and could be seen as a sequel to *Storm over the Yangtze River*. Nonetheless, this black-and-white film was poorly made and was not well received, unlike Li's film.

What was more impressive was another spy film that Liang made the same year, *Secret Agent Chungking No. 1* (*Chongqing yihao,* 1970). This film, in color, was an adaptation of another Zou Lang novel. Unlike *Storm over the Yangtze River,* which was a new type of spy film, *Secret Agent Chungking No. 1* bore similarities to earlier Taiwanese spy films. For example, the infiltration of Chinese agents into the Japanese headquarters returned as the main theme of the narrative. The production values in this film were an obvious improvement over Liang's earlier efforts. The film featured a tighter plot, more thrilling action sequences depicting covert missions, and more realistically portrayed characters. The film depicts a family in which the son is the deputy director of the intelligence agency in Nanjing, where his sister works for him as an agent. As the chairman of the Sino-Japanese Friendship Committee, their mother provides ideal cover for them. Little do they know that their own mother—secret agent Chungking No. 1—is actually the chief director of the Nanjing agency where they work and that she has been supervising them incognito all along. When the siblings are captured along with other agents, their mother rescues them. Still in her undercover role, she asks her son to give in and work for the Japanese in order to save his life. The son chastises his mother for betraying the nation to work as a mole for the Japanese. Then, pretending to accept his mother's pleas, he takes his first opportunity to try to suffocate her. When that fails, he bites her arm, causing profuse bleeding. The sequence is charged with Nationalist ideology, which puts the love of country above love for one's own mother. The mother eventually reveals her true identity, and everyone escapes. At the film's climax, the mother blows up the Japanese military base, and her children beg for her forgiveness. She in turn assures them that they have done nothing wrong. This ostentatious display of patriotic ideology won the film a special award at the Eighth Golden Horse Film Festival (1970) for Advocating Nationalist Spirit.

Sino-Japanese War Epics and National Heroes

In the 1970s, a series of setbacks in the realm of foreign affairs—Taiwan's withdrawal from the United Nations in 1971, President Richard Nixon's visit to China, Japan's severance of diplomatic relations with Taiwan in 1972, to be followed by the United States doing the same in 1978—would have dramatic repercussions on the cultural front and the ideology behind anti-Japanese films. As Taiwan's diplomatic situation worsened, anti-Japanese war films quickly replaced spy war films to become the main genre of films produced by state-owned studios. The key person who championed this significant change was Mei Chang-ling, the producer of *Storm over the Yangtze River*. Mei was appointed general manager of the CMPC in 1972. Two years later he made an important film biography of General Zhang Zizhong, who died fighting the Japanese during the War of Resistance, *The Everlasting Glory* (*Yinglie qianqiu,* 1974), directed by Ding Shanxi. The film received the full support of the Ministry of Defense, which facilitated the inclusion of a series of extraordinary battle sequences. To portray the general as a national hero, it highlights three aspects of his military career. First, he sacrifices his reputation and agrees to become the mayor of Beiping[22] (now Beijing) while it is under Japanese occupation. Despite being wrongly accused of being a traitor (even by his own daughter), he perseveres and helps the Nationalist leader, Chiang Kai-shek, to earn more time to prepare for the coming war with Japan. Second, to demonstrate his skilled leadership as an army commander, the film shows that he led the Thirty-Eighth Division of the Nationalist Army to achieve China's first major military victory over Japan at Xifengkou. Third is his heroic death on the battlefield of Nanguadian in northern Hubei Province. *The Everlasting Glory* was well received, and the government also openly promoted the film. It broke box-office records, earning more in ticket sales than any other film in Taiwan up to that time. In just five days after its initial release, *The Everlasting Glory* earned more than NT$1 million in domestic ticket sales. Ke Jun-xiong, who was known for his many leading roles as a charismatic playboy and womanizer, played the role of General Zhang. His performance in this film was so good that it completely changed his screen persona for the rest of his acting career. The prime minister at the time, Chiang Ching-kuo (Jiang Jingguo; Chiang Kai-shek's son), not only praised the film as "the most successful film the CMPC has ever made" but also told his cabinet members that they should go to see the film and "emulate General Zhang Zizhong's spirit of willing sacrifice and unyielding determination."[23]

In 1975, at the twenty-first Asia Pacific Film Festival, *The Everlasting Glory* won awards for best director, best performance by an actor, best script, and best editing. The Twelfth Golden Horse Film Festival that year also gave it a special award for advocating the national spirit. The positive response to the film as well as its popularity encouraged the CMPC to make two more film biographies on anti-Japanese war subjects: *Eight Hundred Heroes* (*Babai zhuangshi,* 1975), also directed by Ding Shanxi, and *Heroes of the Eastern Skies* (*Jianqiao yinglie zhuan,* 1977), directed by Zhang Zengze. *Eight Hundred Heroes* recaptures the heroic 1937 battle at Sihang Warehouse in Shanghai that initiated fighting with Japan by a battalion of Chinese soldiers led by the regimental commander Xie Jinyuan (portrayed by Ke Junxiong).[24] *Heroes of the Eastern Skies* turns its camera to the skies and shows how the Air Force Commander Gao Zhihang (portrayed by Liang Xiushen), leads his pilots in winning air battles against pilots flying Japan's more advanced fighter aircraft. The first Taiwan film to show extensive air battle scenes, it caused quite a sensation. Neither of the films, however, reached the artistic heights of *The Everlasting Glory,* which the film critic Liang Liang considers "a landmark of war films." At the Thirteenth Golden Horse Festival in 1976, *Eight Hundred Heroes* was only given the special award for advocating national spirit. And *Heroes of the Eastern Skies,* despite winning five awards including those for best director and best script, at the Fourteenth Golden Horse Film Festival in 1976, was also described as one of the "Ten Worst Films of the Year" by film critics at *Yingxiang zazhi* (Influence Magazine) in 1977.[25]

Chiang Ching-kuo had good reasons for praising *The Everlasting Glory* so enthusiastically. At the time, Taiwan was facing its most severe national crisis since the Nationalist government had first arrived there in 1949. The "dignity of the Chinese," as the veteran film critic/producer Peggy Chiao (Jiao Xiongping) put it—which was precisely what Zhang Zizhong demonstrated while he was the mayor of Beiping—was what Taiwan desperately needed from its people during the turbulent 1970s.[26] The Ministry of Education implemented a plan for "Education of the National Spirit" in 1971. Maintaining "national confidence and dignity" among the citizens and retaining an "unyielding national force" were two key principles.[27] In this sense, *The Everlasting Glory, Eight Hundred Heroes,* and *Heroes of the Eastern Skies* were excellent contributors to the elevation of the ROC's national spirit. The War of Resistance as portrayed in these films can be read as an allegory for Taiwan's national situation in the 1970s. If Zhang Zizhong, Xie Jinyuan, and Gao Zhihang could endure the hardships of the War of Resistance to achieve a final victory, then Taiwan could also overcome hard times as long as its citizens maintained their national spirit. Nowhere was the success of this education articulated more clearly than in this review by Li Zhongdao in the *Overseas Chinese Daily News:*

> We felt so tremendously confident about our nation's bright future. The difficulties our nation faces today are worse than the invasion of the Japanese. And the killing and raping of our compatriots in China by the Communist Chinese surpasses the Nanjing Massacre (1937) many times

over. As long as we all have the spirit of Zhang Zizhong, we shall overcome the difficulties of our nation. . . . We need more Zhang Zizhongs.[28]

It is not surprising that all three films contained scenes in which even
the Japanese and the British were moved by the Chinese heroes' spirit. At
the end of *The Everlasting Glory,* before he kills himself so that he will not
be taken prisoner, Zhang Zizhong, severely wounded, lectures the Japanese
commanding officer, who goes to ask him to surrender so as to save his life.
Instead of surrendering, Zhang delivers the following monologue:

> The reason I am still alive, after bleeding from six gunshot wounds, is
> to save my last breath to ask you to tell Seisirou Itagaki [the commander
> of the Fifth Division of the Imperial Japanese Army] and your emperor
> that I have refused to yield even up until the last minute. I, Zhang
> Zizhong, am merely a veteran soldier of China. There are thousands and
> tens of thousands more young soldiers and generals who will continue
> fighting until every last drop of blood has been paid back. Go home!
> China is too great for you to conquer.

The film cuts to a reaction shot of the Japanese commanding officer, who—
truly moved by Zhang's words—replies that the apples his government has
encouraged them to go to China to enjoy are too bitter to swallow. The images
of the bodies of dead Japanese soldiers reinforce the great cost the Japanese
had paid for their invasion. He then salutes Zhang and says to him, "May the
commander-in-chief's brave soul always be with us to teach our military government to shut off the killing machine and get rid of the pain of war." When
Zhang finally ends his life by impaling himself on a dagger, the Japanese commanding officer calls out to his soldiers: "To the Chinese war god, salute!" The
film then shows even Seisirou raising his hand to salute Zhang. It is of no
consequence that the scene is not historically accurate (for one thing, the name
"war god" was given to Zhang by Chiang Kai-shek posthumously); the point is
to demonstrate the invincible power of the national spirit.

In *Eight Hundred Heroes,* the British in their enclaves are also touched
by the courage of a young girl scout, Yang Huimin (portrayed by Brigitte
Lin), who risks her life to sneak into the warehouse. After allowing Yang
and her friends as well as several trucks with supplies to get through to the
warehouse, the British general tells his subordinates, "Don't let the Japanese
capture these brave people. Just think, because of these brave boy scouts and

girl scouts, the whole relationship between Japan and the Great Britain will be completely and drastically changed." *Heroes of the Eastern Skies* goes on to show Japanese soldiers saluting a Chinese pilot, as in the final scene in *The Everlasting Glory.* In the scene in which Air Force Lieutenant Yan Hai-wen, having managed to get out of his damaged aircraft, is surrounded by Japanese soldiers who are pursuing him, he takes down a few of them with his handgun and then stands up to face them. With the last bullet in his gun he takes his own life after screaming "Long live the Republic of China!" Then the screen goes black for a second, followed by an image of his grave. On the wooden memorial tablet is written "Tomb of a brave Chinese pilot." The camera then pulls back for a wide shot, showing a Japanese officer directing his soldiers to salute the tomb and call out: "To the spirit of the brave Chinese pilot, Salute!"

In the 1960s the War of Resistance provided spy films in Taiwan dialect and Mandarin with a convenient narrative structure to create cold war stories in the fashion of James Bond–style spy films. In the 1970s, when Taiwan found its national identity challenged, the War of Resistance was once again employed to boost the Taiwanese people's national spirit on screen. As Emilie Yueh-yu Yeh (Ye Yueyu) points out:

> Anti-Japanese films were very popular in the 1970s. Renowned block-buster films of this period . . . all accentuated the unyielding Chinese national spirit and the conviction that the nation was to be protected even with one's own life . . . , [because] the setbacks in foreign affairs during the 1970s demanded that the issues of national identity being questioned in the international arena be reconfirmed and that the sagging national spirit be reconsolidated.[29]

In addition to these three war films, another renowned blockbuster film of the 1970s was *Victory (Meihua,* 1976), directed by Liu Jiachang, which Yeh extensively discusses in her book. The film depicts a Taiwanese family's experiences during the anti-Japanese war. The film begins with the brutal death of the father and three other townspeople. They are decapitated after refusing to move their ancestors' tombs to make way for a road connecting a power plant to a nearby dam. The elder son, who has worked as a schoolteacher, secretly joins the Nationalist army in China to fight the Japanese, while the younger prodigal son (Ke Junxiong) takes a job at the power plant. To cut off Japanese military supplies from Taiwan, an assault unit of four (consisting of Taiwanese living on the mainland) is sent back to Taiwan to destroy the power plant. However, the mission fails after the younger brother working at the factory refuses to support it. In the process, three die and one other person is wounded. Only after witnessing his neighbors be executed for helping the wounded man is the young brother's national spirit awakened, and he ultimately risks his own life to blow up the power plant. The film ends with the elder brother finally returning home after the victory over Japan.

Victory successfully combines romantic and melodramatic elements in its main patriotic plot with a popular theme song, "Meihua" (Plum Blossoms), written and composed by the director. The interweaving of romance, melodrama, and patriotism proved an effective formula for a film intended to promote the national spirit. One of the film's subplots involves the younger brother's tireless pursuit of a childhood friend, played by Sylvia Chang. While she never much cared for him, she despises him even more after he begins to work for the Japanese. But after he blows up the power plant and is dying in jail, she goes to visit him and tells him she feels that she is not good enough for him. She says, "You are so strong, so much like a real man that I wish to be married to you right away and give birth to ten sons, everyone of them as brave and as great as their dad." The feelings of Chang's character for the younger brother greatly enhance the audience's identification with his patriotic act. In an even more dramatic scene, the local butcher is arrested together with several other people for helping the wounded soldier to escape. When the interrogating Japanese officer knocks him down and contemptuously mocks them, saying, "You Chinese people are so weak," he gets up, only to be knocked down again. He then gets up and is knocked down again several more times before the Japanese officer finally stops and asks in amazement who he is. The response: "I am Chinese." This kind of melodramatic demonstration of the national spirit is characteristic of *Victory*.

Liu Jiachang apparently was one of the most effective directors in terms of his ability to manipulate the audience's emotions with music and images. The simple lyrics of the film's theme song that he penned use plum blossoms to symbolize the nation:

> Plum blossoms, plum blossoms are everywhere.
> The colder the weather, the better they bloom.
> Their perseverance is a symbol of our nation,
> The great, great nation of China.
> Look! Plum blossoms are blooming everywhere.

Wherever there is earth there are plum blossoms.
They are afraid of neither the snow nor the storm.
They are our national flower.

In two sentimental scenes, the film shows a great chorus of people singing the theme song to enhance patriotic feelings. One such chorus marks the townspeople's honoring of the elder brother's wife, after they realize they made a mistake in accusing her of being a traitor. Despite threats by the Japanese soldiers' to open fire, they assemble at the dam where she drowned herself and throw plum blossoms into the water while singing the song. In the other sequence, the townspeople gather in the street to watch the butcher being paraded around before his execution. The butcher tells his crying child, "Sons of China do not cry." When the son answers that he feels bad, the father says, "You feel bad? Sing!" The son thus begins to sing the theme song to see his father off. The film then cuts to the butcher, who is also singing, and then to the bystanders singing together with them. Commenting on the ideological effectiveness of the song, Yueh contends, "the song has replaced the narrative and become the subject per se of this film."[30] Disregarding the imperatives of fictional realism, the film in these scenes seeks to join the audience and the characters in the national identity expressed in the song: "the great, great nation of China."

Compared with the three war films, which focus on actual historical personalities who are remolded as national heroes, *Victory* is a unique anti-Japanese film produced by the CMPC. One important aspect of its uniqueness is the shift to telling anti-Japanese stories set in Taiwan while emphasizing the cooperation between Taiwan and China in the War of Resistance. In the 1970s, the CMPC went on to make four anti-Japanese films set in Taiwan, namely *My Sweet Memory* (*Mimi xiangsilin*, 1976), *The Operations of Spring Winds* (*Wang chunfeng*, 1977), and *Gone with Honor* (*Xianghuo*, 1979). In addition to the local settings, many Taiwanese cultural elements are added to these films to increase the local color. *My Sweet Memory*, for example, takes the audience to appreciate the Ten Constructions (*shida jianshe*) (a series of major state-sponsored engineering projects carried out in Taiwan from the late 1960s through the 1970s) and then to Alishan, a famous scenic mountain in Taiwan, to recall the romance and heroic sacrifice of an old engine driver. *The Operations of Spring Winds* employs the famous Taiwanese song "Wang chunfeng" (Looking for Spring Wind) in its title to depict a mission involving sabotage. The mission to destroy a kamikaze airport base is carried out by of a group of Taiwanese villagers in cooperation with activists from China. The film also invites the Taiwanese opera singer Yang Lihua to play an opera performer in order to further accentuate the film's local color. *Gone with Honor,* however, adopts an epic form to narrate the history of a Taiwanese family, starting with the immigration of the first generation from China, to emphasize the genealogical connection between Taiwan and China. In the film, the worst crime of the Japanese is to force the Taiwanese people to give up their wooden ancestral memorial tablets to the Japanese to be burned. The young son, a member of the third generation, goes to Japan to study, where he is inspired by a Chinese anti-Japanese activist but, instead of returning to Taiwan, he goes to China to join the War of Resistance. The bag of incense (*xianghuodai*) he receives from the Chinese student is a symbolic object to signify the connection to one's ancestors. The film—whose title translates literally as "Bag of Incense"—uses this bag of incense as a prop for Taiwan to remember its connection with China.

Conclusion

In a way, these films produced by the CMPC in the second half of the 1970s reflect the increasing democratization and Taiwanization, which began in the early 1970s, and the Nationalists' anxiety concerning emerging voices calling for Taiwan's independence. The "debates over native literature" in 1977 demonstrated clearly the intensity of the ideological clashes in Taiwan, to which these later anti-Japanese films by the CMPC refer only subtly. As the 1970s proceeded, the CMPC found itself increasingly out of touch with audiences, and many regarded their films as little more than propaganda. Since the CMPC was the largest production company in Taiwan, its decline eventually brought down the entire movie industry in the country. By 1980 only light urban comedies by directors such as Hou Hsiao-hsien and Chen Kun-hou seemed to enjoy some degree of popularity. In this shifting climate, two very different anti-Japanese films were released that were directed by Chen Junliang and produced by a local film company: *Love in a Chilly Spring* (*Chunhan,* 1979) and *White Jasmine* (*Molihua,* 1980). They examine the Japanese invasion of China and Japanese colonial rule over Taiwan from the perspective of women, portraying history as a traumatic experience. Unfortunately, at the time of their release, neither film received the attention it deserved. Chen's films should be recognized for their unique contribution to the continued renegotiation with the collectively intertwined traumatic history of China, Taiwan, and Japan.

The Taiwan New Cinema movement started in 1982 with two small-budget portmanteau films produced by the CMPC. Although the movement lasted only a few years, its personalized and auteurist approach to filmmaking would become the dominant style of Taiwan cinema in the 1980s and 1990s, with the rise of Hou Hsiao-hsien, Edward Yang, and Tsai Ming-liang. Understandably this shift from the (state-sponsored) studio system to the auteur system made the historical subject of the War of Resistance—which normally requires large budgets to recreate battle sequences and historical set designs—difficult to undertake. That continued to be the case for the next few decades, at least until Wei Te-sheng (Wei Desheng) had a surprise blockbuster with *Cape No. 7* (*Haijiao qihao*, 2008), which broke box-office records when it earned NT$530 million (about $16.5 million) in ticket sales. And although the film did have a subtext referencing the Japanese colonial era, even more significant for the Taiwan's cinematic history of the War of Resistance was the fact that the film enabled Wei Te-sheng to fund his dream project, an epic film about the Musha Incident. The film, which recounted a bloody conflict between aboriginal Taiwanese tribes and the Japanese colonizers in 1930 that led to a massacre of the tribal people, was produced by John Woo and released in two parts. At the same time, Wei's film can also be seen as a return to the roots of the first anti-Japanese film in Taiwan, He Jiming's 1957 film *Bloodshed on the Green Mountains,* which also depicted the Musha Incident. Thus, in late 2011, after an absence of many years, another big-budget anti-Japanese film was viewed in Taiwan's screens: *Warriors of the Rainbow: Seediq Bale* (*Saideke balai*), an epic film that would write a new page in Taiwan's cultural memory of war and create a new breed of national hero.

Notes

1   Wang Chaoguang, "Kangri zhanzheng lishi de yingxiang jiyi: yi zhanhou Zhongguo dianying wei zhongxin," (Visual Memories of the History of the War of Resistance Against Japan: With a Focus on Post-War Chinese Films), in *Xueshu yanjiu* 6 (2005): 92.

2   Yu Mo-wan (Yu Muyun), "The Relationship between Chinese Films and Hong Kong Films," in *Huayu dianying lishi yantaohui lunwenji* (Symposium on Chinese Film History) (Taibei: Taibei Film Archive, 2003), 11.

3   Liang Liang, "Xianggang kangri dianying" (Hong Kong Anti-Japanese Films), *Dianying biji,* August 23, 2005.

4   Wang, "Kangri zhanzheng lishi de yingxiang jiyi," 92.

5   Shi Bogong, "The Anti-Japanese Movies from 1932 to 2005," *Contemporary Cinema* 5 (2005): 82.

6   Shiu Ruei-mei (Xu Ruimei), *Zhizuo "youda": zhanhou Taiwan dianying zhong de Riben* (A Constructed "Friend": Japan in Postwar Taiwan Cinema) (New Taibei City: Daw Shiang, 2012), 112.

7   Huang Ren, *Beiqing taiyu pian* (Taiwanese-Language Films of Sadness) (Taibei: Wanxiang tushu, 1994), 100.

8   Ibid., 102.

9   Chen Ying, "Yi wushe shijian weizhu de taiwan dianying zuopin" (Taiwan Films about the Musha Incident), *OttoCat bangqiu xinwen zaji*, June 27, 2011.

10   To know more about the incident and Japanese propaganda campaign, see Wan-yao Chou, "Shayong zhi zhong de gushi ji qi zhoubian polan" (The Story of "Sayon's Bell" and Its Subsequent Development), in *Hai xin xi de niandai: Riben zhimin tongzhi moqi Taiwan shilun ji* (Collected Historical Essays on the Final Years of Taiwan's Colonial Period Under Japan) (Taibei: Yunchen wenhua, 2003).

11   See Zhao Min and Lu Ye, "Wenhua shenfen de shengcheng yu zaizao: cong shayang zhizhong dao yueguang xiaoyuqu" (The Creation and Reconstruction of Cultural Identity: From "Sayon's Bell" to "Moonlight Serenade"), *Xinwen daxue* 1 (2007), for a detailed account of the manufacturing of Sayon's public image as an imperial subject.

12   Wu Junhui, "Xin Qi fantanlu: lishi, ziwo, xiju, dianying" (Interview with Xin Qi: History, My Life, Theater, and Film) in *Taiyu pian shidai* (The Age of Taiwanese-Language Cinema), ed. Dianying ziliaoguan (Taibei: Taibei Film Archive, 1994), 120.

13   Xue Huiling and Wu Junhui, "Taiyu pian pianmu," (Taiwanese-Language Cinema Filmography) in ibid., 381–398.

14   Shiu (Xu), *Zhizuo "youda."*

15   See Poshek Fu, "Japanese Occupation, Shanghai Exiles, and Postwar Hong Kong Cinema," *China Quarterly*, no. 194 (2008), for a detailed discussion of *Flower Street* and the issue of Han traitors in postwar Hong Kong cinema.

16   See Homi Bhabha, *The Location of Culture* (New York: Routledge, 2004), 85–90.

17   According to Wang Dao, the commander-in-chief of the First Advance Column of the Sixth War Zone, the area depicted in the novels/film, was a very complicated place. He estimates there were as many two thousand secret agents working for the Nationalist central government and local government, the war zone commander-in-chief's office, the field army headquarter and other military units, the Japanese army, the puppet army, and the Chinese Communist Party.

18   Gu Zhen, "Minzu dayi," Zhongguo dianying zhipianchang, 41.

19   See the top ten box office chart in *Taiwan dianying bainian shihua* (One Hundred Years of Taiwan Cinema), ed. Huang Ren and Wang Wei Taipei: Zhonghua yingping ren xiehui, 2004.

20 Huang Ren, "Yangzijiang fengyun guanhougan" (After Watching *Storm over the Yangtze River*), in *Yangzijiang fengyun yingpingji* (Essays on *Storm over the Yangtze*) (Taipei: Zhongguo dianying zhipianchang, 1969), 48.

21 Among all the film titles listed in this chapter, only *Secret Agent Yangtze River No. 1* is still available. All others cannot be traced on the online database of either the Taipei Film Archive or the Hong Kong Film Archive. Further research has to be conducted to verify whether they were actually made and released.

22 Beiping was the wartime name for Beijing.

23 The quotation is from the page after the cover page of Zhongyang dianying shiye gongsi, ed., *Yinglie qianqiu yingping ji* (Collection of Reviews of *The Everlasting Glory*) (Taibei: Zhongyang dianying shiye gongsi, 1973), unpaginated.

24 The number eight hundred was not the correct number of soldiers in the warehouse. It was used to mislead the attacking Japanese.

25 Yu Yeying, *Cuican guangying suiyue: Zhongyang dianying gongsi jishi* (The Glorious Age of Cinema: A Historical Record of Central Motion Picture Corporation) (Taibei: Zhongyang dianying shiye gufen youxian gongsi, 2002), 196.

26 Jiao Xiongping (Peggy Chiao), *Shidai xianying: Zhongxi dianying lunshu* (Images for the Age: Essays on Chinese and Western Cinema) (Taibei: Yuanliu, 1998), 158.

27 See Long Baoshan, "Guojia jingshen jiaoyu" (National Spirit Education), in *Zhonghua baike quanshu diancangban* (Chinese Encyclopedia Online), http://ap6.pccu.edu.tw/Encyclopedia/data.asp?id=1620 for details of the implementation plan, see the *Disici Zhonghuaminguo jiaoyu nianjian* (Fourth Education Yearbook of the Republic of China) available at: http://www.naer .edu.tw/files/15-1000-7983,c1311-1.php?Lang=zh-tw explains how the plan should be put into practice in vol. 17, on civic and moral education.

28 Li Zhongdao, "Zhang Zizhong jingshen yongchui buxiu: Guanshang 'Yinglie qianqiu' you gan" (Long Live the Undying Spirit of Zhang Zizhong: My Thoughts on *The Everlasting Glory*"), in *Yinglie qianqiu yingping ji* (Collection of Reviews of *The Everlasting Glory*) (Taibei: Zhongyang dianying shiye gongsi, 1973).

29 Yeh Emilie Yueh-yu, *Gesheng moying: Gequ xushi yu zhongwendianying* (Phantom of the Music: Song Narration and Chinese-Language Cinema) (Taibei: Yuanliu, 2000), 20–21.

30 Ibid., 20.

CHAPTER 3

The "Division Blockbuster" in South Korea
The Evolution of Cinematic Representations of War and Division

Hyangjin Lee

Popular culture reflects dominant ideologies as well as challenges to them in a society. This chapter explores this dialectical dimension of cultural politics, focusing on three interrelated phases of South Korean films on the Korean War and national division: (1) state censorship from the 1950s and resistance by filmmakers in the context of a rising democracy movement in the 1980s; (2) nationalism in the arena of cultural consumption in reaction to the forces of globalization that swept Korea during the 1990s; and (3) the emergence of what I call the "division blockbuster" in the late 1990s and early 2000s.

Tracing changing cinematic portrayals of North Koreans in South Korean cinema, this chapter seeks to illustrate national identity and historical consciousness in transition. South Korean films on war and division reflect stresses and transformations in the political-economic context. Their cinematic imaginations, moreover, echo the renegotiation and redefinition of ideological norms. Yet, as we shall see, the films under consideration are ambiguous texts that contain both radical and conformist elements.

1950s–1980s: Films and State Ideology North and South

For several decades after the partition of Korea into two mutually antagonistic regimes, films in both the north and the south were subject to strong state censorship, reflecting each side's prevailing political orthodoxy. The two most common themes in North Korean films, which often appear in combination, are class struggle by the landless or proletarian class against exploitation during the feudal era and the anti-Japanese resistance to achieve national independence. North Korea's Korean War films were produced primarily by the Korean 2.8 Film Studio, which was run directly by the North Korean Army.[1] These war films are filled with the heroic actions of North Korean patriots during the war. The Film Production Division of the Korean People's Army, the predecessor to the Korean 2.8 Film Studio, produced five feature films during the three years of the war, all of which were intended to boost morale among the people engaged in military action. After the ceasefire was declared in 1953, films focusing on the Korean War continued to be made, but the objective shifted to whipping up anti-American sentiment and preparing the people for the ultimate war of reunification. Notable films in this latter category are *Ch'oe Hakshin's Family* (*Ch'oe Hakshin-ŭi ilga,* 1966), *Unknown Heroes I–IIX* (*Irŭmŏmŭn yŏngungdŭl I–IIX,* 1979–1981), and *Wŏlmi Island* (*Wŏlmido,* 1982).[2] Filmmaking even today remains subject to tight state control in the north.

Until the 1980s, the South Korean government also sought to exercise rigid ideological control over the film industry. Numerous directors were arrested or blacklisted, and many films were banned for alleged violations of national security. Moreover, after the military's overthrow of the Second Republic in April 1960, the new regime denied filmmakers one of the most important functions of art: social criticism. The Korean Motion Picture Law of 1962 empowered the government to censor or ban cinematic representations of political and economic conflicts in South Korean society, especially the poverty and suffering of the working class. In this restrictive environment, it is hardly surprising that filmmakers tended to stick to safe genres, notably melodramas portraying upper-class life, love affairs, or the lives of bar hostesses. Prominent in this respect was a group of films that dealt with the relationship between a rich man and a poor barmaid. By focusing narrowly on personal relationships, these films enabled South Korean filmmakers to avoid sensitive topics related to their immediate social environment and political circumstances.

In accordance with the military government's film policy, propaganda films were also produced. The most successful military film was *Red Scarf* (*Ppalgan mahura,* 1964). Directed by Shin Sangok, *Red Scarf* is a story about Korean Air Force fighter pilots. Another subgenre of propaganda films portrayed the economic prosperity brought by the administration of President Park Chunghee and his development plan. A quasi-travelogue, *Sights of the Eight Provinces* (*P'aldogangsan,* 1967), directed by Pae Sŏkin, is representative of this subgenre. State censorship was crude and unyielding—as exemplified by the confiscation of Yi Manhŭi's *Seven Women Prisoners* (*Ch'ilin-ŭi yŏp'oro,* 1965), and the arrest and subsequent trial of the director, who was charged with exhibiting communist sympathies. Though Yi sought to allow North Korean soldiers a measure of humanity in this film and his *The Marines Who Never Return* (*Tolaoji annŭn haebyŏng,* 1963), these works, in fact, did not directly challenge the prevailing anticommunist ideology.

State censorship became even more severe in the 1970s with the promulgation of the Yushin Constitution in 1972, which was essentially martial law. The revision of the Korean Motion Picture Law in 1973 instituted a form of double censorship—that is, all film scripts had to be approved by the censors *prior to* production and then the final film had to be submitted for a second round of approval before its public release. Furthermore, by imposing a heavy tax on filmmakers and theater owners, the revised law hindered the importation of expensive foreign films. The general decline of the film industry is clearly reflected in the overall production of films during this period; the number of feature films made between 1969 and 1977 decreased from 229 to 101. The size of audiences also shrank, by nearly three-quarters—from total ticket sales of approximately 170 million in the 1960s to 44 million in 1981.

1980s–1990s: The South Korean Cinematic Renaissance and New Challenges

With the upsurge in the democracy movement in the 1980s (after the 1979 assassination of President Park and the brutal crackdown in Kwangju by his successor, General Chun Doohwan in May 1980), South Korean filmmaking entered a period of dynamism. A new generation of socially conscious filmmakers emerged,[3] and by the end of the decade South Korean films began to draw the attention of international critics. To cite just a few examples, three of Im Kwontaek's films—*Surrogate Mother* (*Ssibaji,* 1986), *Adada* (*Adada,* 1987), and *Come, Come, Come Upward* (*Aje aje para aje,* 1989)—won awards at international festivals. War films also began to deviate from mainstream ideological conformity and receive wide acclaim. Chung Jiyoung's *White Badge* (*Hayan chŏnjaeng,* 1992), which grappled with South Korea's involvement in the Vietnam War, won the Grand Prix at the fifth Tokyo International Film Festival in 1992. Yi Kwangmo's *Spring in My Hometown* (*Arŭmdaun sijŏl,* 1998), which depicts the corrosive social impact of the Korean War as seen through the eyes of children, was honored at the fifty-second Locarno International Film Festival in 1998.

Within this atmosphere of iconoclasm and experimentation, one film in particular challenged the anticommunist ideological hegemony—paving the way for works such as *Spring in My Hometown* as well as other films considered below. Chung Jiyoung's *Southern Guerrilla Forces* (*Nambugun*, 1990) is a humanistic story about communist partisans fighting against the South Korean and the UN forces during the war. Tackling one of the forbidden subjects in South Korean cinema, and calling into question the legitimacy of anticommunism as the state ideology, this film marked a new phase in Korean film history. Communist partisans had been erased from official histories and, when portrayed on screen, were usually bloodthirsty villains or pathetic dupes who fell into the trap of North Korean communists because of their naïveté. In war films produced before the late 1980s, the southern communist guerrillas appear as brutal bandits who massacre innocent neighbors and then run off into the mountains.

Southern Guerrilla Forces deviated from this stereotype. Various episodes in the guerrillas' past lives demonstrate that they are people of flesh and blood to whom the audience can relate, not dehumanized ideologues who are out of touch with reality. Moreover, Chung's film draws attention to the brotherly warmth and disciplined attitude they display toward people living at the foot of the mountains. When the guerrilla forces attack or when they retreat, one important concern is the safety of the villagers, who have to continue their everyday lives regardless of ever-changing circumstances brought on by the war. At the end of the film, South Korean regular forces kill the majority of the guerrilla fighters and capture the rest. Despite this ending, none of the survivors consider their efforts to have been in vain. They believe that they acted in good conscience at the risk of ostracism and even death. Their ultimate heroism lies in this honest acceptance of their choice and its consequences.

The unfolding of democratization and cinematic divergence from statist anticommunist hegemony notwithstanding, South Korean filmmakers faced formidable new challenges. In 1988, the South Korean government caved in to pressure from the United States to scale back its screen quota system, which was based on the aforementioned Motion Picture Law, and allow direct distribution of U.S.-produced films in Korea.[4] United International Pictures (UIP)—the international distributor for Paramount Pictures,

Universal Studios, and (until 2000) MGM Studios—filled Korean theaters with Hollywood fare. The results were dramatic. The domestic market share of Korean-produced films fell from just over 50 percent in 1982 to approximately 16 percent in 1993. In response, calls rang out throughout South Korea's mass media to preserve national cinema and resist Western-centric globalization *qua* "cultural imperialism."[5] National cinema, after all, plays a vital role in shaping collective identity, historical consciousness, and even social aspirations.

Facing this onslaught from the West, Korean film studios sought new sources of investment and tried to imitate the Hollywood blockbuster. In the early 1990s, *chaebŏls* (industrial conglomerates), such as Samsung, Daewoo, LG, and SK Group, decisively joined the film industry. As major manufacturers of video players, they needed content for the rapidly growing video rental markets. Seeking to emulate the success of Hollywood blockbusters and Hong Kong action films in Korea, they became the most significant source of financing and changed the nature of local filmmaking with steep rises in production costs and the nurturing of a domestic star system. Counter to expectations, however, these investments did not immediately reap impressive financial returns. When the IMF (International Monetary Fund) crisis of the late 1990s forced *chaebŏls* to embark on structural reorganization, they closed media and film related businesses to focus on the more profitable sectors. Thereupon followed the emergence of midsize production and distribution companies, such as CJ Entertainment, Cinema Service, Show Box, and Lotte Entertainment.[6] Venture capital companies entered the film industry as well. In tandem with these transformations with respect to financing, further innovations became possible as a new generation of filmmakers—mostly university graduates who had been involved in the democracy movement as students and were familiar with the idioms of global visual culture—entered the industry. The creation of a new form of local blockbuster was one of the most ambitious projects launched by these new filmmakers.

Glocalization and the Making of Korean Blockbusters

The creation of local blockbusters can be seen as the response by a national cinema caught in the cross currents of localization and globalization. Imitation as well as hybridity and innovation are key elements for success in this complicated context. Successive failures during the mid-1990s of *chaebŏl*-backed "big" film projects underscored that expensively produced action sequences and special effects were not sufficient for success. Kang Jegyu's *Shiri* (*Swiri,* 1999)—the first so-called division blockbuster—distinguished itself from previous failed attempts by pursuing an amalgamation between the local and the global. It combined a uniquely Korean story with a familiar Hollywood/Hong Kong style. Indeed, *Shiri* presented a story that suited the mood of détente between the north and the south at that time, which resulted in the Joint Declaration in 2000.[7] In the film, a South Korean secret service agent falls for a woman who appears to be the quiet owner of a fish and aquarium supply store but is actually a trained sniper and sleeper agent from the north, awaiting orders to carry out a dramatic terrorist attack. The widespread resonance the film had with local audiences indicated that the story reflected popular discourses on national division. Marketed, furthermore, as a Korean challenge to the Hollywood blockbuster, *Shiri* appealed to nationalist antipathy toward globalization centered on the United States.[8]

The following year, Park Chanwook's *Joint Security Area* (*Kongdong kyŏngbi kuyŏk* [*JSA*], 2000) joined the evolving mainstream discourse on national division. This work veers from a buddy film to a crime mystery before its ultimate turn to tragedy, all the while skillfully communicating the story of a forbidden friendship in a divided nation. *JSA* dramatizes the lives of young men from the north and the south who are doing their compulsory military service along the demilitarized zone (DMZ) between the two states.

Sleeper agent receives her orders

A forbidden friendship

The soldiers end up crossing the line because of loneliness and their yearning for companionship, but the state defined their friendship as treason. This film drew an audience of more than 5.8 million. While compulsory military service is a familiar subject to Korean filmgoers, they had never seen a film that dealt with it and the tragedy of national division in such an entertaining way. The film, however, offered no fantasy of reunification that could provide psychological distance or emotional relief from the disturbing story. Furthermore, the film reminded audiences of their own memories of family separation and their own fear of confinement and punishment.

The success of *Shiri* and *JSA* inspired additional division blockbuster films in the following years. In 2004, Kang Woosuk's *Silmido*—which brought to light a long-suppressed story of an ill-fated commando unit— and Kang Jegyu's *Taegukgi: The Brotherhood of War* (*T'aegŭkki hwinallimyŏ*, 2004)—about two brothers separated by war—successively shattered box-office records within a few short months of one another. Each film attracted more than 11 million filmgoers, equivalent to roughly one-quarter of the South Korean population at the time. In many ways, the two stories express different ideas and perspectives in narrating the history of the postwar division. Yet both embrace a clear humanism that overcomes present conflicts, echoing the changed social atmosphere regarding the reunification of the country. And as explained below, both films reminded audiences about those swept up in the tide of official history.

Welcome to Dongmakgol (*Welk'ŏm t'u tongmakgol*, 2005), directed by Park Kwanghyun, represented a new type of division blockbuster. Unlike the previous works, the film did not rely on the name value of its stars or director. This parodic fairytale set in a peaceful village during the Korean War drew more than 8 million to theaters, earning the biggest box-office receipts of the year. Set in 1950, it is about the villagers of Dongmakgol, who do not know about the war because of their geographic isolation; instead, they live in blissful ignorance. One day, the villagers save a disparate group of soldiers left behind the front lines but are utterly shocked by the violence and hatred between the soldiers. The group comprises three North Korean soldiers who survived a firefight with South Korean forces, two South Korean deserters, and a wounded U.S. Navy pilot who was caught in a mysterious storm and crash-landed his plane in the deep forest. Isolated from the battlefront, the soldiers first condemn each other but soon learn how to live together as a part of the peaceful village. Meanwhile, commanders in the U.S.-led United Nations Command mistakenly identify the remote village as a hiding place for enemy units and plan an attack to rescue the wounded pilot. The soldiers decide to protect the innocent villagers by undertaking a united operation to draw the attackers away from the village. The story of the soldiers, who despise the war and disobey orders to kill innocent civilians, conveys the meaninglessness of war to the divided nation. The utopian image of village life is the history they wish to remember, suggesting the dystopian image of present-day society. The success of this and other films shows that, within a few years, the division blockbuster had emerged as a major genre in contemporary Korean cinema.[9] But what did this phenomenon really mean?

History, Memory, and Cinematic Imagination

Division blockbusters reflect larger movements in the historiography of the Korean War and its consequences. The stories explore what that traumatic history continues to mean to Koreans. The portrayal of national division in these films also reflects new trends in the study of the Korean War.[10] For a long time, scholarly inquiry had focused on the origins and development of the war, the nature of foreign interventions, the casualties on each side, and so on. However, in recent years, collective memories of war victims and ordinary citizens have emerged as subjects worthy of attention in Korean War studies. The five films discussed here (along with other, less prominent works) helped not only to surface the memories of those who have suffered from national division but also to explore how those memories have refused to submit to attempts at erasure in the official history.

T'aegŭkki most succinctly communicates the limitations of official accounts of war and national division. In the opening scene, a South Korean army excavation team preparing a former battle site for the creation of a memorial discovers a set of remains, which are identified as those of Yi Chinsŏk. In reality, they were those of his older brother, Yi Chint'ae, who had perished while in possession of a fountain pen engraved with his younger brother's name. The official history lists Chinsŏk's death—based on one "fact." The truth is eventually discovered after the perspectives from those who actually witnessed the battle are introduced to reconstruct what happened.

Silmido (*Silmido,* 2003) likewise challenges the authority of official history. Silmido is a small uninhabited island off the western coast of South Korea (about five kilometers southwest of what is now Incheon International Airport). The island became the training ground for Unit 684—a team of thirty-one social outcasts, including death row inmates who were recruited by the South Korean army to infiltrate North Korea in early 1969 and assassinate its leader, Kim Il Sung in retaliation for the north's failed 1968 attack on South Korea's presidential palace. For reasons that are still not entirely clear, Unit 684 was never deployed but remained on the island nonetheless, and two years later its members mutinied and escaped to Seoul. There, most of them were killed, others took their own lives, and only four were taken alive. The government portrayed the incident as another terrorist attack by North Korean agents and then offered a revised account a few days later, when the incident was characterized as a "military disturbance," without any further explanation. Military authorities at the time destroyed much of the evidence, executed the four survivors, and labeled the entire incident "classified." After the end of the military dictatorship and the democratization of society, the incident became public in 2003, but the authorities refused to release the extant records to the filmmakers. It was not until 2006 that an official government report was finally made public.

The story reconstructed in *Silmido* is based on the memory of witnesses and relies heavily on dramatic license taken by the director. According to the logic of the film, official history is full of fabrications and the collective memory reconstructed by the film frees history from its theft at the hands of the state. At the same time, the cinematic apparatus works to transcend the dispute between whether something is true or false and communicate the subjective dimension of human experience.[11]

Significantly, the perception of the north in division blockbusters has evolved from that of enemy to victim and, ultimately, to that of companion.

The transitional status of Korean identity requires companionship in order to overcome hostile threats from an old enemy. The strength of familial bonds melts away the opposing images of "north" and "south," leaving behind the shared grief of separation. Instead, the northern "other" is replaced with the "foreign" presence of U.S. forces. In *Shiri,* the leader of North Korean's guerrilla forces, Pak Muyŏng, delivers a speech on South Korea's colonial status under American domination and the necessity for reunification by force, which ultimately trumps secret agent Yu Chungwŏn's justification for division and peaceful reconciliation. The united operation of northern and southern soldiers against the UN forces in *Welcome to Dongmakgol* is also representative of this conceptual shift.

Conclusion: Cultural Conservatism in Division Dramas

Recent division blockbuster films comprise an ambiguous tool for narrating history. On the one hand, many of these stories offer radical critiques of the ideological orthodoxy concerning war and division that had prevailed during the period of military rule. On the other hand, division blockbusters are not entirely transformative because they have tended to rely on "traditional" notions of Confucian morality to inspire emotional identification among audiences. As expressed in the film titles—*Shiri* and *Taegukgi: The Brotherhood of War*—the nation is equated with the family.[12] In fact, all five films featured in this chapter employ well-worn conventions of family melodrama to posit an inseparable relationship between the north and the south. In *Shiri,* Yu Chungwŏn, the South Korean secret agent, in the end mercilessly kills Yi Panghŭi, the North Korean sniper. In the film, Panghŭi disguises herself as a South Korean named Yi Myŏnghyŏn and approaches him. However, unable to control her affections, Panghŭi falls in love with him and ultimately chooses love over duty. She divulges the plan just before the mission to get under way; however, Chungwŏn chooses duty to his country over love, although he continues to have deep feelings for Panghŭi. In *Taegukgi,* the family motif is more obvious. Chint'ae's savagery in killing so many people regardless of which side he belongs to is understandable only because of his devotion to his younger brother, Chinsŏk. The family has no father, so the eldest son has to take responsibility for protecting his younger brother.

Nevertheless, the division blockbusters, to a great extent, challenge any form of justification for war in the divided nation. This antiwar message, which seems to reappear in numerous films in the division blockbuster genre, urges a reassessment of national division as it is framed in the official history. The success of division blockbusters also demonstrates a nationalistic response by Koreans to cultural globalization led by the West. The division block-buster phenomenon confirms that film is not a mere commodity but a commentary by the Korean people on their own society and themselves.

Notes

1   2.8 refers to the foundation day of the North Korean People's Army on February 8, 1948. The studio's name was later changed to 4.25 to commemorate the formation of the anti-Japanese guerrilla forces led by Kim Il Sung on April 25, 1932.

2   For interpretations of these North Korean films, see Hyangjin Lee, *Contemporary Korean Cinema: Identity, Culture, Politics* (Manchester, UK: Manchester University Press, 2000), chap. 3.

3   Following the Kwangju Massacre in May 1980, a group of radical young directors centered on university communities emerged to challenge the existing film production system. The more radical among them defied the conventions of mainstream Korean films, refusing to not only to make commercial films but also to distribute their works in the existing film market. Their favorite subject matter included the struggle of the working class and the contradictions of capitalism.

4   The Motion Picture Law, which was revised in 1973, enforced a required minimum of screening days for domestically produced films as a way to limit spending on the importation of foreign films. The screen quota system was amended from 146 to 73 days in 2006 due to pressure from major Hollywood studios. The controversy originally stemmed from the South Korea-U.S. Bilateral Investment Treaty in 1997.

5   Globalization has inspired much resistance throughout the world. See, for example, Roland Robertson, *Globalization: Social Theory and Global Culture* (London: Sage, 1992).

6   In contrast to *chaebŏl*s, these medium-sized firms focused on film production and distribution. In addition, CJ Entertainment and Lotte Entertainment also own a chain of movie theatres.

7   The June 15 Joint Declaration was adopted at a 2000 summit meeting of the then leaders of North Korea and South Korea—Kim Jong Il and Kim Daejung, respectively—which was held in Pyongyang to discuss the peaceful reunification of the country.

8   There were cinematic precedents. A series of films dealing with issues of separate families appeared in the late 1980s clearly reflecting popular unification movements at that time. In addition, aforementioned works such

as Chung Jiyoung's *Southern Guerrilla Forces* (*Nambugun*, 1990), and Yi Kwangmo's *Spring in My Hometown* (*Arŭmdaun sijŏl,* 1998) provided innovative views on division issues.

9   Of course, it was not only division blockbusters that enjoyed great popularity. Comedy, action films, and melodrama were the most common genres. Indeed, the new South Korean cinema was characterized by the hybridization of these genres—with the mashing together of, say, costume drama, historical fantasy, monster-disaster flicks, horror, and social-political films.

10   For example, see Kyunghak Kim et al., *Korean War, Community, and Residents' Memories* (Seoul: Hanul Academy, 2005); Dongchun Kim, *War and Society: What Was Korean War to Us?* (Seoul: Tolbegae, 2000).

11   For example, according to the historical records, Vice Admiral Choi Jaehyeon did not commit suicide—he was killed. The communist family background of Inchan was also "created" by the need of the narrative. The heroic death of Jaehyeon and the misery of Inchan as a family member of a communist is a valid approach to the truth rejected by the official history.

12   Shiri is the name of a fish that is said to live as a couple and exists only in Korea. In the film, it is used as a metaphor for the unification of Korea, likened to the common fate of a divided nation. One cannot live without the other.

CHAPTER 4

Under the Flag of the Rising Sun
Imagining the Pacific War in the Japanese Cinema

David Desser

In Fukasaku Kinji's intense World War II–themed mystery *Under the Flag of the Rising Sun* (*Gunki hatameku motoni,* 1972), a widow who has been denied survivor benefits relentlessly interviews her husband's surviving comrades some twenty-five years after the war. *Rashōmon*-like, each man tells a story that is as much self-serving as truthful. And although she ultimately learns something approaching the real truth, she also learns that sometimes the truth is no more comforting than ignorance or lies. She uncovers a pattern of unbelievable cruelty by the officers toward their own enlisted men. Her husband ultimately rebelled against this system by killing a particularly vicious and cruel officer, but only after he committed what can only be called atrocities and behaved in a way that only men in extreme conditions can act. Thus, he had been as much a victimizer as a victim. Fukasaku intercuts archival photographs with his fictional story, going so far as to begin the film with footage of the emperor paying homage to the casualties of Japan's East Asian war. This same structure of a relentless interviewer confronting former soldiers about their wartime actions—and meeting with resistance, repression, and denial—is seen in the successful and controversial documentary *The Emperor's Naked Army Marches On* (*Yuki yukite shingun,* Hara Kazuo, 1987).

What these films have in common is both an admirable attempt to come to terms with Japanese aggression against its neighbors and an almost simultaneous slippage into seeing the Japanese as no less a victim of their own wartime actions. In this respect, the films repeat a pattern observed in other media discourses on Japan's modern history, which similarly swing between representations of Japan as perpetrator and Japan as victim. This chapter explores the duality or tension in two parts: first, through a survey of Japanese variations on the "World War II combat film" genre and, second, by focusing on how postwar Japanese cinema has grappled—or not—with four recurring icons in larger public debates about Japan's war responsibility: the "comfort women," the Nanjing Massacre, Yasukuni shrine, and the atom bomb.

Japanese Variations on the "World War II Combat Film"

During the war years, the Japanese film industry produced films with fictional stories that arguably fit the flexible and evolving genre that the film critic Jeanine Basinger has dubbed the "World War II combat film."[1] Films such as *Five Scouts* (*Gonin no sekkōhei,* Tasaka Tomotaka, 1938), *Mud and Soldiers* (*Tsuchi to heitai,* Tasaka Tomotaka, 1939), *Chocolate and Soldiers* (*Chokoreto to heitai,* Sato Takeshi, 1938) and *The Naval Brigade at Shanghai* (*Shanhai rikusentai,* Kumagai Hisatora, 1939) contain little overt propaganda (in marked contrast to Hollywood films made during and just after the war) and, instead, focus on a small group of soldiers and the harsh, dangerous conditions in which they are fighting. They also produced semidocumentary films that focus on real battles but rely on fictionalized accounts along with professional actors. The most famous of these films is probably *The War at Sea from Hawai'i to Malaya* (*Hawai'i Mare oki kaisen,* Yamamoto Kajirō, 1942), with its spectacular battle effects by Tsuburaya Eiji, who would go on to help "destroy" Tokyo over and over with his special effects in the *Godzilla* series. And they produced numerous documentaries, many of which relied heavily on newsreel footage, in the genre known as *bunka-eiga* (culture films). Films such as *Holy War* (*Seisen,* 1938) and *Advancing upon French Indo-China* (*Futsuin shinchū,* 1941) paint the war against China in millenarian terms. Also in this group is a 1938 trilogy about the taking of China's major cities: Shanghai, Nanjing, and Beijing.[2] We might say that the whitewashing (or historical revisionism) of the Nanjing Massacre began as it was occurring.

Few, if any, combat films were produced during the U.S. Occupation of Japan (1945–1952). This is understandable, given that—as Kyoko Hirano notes—American censors tried to prohibit the use of military characters in films.[3] Interestingly, combat films, unlike period films featuring sword-wielding samurai, did not return to prominence in the booming film industry of the 1950s. Even though wartime Japanese combat films (e.g., *Five Scouts* and *Mud and Soldiers*) did not celebrate war itself, they nonetheless celebrated the values that enabled Japan to mobilize for battle in Asia and the Pacific. While some of these values are shared by Hollywood war films—heroic sacrifice, male camaraderie, group cohesion—the Occupation's mistrust of such qualities in the Japanese context as well as the Japanese people's own postwar ambivalence about them made the revival of this genre unlikely, at least for a few years. Thus war-themed films in the early postwar years tended to be antiwar works that do not focus on combat.

The point of emphasis became, instead, the trope of victimization or, rather, "self-victimization," which, many claim, was enabled by the Occupation. American authorities not only refused to prosecute Emperor Hirohito as a war criminal, they eventually scaled back the "purge" of public figures who were initially removed from high-profile positions in politics and industry. Indeed, the Occupation explicitly allowed the great majority of the Japanese populace to escape much of their war guilt and re-interpret themselves as essentially war victims.[4] The official line promulgated by the Americans went something like this:

> According to "The History of the Pacific War" [a series of newspaper columns that appeared in the Japanese press beginning on December 8, 1945], neither Hirohito nor the ordinary public bore any blame for the war. Rather, the military leaders were solely responsible for the abuses of power, the deprivations of the people's freedom, the inhumane treatment of civilians and prisoners of war, and other violence that had occurred during the war.[5]

Thus, the antiwar films of the Occupation era emphasized civilian deprivation and victimization. And in the post-Occupation period, this victimization was extended to Japan's fighting men.

Films like *Beyond the Clouds* (*Kumo nagaruru hateni*, Ieki Miyoji, 1953) and *The Human Torpedoes* (*Ningen gyorai kaiten*, Matsubayashi Shue, 1955) attempt to use the image of the kamikaze to view the war effort with skepticism. (The former film features airplane pilots, and the latter "human torpedoes"—men who are strapped into a minisubmarine that consists largely of a torpedo and set adrift in the ocean until they spot an enemy ship and launch a suicide attack.) In these films, the young men who volunteered for the Special Attack Forces move from idealism to cynicism; but, in this way, the films reproduce the pattern of victimization of the Japanese, especially in films that focus almost exclusively on scenes of the soldiers or sailors awaiting deployment in what must surely be their last mission and flashbacks that show a gradual progression to the present. The enemy and combat are virtually absent. As Isolde Standish perceptively notes, the ambiguity we might detect revolves around a tension between condemnation of Japanese wartime attitudes of self-sacrifice and a reproduction of the very ideals of male bonding and camaraderie that underpinned most wartime films.[6]

Far more famous are the ostensibly antiwar films that are part of the canons of the influential and respected directors Ichikawa Kon and Kobayashi Masaki. These directors have a decidedly humanist take on the subject but have a marked tendency to go from the particular—the Japanese fought the war in a specific way that led to destruction and devastation—to the general—war is bad, especially for the ordinary soldier. Ichikawa created two powerful films, both based on popular novels (which have been translated into English), and each of which contain critiques of Japanese military culture and the conduct of Japan's war. Yet ultimately it can be argued that each ignores the larger context of the war by focusing on a period when the war has just ended or is clearly already lost; thus, the origins of the war in Japan's imperialist aggression are repressed. Similarly, though some attention is paid to the devastation wrought by the Japanese military on the land and people that they occupied, ultimately, the victims are the Japanese soldiers and, moreover, victims less of a militarized culture than of the cruel nature of war itself.

The first of Ichikawa's critically acclaimed but thematic ambiguous antiwar films was *Harp of Burma* (*Biruma no tategoto,* 1956). The film was entered into competition at the Venice Film Festival of that year (along with Mizoguchi's *Red Light District* [*Akasen chitai*]), where it won the San Giorgio Prize, an award given to films considered especially important for the progress of civilization. The film focuses on a platoon under the command of Captain Inouye, a music teacher in civilian life who has brought his music and gentle sensibilities to his combat command. Right before his troop is to fight the British, they learn that the war is over.

The first condemnation of military ideology comes when Captain Inouye sends Corporal Mizushima to persuade a group of Japanese soldiers holed up in a cave to give up their arms. This is where the notorious wartime credo against surrender comes into play. When the group's leader refuses to surrender, the men are attacked by Allied forces; only Mizushima survives. Thus, we see already the victimization of the ordinary soldier by Japanese ideals. So, on the one hand, the film reminds us of the cruel ideology of militarism and the fanaticism that accompanied it, but, on the other hand, the victims of that ideology are the Japanese themselves.

Following his recovery from wounds sustained in the attack, Mizushima becomes a mendicant Buddhist monk and remains in Burma (now Myanmar) to tend to the souls (and, to some extent, the bodies) of Japanese soldiers. In so doing, he becomes the ultimate symbol of heroic self-sacrifice and thus something of a victim, too. Mizushima chooses to remain in Burma and thus not to return to Japan. And that is the ultimate sadness, being separated from his beloved homeland. His comrades, who search for him throughout the rest of the film, recognize his sacrifice, and they weep at the thought not only of never seeing him again but of his lifelong separation from his family and from Japan.

Though *Fires on the Plain* (*Nobi,* 1959) is very different in tone, mood, and effect from *Harp of Burma,* it likewise projects an ambiguous stance toward Japan's war experiences. A prize winner at the Locarno International Film Festival in 1961, *Fires on the Plain* also won a number of awards in Japan. It is undeniably a grim, gritty, powerful, and shocking film. It is relentless in its portrayal of the collapse of the Japanese Army in the Philippines and how this affected the enlisted personnel. On the run from an American advance in Leyte, the Japanese Army has run out of ammunition and supplies, and reinforcements are all gone. Private Tamura comes down with tuberculosis, and is told to go to the hospital or commit suicide. As he tries to make his way first to the hospital and then simply out of harm's way, he encounters not just an army in disarray but soldiers who lack everything but the most basic instinct for survival. Hunger is staved off, at least temporarily, by cannibalism (this issue has been raised in public discourse in Japan).[7] Eventually, Tamura is left alone to face scared civilians and hostile guerrillas. He does not survive.

Fires on the Plain can be criticized for failing to provide sufficient context. Notably, the matter of why Tamura is in the Philippines in the first place is elided. The devastation wrought by the Japanese military on the civilian population is at best marginally alluded to, and while military culture is condemned (e.g., our horror at an officer who slaps Tamura for returning to his unit), the film also glosses over the issue of what would have happened had the Japanese Army not been on the run. The film, then, like so many others, slowly changes from a condemnation of Japanese militarism to a more general look at the horrors of war and the depths to which anyone (not just the Japanese) would sink under cruel and inhuman conditions. Saying that war is hell is not the same as saying that Japan's war aims led to hell.

Kobayashi Masaki's contribution to the humanistic antiwar ideology of the 1950s came in the form of a still-underappreciated, unprecedented epic. *The Human Condition* (*Ningen no jōken*), released as a trilogy from 1959 to 1961, occupies almost ten hours of running time. It is an admirable attempt to come to terms with many repressed issues of Japan's wartime conduct, to lay blame on aspects of Japanese culture, not just military culture, and to show how an individual could make at least some kind of attempt at resistance to military ideology and the exploitation of non-Japanese civilians. Yet, ultimately, it succumbs to victim consciousness as the main character, Kaji, is subjected step-by-step to the forces of fascism, militarism, and the degradations of war. When, after nine or so hours of a descent into wartime hell, he finds himself a prisoner of war at the hands of the Soviet army, he comes close to repudiating his Marxist beliefs and, more importantly, he becomes a victim not just of the military system that he tried to oppose but of an invading army.

To be sure, the film comes closer than most Japanese films to detailing the reality of Chinese conscript labor in Manchuria. The virtual enslavement of Chinese and Korean men during the war years was first broached in this film (though underrepresented subsequently), and Kaji's attempts to hold on to his humanity, not to mention his socialist beliefs, represents an admirable struggle between individualism and conformism. Even if Kaji is ultimately unsuccessful in reforming conditions in the slave-labor camp, at least he made an effort, more than most others at the time. But when he is subjected to the absurd rigors of Japanese military training (more than in *Fires on the Plain,* we see the distinction between officers and enlisted men and the brutalization that military training entails   a motif taken up with vigor in the more radical 1960s films to follow), the film inexorably drifts toward the victimization of Kaji.[8]

The Human Condition uses China, specifically Manchuria, as its primary setting. As public discussions in Japan and around the world over the Nanjing Massacre increased throughout the 1960s, China came to signify Japan's military adventurism, and many of the most important films in the decade were set on the Chinese frontier. Two films by Masumura Yasuzō and one by Suzuki Seijun use the campaign in China to condemn military culture, show the hypocritical differentiation of the officers from the enlisted men, reveal something about the exploitation of women, including foreign women, and generally take a more cynical attitude toward the war. Suzuki's version of *Story of a Prostitute* (*Shunpuden*, 1965), moves beyond focusing on Harumi, a Korean prostitute serving on the Manchurian front, and includes portrayals of two different enlisted men to show not just their victimization but also their rebellion. One falls in love with her; the other, reading his books and refusing the military line of thought, evinces sympathy for the Chinese (and even willingly joins their cause). Because it features elements of the sexual exploitation film, along with Suzuki's outré style, the film is a cogent critique of a culture that exploits men as well as women, the kind of culture that could easily go to war. Suzuki's *Elegy to Violence* (*Kenka erejī*, 1966) could be seen as a prequel to this film because of its understanding of how masculinity and sexuality can be perverted into militarism. It ends, of course, with the protagonist witnessing a military parade.

Also set in Manchuria is Masumura's *Hoodlum Soldier* (*Heitai Yakuza*, 1965). As is typical of virtually every film mentioned so far, in this film, actual combat is either minimized or never seen. Instead, it emphasizes the soldiers' lives away from the battlefield. They fight among themselves or against other Japanese units. Military life is seen as monotonous, but grim; military discipline as absurd. The great Katsu Shintarō, who plays the hoodlum soldier of the title, is incorrigible, undisciplined, and seemingly indestructible. He takes under his wing a soldier who is his exact opposite: an intelligent, pacifist sergeant. They are individuals in a sea of conformists, men who reject military ideology (though for different reasons) and who have no illusions about the nature of their cause. That they are doomed seems clear—no amount of individuality can withstand the complete brutalization of army life, nor can two lone figures fight a whole system. Similarly, as tough as the hoodlum soldier might be, he can be no match for bullets or artillery.[9]

Another of Masumura's war-themed films is *Red Angel* (*Akai Tenshi*, 1966). Though set on the Chinese front, the film takes place early in the war and focuses not on combat or even combat troops but on an army nurse and her interaction with patients and the surgeon with whom she falls in love. Through Nurse Nishi Sakura (much is made of her name—*sakura* means cherry blossom, the most prized image in Japanese aesthetics for its transitory nature) the audience gains entrée to the horrors of war and the collateral damage it inflicts, specifically on the army doctors and nurses who care for the wounded Japanese soldiers. The film is relentless in its depiction of the gruesome injuries the men suffer, in particular, the never-ending number of amputated limbs. The relationship between war wounds, especially amputation, and blighted sexuality seems to be the film's major motif. In the film's first scene, Sakura is raped by a soldier in the hospital (though she reports it, she is not overly traumatized by the event), and although he jauntily goes off to fight, when he next sees Sakura, he is gravely wounded and, needless to say, far less jaunty. His desperate pleas to be saved are in stark contrast to his earlier happy-go-lucky attitude. And rather than take any revenge against him in his weakened condition, Sakura begs the doctor to try and save him. The doctor's efforts are to no avail.

In another instance, a soldier who has had both arms amputated at the shoulder begs Sakura for sexual release. She provides that and more, even taking him to a hotel in the city where they spend the day making love. Realizing that this will likely be his last opportunity to be a "real man," he kills himself. He also brings home to Sakura (and us) the wartime situation in which gravely wounded soldiers, especially early in the war, were held in military hospitals, prevented from going home, lest the civilian population see the effects of a war they were being asked to blindly support.

Yet it is not just the soldiers who lose their sexual potency because of their war injuries. The surgeon, too, has become impotent through a combination of psychological trauma resulting from all the operations he must perform and addiction to morphine, which he uses to take his mind off his duties. Here, too, Sakura becomes a ministering angel, returning him to his manhood, ironically and symbolically, on the night before a Chinese attack that wipes out the whole platoon. A shot of Sakura laying across his body, his broken samurai sword beside him, presents an overripe symbol.

In *Red Angel,* like the films discussed above, much is ambiguous or problematic. The connections drawn between war wounds and sexual dysfunction and the importance of women in healing these wounds arguably trivialize the wartime setting. Equally problematic is the fact that, once again, no context is provided for the Japanese presence in China—considering that the film is set in the years 1937–1938. The massive number of Japanese wounded clearly implies that the Chinese are winning the war at this point, and there is the constant carping that the Japanese are outnumbered and outgunned by the Chinese. And if the soldiers are not heroes (and they are not), we are asked to sympathize with the doctor because of his inability to practice real medicine instead of being little more than a butcher removing

Red Angel (1966) battlefield

limbs. Thus the film seems to suggest that the Chinese are the aggressors as well as to encourage viewers to focus more on the nurse's sexual healing prowess than on the causes for all the bloodshed. Nonetheless, the vision of battleground as slaughterhouse is unforgettable, and the idea that war emasculates men who cannot recover from their trauma is an equally striking proposition.

At least one more film should be mentioned as taking a caustic, critical look at the war: *The Human Bullet* (*Nikudan,* 1968) from the stylish, underrated director Okamoto Kihachi. The film seems to capture the same spirit as *Catch-22,* or perhaps even that of *Dr. Strangelove.* It is certainly a demythologized look at the kamikaze squadrons that still inspire admiration for their "cherry blossom" existence. The spirit of the 1960s, very apparent in the works of Suzuki, clearly finds its way into this irreverent film. This was not Okamoto's first foray into war cinema. A year before this film, he released *Japan's Longest Day* (*Nihon no ichiban nagai hi*). The longest day in question concerns the events, discussions, and recriminations leading up to the surrender on August 15, 1945.

Even the radicalism of the 1960s could not keep others from valorizing the kamikaze fighters. Films that continued to celebrate the camaraderie and spirit of self-sacrifice that make these men icons of the nobility of failure for the Japanese included *Ah, Special Attack Corps* (*Aa tokubetsu kōgekitai,* Inoue Yoshio, 1960); the big-budget spectacular *Wings of the Pacific* (*Taiheiyō no tsubasa,* Matsubayashi Shue, 1963), starring Mifune Toshirō and Kayama Yūzō, with special effects by Tsuburaya Eiji; and the testosterone-heavy *The Last Kamikaze* (*Saigo no tokkōtai,* Satō Jun'ya, 1970), whose cast included a who's who of Toei tough guys like Tsuruta Kōji, Takakura Ken, Sugawara Bunta, Wakayama Tomisaburō, and Sonny Chiba.

The 1970s got off to an interesting start in terms of war films with Ya-mamoto Satsuo's three-part adaptation of the same Gomikawa Junpei novel that was the source for the *Human Condition* trilogy just a decade earlier. Called *War and Humanity* (*Sensō to ningen*, 1970–1973), it follows the same basic storyline of the novel and first film adaptation. However, its large bud-get also allowed for some spectacular battle scenes. This adds a new dimension to the film that set a trend for many 1970s war epics. Okamoto Kihachi got into the act with his two-and-a-half-hour combat epic *The Battle of Oki-nawa* (*Gekido no shōwashi: Okinawa kessen*, 1971). An all-star cast (Nakadai Tatsuya, Tamba Tetsurō, Kayama Yūzō, Kobayashi Keiju, and others) and the use of newsreel footage combine to tell the complex and bloody story of the battle that many believe was the impetus for the American decision to drop the bomb. The film makes a gallant effort to detail the battle from the military high command on down. Civilians and soldiers alike fall before the inexorable might of the U.S. armed forces and many of them by suicide. In particular, the mass suicides of Okinawan civilians, who had been told that a horrible fate awaited them if they were captured by the Americans, along with the drumbeat of militaristic ideology to which they had been exposed, clearly makes these civilians the victims of Japanese ideology and aggression. The February 26 Incident (a failed coup d'état by young army officers in 1936) was also a popular topic in the military-themed tales, in-cluding the avant-garde treatment it received from Yoshida Kijū in *Coup d'Etat* (*Kaigenrei*, 1973) and the rather more prosaic but compelling treat-ment from director Moritani Shirō working with the star Takakura Ken in *Disturbance* (*Dōran*, 1980).[10]

A perceptible increase in war films was apparent in the 1980s, a period when commercial Japanese cinema was struggling to find, let alone main-tain, a mainstream audience. No fewer than eight films with wartime sub-jects were released between 1982 and 1985, suggesting that this moment of economic solidity, even triumph, allowed for revisionist representations of Japan's wartime past. Perhaps the most famous example of economic trium-phalism came in the form of the publication of Ishihara Shintarō and Mo-rita Akio's "*NO*" *to ieru Nihon: shin Nichi-Bei kankei no kādo* in 1989. Major films that find new excitement in the war and its aftermath, and take a re-visionist stance, include *The Great Empire of Japan* (*Dai-Nippon teikoku*, Masuda Toshio, 1982); *Zero Fighter Burns* (*Zerosen moyu*, Masuda, 1984), which traces the manufacture and testing of the famed war planes; and *Tokyo Trial* (*Tōkyō saiban,* 1983), Kobayashi Masaki's painstaking documentary that raises questions not just about war guilt but about the legitimacy of the war crimes trials.[11]

Not all 1980s war films take a revisionist approach or repress the question of Japan's wartime aggression. *Shanghai Rhapsody* (*Shanhai bansu kingu,* 1984) "roundly condemns Japanese actions during wartime on Chinese soil,"[12] which is perhaps no surprise because it emanates from the sympathetic canon of Fukasaku Kinji. Similarly, *Southern Cross* (*Minami jūjisei,* Maruyama Seiji and Peter Maxwell, 1982) examines the killing of 5,000 ethnic Chinese in Singapore. A Japanese-Australian co-production, the film does not shy away from placing blame squarely on Japanese forces for the murders (at the hands of the notorious military police, the Kempeitai), but it also makes a hero out of a Japanese bureaucrat stationed in Singapore. *The Go Masters* (*Mikan no taikyoku,* Satō Jun'ya and Duan Jishun, 1982) was a Sino-Japanese co-production about the wartime era and the breakdown of relations between the two countries amid Japanese imperialism. The co-production marked an attempt to repair relations between the two countries.

The 1990s found the kamikaze flying yet again in a handful of sentimental, yet effective melodramas. *Summer of the Moonlight Sonata* (*Gekkō no natsu,* Koyama Seijirō, 1993) utilizes a common structure of seeing the war from the perspective of the present in telling a story about two kamikaze pilots who visit an elementary school in order to play the titular musical piece on the school's grand piano. A search for the two pilots in the present day reveals that one of them did not perish in the war, after all. The fact-based *Wings of a Man* (*Ningen no tsubasa,* Okamoto Akihisa, 1995) tells the story of a young professional baseball pitcher who enlisted as a kamikaze pilot and died in combat in 1945. It uses another common motif in war films—actual footage to lend the film a documentary flavor. Though this independent film had no commercial distribution in Japan, it had frequent nontheatrical showings and was awarded a number of prestigious cultural prizes (e.g., from the Ministry of Education and the National Congress of Parents and Teachers). *The Firefly* (*Hotaru,* Furuhata Yasuo, 2001) is certainly the best of these more recent kamikaze films, thanks to the presence of Takakura Ken and its interesting story of a Korean kamikaze pilot who died in combat and his surviving Japanese comrades. It was nominated for awards from the Japanese Academy in a dozen categories, including best film (though it did not win in any). This film, too, sees the past from the perspective of the present, focusing in particular on the aged surviving pilot and his wife, who had been the fiancée of the deceased kamikaze fighter. Its attempt to deal also with Japanese-Korean issues is admirable.

Yet even as the 1990s witnessed a renaissance of Japanese cinema with respect to artistic excellence and commercial viability, the period produced relatively few war films. Directors as varied as Kitano Takeshi, Iwai Shunji, Kurosawa Kiyoshi, Aoyama Shinji, Tsukamoto Shinya, and Miike Takashi came to national and international prominence. Where are the war films from this varied group? Given both Kitano and Miike's avowed interest in explorations of violence and masculinity, such a genre would seem ideal. Tsukamoto and Kurosawa, in different ways, are interested in reactions to extreme situations; yet the war film has not proved of interest to them. Thus, the genre has been relegated to the occasional production of typically revisionist fare.

Resurgent nationalism, not to mention revisionism, is certainly apparent in the new millennium. Along these lines, we find a film like *Merdeka* (*Murudeka 17805*, Fuji Yukio, 2001), which imagines the positive role of the Japanese Army in Indonesia's struggle for independence from the Netherlands. Businessman-turned-producer Asano Katsuaki made the film in order to "restore national pride among Japanese people in being a Japanese national."[13] The big-budget *Yamato* (*Otokotachi no Yamato*, Satō Jun'ya, 2005) also uses the perspective of the present to examine the past, but it features spectacular scenes of naval combat in its tribute to the largest warship ever built.[14] This film was released amid a flurry of war-themed fantasy films, like the alternate history *Lorelei: The Witch of the Pacific Ocean* (*Rorerei*, Higuchi Shinji, 2005). It should be noted, of course, that many progressives in Japan have resisted such revisionism and nascent nationalism and looked honestly at Japan's wartime actions and reported the truth about them. While it is easy to overlook revisionist drivel like *Merdeka* and *The Truth of Nanjing* (discussed below), the most revealing texts are those produced with a sense of honesty and humanity, films that attempt to examine the war with sensitivity and insight. The contradictions and slips in these films, like *Harp of Burma, Fires on the Plain, The Human Condition, Red Angel,* and *Black Rain* (see below), tell us much about the struggle over the war in Japan's ongoing, contentious postwar.

Icons of War

Large-scale, complex, and traumatic events are difficult to grasp in their entirety. They are, therefore, typically reduced to a single image, place, or occurrence—a synecdoche for the larger whole. For the Pacific War, a small constellation of images has been used to cinematically narrate the war and Japan's responsibility in it. This constellation of images has much to do with the war memories of Japan's Asian neighbors, particularly the Chinese and the South Koreans, who insist, in varying degrees, on Japan's role as perpetrator. In contrast, we find images in which the Japanese attempt to portray themselves as victims, or, more problematically, to explicitly deny the charge of having been perpetrators or aggressors. In this cauldron of contending representations, four main motifs emerge: the "comfort women," the Nanjing Massacre, the Yasukuni shrine, and the atom bomb.[15]

The "Comfort Women"

The question of the euphemistically labeled "comfort women" (*ianfu*) was slow to emerge into public discourse and consciousness as an indication of Japanese war crimes. A war-crimes trial in Indonesia in 1948 convicted a number of Japanese military officers for the enforced prostitution of a few dozen Dutch women (ignoring the similar fate of Indonesians). This issue was not raised at the Tokyo War Crimes Trials (1946–1948).[16] The issue lay dormant until the late 1980s, when it arose in South Korea at the insistence of many former comfort women and their supporters. The filing of a class-action lawsuit in 1991 put the issue on the front page of major newspapers the world over. The Japanese government responded that, first, there was no evidence of official complicity by the Japanese military high command or the government; and, second, no compensation could or should be paid in any case, because of a 1965 treaty between Japan and South Korea. However, shortly thereafter incontrovertible documentation of official complicity began to emerge. The Japanese government soon issued an admission of some responsibility, and the then–Prime Minister Miyazawa Kiichi even offered a qualified apology. Over the years, other government officials have expressed apologies for the military activities in this matter and gave assurances of Japan's sincere regret without ever fully admitting complicity. The establishment of a quasi-public fund (the Asia Women's Fund) to pay compensation nonetheless has been another way the government has managed to skirt the issue. Unfortunately and, some would say, predictably, high-level revisionist responses or outright denials continue to be made.[17]

Korean documentaries—especially the brilliant three-part series from the director Byun Young-Joo, *The Murmuring* (*Najŭn moksori*, 1995), *Habitual Sadness: Korean Comfort Women Today* (*Najŭn moksori II*, 1997), and *My Own Breathing* (*Najŭn moksori III*, 1999)—have done much to keep the issue alive in a very forceful way. The films have had wide exposure at international film festivals. *The Murmuring* premiered in Japan at the Yamagata International Film Festival in 1995 and won the prestigious Ogawa Shinsuke Prize.[18]

But for the Japanese, the issue of *ianfu* has been repressed. To be sure, the novelist Tamura Taijirō, of the famous postwar *nikutai bungaku* ("literature of the flesh"), not only dealt rather clearly with the prostitutes who served soldiers in the war and postwar eras—*Shunpuden* and *Gate of Flesh* (*Nikutai no mon*, Suzuki Seijun, 1964), respectively—but acknowledged the presence of Korean women on the front lines of the comfort stations in China. His protagonist in *Shunpuden,* Harumi, is Korean, though not exactly pressed into service as the vast majority of Korean comfort women were. Film versions of *Shunpuden,* however, have greatly played down that aspect. Important adaptations include *Escape at Dawn* (*Akatsuki no dassō,* Taniguchi Senkichi, 1950—a film well worth examining, if only because it stars Yamaguchi Yoshiko as Harumi) and *Shunpuden*, in which, again, the question of the sexual slavery of foreign women remains nearly out of sight. Kyoko Hirano discusses the problems that Taniguchi's film had with the Occupation censors and points out not only the repression of Harumi's Korean background but the change in her character from a prostitute to a singer.[19] "Comfort women" appear briefly in a single scene in Masumura Yasuzō's confused sex-and-war tale *Red Angel*, but it is unclear whether the women are Japanese or Chinese—the women are given no voice, save for one who moans in agony as she is stricken with cholera. One is tempted to say this voicelessness is all too symbolic of the plight of both foreign and Japanese military comfort women.

The Rape of Nanjing

During the war, reports of Japanese atrocities were frequent, and American and British war films of the period often used such atrocities for propaganda purposes. The "Bataan Death March" and the construction of the Burma

Railway and the infamous bridge over the River Kwai (and the 1957 Oscar-winning film about it) provided cinematic fodder in the postwar era as well. The use of Chinese and Korean men as slave labor is also well known, as has become, in recent years, the activities of Unit 731. The Imperial Japanese Army practiced a policy of raping, pillaging, and looting in the theater of war, giving rise to such incidents as the Manila Massacre of February 1945, along with many documented incidents of systematic terror aimed at local and other civilians in China. Yet it is clear that the most potent image and rallying cry for the commission of Japanese war crimes has been the Nanjing Massacre, more tendentiously but unarguably best described as "the Rape of Nanjing." Though the Nanjing Massacre was reported on at the time of its commission and used in American propaganda films, it did not always possess the metonymic value that it does today. Yoshida Takashi has traced in detail the way in which the incident came to represent the kind of imagery and significance it possesses today and he writes that successive historical developments led to shifts in its meaning and emphasis. Various historical events—including the establishment of the People's Republic of China (PRC) in 1949, the cold war, the Vietnam War, the normalization of relations between the PRC and the United States and Japan in the 1970s, Japan's rise to economic preeminence in the 1980s—led to revisions in thinking about and increased attention to the issue. For Yoshida, the issue begins to enter Japanese public discourse about twenty years after the conclusion of the war.

> For practical purposes, the 1960s may be considered as marking the beginning of the historiography of Nanjing. In 1965, the veterans of the Kumamoto Units published their military history and included a brief discussion of the "Nanjing Incident" (*Nankin jiken*). Its editor agreed that Japanese must reflect on the Nanjing Incident and accept responsibility for the killing of innocent civilians.[20]

Thereafter, those who insisted on acknowledging, explaining, and making amends for the atrocities competed with those who claimed that reports of atrocities were either exaggerated or outright fabrications. A perhaps typical revisionist sentiment claims that the "so-called Rape of Nanjing" was invented in order to create a counterpart to the Nazi crimes in Europe.[21]

Understandably, Nanjing has not occupied much of a cinematic presence in Japan. However, a 1995 Chinese-Taiwanese co-production titled

Nanjing 1937 (directed by Wu Ziniu) had a short theatrical run in Japan. The general consensus seems to be that the Japanese responded to this film with *Pride: The Fateful Moment* (*Puraido—unmei no toki,* Ito Shunya, 1998). Financed in part by the businessman Nakamura Isao and directed by Itō Shunya (whose major claim to earlier cinematic fame is the "Female Convict Scorpion" series, deliriously stylish exploitation films in 1972–1973), the film was a big-budget affair with an impressive international cast, led by the Japanese star Tsugawa Masahiko and the Hindi-language cinema stalwarts Suresh Oberoi and Anupam Kher, along with veteran Hollywood actors Ronny Cox and Scott Wilson. Such an impressive international cast is rare in Japanese films, and it is interesting that American actors agreed to appear in a film with such an obviously revisionist ideology. The film clearly claims that Japan was forced to go to war against the United States; that eyewitness accounts of the Nanjing Massacre are merely hearsay; that the Japanese were instrumental in helping India gain its independence; that the bombings of Hiroshima and Nagasaki were as serious as any supposed Japanese war crimes; and that Tōjō Hideki, the prime minister of Japan during the war, was simply a decent family man who, at the war's end, only wished to tend his garden in peace. Instead, he is sacrificed on the altar of victor's justice despite the dissenting opinion of the heroic Justice Radhabinod Pal at the Tokyo War Crimes Trial.[22]

A more obvious, cinematically less-assured attempt to debunk the Nanjing Massacre came in the form of an even more forthrightly revisionist work, *The Truth of Nanking* (*Nankin no shinjitsu,* 2008). Directed by the right-wing filmmaker Mizushima Satoru and sponsored by the conservative Channel Sakura, this film, too, was made in response to another film—in this case, *Nanking,* an American documentary, co-directed by Bill Guttentag and Dan Sturman, which had been screened at the prestigious Sundance Film Festival in 2007 and subsequently had been shown in many countries around the world, including China, Singapore, and Taiwan. *The Truth of Nanking,* has been described in official press releases as follows:

> A movie [that] investigates the "real truth" behind the Massacre of Nanking. . . . While the rest of the world identifies the Japanese as the culprits of the Massacre, this film investigates the involvement of the Chinese in this matter. The film is shot from a different point of view with the belief that the event was overemphasized. A movie like this allows people to see a new perspective on a one-sided event.[23]

Like *Pride,* the film focuses on Tōjō and six other men convicted of war crimes in the Tokyo trials, depicting them as "seven honorable martyrs who sacrificed themselves for the fatherland." Like Fukasaku's *Under the Flag of the Rising Sun,* this film, too, interweaves period footage to try to present some historical authenticity and context.

The failure of the film (*Pride* performed far better at the box office) to strike a chord with Japanese audiences is due in part to its obvious artistic inferiority but also to its extreme viewpoint. The website devoted to the film (in English and Japanese) makes much of the "truth of Nanking" as they see it, rather than focus on the film itself. The website presents the now-standard revisionist arguments regarding the Nanjing Massacre: that mass murder never took place; that it was a Chinese propaganda ploy at the time and thereafter; that the Occupation and its sham war crimes trial needed to find a way to condemn the Japanese for genocide as the Allied forces had condemned the Nazis; that the Chinese were guilty of waging a guerrilla war; and that Iris Chang's popular book, *The Rape of Nanking: The Forgotten Holocaust of World War II* (1997) was not only written in support of Chinese political ends but filled with errors and distortions.[24] This film, and others less outrageously revisionist, obviously attempts to deny Japan the label of perpetrator.

Yasukuni Shrine

Few symbols have proved as potent a lightning rod for controversy as the official visits undertaken by prominent Japanese politicians (including prime ministers) to the Yasukuni shrine. The shrine began as a memorial to commemorate those who fell in support of the Meiji Restoration (1868). Thereafter, those who fought in service to the emperor were enshrined therein. Before Japan began the "China Incident" (i.e., invasion) in 1931, little more than 100,000 memorialized heroes were there. By the end of World War II, over 2 million had been added. Arguably, it was the enshrinement and commemoration of over 1,000 war criminals, including about a dozen "Class A" criminals (especially Tōjō) that began the regular Asian protests against visits to the shrine by Japanese government officials and, in turn, Japanese resistance against those protests. The Occupation insisted that the shrine itself be decoupled from official state sponsorship and support, and so it has officially been maintained using private funds ever since. One sign often pointed to in support of the idea that Japanese revisionists and atrocity-deniers wield power in Japan is what Harry Harootunian claims is the "un-

Yasukuni shrine

doubtedly authorized . . . countrywide movement to induce the government to once more assume responsibility for the financial and administrative maintenance of [the shrine]."[25] While many governmental officials visit the shrine, some claim to do so in the guise of their "civilian" life. The howls of protest in response from China, the two Koreas, and Taiwan are met with equal derision by the Japanese Right, in what seems an endless game of reaction and recalcitrance.

Somewhat less remarked upon than the visits of high-level politicians to the shrine is the war museum within the shrine, the Yūshūkan. The exhibits here assert that Japan fought the war to liberate Asia from Western imperialist powers. Such an idea remains a standard feature of revisionist histories of the war and was, as is well known, a central part of Japan's wartime propaganda (the Greater East Asia Co-Prosperity Sphere [*Dai Tōa Kyōeiken*]). That such a notion should so brazenly appear in a modern museum setting is perhaps both shocking and also fitting for its placement in the shrine.

For the scholar John Breen, the Yūshūkan has other disturbing features:

What is perhaps unique to the Yūshūkan war museum—it certainly offers a striking contrast to, say, the Imperial war museum in London—is the curious absence of the enemy. The visitor to the galleries on the Sino-Japanese war, the Russo-Japanese war, the Manchurian "incident" and the Pacific war looks in vain for a sighting of the enemy. There are no representations of Chinese, Russian, Korean, American or British soldiers; no weaponry, uniforms, flags or other trophies of war. . . . The exhibits prompt reflection only on heroism, loyalty and self-sacrifice.[26]

Of course, the whole point of the shrine is to transform the spirits of the war dead, who, by definition, died defending "Japan," into *kami* (gods), and thus heroism, loyalty, and self-sacrifice are never in vain, for the enemy is, in some sense, irrelevant.

Breen has another point to make as well, one that recurred in films: the Tokyo War Crimes Trial and the way in which it has also been used as a weapon by Japanese war revisionists. He writes:

The visitor reaches the end of the Yūshūkan gallery on the Pacific war to discover that, though the enemy is entirely absent, there is a striking foreign presence. The gallery concludes with a photograph, magnified perhaps ten times, of Justice Radhabinod Pal. Justice Pal was the one Asian judge at the war crimes tribunal in Tokyo, and it was his considered view that the Japanese were innocent of all war crimes, and that the real aggressors in Asia were British and American imperialists. Justice Pal's views are reproduced by the side of his portrait. They make for a striking and a dramatic end to the gallery.

The point here is that such a blatant attempt to shift the responsibility for war crimes from the Japanese to the victors is consistent with other attempts to relativize, ignore, or deny the commission of any crimes.[27] In this instance, the failure to acknowledge the enemy (and thus potential war crimes and Japan's defeat) leads to a denial of the legitimacy of the war crimes trial.

Yasukuni, like the comfort women, has not been a popular or significant subject in films. Yet a documentary released in 2007 and directed by a long-time Chinese resident in Japan, Li Ying, with a Japanese production crew and some Japanese financing, in particular a 7.5-million-yen (roughly, $62,500) grant from the Agency for Cultural Affairs, did spark discussion and some controversy. As Philip Brasor wrote in the *Japan Times,* scheduled screenings of the film, titled simply *Yasukuni,* had been canceled in Tokyo and Osaka out of fear of protests and violence by right-wing extremists. In addition, the government funding for the film also created some raised eyebrows because of its alleged anti-Japan bias. Apparently, the film played in Japan without much further controversy thereafter.

The Atom Bomb

One does not enter lightly into any discussion of the dropping of the atom bombs on Hiroshima and Nagasaki. The sad fact is that they were dropped, and with devastating consequences. The use of nuclear weapons against these cities perhaps more than anything else has lent credence to the Japanese people's sense of themselves as victims—indeed, as the children of the atom bomb. Interestingly, there is little of what might be called an atom-bomb film genre in Japan. A handful of films were produced in the 1950s, ranging from documentaries to fiction films, all of them dealing with what we might call "the legacy" of the bomb. Therefore, the makers of these films felt no need to contextualize the bombings, because their works address the effect of the bombings (short term and longer) and not the war that led up to them. Virtually none of these films were distributed overseas, and most are largely forgotten today. Though the atom bomb was a subject strictly forbidden by the Occupation authorities, they had, after much discussion, allowed the publication of Nagai Takashi's memoir *The Bell of Nagasaki* (*Nagasaki no kane*) in 1949. It seemed that the authorities could not, then, deny production of a film version, released in 1950, directed by Oba Hideo with a script by Shindō Kaneto.[28]

Shindō, whose interest in the atom bomb would recur throughout his lengthy career, released *Children of the Atom Bomb* (*Gembaku no ko*) in 1952. With respect to the making of the film, Kyoko Hirano notes "as soon as the occupation was terminated, Shindō's crew headed for Hiroshima in May 1952 and the film was released later that year.[29] The film was entered and accepted into competition at the Cannes Film Festival in 1953 and remained among the few non–period dramas sent to a major European festival until late in the decade. While the Japanese used the period drama to soften their image by creating Orientalist images of their past, it is significant that among the first non–period films to be sent to Cannes were stories about the atom bomb; Shindō's film was followed in 1956 by Kurosawa Akira's *Record of a Living Being* (*Ikimono no kiroku*).

The film is typical of most of the atom bomb cinema, in that it deals with *hibakusha* (survivors of the bombings), and it relies, at least somewhat, on real-life accounts. A deft use of flashbacks gets at the issue of rupture or break that is central to most depictions of the bomb: that there was vibrant life before the bomb was dropped; and then everything changed. After the bomb, nothing would be the same. Thus, for Shindō those moments before the bomb was dropped are crucial, seen in this film in flashback sequences. The same is also true in Imamura Shōhei's *Black Rain* (*Kuroi ame,* 1989). Similarly, *Tomorrow* (*Ashita,* Kuroki Kazuo, 1988) focuses on the twenty-four hours before the bomb was dropped on Nagasaki. Donald Richie discusses a handful of other bomb-themed films of the 1950s in his essay "'Mono no aware': Hiroshima in Film," so I will not repeat that discussion here.[30] Similarly, one could discuss allegories of the bomb, for instance, seeing *Rashōmon* (Kurosawa Akira, 1950), with its images of ruination and metaphysical shock, or *Godzilla* (*Gojira,* Honda Ishirō, 1954), with its obvious nuclear anxiety and scenes of massive destruction, as a function of the legacy of the bomb.[31] Anime, with its frequent images of apocalypse, must also be reckoned as a significant arena where the atom bomb and nuclear anxiety are worked out in cinematic form.[32] Indeed, perhaps the best-known film on the subject of the bomb and *hibakusha* remains a work of anime: *Barefoot Gen* (*Hadashi no Gen,* Mori Masaki, 1983), which approaches the subject directly, but relies on animation to create some distance from the horrors.

The legacy of the bomb seen in the films of the early postwar years became a more overt form of victim consciousness (*higaisha ishiki*) following the atom bomb tests on the Bikini atoll in March 1954.[33] The irradiation of the fishing vessel *Daigo Fukuryū Maru* (Lucky Dragon No. 5) was a shock to the national body, a reminder, if one was needed, of the victimization of the Japanese by American nuclear weapons. Shindō, evincing his continued interest in the bomb, made a film version of the ill-fated fishing vessel affected by American atomic testing in 1959, which takes the name of the boat for its title. Perhaps this is the best context in which to view Kurosawa's *Record of a Living Being,* a film that seems to claim that, far from merely having a legacy, the bomb is very much a reality in the Japanese psyche.

Because relatively few films on the bomb were made overall in the stream of Japanese cinema, it is interesting that two major films were released only two years apart, the aforementioned *Black Rain* in 1989 and Kurosawa's *Rhapsody in August* (*Hachi-gatsu no kyōshikyoku*) in 1991. Given the stature of these two filmmakers, and the wide release given the films, not to mention the discussion they provoked in Japan and overseas, no discussion of the atom bomb in Japanese cinema can fail to include them.

Black Rain (1989) and Ozu Yasujirō

That Imamura's film is so artistically successful and Kurosawa's at best uneven owes to Imamura's channeling, if you will, of the spirit, style, and themes of Ozu Yasujirō and to Kurosawa's inability to get beyond the amateurishness of the performances by the young cast and the use of his vaunted style of handling action in a film that contains none. *Black Rain* is best understood less in the context of an adaptation of Ibuse Masuji's enormously successful and influential novel (available in English translation) than as a film that imagines Ozu in light of the bomb.

Ozu is the avatar not only of an innovative approach to cinematic storytelling and a set of stylistic tendencies that accompany it (everything from the use of narrative ellipses to tatami-floor-level camera placement) but also as a director concerned with the continuity of Japanese life. This does not mean Japanese culture; he is a decidedly apolitical (though not ahistorical) director. This means daily life   thus the focus on daily activities and ordinary people in his films. For Ozu, there is simply a cultural imperative to complete the life cycle, especially in his handful of postwar films that deal with the necessity for a twenty-something daughter to leave her ordinary household and marry. The plot of *Black Rain* concerns the desire of Shizuma Shigematsu and his wife, Shigeko, to see to the marriage of their niece Yasuko, for whom they have parental responsibility in the postwar era. This simple plot unfolds Ozu-style, with numerous interior scenes of the family sitting around a table on tatami, eating, talking, or listening to the radio. But despite the plot and style, this cannot be an Ozu film, for there has been a rupture in the form of the blinding light of the atom bomb and its inescapable legacy. Yasuko will not be married; she cannot be, for she is stricken with radiation sickness, contracted during an ill-fated trip to Hiroshima, and her exposure there to the poisonous black rain from which the story derives its title. Of course, Yasuko is a victim, indeed, an innocent one, and, in placing the film so clearly in the shadow of Ozu, all of Japan becomes a victim and the bomb a rupture that cannot be closed.

The film is not, however, simply another example of victim consciousness. Imamura does provide some context. For instance, Shizuma wears a uniform to work in a factory that presumably makes war munitions. The added character of Yuichi (which Imamura takes from Ibuse's short story "Lieutenant Lookeast") is a World War II veteran who served in the antitank squad. His posttraumatic stress disorder (and thus his own victimhood) notwithstanding, his presence is a stark reminder of the conflict that culminated in the dropping of the bomb.

In what is possibly a coincidence, these two major films by two of Japan's most important directors consider first, Hiroshima and, second, Nagasaki. The legacy of *Rhapsody in August* is likely to be the recognition of the dwindling of Kurosawa's artistic power on view in his penultimate film and the controversy the film sparked as early as its first screening at the Cannes Film Festival. The late Roger Ebert reported that, at a press conference after the screening, one journalist cried out, "Why was the bomb dropped in the first place?" American audiences reacted with anger at a scene in the film in which Clark (portrayed by Richard Gere), the Hawaiian-born half-Japanese–half-Caucasian nephew, apologizes for the death of his uncle in the Nagasaki bombing and, in larger terms, for America's crime in dropping the bomb.

The film attempts to accomplish two goals, failing in one but succeeding in the other. As for the first aim: it attempts to teach a history lesson—that of the bombing of Nagasaki, to a generation, represented by the heroine's teenage grandchildren. Poor performances by the child actors and an obviously didactic tone harm this element of the film. Where the film succeeds is in its presentation of rupture, loss, and the need to mourn and forgive. An old woman whose husband died many years earlier possesses a quietude that puzzles her grandchildren. Yet she seems to be drifting into a kind of senility, her memory of the day the bomb fell slipping into the present. Of course, this is precisely the point; that the memory cannot be repressed yet is in danger of being forgotten. Thus the use of the children to be the repository of the collective memory that is in danger of fading away with time and old age.

Films about the bomb carry a heavy load of representation. In this case, comparisons to films about the Holocaust are apt. What can be said in the face of such overwhelming tragedy, death, and destruction? It may be no surprise that so few films have been made on the subject and very few by major artists adequately grapple with such profound issues. Films dealing with soldiers in combat or the women who served them are more typical. Collectively, even these films have a heavy burden as well: how to remember Japan's ill-advised, ill-fated, and aggressive war—and thereby seriously address historical injustices and move toward reconciliation.

Notes

1   Jeanine Basinger, *The World War II Combat Film: Anatomy of a Genre* (Middletown, CT: Wesleyan University Press, 2003).

2   The best known of these three films is *Nanking* (*Nankin*, 1938), which was directed by Akimoto Ken, filmed by Shirai Shigeru of Tōho Films, and produced in association with the Army Special Services Division. Long thought lost, a nearly complete copy of the film was discovered in Beijing, China, in 1995.

3   Kyoko Hirano, *Mr. Smith Goes to Tokyo: Japanese Cinema under the American Occupation, 1945–1952* (Washington, DC: Smithsonian Institution Press, 1992), 49.

4   The comparison with postwar Germany is often mentioned in this regard. For instance, Ian Buruma argues that while the Germans have engaged in collective self-criticism and examination, the Japanese have not especially followed suit to the same extent (*The Wages of Guilt: Memories of War in Germany and Japan* [New York: Farrar, Straus & Giroux, 1994]).

5   Yoshida Takashi, *The Making of the "Rape of Nanking": History and Memory in Japan, China, and the United States* (New York: Oxford University Press, 2006), 48.

6   Isolde Standish, *A New History of Japanese Cinema: A Century of Narrative Film* (New York: Continuum, 2005), 184–185.

7   This motif appears in *Under the Flag of the Rising Sun* as well as in *The Emperor's Naked Army Marches On*.

8   In the presentation of this paper at the conference held at Stanford University, an audience member noted the repeated motif of soldiers who do not return to Japan following the war, as if to banish from the nation these representatives of the disastrous military campaign. Indeed, we can note that

a major motif in postwar Hollywood cinema is the emotional and physical struggle of returning veterans. Yet in Japan, such a theme is notable by its absence. One can think of Kurosawa's *Stray Dog* (*Nora Inu,* 1949) as one exception to this rule, although it is hardly highlighted as it is in Hollywood films, such as *The Best Years of Our Lives* (William Wyler, 1946) or *The Men* (Fred Zinnemann, 1950).

9   Daiei Studios released a sequel to the film, dissipating some of the nihilistic energy of the original. The reduction of the series of films that followed to a buddy-buddy structure weakened the theme of individuals doomed by an oppressive military system and by combat in a meaningless cause.

10   In the February 26, 1936, "incident," a group of young military officers launched a coup d'état against the civilian government of Prime Minister Okada Keisuke. An army general and two prominent ministers were killed, and others were wounded. Martial law was declared, and two days later the soldiers were forced to surrender. A number of them were later executed, as was Kita Ikki, whose radical right-wing philosophy was a major justification for the attempted coup.

11   This is not to say that Kobayashi's narration or choice of footage denies the trial's efficacy and legality—merely that the issue of their legitimacy is raised. Kobayashi did not repudiate his antiwar, antifeudal, and humanist stance of the 1950s and 1960s.

12   James Bailey, "War Films Depict Japan as Misunderstood Victim," *New York Times*, November 10, 1985.

13   Kitamura Masayuki, "War Flick Touting Japan's Role in Indonesia's Birth Irks Jakarta," *Japan Times*, March 27, 2001.

14   Satō Jun'ya, whose name appears a number of times in this chapter, made his directorial debut with a war-themed drama that is quite explicit in condemning the behavior and character of the Japanese army: *Cruel Story of War* (*Rikugun zangyaku monogatari*, 1963). He is thus something of a specialist in war films, a rarity in the postwar Japanese cinema and, considering the ambiguities of the genre, and his own movement from outright antiwar, antimilitary films to something a bit more nationalistic, might be worth a closer look.

15   There is at least one more major motif in the perpetrator/victim continuum and that is the issue of the "textbook controversy." This has been the subject of much public discourse, but one that has no cinematic component. Of course, one could find other symbols of Japan's wartime conduct: for the United States that would include such things as Pearl Harbor and the Bataan Death March; and for both the United States and Japan, the kamikaze fighters. Yet it seems clear that these four images have the greatest hold from

inside and outside Japan. For purposes of this chapter, the kamikaze fighter is subsumed within the larger genre of the war film, but has not in itself come to take on powerful metonymic or condensed qualities.

16 One compelling theory as to why this was so maintains that there was complicity on the part of the U.S. Occupation in the suppression of the comfort women issue because the Occupation forces availed themselves of comfort stations set up by the Japanese government.

17 Demands periodically arise to revoke the 1993 apology. One such effort came from Prime Minister Abe Shinzō, who claimed, initially, that the comfort women were not coerced into their sexual slavery. He did not deny the use of comfort stations but insisted that there was no evidence of enforced slavery or coercion. Facing international outrage, he backed off slightly from those comments shortly thereafter but, again, fell far short of acknowledging the official complicity in setting up the comfort stations. And he refused to issue an apology, saying merely that the 1993 statement could stand.

18 For an analysis of these films and their place in recent Korean cinema, see Frances Gateward, "Waiting to Exhale: The Colonial Experience and the Trouble with *My Own Breathing*," in *Seoul Searching: Culture and Identity in Contemporary Korean Cinema*, ed. Frances Gateward (Albany, NY: SUNY Press, 2007).

19 Hirano, *Mr. Smith Goes to Tokyo*, 87–95. Hirano claims that the film was selected as an official entry at the Cannes Film Festival in 1951. This is a vague assertion, unfortunately, as it is not listed as "in competition" for the festival in 1951. It might mean that the Japanese themselves submitted it to the festival, but the festival programmers chose not to enter it for prize consideration. The film did have distribution in Asian countries where Japanese cinema was not banned.

20 Takashi, *The Making of the "Rape of Nanking,"* 59.

21 Ibid., 96.

22 Michael J. Green, "Can Tojo Inspire Modern Japan," *SAIS Review* 19, no. 2 (1999).

23 http://japanvisitor.blogspot.com/2008/10/truth-about-nanking-movie.html.

24 There is some controversy and ambiguity over the cancellation of a Japanese translation of Iris Chang's book *The Rape of Nanking* (New York: Basic Books, 1997) during her lifetime. Though popular opinion has it that the cancellation was due to right-wing pressure, the story is apparently far more complicated, revolving around Chang's unwillingness to correct certain minor errors; of having a foreword to the Japanese edition; and having a simultaneous, separate book appear with such corrections and discussion.

The book was eventually translated and published in 2007, a few years after Chang's sad death.

25 Harry Harootunian, "Japan's Long Postwar: The Trick of Memory and the Ruse of History," *South Atlantic Quarterly* 99, no. 4 (fall 2000): 718.

26 John Breen, "Yasukuni Shrine: Ritual and Memory," *Asia-Pacific Journal: Japan Focus*, June 3, 2005, http://www.japanfocus.org/-John-Breen/2060/.

27 For further ways in which Justice Pal has been used in recent years by the right in Japan and something of his legacy in India, see George Nishiyama, "Abe Risks Ire by Meeting Son of Indian Judge," Reuters, August 23, 2007; Norimitsu Onishi, "Decades after War Trials, Japan Still Honors a Dissenting Judge," *New York Times*, August 31, 2007.

28 For a discussion of the negotiations involved in getting the film produced, see Hirano, *Mr. Smith Goes to Tokyo*, 63–65. In his fascinating and detailed essay "The Body at the Center—The Effects of the Atomic Bomb on Hiroshima and Nagasaki," Markus Nornes discusses the attempts by the Occupation to suppress and even try to destroy all copies of a documentary film that featured footage shot in the ruined cities just a month after the surrender. See Broderick, ed., 121–160.

29 Hirano, *Mr. Smith Goes to Tokyo*, 62.

30 Donald Richie, "'Mono no aware': Hiroshima in Film," in *Hibakusha Cinema: Hiroshima, Nagasaki and the Nuclear Image in Japanese Film*, ed. Mick Broderick (London: Kegan Paul, 1996), 20–37.

31 See, for example, Chon Noriega, "Godzilla and the Japanese Nightmare: When *Them!* Is U.S.," in ibid., 54–74; William M. Tsutsui and Michiko Ito, ed., *In Godzilla's Footsteps: Japanese Pop Culture Icons on the Global Stage* (New York: Palgrave Macmillan, 2006). Yoshikuni Igarashi has written cogently and convincingly that, far from being an allegory or a metaphor for the atom bomb, Godzilla marks a direct confrontation with it, including America's culpability. The very excision of America in the film indicates its very presence, along with the military hardware employed by the Self-Defense Forces. He even parses the very interesting point that the monster studiously avoids the Imperial Palace, destroying only the prosperous downtown section that arose after the war and that itself elides it. See Igarashi Yoshikuni, *Bodies of Memory: Narratives of War in Postwar Japanese Culture, 1945–1970* (Princeton, NJ: Princeton University Press, 2000), 114–122.

32 Freda Freiberg, "*Akira* and the Postnuclear Sublime," in *Hibakusha Cinema*, 91–102.

33 Takashi, *The Making of the "Rape of Nanking,"* 55–56.

CHAPTER 5

Japanese Manga and Anime on the Asia-Pacific War Experience

Kyu Hyun Kim

This chapter provides a brief overview of how major manga artists in pre- and postwar Japan have engaged with the Second Sino-Japanese War (1937–1945) and the Pacific War (1941–1945). Manga are Japanese cartoons, comic books, and graphic novels. Because of the robustness of the art form and the proliferation of works on the war years, this chapter can touch on only a few recurrent themes in manga. Especially between the mid-1960s and the 1980s in postwar Japan, manga dwarfed traditional literature and news media in terms of quantity. Compared to anime, the distinctively Japanese style of animation, manga from this "golden age" is still not well known in the United States, although that situation may be changing. Some of the artists examined in this chapter, such as Tezuka Osamu and Matsumoto Leiji, are now well represented in the realm of English-translated manga as well as in anime, but even in the twenty-first century, American readers are still overwhelmingly familiar with anime and approach manga as "originals" from which many popular anime were adapted. In other words, the majority of the works discussed below may be unfamiliar to most American readers, even those with more than a casual interest in anime.[1]

Given the impossibility of offering a comprehensive discussion of war manga and anime in this limited space, I focus my attention here on a series of manga that explicitly deal with the Asia-Pacific War by artists who have been "canonized" as significant or who have at least met with popular acclaim among the Japanese reading public, with a few references to anime. The artists spotlighted here are best known for creating narrative comics geared primarily toward male consumers, both adults and children, rather than those working in the subgenre of four-panel or one-panel newspaper or newsmagazine cartoons or exclusively in comics marketed to female consumers.[2]

Before we look closely at individual artists, let us begin with a few general observations. First, the strong orientation toward a "victims' narrative"[3]—the desire to see Japanese as victims of the war and not aggressors—has led most postwar manga artists to condemn "war in general" in their works, rather than actions of the Japanese government. Second, changing international circumstances, especially regarding American involvement in the Vietnam War, have made it possible for them to bring out their repressed anger and resentment toward Americans as (hypocritical) judges of the Japanese past in the context of postwar pacifism. Each manga artist has dealt in his own way with the inherent ambivalence in their position toward Japan's history and the United States as their former enemy (and current benefactor). Few of their attitudes can be reduced to simplistic labels such as left or right wing, or liberal or conservative, although there certainly are exceptions, such as Kobayashi Yoshinori. In my view, however, these artists' nationalism, which defines the United States as an arrogant and hypocritical victor in the Pacific War, in conjunction with repressed memories of Japanese aggression and colonization of East and Southeast Asia, must be taken seriously in order for us to properly understand their postwar popularity among the Japanese.

In addition to the examples explored in this chapter, there is also a rich body of contemporary manga and anime that uses science fiction metaphors for Japan's war experience, especially the bombings of Hiroshima and Nagasaki. Space limitations prevent an exploration here of what Godzilla or Ultra-Seven have to say about Japan's wartime past, but I will, nonetheless, deal with instances in which science-fiction devices for imagining "counterfactual history" have been employed to explore the war experience, the most prominent example of which is Yamagami Tatsuhiko's *Shining Wind* (*Hikaru kaze,* 1970).

Pre-1945 Developments

Manga and animated films were not free of involvement in the overseas expansion of the Japanese empire and the rise of militarism in Japan. In 1931, the Manchurian Incident (aka the Mukden Incident, or Japanese invasion of Northeast China), planned and executed by Japan's Kwantung Army, signaled the commencement of Japan's military aggression in Northeast China. In the late 1920s and 1930s Japan, censorship was tightened and government surveillance intensified, as shown by the creation of the Special High Police, sometimes referred to as the "thought police." At the same time, this period was characterized by the unprecedented growth of an urban-centered mass culture. The advent of "comprehensive magazines" such as *Shōnen* (Boy), *Kingu* (King), and *Shufu no tomo* (Friend of the Housewife) created a mass readership, with sales of these titles averaging between 30,000 and 40,000 copies annually. In 1912, Japan's first movie production company, Nikkatsu (Japan Motion Picture Company), was established. In the 1920s and 1930s, the Japanese watched more Japanese movies than European and American movies, and there were more movie theaters in Japan than in the United States. The publishing house Kōdansha was at the forefront of pushing manga to adapt to this new mass culture. It opened up its flagship children's magazine *Shōnen Kurabu* (Boy's Club) to longer, serialized comics with long, sometimes self-contained narratives instead of four- to eight-panel manga, which had been the norm until then. The serials were then collected in glossy, hardcover books, printed in color.[4]

It is interesting to observe the extent to which many supposedly innocuous children's comics since 1931 have absorbed and internalized the cultural logic of militarism. One good example is the series about the dog *Norakuro* (Stray Black), by Tagawa Suihō (1899–1989), a well-known *rakugo* artist. First serialized in *Shōnen Kurabu* in 1931, Norakuro's adventures revolve around his antics as a brash but charming foot soldier, who is serving with a canine army squadron facing off against enemy monkey soldiers (a take on the proverbial enmity between dogs and monkeys) and other animals. Early parts of the story are gently satirical about various aspects of army life, setting Norakuro up as a foil against his tough and no-nonsense superiors, Colonel Bulldog and Captain Mōru. And yet even in these early parts, Norakuro's genteel world occasionally makes sudden shifts into the strikingly violent world of combat. In one episode of *Senior Private Norakuro* (*Norakuro jōtōhei*, 1932), for instance, Norakuro mistakenly drives an experimental airplane into monkey territory, igniting an all-out war between the two species: not only do Norakuro and other dogs mercilessly kill and destroy the monkey soldiers but a group of them also organizes a voluntary "suicide mission" to blow up the enemy's barbed-wire fence. The dogs all die in a heroic blaze, and a towering monument (which occupies the length of an entire page) is built by Colonel Bulldog in their honor. The juxtaposition of this overt valorization of military heroics, especially the emphasis on death as a necessary sacrifice to win a war, on the cozy world populated by cute canine characters moving about on all fours, is more than a little jarring from our postwar perspective. By 1937, Norakuro has been promoted to the rank of corporal and engages in an all-out war against Chinese soldiers, disturbingly rendered as pigs spouting dialogue in pidgin Japanese.[5]

Mostly, though, Japan's imperial wars were incorporated into and subsumed under the conventions of existing genres of children's comics. This trend is illustrated in another popular manga series, *Adventurous Dankichi* (*Bōken Dankichi*, 1933–1939), by Shimada Keizō. Dankichi took the fairytale of a young Japanese boy engaging in an adventure on a Pacific island (populated by the abjectly stereotypical black "natives"), eventually claiming the latter's throne, and recontextualized it in terms of Japan's "benevolent" (neo) colonialism, against the "white" former rulers. In one telling episode, Dankichi, now a king, leads an expedition with an "elite troop" of native soldiers (who have coconut-shell helmets and white numbers emblazoned on their chests) through his "territory," culminating in the capture of a fierce lion: upon the capture of the lion, Dankichi unfurls and raises the Japanese flag, and he, his rat adviser/minister Mr. Kari, and the native soldiers engage in a spirited celebration, yelling "banzai!"

While not overtly militaristic, this story can certainly be read by children as metaphorically representing and validating the Japanese military conquest of a South Pacific territory (the "lion" perhaps symbolizing Great Britain).[6] At the other extreme of jingoistic fervor, one finds Kiyohara Hitoshi's *The Human Bullet* (*Manga no nikudan*, 1932, cartoon version). Its protagonist, Chikuba Tarō, is a child soldier whose father committed suicide out of shame after he tried to sign up for military service but was turned away by the conscription officer because he was in poor health. Clearly intended for children, the cartoon is, nonetheless, full of extremely violent passages, with a heavy emphasis on the beheading of Chinese soldiers using a sword. It ends with Chikuba perishing in the same sort of suicide mission as carried out by Norakuro's mates in the preceding example, blowing himself up in order to take down the enemy's barbed-wire fence.[7]

In the realm of animation, too, the wartime propaganda machine provided opportunities for wide distribution and state funding, enticing many animators to produce works that were strongly jingoistic and imperialist. These include Murata Yasuji's *Momotarō of the Sky* (*Sora no Momotarō*, 1931) and Nakano Takao's *Hooray for the Black Cat* (*Kuroneko banzai*, 1933), in which the American bombers are piloted by creatures obviously meant to suggest Mickey Mouse. Norakuro was adapted for animation by Murata as *Corporal Norakuro* (*Norakuro Gunsō,* 1934), more or less preserving the humorous tone of the original manga, at least in its early stage of the character's evolution.

As the Japanese advanced on the South Pacific, a children's folktale starring Momotarō, the "Peach Boy," and his expedition to punish or conquer the island of goblins (*oni*), was transposed to the Japanese imperialist expansion, turning the Peach Boy and his animal companions—a dog, a pheasant, and a monkey—into stand-ins for Japanese soldiers engaged in the Pacific campaign.[8] The Peach Boy dressed up as the Japanese naval commander shows up in *Momotarō's Sea Eagles* (*Momotarō no umiwashi,* 1943), a short lasting only thirty-seven minutes. The short was directed by Seo Mitsuyo, a young animator heavily inspired by Walt Disney, whose influence can be seen most clearly in his masterpiece, *The Spider and the Tulip* (*Kumo to chūrippu,* 1944). Its sequel, *Momotarō's Divine Navy* (*Momotarō umi no shinpei,* 1945), was far more ambitious: not only was it twice the length of its predecessor at seventy-four minutes, it included lengthy musical interludes allegedly modeled after Disney's *Fantasia* (1940), accompanied by a full orchestral score. Even though some postwar critics have argued that the Momotarō feature films contain subtle pacifist messages, this is not evident, unless one regards the sage reflection by Commander Momotarō on the sacrifices the animals have to suffer as evidence of "pacifism." Perhaps the defenders of *Divine Navy* are citing the film's stunningly brutal depiction of naval battles as evidence of the filmmaker's desire to depict the war as evil. I am not convinced of this either, as the battles, while undeniably horrific, are also presented in an exciting manner, with the British depicted as cowardly buffoons (all voiced in English, allegedly by captured prisoners of war). The film also includes a lengthy sequence in which Momotarō lectures the animals clearly meant to be "foreign" (kangaroos, elephants, rhinoceroses and so on, presumably representing the "native" population of Asia and Africa) on the righteousness of Japan's cause, based on the ideological programs of the Greater East Asia Co-Prosperity Sphere. Overall, *Divine Navy* is an exemplary propaganda film for the Japanese navy, espousing an optimistic vision of the Pacific War at a time when the tide was obviously turning against Japan. From today's perspective, Japanese live-action war films from the same period, including *Electric-Lightning Squadron Mobilized* (*Dengekitai shutsudō,* 1944), in contrast, can be seen as more melancholy and fatalistic.

"Victim's Narrative" and the Terror and Beauty of War Machines

When Japan lost the war, full disclosure of the empire's wartime activities was not pursued by either the leaders of postwar Japan, some of whom were reinstated despite having been accused of war crimes, nor the U.S. Occupation forces, who needed Japan as a buffer against the Soviet and Chinese communism. Therefore, the Asia-Pacific War remained a taboo subject in visual popular culture during the immediate postwar era. A typical cartoon depiction of the war in 1950s was Maetani Koremitsu's *Robot Recruit* (*Robotto santōhei*), a lighthearted comic romp. This situation was roughly paralleled in films, but it was relatively safer for motion pictures to promote feelings of Japanese national unity by making "epic" war films set in the era prior to 1931, such as *Meiji Emperor and Russo-Japanese War* (*Meiji tennō to Nichi-ro sensō,* 1957).

Despite the fact that Japan was being accused of having committed large-scale atrocities, particularly in China during its undeclared war there between 1937 and 1945, many Japanese have felt that they themselves were also victims of the war. For at least the first two decades following Japan's defeat, the Japanese vividly remembered the poverty and hardship suffered during the war years, as well as the experience of massive aerial bombardment, especially the fire-bombing of Tokyo and other major cities, and, of course, the atom bombings of Hiroshima and Nagasaki. For them, American B-29s, which had a 3,000-mile range and were capable of carrying a load of eight tons, symbolized the war machine par excellence. During the March 10, 1945, bombing of Tokyo, B-29s dropped nearly 1,700 tons of incendiary bombs. One eyewitness reported a pile of victims stacked seven feet tall, casualties not of the fires but a lack of oxygen. The pull of these types of "victim's narratives" is strong precisely because its basic humanism had considerable appeal even for (left-wing) artists who clearly rejected overt forms of Japanese nationalism. Shirado Sanpei (b. 1932), for example, has drawn many manga extremely critical of Japanese militarism and the postwar political arrangement from the radical left-wing perspective, but his short pieces on the horrors of World War II (*Jessica, the Blond-Haired* [*Kinpatsu no Jeshika*], *The Time Bomb* [*Jigen bakudan*] and *A Lopsided Eating Habit* [*Henshoku*], all serialized in *Garo* magazine in 1963) still show the bifurcation between the European-American and Japanese experiences. Although the pieces on the European war theater emphasize the heroic struggles of the Czechoslovakian laborers and Soviet soldiers against Nazi militarism, his portrayal of the Pacific War takes the form of a flashback by a man peacefully living with his family in postwar Japan. He remembers the inhuman conditions suffered by Japanese soldiers during the Pacific campaign, which eventually drove them to cannibalism.[9]

Indeed, memories of the war among many leading manga artists in postwar Japan were deeply affected by terror of Allied (American) air strikes, the horrific conditions of extended campaigns during the Pacific War, and poverty and mental depression in the immediate postwar years. Tezuka Osamu was a middle-school student forced to work at a munitions factory. He continued to draw cartoons whenever the work stopped due to Allied bombings. After he was found out by a superintendent, he was accused of being a "noncitizen" and savagely beaten. Akatauka Fujio lived near the border of Manchukuo and after the war was ended, he was nearly captured and killed by the "bandits." Fujiko Fujio A (Abiko Moto-o, the "adult-oriented" half of the two cartoonists who partnered as Fujiko Fujio, a pseudonym for the creators of the mega-hit characters such as Doraemon, the cat robot from the future) and Takida Yū saw their neighborhoods burn to the ground during air raids in Toyama and Tokyo, respectively. Mizuki Shigeru survived being stationed in the South Pacific only to lose an arm due to American bombings: this did not stop him from being a prolific manga artist. Matsumoto Leiji (his preference for spelling his given name in English, instead of the usual rendition Reiji) spent most of his childhood at his home in the countryside in Ehime, narrowly avoiding a close encounter with American bombs. And Nakazawa Keiji, the author of *Barefoot Gen,* lost most of his family during the bombing of Hiroshima.

Given these terrifying experiences and personal losses by this interwar and wartime generation of manga artists who led the development of the medium in the 1960s and 1970s, it is not surprising that popular culture in this era and its subsequent legacy reflects a dual consciousness about Japan's war experience: on the one hand, strong negative feelings against their own nation for waging such a destructive and meaningless war and, on the other, the often sublimated hatred of the Americans or, more precisely, the "American war machine." An acceptable compromise between these two sentiments was to "blame the war itself" and blunt the sharpness of political criticism from either the left or the right. This position dovetailed with the ideological direction taken by postwar Japanese society, with its new "peace" constitution forever renouncing the military, even though in reality Japan is protected by a de facto military force, the Self-Defense Forces (SDF; created in 1954 with the approval of the American Occupation).

During mid- to late 1960s, particularly with the expansion of the Vietnam War, Japan's wartime experience became a topic openly depicted in comics and films.[10] The hundredth anniversary of the Meiji Restoration (1868) opened up new commercial venues for comic books such as *Shōnen King, Shōnen Sunday,* and *Shōnen Magazine* to run "specials," advertising the Japanese military hardware of the past, as well as those of "today," including the F-104 Phantom jets deployed by the SDF. It was definitely not a coincidence that during this period all three magazines began publishing "air-action" comics and "special attack force" comics, such as Kaizuka Hiroshi's *Zero Squadron March* (*Zero-sen kōshinkyoku,* 1967–1968). The romanticization of fighter pilots and airplanes in these comic books can also be traced to prewar popular culture, in which a strong identification between aviation technology and nationalism combined with the popular image of the navy, which did the double duty as a de facto air force during the war, as elitist, aristocratic, and prestigious. An air of quasi-existentialist despair and fatalistic commitment to one's mission prevails in these naval-themed postwar comics.[11] A large proportion of the 1960s manga directly dealing with the Pacific War belong to this subgenre: some other notable examples include Chiba Tetsuya's *The Hawk of the Purple Thunder* (*Shidenkai no taka,* 1963–1965), Mochizuki Mikiya's *The Untamed Eagle Boy Squadron* (*Arawashi shōnendai,* 1964), and Kaizuka Hiroshi's *The Zero Fighter's March* (*Zero-sen kōshinkoku,* 1967–1968).

Nakazawa Keiji and the Atom Bombings

As for the atom bombs, the best-known and earliest example of a manga directly confronting Hiroshima and Nagasaki is surely *Barefoot Gen,* Nakazawa Keiji's magnum opus originally serialized in *Shūkan Shōnen Jump* beginning in June 1973. Nakazawa's work in fact does not subscribe to the "Japanese-as-only-victims" narrative. It is true that his graphic and horrific renderings of the bombing victims, with their molten skin dragged on the ground like tattered shrouds, leave little to the imagination. More than once the protagonist, Gen, vents powerful feelings of anger toward the Americans for bringing this unprecedented atrocity down upon Japan's civilian population. Yet, unlike some other popular accounts of Hiroshima and Nagasaki that treat the experiences of being bombed as an event akin to a natural disaster or random burst of human savagery without delving into its historical meaning, *Barefoot Gen* clearly contextualizes these bombings in terms of Japan's long-term war efforts, as a culmination of the misery and destruction that the Japanese people had suffered at the hands of their own government (and not merely a handful of militarists, either). Not only does Nakazawa detail hypocrisies, abuses, and lies perpetrated by the Japanese military and government against their own people (no romanticized portrayal of the Japanese soldiers here), he also introduces a Korean character named Mr. Park to emphasize the closed-minded, discriminatory, and subservient nature of ordinary Japanese citizens.[12]

The images of "blinding light," a "mushroom cloud," and the utter devastation resulting from the bombings, as well as those of human beings reduced to black imprints scorched onto the rubble of Hiroshima and Nagasaki have so deeply penetrated the Japanese popular consciousness that almost any visually oriented popular cultural work of science fiction or horror that touches upon apocalyptic themes or large-scale devastation of a city feature some variants of these images.[13] Yet, a surprisingly small number of manga during its postwar zenith directly tackled the experience of the atom bombings. This contrasts with the significant body of canonized literature on the bombings, including Ibuse Masuji's *Black Rain* (1966), Ōe Kenzaburō's *Hiroshima Notes* (1965), and Kurihara Sadako's poetry collection *Black Eggs* (1946).[14] Indeed, in addition to the work of Nakazawa, other important postwar works that deal directly with the Hiroshima and Nagasaki bombing experiences are mostly done in the "girl's comics" genre.

For instance, what is now recognized as the first extended comic book to tackle the story of an atom bombing survivor is Tanikawa Kazuhiko's *The Stars Are Watching* (*Hoshi wa mite iru,* 1957), about a young girl in Hiroshima who loses both parents in the bombing. Other notable recent works in this vein include Kōno Fumiyo's *The Street of Evening Calm, The Country of Cherry Blossoms* (*Yūnagi no machi sakura no kuni,* 2003) and Matsuo Shiori's *The Sun You Gave Me* (*Kimi ga kureta taiyō,* 2008). Kōno does not dwell on the carnage of the bombing itself and focuses instead on the lives of three women from different generations living in the slums of Hiroshima. Drawn in a watercolor-like, serenely evocative style, *The Street of Evening Calm, The Country of Cherry Blossoms* weaves a complex story with its flashback-within-a-flashback structure. It references existing literary works, such as Ōe's *Hiroshima Notes,* and strives to capture the everyday details of the survivors. They are as far removed from the vibrantly boyish and in-your-face graphic realism of *Barefoot Gen* as one can imagine, but they are also stripped of overt signs of a "victim's narrative." In these works, the bombings, tragic and cruel as they might have been, do not appear with the apocalyptic weight and traumatic force that they play in many male-oriented manga and anime. Beyond the primary trauma of the bombing, women also had to deal with a variety of other challenges as survivors, including the way in which bomb victims were treated by the rest of the Japanese society, a concern in line with that of Ibuse Masuji's *Black Rain*. Finally, they evince a strong sense of locality and resist the trend toward having their narratives incorporated into the national narrative of victimhood or reconstruction.

Mizuki Shigeru: Clear-Eyed Elegy for the Japanese War Dead

Mizuki Shigeru (b. 1922), who would later gain fame for his acclaimed series of supernatural comics, is one manga artist whose war-related comics have continued to expose the real horrors of war as well as explore the difficulties faced by the soldiers in making moral choices. His early short masterpiece, *White Flag* (*Shiroi hata*), first published in the collection *Chronicle of the Sun Flag Wars* (*Hinomaru senki,* 1964), is set during the last stages of the Battle of Iwo Jima and is strikingly similar to Clint Eastwood's film *Letters from Iwo Jima* (2006) in its sympathetic yet unflinching portrayal of Japanese soldiers on the cusp of defeat and death. A hopeless charge at the American forces leaves only a handful of severely wounded survivors. In order to buy time for his men to retreat, a young navy lieutenant decides to wave a white flag at the American soldiers. His men object, but the navy lieutenant does not budge, telling them:

> You have done all you could for our country. There is no reason for you to remain here and die for our fatherland. I don't believe that our country will demand that from you. It is now my duty to protect your lives.

An army lieutenant threatens to shoot him, arguing that their fighting, even if futile in the short term, can still save more lives on the mainland. Mizuki does not present the army lieutenant as the villain of the piece: each character has logical arguments to back up his position. The two never reconcile their differences, and, during the story's climax, the army lieutenant shoots and kills the navy lieutenant. Still, the navy lieutenant's efforts result in the survival of his men, six soldiers make their way to the sea and escape on a raft, weeping tears of joy and sorrow, while others are blown to bits by the American artillery.[15]

As a survivor of the South Pacific campaign, Mizuki is relatively non-judgmental when it comes to patriotic belief in the cause of the war, especially in his early works. But he is ruthlessly unsentimental in showing the terrible human cost of wartime ideology and ideologically motivated practices such as "glorious mass suicide" (*gyokusai*). In *All Soldiers to Their Glorious Death!* (*Sōin gyokusai seyo!,* 1973), a mind-bogglingly detailed (354-page) chronicle of the largely fruitless fight waged by the Japanese soldiers during the Pacific campaigns, Mizuki dwells on the time-lapse panorama of the torn, decapitated, crushed, and mangled bodies of the soldiers decomposing into skeletons and then blown into wafts of dust in the wind, forever lost and forgotten.[16] This seemingly cold but ultimately understanding gaze used by Mizuki to observe the Japanese military is turned on himself as well. He published a series of autobiographical comics centering on his own experiences in the Pacific War, including *Chronicle of Defeat* (*Haisōki,* 1970), which culminated in the eight-volume *Comic History of Shōwa Era* (*Komikku Shōwashi,* 1988–1989).

Narrated by the Rat Guy (Nezumi-otoko), a famous sidekick goblin character from the popular supernatural-satirical comic *Kitarō of the Graveyard* (*Hakaba no Kitarō*) series, the first six volumes of the *Comic History of Shōwa Era* is a sprawling indictment of almost all aspects of Japan's imperial war against China, its colonization of Korea, Taiwan, and the Southeast Asia, and the Pacific War. Intertwined with droll commentaries by the Rat Guy (he "interviews" historical figures and Mizuki's family members as if he were a time-traveling news anchor) and straightforward exposition of the political and military history of Japan from 1931 to 1945 are episodes of Mizuki and his family grappling with the war. Mizuki makes absolutely no effort to hide enthusiastic—and, in many cases, privately motivated—support for Japan's wars from his relatives and family members. In one scene, his father lets out a loud guffaw at the news of the attack on Pearl Harbor, until his mother reminds him that the Mizuki family has three sons, all reaching draft age. He portrays a younger version of himself as a disinterested outsider to the Japanese empire, aware that the Pacific War could claim his life at any moment but not stating any political opinion about the war.[17]

As seen in the poet Takamura Kōtarō's *Brief History of Imbecility,*[18] there is a sense of bittersweet irony as the older Mizuki looks upon his younger self and chastises the latter for being so gullible and unreflective while sympathizing with him for having been swept up in the torrent of historical change over which he had so little control. His massive manga depicting the Pacific War is, in the sense that it is firmly grounded in his own personal experience, an effort to write a "history of selfhood" (*jibunshi*), deconstructing the grand narrative of national history but, at the same time, refusing to subordinate the narrative to ideological configurations of the left or right.[19] In one area, though, Mizuki never suffered from the same kind of internal struggles as "Americanized" comic book artists/animators like Tezuka Osamu. For Mizuki, the United States, if not ordinary American people, has always been the enemy in his comics, whether represented by a sinister-looking Franklin D. Roosevelt or a supremely arrogant Douglas McArthur. Not surprisingly, this perspective is extended to his works in genres other than war comics, for example, in his *Kitarō* series, in which U.S. might is often chastised and derogated as the physical manifestation of rampant Western modernity, which poses far greater threats to mankind than the supernatural demons in Japanese lore ever could.

Matsumoto Leiji and the Technoromanticism of the Navy

A member of a slightly younger generation than Mizuki Shigeru, Matsumoto Leiji (b. 1938) went in the opposite direction from him, rehabilitating wartime military values by highlighting the attraction of the technological and mechanical aspects of war. His greatest hit was the animated television series *Space Battleship Yamato* (*Uchū senkan Yamato*), which was later changed to the nonhistorical *Star Blazers* when it was imported to the U.S. market. In *Space Battleship Yamato,* the battleship sunk during the Pacific War is salvaged and refitted for space travel. First serialized in 1974, *Space Battleship Yamato* dutifully evinces pacifist rhetoric, yet remains an updated, romantic re-imagining of the wartime "society" of male warriors committed to a lost cause—under the command of a taciturn, immaculately dressed captain and populated by stalwart young technicians and soldiers, wallowing in a locker-room–like atmosphere of male bonding, with only one female crew member serving as an all-purpose communications officer and nurse. Matsumoto does not forget to decry the futility of war, but nearly all his comics and animated films indulge in this brand of hypermasculine technoromanticism, focusing on glamor of the war machines.

Matsumoto's own father was in many ways a model for his authoritative "navy captain" characters (e.g., Captain Okida in *Yamato* and Captain Herlock, the eponymous pirate of the popular space opera). The elder Matsumoto was a training official for student fighter pilots: having survived the war, he allegedly refused to join the SDF because that meant "riding the enemy planes." Leiji's grandmother prepared to join in committing mass suicide when Japan declared its unconditional surrender to the Allies. With occupation by foreign forces imminent, she dug old Japanese swords and other family heirlooms out of storage in preparation for the ultimate sacrifice. It is clear, however, that the influence of this Japanese militarist ethos coexisted with Matsumoto's privileged background, which gave him easy access to Disney cartoons, the Fleischer brothers' *Popeye the Sailor,* and other American animation.[20] Therefore, despite the romantic and sometimes militaristic quality of *Space Battleship Yamato,* it expresses a profound ambiguity when it comes to treating its "enemy" as inhuman. The *Yamato*'s alien enemies, such as the Gamiras empire, can be read as representing the "white races," but even so, Matsumoto, out of genuine hatred for war or a canny calculation to appeal to the maximum number of consumers in the world, has erased obvious ethnic or cultural markers that could make *Yamato* and its crew's heroics a counterfactual replay of the Pacific War. His strikingly archetypal drawings of characters also tend to blur the distinction between "heroes" and "villains"—Captain Herlock may sport facial scars and the black cape usually associated with villains, while Gamiras generals may be attired in ways that are reminiscent of the Imperial Japanese Army—further diluting racial antagonism and nationalism.

Matsumoto prefers to use science-fiction trappings to advance his romantic fantasies, but he also produced a few straightforward short works and animated films set during the Pacific War. The most notable among them is *The Cockpit* (*Za Kokupitto,* 1993), composed of three short segments, two of which involve Japanese pilots. The second segment, "Sonic Boom Squadron" (*Onsoku raigekitai,* directed by Imanishi Takashi) deals with a kamikaze pilot, but Matsumoto purposefully tells a parallel story with a shifting point of view between Japanese pilots and American sailors, even having one of the latter mourning the death of an aspiring comic book artist killed by a "crazy Jap." In this way, Matsumoto and his staff explicitly purge the question of Japanese imperial aggression from *The Cockpit* and allow both the Japanese and the Americans to gain equal footing in their denunciation of the "war" in an abstract sense. This serves as an interesting reminder of the compromise with respect to Japanese nationalist expression necessitated by the overwhelming global success of anime.

Tezuka Osamu: Ambivalence of the Exemplary Humanist

Tezuka Osamu (1928–1989), perhaps the world's best known and most read manga artist, not to mention one of the pioneers of modern animation, boasted a broad and in-depth knowledge of Euro-American cinema, cartoons, and popular culture, explicitly modeling his most popular characters, such as the boy robot Atom (Astro Boy), on Western icons such as Mickey Mouse. He studied medicine at Osaka University before launching his career as a manga artist. Consequently, his familiarity with the technological aspects of Euro-American modernity greatly influenced the themes and subjects of his manga works, although this Euro-American disposition sometimes resulted in clashes with his personal orientation as an in-your-face *Edokko* (Tokyo native), down-to-earth and unpretentious. For instance, he created a flagrantly Gothic character *Black Jack* (serialized from 1973 to 1983), a mysterious surgeon with hideous facial scars who operates without a medical license, charging an exorbitant amount of fees to wealthy clients, but did not hesitate to drop him in the middle of contemporary Japanese society and make him interact with, say, sushi chefs from the Kansai region. While on surface Tezuka was much more enthusiastic about promoting the tenets of postwar democracy and supposedly Euro-American liberal values than, for instance, Mizuki Shigeru, in some ways he was more explicitly conscious of his problematic identity as a citizen of a postwar Japan partially built on denial of continuity with its prewar incarnation.

Tezuka's most popular work relating to World War II is *Tell Adolf* (*Adorufu ni tsugu*), referred to as simply *Adolf* in English and German, 1983–1985).[21] The manga's central narratives revolve around the internal conflicts of Adolf Kaufmann, a half-Japanese Gestapo officer, over his friendship with a Jewish baker called Adolf Kamil. The major Japanese character, a reporter named Tōge Sōhei, is distinctively placed in a subordinate role. There is no question that *Adolf* is a major showcase of Tezuka's ability to tell a long-form fictional narrative at an epic scale and to populate it with completely believable non-Japanese characters. The artist effectively blends cartoonlike exaggerations and deformations with cinematic verisimilitude in harnessing a complicated narrative with many turns and stops. Moreover, the potentially controversial touches that "humanize" Adolf Hitler, the "third" Adolf of the comic, are handled rather skillfully (mostly seen from the admiring eyes of Adolf Kaufmann), even in comparison with the ways in which more recent German popular media have represented Hitler in films such as

Downfall (*Der Untergang,* 2004) and the satirical cartoons of Walter Moers.[22] However, while Tezuka does not shy away from tackling Japan's complicity in Nazi persecution of the Jews, he does not go so far as to draw any parallels between their racist policies and Japanese racism toward colonized populations not only of Korea and Taiwan but of China.

Like many other manga artists of his and younger generations, Tezuka has touched upon the Pacific War by generally redressing it in a safer form, for instance, through the modality of science fiction. He has produced only a few short pieces that tell about his experience as a Japanese boy during the war directly. Yet in these works, and in his post-1960s anti–Vietnam War pieces, his portrayal of Americans betrays a deep ambivalence: Americans are at one point depicted as a vast, anonymous war-conducting machine and at another as evil hypocrites steeped in quasi-racist stereotypes. At one point, he turns Astro Boy into an ally of the North Vietnamese fighting American "invaders."

In *Kanon* (1974, originally serialized in *Manga Akushon*), the protagonist has been traumatized after witnessing the death of his friends in the Pacific War, especially that of a beautiful female teacher on whom he had developed a crush. Tezuka does not pull punches: when the teacher dies, her face is literally blown apart by the bullets from an American plane "as if it were a smashed watermelon."[23] In another story, *An Empty Stomach Blues* (*Sukippara no burūsu,* 1975), a uniformed student determined to succeed as a manga artist—an obvious double for Tezuka—is subjected to humiliation by American soldiers, who contemptuously throw chocolates, cookies, and other sweets to the hungry Japanese. The hero, Ōsamu (mirroring Tezuka's given name), receives some food from a black American soldier (drawn as a borderline-racist caricature, featureless and idiotically grinning), but both of them ultimately become the objects of physical abuse and violence at the hands of white American soldiers. At the moment of this beating by a white soldier, a narration is inserted, claiming that "[the U.S.] occupying army was a lawless bunch of hooligans. Everywhere innocent Japanese were beaten up, sometimes killed, and especially Japanese girls were made objects of fun."[24] At these moments, no real distance exists between Tezuka's view of Americans and the most belligerent Japanese "patriotic" view of the demonic and animalistic British America (*Kichiku beiei*) during the Pacific War.

To be sure, in his manga Tezuka has been a consistent promoter of "Americanized" values, such as technological nationalism and faith in universal human rights, preferring to view the prewar Japanese militarists as ignorant, anti-intellectual, and quick to resort to violence. Yet there is an un-mistakable undercurrent of anti-American sentiment in his works that can be traced in part to his personal experiences. Like Mizuki, Tezuka did not really abandon the imagery of Americans as hated enemies, but in his case, the Vietnam War and American racism against Asians and blacks was mobi-lized to justify his hostility morally and politically. The problem is that, despite his avowed and (no doubt) sincere antagonism toward prewar mili-tarist values, Tezuka's stance leads to inadvertent legitimization of the wartime ideology of the "Japanese standing up for the non-white victims of the white racists." He cannot bring Americans to task for being hypocrites without also addressing the hypocrisy of the wartime Japanese leaders: but while he denounces the ignorance and stupidity of those leaders, the *hypoc-risy* of their ideology and rhetoric remain largely unchallenged in his comics. In other words, one cannot shake the disturbing sense that Tezuka's exem-plary humanism and commitment to universal values, as evident in works such as *Adolf,* do not necessarily extend to portrayal of those colonized by the Japanese empire. The exoticized, pidgin-Japanese–speaking "Vietnamese" of his anti–Vietnam War comics, abused or massacred by the grotesquely "white," preternaturally violent American soldiers, are never raised to the level of "ordinary Japanese." Such portrayals cannot avoid the criticism that in many ways they reproduce stereotypes of the colonized "exotics" of the Japanese empire—which, of course, included the Vietnamese themselves, as well as the Chinese, the Taiwanese natives, the Koreans, Southeast Asians, and South Pacific islanders.

Yamagami Tatsuhiko: Militarism Is Still with Us

Yamagami Tatsuhiko (b. 1947) is a perhaps surprising subject for this chap-ter. He is virtually unknown to English-language readers of manga, perhaps due to the fact that his most famous works are in the subgenre of "gag" comics, in which nonsensical, deliberately non sequitur humor plays an important role. The representative works in this vein are *The Compendium of the New Comedic Thoughts* (*Shin kigeki shisō taikei,* 1972–1974), which combine fairly realistic *gekika* (dramatic comic)–style drawings with gro-tesquely obsessive sexual content and plenty of lowbrow, bathroom humor. *The Kid Cop* (*Gaki deka,* 1974–1980) stars a strangely proportioned (his head is much bigger than his body) adolescent police officer, who, spouting hilariously foul babble and, of course, obsessed with sex, gets embroiled in a variety of misadventures with his friends. Since the 1990s, Yamagami has focused his attention on the second career as a novelist, only occasionally returning to comic books. However, prior to the runaway success of *The Kid Cop,* which reportedly sold 30 million copies in its initial printing as a stand-alone graphic novel, Yamagami had been best known for his pronouncedly dark and ironic science fiction-fantasies.

It is in this mode as an essentially "serious" sci-fi fantasist, albeit with black humor, that he wrote what many Japanese connoisseurs of manga consider his masterpiece, *The Shining Wind* (*Hikaru kaze,* serialized in *Shukan shōnen magajin* in 1970). Although Yamagami has never clearly aligned with any political position, left or right, he has repeatedly demonstrated his radical stance when it comes to questioning the postwar pacifist arrangement and its whitewashing of Japan's military past. For example, in 1973, he serialized an astonishingly avant-garde manga titled *A Collection of Documents on the Twelve Rioting Crimes* (*Jūni innen bōto hanzai ni kan suru shorui hensatsu,* 1973) in *Gekiga serekuto* magazine. In it, Yamagami problematized the unspeakable atrocities committed during biological experiments conducted by the Kwantung Army's Unit 731's and the inability of postwar Japanese to address these atrocities in any meaningful way. His critique was expressed by deliberately breaking down traditional narrative structures, illustrating fragmented memories as puzzle pieces, shattered because of the trauma of the human experiments and subsequent denial by the main characters of participation in them (the story ostensibly unfolds through the narration of a nurse stationed at one of the germ-warfare laboratories). Yamagami uses a variety of innovative techniques, such as the employment of fragmented dialogue that read like Zen kōan, cut off from the context in which they are spoken, challenges to traditional comic representation through absence or erasure (e.g., leaving an entire page nearly blank, except for a few rudimentary drawings of human skulls) coupled with the hyperrealistic duplication of actual wartime photographs (usually of Japanese soldiers imposing themselves on Chinese victims). Collectively, these strategies of representation wreak havoc on the narrative logic of a commercial manga, rendering the activities at the Japanese medical facility, "normal" in the context of wartime Japan, unbelievably grotesque.

The Shining Wind is set in a counterfactual Japan of 1970.[25] Any knowledge about prewar Japanese imperialism and atrocities is rigorously suppressed, and the police are given fascist power over the civilian population, including the right to carry out summary executions on those considered "enemies of the state." The main protagonists are Gen, a free-spirited student, and Mitsutaka, his brother, enrolled at a preparatory school for the (fictional) National Defense Forces, both children of the staunchly conservative Rokkōji clan. Gen runs afoul of the police and the Japanese state when he and his classmates investigate a strange ritual performed by the mutant victims of a mysterious genetic disease, leading him eventually to be incarcerated with other political prisoners critical of the state. Mitsutaka, meanwhile, is sent off to fight in a Southeast Asian conflict, which in this alternate reality has escalated into a potentially genocidal war with the deployment of a neutron bomb and other weapons of mass destruction by American forces.

The Shining Wind is a shocking portrayal of 1970s Japan overcome by fascism and militarism. The work mercilessly skewers the bourgeois complacency and fanatical patriotism of "ordinary" Japanese, although it does occasionally reach for melodramatic heights in the sequences involving the police and archmilitarists such as Lieutenant Amakatsu. It is also prophetic in detailing how the Japanese right wing would win public support for Japan's (de facto) military forces by performing "supportive action" for a U.S.-led war: in "real" history, it was, of course, the Gulf War (1990–1991) that fulfilled this function. However, *The Shining Wind,* like Tezuka's other works discussed above, also conflates the evils of Japanese militarism together with those of American imperialism, and in certain sections of the piece "nativist" militarism almost gains a sense of emotional legitimacy, if not heroic status, against the hateful (white) Americans who are the *true* villains of the work. When Mitsutaka returns home as a limbless torso and a head (obviously influenced by the horrific Edogawa Ranpō story, *Caterpillar* [*Imomushi*, 1929], set in the aftermath of the supposedly glorious 1904–1905 Russo-Japanese War) and his condition is revealed as the outcome of an unfortunate encounter with an American biological weapon, the elder Rokkōji cuts down the American officer responsible with a Japanese sword and commits seppuku along with his wife. Likewise, the fanatical Japanese officer Lieutenant Amakatsu ends up dying while fighting American scientists and soldiers who were building a germ-warfare laboratory on Japanese soil.

Amakatsu's racist epithets and attitudes, ultimately seeing the world divided between the white and "colored" races, and concluding that the twain shall never meet, are implicitly portrayed as positive attributes: in *The Shining Wind* the United States is really nothing more than a belligerent white man's empire, still trying to impose a pre–Civil War vision of Manifest Destiny on the world. While Yamagami's critique of the continued relevance of wartime ideology in postwar Japan is salient and provocative, it is also partially reconfigured into the axis of West vs. East or the white vs. colored races, following the criticism of the U.S. militarism now made "legitimate" by the Vietnam War. As a result, like Tezuka's criticisms of the Vietnam conflict, Yamagami's protest loses potency as a commentary on Japan's failed relationship with other Asians. In the end, Yamagami forcibly "resolves" this potential self-contradiction by interjecting a massive deus ex machina into the narrative, a Great Kantō Earthquake–like seismic disaster that ends up destroying heroes and villains and Japanese and Americans alike in a supremely nihilistic denouement.

Kobayashi Yoshinori and "Conservative Revisionism"

During the 1980s, Japan's economy experienced sustained growth, while many industrial democracies experienced a surge of political conservatism, represented by such leaders as U.S. President Ronald Reagan, British Prime Minister Margaret Thatcher, and Prime Minister Nakasone Yasuhiro in Japan. The victim's narrative remained prevalent in Japanese popular culture. This narrative, while preventing the Japanese from integrating their country's history of imperialist war and colonial experience into a "modern history" proper, continued to provide a moral center for the Japanese to hold on to as they reoriented themselves toward a pacifist and humanitarian perspective. However, in the 1980s manga finally began to show signs of being comfortable with the idea of Japan as a militarized nation, and jingoism re-infiltrated the domain of popular culture. In Kawaguchi Kaiji's *The Silent Service* (*Chinmoku no kandai,* 1988–1996), for instance, the captain of a newly launched nuclear submarine declares his vessel an independent nation called "Yamato," turning against both Japan and the United States. However, aside from indulging in the macho fantasy of a Japanese hero besting Americans at their own game (technological warfare)—as in *Space Battleship Yamato,* few female characters appear in the thirty-two-volume narrative— *Silent Service* has little use for the nostalgic invocation of Japan's imperial past, ultimately disappointing right-wing readers.

In 1996, the Association for the Publication of New Textbooks was formed by Fujioka Nobukatsu, a former member of the Japanese Communist Party and a faculty member in the Department of Education at the University of Tokyo. Fujioka started "small," with criticism of negative views of the SDF and the "peace-oriented education" that he saw as responsible for producing such views, but soon he and his compatriots began to vociferously denounce what they claimed to be the "masochistic historical perspective" in history textbooks, seeking to rehabilitate much of Japan's imperialist and colonialist conduct and extolling the "lost" virtues of patriotism and nationalism.

Around 1996 the manga artist Kobayashi Yoshinori (b. 1953) joined this organization and presented a highly controversial "defense" of the practice of "comfort women," the Japanese military mobilization of young Asian women for sexual services often under horrific conditions, in his manga *The New Gōmanism Manifesto* (*Shin Gōmanizumu sengen*, vol. 3, 1997), which enjoyed great success. Afterward, Kobayashi rapidly took up the role of visual propagandist for the right-wing group, publishing *On War* (*Sensōron*, 1995) and *On Taiwan* (*Taiwan-ron*, 2001). It is interesting that Kobayashi's initial fame as the author of *The Gōmanism Manifesto* was as a loud social critic unafraid to address issues—HIV infection, the Imperial Household, "foreigners" and Japanese women, and so on—thought to be considered taboo by the mainstream media. His stance until 1996 was, in fact, vaguely left wing, although it has always been marked by vicious misogyny (including an almost comically exaggerated disdain for "feminism") and xenophobia.[26]

Most of Kobayashi's arguments do not stand up to close scrutiny by historians and, in many ways, are rehashes of the same old justifications for the Asia-Pacific War commonly observed until at least the late 1960s. What is fresh is his style: a free-form visual essay that eschews logic, rational argument, and fidelity to facts in favor of the emotional affectation that offers the reader a catharsis of taboo breaking. Kobayashi is almost neurotically obsessive in finding fault in "conventional truths" as well as expressing hostility to "political correctness" of any kind.[27] Kobayashi then combines this emotionally manipulative narrative strategy with the shock-jock tactics of political poster arts in his comic panels, including the manipulation of the size and flow of written characters in what can only be described as hyper-sloganeering.[28] You do not get a coherent argument or story in his manga, but he certainly knows how to get your adrenalin to flow by stoking your vague resentment of schools, Americans, liberal academics, and other "authority figures." This effective strategy has led many Japanese to see in his enterprise a refreshing, if not liberating, alternative to the rigid conventionality of mainstream views on the Asia-Pacific War. In sum, Kobayashi's works can be seen as a successful deployment of the manga form for the purpose of political propaganda, shrewdly associating and conflating the cathartic thrills of taboo breaking with their right-wing views.

Yet Kobayashi's rhetoric is predicated on the fact that his generation of postwar Japanese never experienced war at first hand, resulting in a sometimes highly abstract discourse on the war experience that adds an air of counterfactual fantasy to even his most vicious or frankly racist outbursts.[29] This aspect has been accurately pointed out by a critique of *On War* by Mizuki Shigeru, who contributed a short piece rather sympathetically chiding Kobayashi for his "lack of understanding" of the terrible realities of the war experience.[30] In other words, the fact that little verisimilitude or gravitas of real-life experience can be felt is an indication of the clear limitation of Kobayashi's essay form manga. They are like a graffiti of a flipped finger drawn at a massive scale on a white wall, with little power to move a reader or compel him or her into reflection.

However, one must acknowledge that Kobayashi's works have become popular partly because they successfully addressed the vacuum left by the postwar popular discourse on Japan's recent past. Thus, they raise the question of whether praising "peace" whenever possible and bad-mouthing "war," as was a reflexive practice in postwar Japan, has been truly effective in inoculating the younger generation of Japanese against the inevitable "revisionist" glorification of the now-defunct Japanese empire: food for thought, not only for historians but also for those concerned about the future of Japan.

Conclusion

We have briefly examined how a select roster of manga artists and a few representatives of feature and television animation based on their works have depicted the Second Sino-Japanese and Pacific Wars. Through this overview, I hope to provide readers with a glimpse of the diversity and complexity of Japanese artists' responses to the war experience, in which some major thematic threads and leitmotifs emerge. Overall, it has been rather uncommon for a manga artist to place responsibility for the wars squarely on Japanese leaders and the ruling elite, as Nakazawa Keiji does in *Barefoot Gen*. It has also been uncommon, as Mizuki Shigeru does in at least some of his works, to openly express sympathy for dead soldiers, while clearly denouncing the militarist regime and displaying unresolved hostilities toward the American enemy. In this sense, neither Mizuki nor Nakazawa can be seen as belonging to the mainstream "pacifist" discourse prevalent in the world of postwar manga, exemplified by the works of Tezuka Osamu and Matsumoto Leiji, in which there is a clear shift from Japan's imperial wars to "war" in the abstract. This does not mean that Japanese manga artists have been in denial in any way when it comes to the issue of Japanese "war responsibility." Indeed, they have left a corpus of works that deal with, for instance, wartime Japanese persecution of Koreans and Japanese mistreatment of the Chinese (despite a nagging vestige of ethnic stereotypes that creep into even their best-intentioned works). Yet one has to reach deep down, beyond the established canon and those most commercially popular works of anime and manga, to access and appraise some of the more personal engagements with the Asia-Pacific War.

It might have come as a surprise to some North American readers that thoroughly "Americanized" manga artists like Tezuka Osamu could display or harbor strong anti-American sentiments, but considering that these doyens of Japanese manga actually lived through the Pacific War and the immediate occupation of Japan by the U.S. forces, it would be unrealistic not to expect such sentiments. Other readers might bristle at the "victim's narrative" pervasive in Japanese popular culture; a few might even find this narrative hypocritical, considering the largely inadequate reappraisal of Japan's imperialist and colonial past. Nonetheless, this narrative can also stimulate American thinking about its complicity in suppressing reflections on the wartime experience, not to mention in its direct involvement in the rehabilitation of the remnants of militarism, which was done in the name of "resisting communism" and "rebuilding democracy" in Japan and East Asia.

The truth is that a dynamic in postwar Japanese culture has prevented the proper understanding of prewar Japan as a global empire. Moreover, Americans have been complicit in giving rise to this dynamic by forcibly configuring the "war experience" as that between Japan and the United States alone and helping the Japanese to avoid confronting their colonial and imperialist legacy. Even the Japanese manga's expression of anger and hate toward the American "victors," in the guise of criticism of U.S. policy in Vietnam, has seldom motivated them to rethink their colonial and wartime policy toward the rest of Asia. In a way, Kobayashi's gloating interpretation of the Japanese "success" in its erstwhile colonies—Korea, Japan, Manchuria, Southeast Asia, and the Pacific Islands—as disgustingly racist and chauvinistic as it is, is one of the few Japanese popular-cultural attempts to advance the discussion of the war experience beyond that of the Pacific War as merely a U.S.-Japanese confrontation. It is hoped that the currently active comic/manga artists in Japan and the United States will confront this challenge and produce comic books, manga, and animation that subvert the complacency of the postwar "global peace" yet does so in a way that honors and brings dignity to the victims of the imperial wars and colonial exploitation.

Notes

1   See, for instance, Julius Wiedemann and Masanao Amano, ed., *Manga* (Cologne: Taschen, 2004), which has introductions to some 140 manga artists. But even this hefty (576-page) compendium is far from comprehensive. While it includes a good deal of somewhat obscure manga artists working in overtly pornographic idioms, it has no entry, for instance, on major figures like Yamagami Tatsuhiko, discussed below.

2   This is by no means intended to suggest that women artists or the genre of "girl's comics" have never dealt with the Asia-Pacific War. My decision to focus on male artists and "boy's comics" is simply due to the lack of ability on my part to conduct properly nuanced and extensive research in the other corner of the comic universe. This is in part due to the fact that, in Japanese manga, gender segregation based on the projected consumer demographic, rather than the actual gender of the artist, has been quite strongly enforced, although there are women artists who broke through the gender barrier and tackled male-oriented topics (e.g., as space-travel science fiction), Hagi Mōto being my personal favorite.

3   The "pacifist" view of the Japanese as victims have been well known via anime to American viewers, especially through two extremely popular anime films, *Grave of the Fireflies* (*Hotaru no haka,* 1988) and *Barefoot Gen* (*Hadashi no Gen,* 1983). Cf. Susan Napier, *Anime: From Akira to Princess Mononoke* (New York: Palgrave, 2000), 161–174.

4   Frederik L. Schodt, *Manga! Manga!: The World of Japanese Comics* (New York: Kodansha International, 1986), 51–52.

5   See the cartoon excerpted from *Norakuro sōkōgeki* (Norakuro all-out attack, 1937), in Akiyama Masami, *Maboroshi no sensō manga no sekai* (Tokyo: Natsume shobō, 1998), 40–41. This episode from *Norakuro* and a similar one mentioned below from *Human Bullet* are based on the real-life deaths of three Japanese soldiers during the Shanghai campaign, February 22, 1932. Some accounts claim that their deaths were mere accidents and were not planned as a "suicide mission," but the news media advertised it as such.

6   Shimada Keizō, "The Adventures of Dankichi," in *Reading Colonial Japan: Text, Context and Critique,* ed. Michelle M. Mason and Helen J. S. Lee (Stanford, CA: Stanford University Press, 2002), 263–270. See also Kawamura Minato, "Popular Orientalism and the Japanese Views of Asia," in ibid., 271–298.

7   Ishiko Jun, *Manga ni miru sensō to heiwa 90-nen* (The ninety years of war and peace seen through comics) (Tokyo: Horupu shuppan, 1983), 46–47, 53.

8   Robert Tierney, "The Adventures of Momotarō in the South Seas: Folklore, Colonial Policy, Parody," in *Tropics of Savagery: The Culture of Japanese Empire in Comparative Frame* (Berkeley: University of California Press, 2010), 110–146.

9   Shirado Sanpei, *Nanatsu-oke no iwa: Shirado Sanpei ishoku sakuhinshū* (The rock of seven pails: A collection of Shirado Sanpei's unusual works) (Tokyo: Shōgakkan, 2000).

10   Cf. Itō Kimio, "Sengo Nihon otoko no ko bunka no naka no sensō" (The war in the male children's culture in postwar Japan) in *Sengo Nihon no naka no sensō* (The war in postwar Japan), ed. Naka Hisao (Tokyo: Sekai shisōsha, 2004).

11   Not surprisingly, this existentialist fatalism is missing in prewar comics romanticizing the aviation technology and war pilots. For instance, a prewar comic by Niizeki Seika called *The Patriotic Comic Commandos* (*Aikoku manga kesshitai*, 1938) depicts a civilian boy's dream, in which he develops a propeller in his lower back and acquires an ability to fly, joining Japanese bombers in their raid of a Chinese air base. The comic, while generally comedic and juvenile in tone, also jarringly metes out extremely cruel fates to the Chinese pilots: one of them is literally torn apart into small pieces by the protagonist Hanamaru's buttock-propeller in midair! Even in this goofy-but-strangely-dehumanizing context, the author's effort to present the Japanese airplanes as a highly aestheticized yet realistic totem of Japan's military superiority is obvious. Niizeki Seika, "Aikoku manga kesshitai" (Patriotic comic commandos), in *Maboroshi no sensō manga no jidai*, ed. Akiyama Masami (Tokyo: Natsume shobō, 1998), 162–173.

12   Nakazawa Keiji, *Barefoot Gen: A Cartoon Story of Hiroshima* (Philadelphia: New Society, 1986), 206–223.

13   An excellent example is Kurosawa Kiyoshi's *Kairō* (Pulse, 2001), about Japan's takeover by dead spirits who overflow out of their realm into that of the living via select computer terminals. In the film, the living characters "marked" by the dead are eventually reduced to a human-shaped layer of ashes on the walls, a direct reminder of the instantly incinerated victims of the atom bombs.

14   For a discussion of the Japanese literary exploration of the Hiroshima and Nagasaki experience, see John Whittier Treat, *Writing Ground Zero: Japanese Literature and the Atomic Bomb* (Chicago: University of Chicago Press, 1995).

15   Mizuki Shigeru, *Shiroi hata* (White Flag) (Tokyo: Kōdansha, 2010).

16   Mizuki Shigeru, *Sōin gyokusai seyo!* (All toward glorious deaths!) (Tokyo: Kōdansha, 1995).

17   Mizuki Shigeru, *Komikku Shōwashi* (A comic history of Showa Japan) vol. 3: *Nitchū zenmen sensō- taiheiyō sensō kaishi* (The Sino-Japanese War-The Pacific War start) (Tokyo: Kōdansha, 2008).

18 Takamura Kōtarō, *A Brief History of Imbecility: Poetry and Prose of Takamura Kōtarō,* trans. Hiroaki Sato (Honolulu: University of Hawaiʻi Press, 1992).

19 The best-known example of "history of selfhood" is possibly the famous historian Irokawa Daikichi's *Aru Shōwashi* (A certain history of Showa Japan) (Tokyo: Chūō kōronsha, 1975), which is generally considered to be responsible for popularizing the term *jibunshi* among the Japanese public.

20 "Aramata Hiroshi Matsumoto Leiji taidan" (Aramata Hiroshi interviews Matsumoto Leiji), Part 1," *Aramata Hiroshi no denshi manga nabigētā, ebookjapan,* October 7, 2011, http://www.ebookjapan.jp/ebj/special /manganavi/manganavi_11–1a.asp, accessed May 21, 2013.

21 Tezuka Osamu, *Adolf,* 5 vols. (San Francisco: Viz Media, 1995–1997). It is notable that the covers of the English-language Viz Media/Cadence Books editions reveal little to indicate that these tomes are Japanese manga drawn by the creator of Astro Boy, whereas the German editions published by Carlsen in 2005–2007 reproduce dramatic panels from the comic on their covers.

22 Bettina Gildenhard, " 'Tasha' to shite no 'hittorā" (Hitler as "the other"), in *Manga no naka no "tasha,"* ("The other" in comics), ed. Itō Kimio (Kyoto: Rinsen shoten, 2008).

23 Tezuka Osamu, "Kanon" (Proper name), in *Sensō manga kessakusen* (The great war comics selection) (Tokyo: Yōdensha, 2007).

24 Tezuka Osamu, "Sukippara no burūsu" (Sukkippara blues), in ibid., 224–231.

25 Yamagami Tatsuhiko, *Hikari no kaze* (The shining wind) (Tokyo: Shōgakkan, Creative Imprint, 2008).

26 For instance, he flippantly derogated *Sankei shinbun*'s affirmation of the "good intentions" of the Greater Pacific War (Second Sino-Japanese War and the Pacific War, as it was known by the Japanese during wartime) in an earlier volume of *The Gōmanism Manifesto* (vol. 4, 1997).

27 It is fascinating that in the United States a verbal comic such as Bill Maher, who also started out by mocking "political correctness," has now become spokesperson for liberalism, in a career trajectory completely opposite that of Kobayashi.

28 See a discussion of this visual/writing strategy employed by Kobayashi in Obinata Sumio, "Sensōron wa nani wo dō katatte iruka" (What and how does "On War" talk about?), in *Kimitachi wa sensō de shineruka: Kobayashi Yoshinori 'sensōron' hihan* (Are you willing to die in a war?: Critiques of Kobayashi Yoshinori's "On War"), ed. Obinata Sumio, Yamada Akira, and Yamashina Saburō (Tokyo: Ōtsuki shoten, 1999), 28–33.

29 Kobayashi Yoshinori, *Sensōron* (On war) (Tokyo: Gentōsha, 1998).

30 Miyadai Shinji et al., ed., *Sensōron bōsōron* (Delusions of "On War") (Tokyo: Kyōiku shiryō shuppansha, 1999), 85–94.

CHAPTER 6

Continuity and Change in Hollywood's Representations of American-Asian Relations in War and Peace

Robert Brent Toplin

South Pacific, a 1958 movie based on Rodgers and Hammerstein's 1949 Broadway musical, itself based on a 1947 book by James Michener titled *Tales of the South Pacific,* criticized racial intolerance. It showed American military service personnel struggling in romantic relationships because of prejudices they inherited. A song in the musical, "You've Got to Be Carefully Taught," suggested that intolerance was not a natural condition; it had to be learned. Like many stories about human relationships in Broadway and Hollywood productions, *South Pacific* communicated symbolic messages. Its story hinted of American problems with racial segregation in the South and of Europe's problems with anti-Semitism. More specifically, *South Pacific* depicted prejudice toward Polynesians. Those scenes hinted at America's troubled history in dealing with Asians. Back in 1882, the United States prohibited the immigration of Chinese laborers, and in 1924 the United States angered the Japanese by barring them from immigrating to the United States. Moreover, during World War II, the U.S. government sanctioned the forceful removal of Japanese-Americans from their homes and their relocation to internment camps.

American attitudes toward Asians needed adjustment in the post–World War II era. Movies, it seemed, could play an important role in effecting changes. Cinema could entertain the millions but at the same time deliver subtle messages about the importance of tolerance and cross-cultural understanding. Hollywood had recently demonstrated the potential of cinema to change attitudes. During World War II, the motion picture industry served America's patriotic cause by depicting the Japanese enemy in a strongly negative light and by portraying Chinese allies sympathetically. A peace treaty with Japan and Mao Zedong's communist revolution in China presented new challenges. In the postwar era, Hollywood filmmakers needed to deal with a rapidly shifting international environment.

This analysis concentrates on a few of the salient differences between depictions of the Japanese in American film during World War II and in the postwar period as well as some major differences between Hollywood's characterizations of the Chinese before World War II, during the war, and in the period of the Korean War and its aftermath. To a much smaller degree, the discussion includes some references to the treatment of Koreans in American cinema.[1]

The Power of Cinema to Promote or Undermine Prejudice

During World War II, authorities in the U.S. government's Office of War Information (OWI) expressed concern that the frightening depictions of Japanese soldiers in Hollywood's wartime movies could promote bigotry in the long term. Officials at the OWI wanted movies to promote the war effort, but these leaders were troubled by the intensely negative stereotypes portrayed in America's cinema. Particularly disturbing were numerous motion pictures that showed disloyal Japanese-Americans secretly providing support for the attack on Pearl Harbor on December 7, 1941. Most Japanese-Americans had not made any trouble in the United States, one OWI authority noted, yet these "rabidly unbalanced," movies "can open the floodgates of prejudice," he wrote. A U.S. official who worked at the War Relocation Authority showed related anxieties about the influence of the movies. He wanted Hollywood films to demonstrate that many *Issei* and *Nisei* (first- and second-generation Japanese) in the United States had been loyal to the country. He warned that movies about spies in Hawai'i made American audiences distrustful. The official pointed out that many Japanese-Americans had been forced from their homes on the West Coast and relocated in the nation's interior. Their resettlement in American communities after the war would likely prove difficult. These movies stoked prejudice, he warned. Motion pictures about sinister Japanese characters might affect the public's attitudes toward the Japanese minority in the United States in profound ways for years to come.[2]

John Dower's informative book about both American and Japanese propaganda during World War II, *War without Mercy,* provides memorable examples of the forms that such ugly prejudice could take. Dower shows that American films, posters, cartoons, and other sources of propaganda characterized the wartime Japanese as ugly, vicious, bloodthirsty, and cruel (and Japanese propagandists promoted their own types of racist stereotyping). These depictions were cleverly crafted to arouse hatred for the enemy. A review of Dower's disturbing evidence leaves the impression that wartime propaganda on both sides whipped up contemptuous images of the "Other," and it would be difficult to challenge these negative impressions after the war ended.[3]

Yet as Dower demonstrates in his book and Hollywood movies reveal in their storytelling after the war, human emotions and impressions of foreigners can shift with surprising speed. Despite the intense hatred aroused by wartime artists in the two societies, benign and often friendly relations developed in the postwar years involving Americans, Japanese-Americans, and the people of Japan, who lived under the U.S. Occupation. Dower finds that the racial imagery was "surprisingly adaptable" to the needs of the postwar occupation. The Americans' aggressive images of the Japanese transferred rather quickly to passive ones that needed U.S. protection and tutelage of a defeated people.[4]

Of course, wartime animosities could not be erased in a fortnight, but the coming of peace afforded new opportunities for the growth of more positive images. By the 1950s, Americans viewed the Japanese much more favorably than they had a short time before, although sometimes condescendingly. Hollywood movies aided this transformation by offering some strikingly different depictions of the Japanese in the postwar era.

This pattern of flexibility and quick adjustments is abundantly evident in Hollywood's treatment of the Chinese as well, particularly cinema's characterizations of those living in China. Both positive and negative cinema images could change with remarkable speed. Hollywood could serve up endearing depictions or shift rather suddenly to frightening ones, and audiences evidently enjoyed the entertainment and expressed little or no anxiety about the rapid changes. During World War II, American movies often characterized the Chinese people as hearty, freedom-loving democrats who worked the land arduously, and when news stories appeared about the establishment of Red China and the outbreak of the Korean War, American movies often presented sharply contrasting images, showing tyrannical Chinese communists oppressing the masses and slaughtering U.S. soldiers in North Korea. Audiences readily accepted the altered depictions of movie heroes and villains. With respect to broad images of friends and enemies in foreign policy, American moviemakers and their audiences rather easily abandoned old prejudices and adopted new ones.

The Japanese in Hollywood's Wartime Cinema

The attack on Pearl Harbor created a new challenge for Hollywood's dramatists, since they had not paid much attention to Japanese militarism in their earlier moviemaking. The leaders of Hollywood's studios and their production personnel had plenty of experience depicting Germans as militaristic enemies in films about American engagements in World War I. By contrast, the Japanese soldier was not a familiar figure in movie drama. Hollywood showed little interest in the Japanese army's invasion of Manchuria in 1931 or in the Japanese invasions of Shanghai and other Chinese locales in 1937. Moviemakers avoided the subject, in part, because U.S. soldiers had not been significantly involved in those military actions. Furthermore, Hollywood executives were acutely sensitive about taking risks that could harm profit-making during the difficult depression years. Hollywood's business leaders did not want to make movies that would alienate political authorities in various countries, a provocation that might provoke an embargo of American-made entertainment.[5]

Consequently, Hollywood filmmakers began the job of giving American and foreign audiences sharply critical cinematic images of the Japanese enemy rather late. They began to demonstrate greater readiness to take some risks and produce controversial stories about German Nazis in 1939–1940, especially at Warner Brothers, but most of their production activity related to the Japanese military threat got under way in the months and years following the December 7, 1941, attack on Pearl Harbor.

Interestingly, one of Hollywood's most notable screen characters of Japanese ancestry was Mr. Moto, a respectable international detective who operated somewhat like the more familiar American-based movie detective of Chinese ancestry, Charlie Chan. In these films, Kentaro Moto (played by Peter Lorre in eight movies in the late 1930s) was a handsome, well-dressed, private detective who spoke several languages and could offer brilliant deductions when investigating crimes. He was also an expert at judo. This attractive image of Mr. Moto contrasted sharply with Hollywood's characterization of the Japanese after Pearl Harbor. As portrayed by Lorre, the detective demonstrated love for his country's culture, people, and emperor. Lorre played a gentleman of fine character who was a tribute to his people. While the very casting of a Caucasian actor in the Japanese role reinforced

Hollywood's deep-rooted conceptions about race on screen, overall the character was presented in a positive light.

After U.S. soldiers began to battle against Japanese soldiers in the Pacific islands, Hollywood's filmmakers borrowed from earlier movie genres to create a new perspective of a dangerous enemy. They drew upon genre traditions that had applied to movie westerns. U.S. soldiers in the new war films acted much like the pioneers in traditional cowboy cinema, while the Japanese attackers behaved much like the Indians, who attacked en masse and surrounded wagon trains and stage coaches in the old Hollywood westerns. These war movies, set in the jungles of the Pacific islands, presented stories of massacres and atrocities. Like the Indians of cinema lore, who pounced on unsuspecting white pioneers to scalp them, moviemakers characterized Japanese soldiers as stealth attackers who readily took a sniper's shot from a tree or surprised a G.I. with a knife or bayonet thrust. These movies about the Pacific conflict left a message similar to the judgment attributed to the noted Indian fighter of the U.S. military, Phillip Sheridan: the only good Indian (Japanese) was a dead one.

Two films from early in America's war against Japan, *Wake Island* (1942) and *Bataan* (1943), featured several elements from the Western formula. The movies appeared in theaters at a time when the American struggle in the Pacific was not going very well. Accordingly, their stories conveyed a sense of difficulty and tragedy. The movies show U.S. soldiers as isolated and surrounded by the enemy. The G.I.s put up a noble fight against the Japanese, who have the advantage of airplanes, superior firepower, and greater manpower. Eventually, the Americans are overwhelmed. The resistance against near-impossible odds resembles cinema's depictions of the desperate efforts of George Armstrong Custer and his men against the Indians at Little Big Horn or of Davy Crockett, Jim Bowie, and others who defended the Alamo against a large force of Mexican soldiers. In *Bataan,* for instance, American heroes are picked off, one by one, but they refuse to surrender. The G.I.s fight tenaciously and die bravely.

In most of these American-made wartime movies, the Japanese attackers are viewed briefly as objects rather than as distinct personalities, and these Japanese soldiers fight viciously rather than honorably. They are nameless, faceless attackers. Audiences rarely hear them speaking or get to know them as individuals. The Japanese soldiers murder Americans in cold blood, kill women and children through bombing and shooting, and often slaughter innocent bystanders. They employ machine guns more than the Americans, who tend to use such weapons in the movies mainly to defend themselves against a rush of swarming killers. Japanese soldiers frequently conduct sneak attacks against Americans in these films. The enemy operates from trees, and the American soldiers sometimes angrily call these surreptitious fighters "monkeys." In *Purple Heart* (1944), one of the rare wartime movies from Hollywood in which Japanese characters have much to say, the enemy's comments sound sinister. The story involves American flyers who participated in the Doolittle Raid over Tokyo and then were captured by the enemy after they crash landed in China. After an obviously unfair trial, the heroes are subjected to both psychological and physical abuse, because the Japanese leader wants to extract information from them about how the Doolittle Raid had been conducted.

The depiction of the Japanese and German enemies in American wartime cinema is intriguingly different in some respects. Although Hollywood's Nazis (as a group) are often seen as cruel and powerful, Hollywood's portrayals of individual German characters often appear in greater complexity. To be sure, most Nazi figures were transparently evil, but the movies often hinted that the German people were not nearly as wicked and might harbor resentments against the Nazis and possibly a distinct interest in resisting them. Sometimes these films hinted that German society, fundamentally good at its foundations, had been hijacked by fanatics. Furthermore, the screen's German soldiers were generally less inclined to commit atrocities than cinema's Japanese warriors. Why the difference?

Americans had a stronger ancestral link to the Germans than to the Japanese, and the moviemakers evidently responded to that distinction in their films. German immigrants had been settling in American society for centuries. Their migrations to the United States had become especially prominent from the 1840s to the early twentieth century, and the Germans had settled in virtually all the major regions of the nation. By contrast, the Japanese were relatively recent arrivals. Most had come to the United States in the late nineteenth and early twentieth century, and they settled primarily on the West Coast. On the eve of World War II, many lived in concentrated neighborhoods, where they had contact mainly with fellow Japanese in their day-to-day activities. They had not fanned out broadly across American society at that time, though the situation has changed dramatically since then. Japanese-Americans and many other national and ethnic groups have migrated to all parts of the country and have assimilated considerably in the past five decades.

Consequently, for many American moviegoers of the early 1940s, the Japanese-Americans seemed like strangers. Most Americans had little direct contact with them, and when wartime tensions sharpened after the shocking events at Pearl Harbor, Americans of European heritage could easily adopt a position of suspicion and hostility. Just as fearful emotions could provide a rationale for the tragic injustices of internment during World War II, angry emotions provided support for the ugly depictions of the Japanese enemy in wartime Hollywood films. Yet because many Americans had some German ancestry, the American people were not inclined to view German characters in movie entertainment with the same degree of negativity.

The nature of the fighting on the two fronts also affected the cinematic characterizations. Fighting in Europe occurred in regions of developed societies. Battles portrayed in the movies took place in open fields, in cities, around churches, and near other familiar sites of "civilization."[6] But cinema depicting the Pacific theater focused on fighting on isolated tropical islands, where there seemed to be no rules of honorable warfare. Savagery and brutality looked like natural components of jungle combat. The sneak attack appeared a likely threat in a steamy, palm-covered environment. Unlike movies about the European theater, which often showed soldiers leaving the front for a little rest and recreation (possibly engaging in romantic encounters with beautiful, French women), the Hollywood soldier on the Pacific front could not escape the enemy's pursuit. Lethal danger seemed to be lurking everywhere. Stories about combat on Pacific islands were often tales about fights to the finish, in which either the American or the Japanese soldiers would prevail. The situation called for a bloody struggle that would end in either survival or death. It is not surprising, then, that movies about the Pacific theater tended to show much more brutality than films set in the European theater.

Also, in the eyes of many Americans, the Japanese enemy appeared to be more deceitful because of the circumstances surrounding the events at Pearl Harbor. U.S. direct participation in the war had been forced by a surprise attack on the Pacific Fleet in Hawai'i. December 7, 1941, would be remembered as a "day of infamy," declared President Franklin D. Roosevelt in his address to Congress. Hollywood moviemakers often invoked the theme of Japanese treachery in connection with the attack on Pearl Harbor. They referenced the deceptions of Japanese diplomats in the peace negotiations. Frequently characters in the war movies revealed a family connection to the events of December 7, 1941. A sailor or soldier would mention that he lost a brother at Pearl Harbor, and he wanted the satisfaction of killing some Japanese. "That one's for Pearl Harbor," said one such character in a Hollywood film of the war period. In several movies, an evidently well-educated Japanese military leader tells Americans that he had studied at a university in the United States (the apparent explanation for his good English). This depiction, too, accentuates the theme of deception at Pearl Harbor. These movies imply that Americans had welcomed Japanese visitors to the United States, and the Japanese returned the favor by spying in support of the surprise attack.[7]

The most notable film about a supposed Japanese enemy living in the United States was *Little Tokyo, U.S.A.* (1942). This movie dealt with the internment of Japanese-Americans living on the West Coast. It portrayed the forced relocation in a rather positive manner. In one scene, a sign appears in a Japanese neighborhood stating, "We are loyal U.S. citizens," but the movie portrays some of the Japanese otherwise. Some remain loyal to Japan's emperor, and they plan to cut telephone lines in the United States in support of Japan's war aims.[8] The U.S. government's evacuation order wrecks their plans for sabotage, and a Los Angeles detective succeeds in apprehending the spies. Other movies depicted related plans for sabotage. In some scenes, for instance, they showed Japanese in Hawai'i and California taking notes about the placement of U.S. military installations and factories.[9]

As mentioned earlier, authorities at the Office of War Information were disturbed by the portrayals in *Little Tokyo, U.S.A.,* and other films that treated Japanese nationals and Japanese-Americans in the United States as sinister plotters. The OWI officials pointed out that no acts of sabotage involving people of Japanese ancestry had been detected in the United States since the Pearl Harbor attack. They counseled Hollywood to desist from such "hate pictures." Nelson Poynter, a liberal newspaper editor and a New Dealer in the OWI who worried about the potential of movies to promote intolerance, urged restraint. He wanted cinema to help the American people understand the war issues, not incite contempt for anyone of Japanese ancestry. The allies were fighting fascism, Poynter stressed, not the Japanese people in general. Poynter tried to pressure Hollywood producers to make films that informed the American public about broad threats to freedom: dictatorship, militarism, and fascism.[10]

Poynter was not very successful in his attempts to help shape Hollywood's portrayals. OWI's influence over moviemaking waned substantially as the war proceeded. The movie industry executives paid less and less attention to OWI's recommendations. They realized that they could not easily attract large audiences to the kind of films that Poynter recommended. Movie patrons did not want cinema-based lectures about fascism. So Hollywood's leaders quickly moved toward the kind of storytelling that had proved successful over the years. Productions that featured starkly sinister villains had worked well in the past, and they served as successful fare in many wartime productions. Movies that showed a brutal Japanese enemy carried the day. These films often portrayed a bloodthirsty, sadistic, enemy that readily participated in cold-blooded murders. The hero/villain formula that had worked so well for western, crime, and detective films became familiar in Hollywood's wartime flicks.

In movies such as *Gung-Ho!* (1943), *Guadalcanal Diary* (1943), and *Blood on the Sun* (1945), Hollywood showed brief glimpses of a vicious enemy. The wartime films usually did not focus on a specific Japanese personality or give Japanese characters major speaking parts. The camera remained principally on American servicemen; the Japanese were usually nameless killers, seen briefly as attacking soldiers or airplanes. *Behind the Rising Sun* (1943) was quite different, however, for it placed a Japanese figure at the center of its story. In the beginning of the film, this character, Taro, attends Cornell University in the United States and seems to be a good-hearted young man. But his personality changes rapidly as he becomes involved in Japan's war effort. By the end of the movie, Taro evolves into a spirited Japanese warrior who finds joy in killing Americans.[11]

Postwar Images of the Japanese

Hollywood filmmaking changed rapidly after World War II ended, in particular with respect to depictions of Japanese. Despite the prolific output of hate-oriented films during the war, California's moviemakers turned rather quickly toward presenting the Japanese as peaceful, responsible, and honorable people. Of course, in some war movies produced in the late 1940s, such as *Sands of Iwo Jima* (1949), the faceless, nameless hordes still fought tenaciously. But by the early and mid-1950s, a more attractive Asian character was often gracing the screen. When moviegoers actually got to see and hear a Japanese character, he or she was not nearly as threatening as those that had appeared just a few years earlier.[12]

Japanese War Bride (1952) illustrates the change well. In this film, some Americans are the troublemakers in the story, while the Japanese woman at the center of the tale appears angelic. At the beginning of the film, a G.I. wakes up in a hospital, where he is recovering from wounds received in the

Korean War. A beautiful and kind-hearted Japanese nurse tends to his needs. The G.I. quickly falls in love with the woman and is determined to marry her. First, he must receive approval from the girl's grandfather, who has taken responsibility for her upbringing. The meeting affords an opportunity for the moviemakers to show people from two cultures learning to recognize their differences and also their common humanity. The lovers marry and then settle in Salinas, California, home of the G.I. Problems quickly emerge in the postwar American community, however. Some family members and neighbors still harbor wartime resentments toward the Japanese, and one of the American women begins to spread mischievous rumors about her. *Japanese War Bride* explores the phenomenon of prejudice toward "mixed" marriage, a theme that appeared in several other Hollywood movies during this period. These films portrayed romances involving white Americans with Asians, Native Americans, Latinos, and African-Americans.[13]

Another important film of the postwar era that reveals newly tolerant and positive images of Asians is *Teahouse of the August Moon* (1956). It features Marlon Brando in the role of a humorous and wise native figure. An American military captain, played by Glenn Ford, arrives at Okinawa intent upon teaching the supposedly primitive Okinawa natives the ways of democracy. He wants them to build a school and plans to put the natives to work making small trinkets for the marketplace. This effort to impose American-style education and business does not go over well with the locals. They prefer the construction of a teahouse, complete with geishas. Eventually Ford's character begins to recognize the value of a more flexible approach to cross-cultural interaction. By selling a beverage that is popular with the islanders, he readily accumulates the cash to build the desired teahouse. Brando, in the role of Sakini, and a woman known as Lotus Blossom (played by Machiko Kyo) assist in the effort.

This funny and well-acted movie, based on a popular Broadway play, cleverly took aim at cultural imperialism. It suggested that the people who fell under U.S. stewardship after World War II were as sophisticated as the Americans, indeed, more clever in some ways. The film shows that Okinawans have an impressive civilization of their own—one that is different from that of the Americans but nevertheless worthy of respect. *Teahouse of the August Moon* was the kind of movie that appealed to enthusiasts of the United Nations in the 1950s. Brando exemplified that spirit in his personal life. When making the film, he announced his intention to donate some of his earnings to support the creation of an UN-based film program in Asia.

Today's moviegoers might find Brando's appearance in the movie as an Okinawan inappropriate. Modern-day audiences expect to see Asians playing Asian characters in films. In the 1950s, however, it was common in Hollywood productions for well-known American actors of European ancestry to be made up to look like people of various ethnic and national backgrounds. Prominent movie stars played Indians (i.e., Native Americans), and as late as 1982 Ben Kingsley appeared as the heroic Indian leader in Richard Attenborough's notable movie, *Gandhi*.

Another Brando film deserves attention, the tender love story, *Sayonara* (1957), based on a novel by James Michener. This film, too, features romances between American men and Japanese women. Brando plays a G.I. with a distinguished military pedigree, who is expected to establish a romantic relationship with the daughter of a prominent military officer, an attachment that could advance his career as well. But a beautiful Japanese woman steals his heart, and experience opens his eyes to the attractiveness of Asian culture. This movie also shows a warm and affectionate marriage between characters played by Red Buttons and Umeki Miyoshi. Umeki won an Oscar for her performance in a supporting role in this picture, the first such award given by Hollywood to an Asian. Evidently, the female Asian character was easier to introduce as an appealing movie personality than an Asian male at this point in U.S. history.

Gina Marchetti has observed connections between movies that explore a fantasy of sexual engagement across cultures. She traces the origins of American society's fears to white Americans' anxieties in the nineteenth century regarding a "Yellow Peril." Americans of European ancestry worried that their Western culture might someday be overwhelmed by Asian immigrants. Marchetti found related concerns communicated in Hollywood entertainment in the twentieth century. The moviemakers' fascination with stories about interracial romance, particularly dramas about white men's love affairs with Asian women, revealed deep-seated racial and social insecurities. Movies in the 1950s that portrayed Japanese war brides invoked the myth of a subservient Asian woman. These stories aimed to shore up the masculinity of white males at a time when some American women were demonstrating greater independence.

Marchetti's interpretation is intriguing, but other factors could be at play in Hollywood's depictions. During the post–World War II era, many U.S.-made films depicted interracial and intercultural romance. To some degree, those movies reflected historical conditions. After a bloody global conflict in which governments and armies oppressed ethnic, racial, and religious minorities, Hollywood produced several movies that criticized prejudice and intolerance. Occasionally, these films made a symbolic case for cross-cultural engagement by portraying white protagonists in romantic relationships with Native Americans (as in the 1950 production *Broken Arrow*), or with an African-American (as in the 1967 film *Guess Who's Coming to Dinner*).

Attitudes toward Asians in the movies changed over time, and that evolution is particularly evident in the way in which Hollywood dealt with an important historical event: the bombing of Pearl Harbor in December 1941. Depictions of the attack shifted, in part, because relations between the United States and Japan changed dramatically. Changes in the foreign policy environment eventually supported a shift in the themes advanced in American cinema. The negative images of the Japanese, promoted vigorously in wartime movies, were not acceptable after the war, when Americans sought to build a friendly relationship with the Japanese people.

In the postwar decades, U.S.-Japanese relations grew increasingly close, largely because of cold war tensions and America's growing involvement in trade with Japan. American worries about Soviet intentions were behind some of the efforts toward amicable relations. Leaders in the U.S. State Department were concerned about Japan's vulnerability. They hoped that the promotion of democracy and economic development in Japan would protect it from communist influence. By the 1960s, Japan had progressed impressively toward economic recovery, and the country was beginning to emerge as one of the most prosperous. An important element of Japan's evolving trade relationship with the United States involved the motion picture industry. The Japanese provided a strong Asian-based market for American films.

In this situation, Hollywood moviemakers did not want to alienate potential Japanese audiences by presenting stories about the Pearl Harbor attack in the 1940s-style format of American heroes slaughtered by foreign villains. The economically and diplomatically wise approach was to advance a cooperative effort toward telling a generally familiar war story. The result in 1970 was an expensive, historically minded war picture *Tora! Tora! Tora!* Japanese filmmakers crafted the Japanese-based half of the movie. They presented history from the perspective of leaders of the Japanese navy, and the filmmakers did not portray the Japanese characters as particularly villainous. The movie demonstrated that some Japanese commanders and planners were naively optimistic about the potential for their secret attack to bring long-term success, but the film certainly did not depict these leaders in the sharply negative manner of earlier Hollywood films that referenced the attack on Pearl Harbor.

Hollywood's characterizations of the Pearl Harbor attack in the 1970s also reflected the producers' concerns about alienating Japanese-Americans. *Midway* (1976) stressed the importance of gaining an American victory in the Pacific in 1942 after the embarrassment and humiliation of Japan's surprise attack on the U.S. Navy's Pacific Fleet. It featured a subplot in which an American fighter pilot was in love with a Japanese-American woman. The girlfriend's family had been sent to a wartime internment camp in the United States. In this way, the film aimed to show some Japanese characters in a favorable light and as victims as well. A few years later, Steven Spielberg's *1941* (1979) characterized American reactions to the news about an attack on Pearl Harbor in a comedic fashion. The Californians in 1941 grossly overreact to the prospect of an invasion on their shores. Spielberg's movie turns the camera's eye toward the Americans rather than the Japanese and makes fun of them.

Economics appears to have figured prominently in the construction of *Pearl Harbor* (2001), a Hollywood production by Michael Bay and Jerry Bruckheimer, two cinema moguls with a reputation for crafting action-oriented blockbusters for both American and international audiences. Bay and Bruckheimer aimed to screen *Pearl Harbor* aggressively with Japanese audiences. They worked carefully to ensure that their story would not alienate them. Unlike most Hollywood movies about history, *Pearl Harbor* did not feature true villains. The Japanese characters in the film are generally decent and admirable. As in *Tora! Tora! Tora!*, the movie dialogue suggests that the Japanese's surprise attack on the Hawai'ian island ultimately was counterproductive, but the movie does not emphasize treachery. An absence of villains in Bay and Bruckheimer's film leaves the movie's drama rather flat.

Far more sophisticated in composition and message were Clint Eastwood's companion films about the American attack on Iwo Jima and the defense of the tiny island in the Pacific by Japanese soldiers. The first of the two, *Flags of Our Fathers* (2006), demonstrated the power of the Iwo Jima experience over the lives of the G.I.s. Several of the principal American characters in the story suffer from long-term depression. They cannot shake the trauma of wartime carnage. Like the traditional Hollywood war pictures, *Flags of Our Fathers* does not characterize members of the enemy army individually. Each Japanese character is seen on the screen briefly as a fighting and often dying enemy. The second of the two films offers an intriguing look at the battle of Iwo Jima from the Japanese perspective. In *Letters from Iwo Jima* (2006), the defensive effort seems like a suicide mission from the beginning, but the Japanese officers and many soldiers nevertheless approached their task with commitment and courage. This film differentiates the Japanese characters, humanizing them in ways that traditional Hollywood war flicks failed to do. Not all of the officers and soldiers are fanatically enthusiastic about the operation. Some want to live rather than die for a lost cause. They have wives and families back in Japan. Audiences get to know the Japanese defenders as real people. This technique makes the characters' travails at Iwo Jima all the more tragic.

Hollywood's treatment of the American dropping of the atom bomb over Japan also reveals evidence of an evolution toward more sensitive treatment of the Japanese. The early films about the bombings tended to justify them, while a more recent Hollywood entry raised serious questions about the use of such weapons. In *The Beginning or the End* (1947), for instance, the film's producers gave Leslie Groves—the chief military officer in charge of the Manhattan Project to develop an atom bomb—script approval. Groves and others requested several changes in the story. At the early stages of the script, the film raised some questions about the American leaders' decision to detonate the bomb over Hiroshima. The writers planned to show the effects of the blast, such as a baby with a burned face and images of the city in ruins. In an early version of the script, the story revealed that some scientists involved in the Manhattan Project raised moral questions about dropping an atom bomb on a location with a large civilian population. A few of them preferred the use of a demonstration blast in a remote area of Japan so that the Japanese leaders would realize that further resistance was futile. Eventually, though, the filmmakers were pressured to avoid raising major questions about the bombing. President Harry S. Truman joined efforts to convince filmmakers to present a positive impression of the bombs' use. To mollify these influential critics, the moviemakers added various elements to the story that put the U.S. military's actions in a favorable light. *The Beginning or the End* claimed the American flyers had dropped leaflets over Hiroshima to warn the Japanese public. It suggested that dropping atom bombs on Hiroshima and Nagasaki helped to shorten the war by about a year and therefore probably saved the lives of from 300,000 to 500,000 American soldiers, who would have been engaged in a land invasion of the Japanese islands if the bombs had not been employed.[14]

A somewhat similar example of powerful influence affected the interpretation of *Above and Beyond,* a 1953 movie about Paul Tibbets and his crew, the American aviators responsible for dropping the bomb on Hiroshima from a B-29 named the Enola Gay. Tibbets served as a paid consultant to the project, and General Curtis LeMay of the U.S. Strategic Air Command had a voice in the story's construction. Not surprisingly, *Above and Beyond* justified American actions at Hiroshima. With the handsome star Robert Taylor in the role of Paul Tibbets, the movie celebrated the aviators' success in completing their difficult assignment. This film, too, maintained that the bombing helped to save the lives of up to half a million U.S. service personnel.

In 1989, when the film *Fat Man and Little Boy* was released, the message was considerably different. Its director, Roland Joffé, was a politically engaged filmmaker who liked projects with humanitarian themes. Prior to making *Fat Man and Little Boy,* he directed *The Killing Fields* (1984), a tragic story about the mass murder in Cambodia during its civil war that suggested a degree of U.S. responsibility for the chaos and mayhem there during the 1970s. Later, he made *The Mission* (1986), which portrayed the efforts of Spanish Jesuits in eighteenth-century Brazil to protect the Indians there from enslavement by the Portuguese. *Fat Man and Little Boy* featured Paul Newman playing against type. As Groves, Newman pushes for development of the bomb without much attention to the implications of its use on Japanese civilians. Because the film includes an accident in a lab that exposes a worker on the Manhattan Project to lethal radiation, Joffé gives audiences a sense of the pain that many Japanese at Hiroshima suffered from the bombing of their city.[15]

Joffé's movie was a product of the late cold war period. Its messages extended beyond the issue of America's use of atom bombs at the end of World War II. The film also raised questions about America's dependence on a huge nuclear arsenal in connection with its arms race with the Soviet Union. The production of *Fat Man and Little Boy* took place in the late 1980s, near the end of Ronald Reagan's presidency. The movie's implied criticism of the bombings reflected the concerns of many people involved in a worldwide movement to reduce the dangers of nuclear confrontation.

This brief review of some major Hollywood films that dealt with World War II and its aftermath shows that portrayals of Asians in American cinema changed substantially over the years. Before the outbreak of World War II, Hollywood had little experience with the depiction of Japanese screen characters. After the attack on Pearl Harbor created emotional shock waves in the United States, Hollywood sprang into action, producing several motion pictures that presented the Japanese enemy as a vicious and inhumane fighter, whether in the air or in the jungle. In the immediate postwar years, Hollywood responded to America's newly friendly diplomatic relationship with Japan. While some of the war pictures continued to portray the Japanese as tenacious fighters, Hollywood filmmakers also portrayed civilized and decent Japanese, especially in love stories involving an American man and an attractive Japanese woman. Further evidence of the evolution toward more positive and sensitive screen images of the Japanese can be seen in the American movies' treatment of diverse themes such as the attack on Pearl Harbor, the battle at Iwo Jima, and the decision to drop atom bombs on two Japanese cities.

Portrayals of the Chinese and the North Koreans as Enemies in American Cinema

As in the case of the movies' shifting depictions of the Japanese, Hollywood's presentation of Chinese characters on the silver screen evolved dramatically in its representations of social and political issues. In the pre–World War II era and during World War II, images of the Chinese in American cinema were generally positive. After the communist takeover of mainland China in 1949 and the outbreak of the Korean War in 1950, however, cold war considerations affected the treatment of Chinese figures as well as depictions of North Koreans. Hollywood's characterizations often took on a distinctly negative tone.

Many of the industry's early movies portrayed Chinese characters with stock images of evil mandarins, bandits, and poor peasants, as scholars such as Dorothy B. Jones and Christine Choy have pointed out, but in the late 1930s and the early 1940s, Hollywood produced more sympathetic and hopeful messages about the Chinese people.[16] Some of that sentiment drew upon the American people's longtime interest in China. During the nineteenth and twentieth centuries, American missionaries had been strongly engaged in bringing their message of Christian salvation to the millions of people in China, and American businessmen had talked excitedly about the potential for selling American-made goods in a huge Chinese market. American scholars also joined in the expressions of hopeful expectation, reporting that China had nursed a sophisticated civilization in earlier centuries, one that appeared to be superior to the culture and science of Western societies at the time. If China could somehow remove the shackles of bureaucratic and imperial rule and emerge as a thriving democracy, the country could move rapidly toward prosperity.

When Pearl Buck's sympathetic novel about life in China, *The Good Earth* (1931), came out as a film in 1937, movie audiences saw a striking example of that sympathy.[17] Paul Muni starred in the popular film, playing Wang Lung, a Chinese farmer who struggles to create a better life. At the beginning of the story, he marries and prospers. But drought and famine begin to plague the land. After his home is looted by intruders, Wang and his family move to the city, looking for work. He faces hard times, and so does the nation, which is caught up in a revolution. Eventually, Wang returns to the land. He faces devastation from a swarm of locusts, but in the end the wind suddenly shifts, and his farm is saved. Throughout the story, moviemakers communicate the idea that many of the Chinese peasants are noble laborers in the soil, somewhat like the poor but honorable farmers in America's heartland. These farmers experience many frustrations in the present, but their internal fortitude may contribute to a much better life someday in the future.[18]

It was an extraordinary coincidence that *The Good Earth* appeared in movie theaters in the United States around the time when the 1937 Sino-Japanese war began. The movie put a human face on the suffering of the Chinese people, showing the kind of individuals who, evidently, had become victims of the Japanese invasion. More than 20 million Americans saw the movie. *The Good Earth* had not been designed as a work of international propaganda, but it seemed to have that effect by arousing American sympathy for the Chinese.[19]

Additional sympathetic treatments emerged from Hollywood in the early 1940s, especially because members of the Nationalist Party in China became important American allies against the Japanese during World War II. Manchuria had been attacked by Japanese troops in 1931, and a new assault began in 1937 on Shanghai, Nanjing, and other cities. News reports about the aggressiveness of the Japanese military and physical abuses and massacres of the Chinese people disturbed Americans. After the United States entered the war against Japan in December 1941, President Franklin D. Roosevelt strongly promoted the idea that China was a valuable wartime ally.

During the war, Hollywood responded to this pro-China outlook by producing films that depicted the Chinese as bold freedom fighters who were determined to resist tyranny. In *China* (1943), David Jones (portrayed by Alan Ladd) is a profiteer who intends to sell oil to the Japanese in China and earn a handsome profit. He is cynical about the Chinese people's effort to resist the invaders until he meets and falls in love with Carolyn Grant (portrayed by Loretta Young), who educates him about the nobility of the Chinese people's struggle. After witnessing an atrocity committed by the Japanese, Jones joins the Chinese resistance.[20] *Dragon Seed* (1944), starring Katharine Hepburn and Walter Huston made up to look like Chinese, also exemplifies the genre. Based on a book by Pearl Buck, it tells the story of a Chinese peasant family that finds itself caught up in the problems of modern warfare. They become involved in the fight to free China from the Japanese invaders. With other members of the rag-tag Chinese army, they retreat inland and struggle against the foreigners by means of guerrilla warfare. Hepburn plays her familiar movie role as a strong woman in this film, challenging the traditional Hollywood image of a compliant and obsequious Chinese woman. Her character displays impressive determination and leadership skills in support of the Chinese resistance effort.[21]

To some degree, Hollywood's effort to portray the Chinese people in a favorable light was aided by a longtime tradition in American cinema of movies about an astute Chinese detective, Charlie Chan. Hollywood produced six of these films during World War II, and in some of them Chan made a contribution to the war effort. Chan is clearly an impressive figure in the series, meant to bring to mind Sherlock Holmes. Wise, intelligent, and honorable, Charlie Chan is the man to whom American authorities turn when confronting a puzzling crime mystery, sometimes invoking the sayings of Confucius as he solves crimes. In comparison to Chan, the American police often look like bunglers in these stories, incompetent and inefficient. Some officials in the Office of War information even expressed concern that these movies put American law enforcement in a harsh light and suggested that Hollywood filmmakers show American police as competent allies of Chan. But the moviemakers did not take this recommendation seriously, as they did not want to alter a story formula that had succeeded with American and international audiences on many occasions. Although actors of European ancestry played Chan in these films, the movies were popular in Asia as well as the United States. Asian audiences enjoyed seeing the Chinese figure in a position of superiority. The depictions of Chinese characters were not uniformly positive in these movies, however. Part of their comic appeal was the characterization of Chan's rather dim-witted son. While Charlie Chan seemed to know everything, "Number One Son" often appeared to know nothing.

In the 1950s, when several films were made that included cross-national, cross-ethnic, and cross-racial romances, the creators of *Love Is a Many-Splendored Thing* (1955) advanced a related theme associated with an Asian character. Like other films about love and marriage between people of different backgrounds, this movie, too, paid a lot of attention to the idea of crossing boundaries through romance. It shows an American journalist in Hong Kong (portrayed by William Holden) falling in love with a physician of mixed European and Chinese ancestry. The woman's social identity appears to be in limbo. Some aristocrats of British lineage view her as an Asian and speak contemptuously about her. A Chinese character considers her Chinese and urges her to forgo romance with the American and, instead, serve the people of communist China. The woman tries to identify proudly with her combined heritage, but her life is made difficult by the complications of mixed identity. Like many American movies at the time that portrayed cross-national and cross-racial love affairs, this romance ends tragically. The heroine's lover is sent off as a correspondent to report on the Korean War, and he dies in early military action there. Evidently, Hollywood filmmakers were not yet comfortable showing couples of "mixed" ancestry living happily ever after.

Although a woman of Eurasian ancestry is the subject of a romance in *Love Is a Many-Splendored Thing,* the portrayal of Asian men was often in the context stories about the Korean War in the early 1950s. In these movies, the North Korean and Chinese characters often represented the communist enemy, the North Koreans who initially invaded South Korea in the summer of 1950 and the "Red" Chinese who poured into North Korea in late 1950 and made life difficult for the American personnel who went there to fight against them. In *Steel Helmut* (1951), Samuel Fuller's economically produced but rather profitable film about the Korean War, the North Koreans are the enemy, but the good Koreans are represented by a little boy who follows a rag-tag group of American soldiers. When the Americans capture a North Korean major, the enemy officer attempts to divide the American soldiers against each other, but they resist. In many respects, the North Korean in *Steel Helmut* resembles the Japanese enemy in the films during World War II. Later in the decade, movies such as *Pork Chop Hill* (1959) focused especially on the enemy Chinese in the Korean War. This story depicts soldiers (led by the character portrayed by Gregory Peck) fighting to capture a hill, since a victory there presumably would aid U.S. peace negotiations at Panmunjom. The movie opens with blaring loudspeakers from a Chinese encampment. A communist propagandist's appeal to the U.S. soldiers asks them to give up and enjoy a peaceful relationship with the Chinese. It is obviously a ruse, and it does not fool the Americans. Later, U.S. soldiers fight against the masses of Chinese fighters. Like the Japanese attackers in World War II–era movies, these communist hordes appear to have no respect for human life.

The Manchurian Candidate (1962), a critically acclaimed film directed by John Frankenheimer, offers an especially disturbing portrayal of both the North Koreans and the Chinese. In the story, North Korean, Chinese, and other communist officials subject American captives in the Korean War to horrible brainwashing. Much of the story focuses on the men's life in the United States after the war, and in these scenes it is evident that manipulations by communist interrogators waging psychological warfare had a lasting effect on the G.I.s personalities. Some of the former prisoners of war are troubled by frighteningly similar nightmares. An investigation of their problems uncovers a dangerous political conspiracy. *The Manchurian Candidate* offered a complex and sophisticated story, yet it did not attract large audiences when it first appeared. Because the narrative includes a plot to assassinate a U.S. presidential nominee, it became problematic after the assassination of President John F. Kennedy on November 22, 1963. Frank Sinatra, who portrayed one of the principal characters in the film, was a friend of Kennedy's, and he tried to buy up copies of the movie after the assassination.

Conclusion

There has been much criticism of Hollywood's role in reinforcing and sometimes creating ethnic, racial, national, and cultural stereotypes, and scholars have devoted considerable space to speculation about the impact of these depictions on the people who watch movies. Students of film have asked whether screen images sometimes stoke powerful and long-lasting prejudices. They have noted that cinema can have a strong emotional impact on viewers. Motion picture entertainment can arouse an audience's sympathies for heroes, and it can incite anger toward a story's villains. When the heavies in these narratives are people of a different race, nationality, or ethnicity, as in many of the popular American-made movies about the Japanese in World War II or in movies about the North Koreans and the Chinese in the Korean War, the emotional impact may be problematic in the long run. The strongly negative depictions of Japanese, North Koreans, and Chinese appears to have a residual effect, keeping American moviegoers resentful, suspicious, and distrustful toward those people long after the wartime hostilities end. Prejudice, it seems, can be stimulated by popular entertainment.

The scholarly literature documenting the apparently nefarious influences of screen images that depicted races, ethnic groups, and nationalities in sharply negative ways is voluminous. Such investigations have inspired useful discussions about the power of popular cinema to create resentment of African-Americans, Italians, Arabs, Jews, Native Americans, Germans, and other groups. Some of that literature has exposed the stereotypical treatment of the Japanese and the Chinese as well. For instance, critics have objected to Hollywood's depictions of Chinese in old movies as mainly warlords, bandits, opium users, as well as weak people traumatized by great poverty.[22] Scholars have also commented extensively on characterizations of a vicious Japanese enemy in Hollywood movies from 1942 to 1945.

Yet what Hollywood delivers it can also take away. Filmmakers began to show less ugly characterizations of various Asian peoples after the conflicts came to an end, and the depictions of female representatives of those cultures turned especially generous in the postwar years. Could these changing portrayals help to break down the prejudices stoked by earlier movies? Did motion pictures have the power to mitigate some of the mischief they created when, in the spirit of wartime propaganda, they dramatized stories about vicious enemies? Evidence of Hollywood's involvement in movies that often countered the messages of war pictures suggests that the postconflict films may have ameliorated some of the emotional damage.

The record of productions examined here reveals that moviemakers shifted their interpretations rather quickly after wartime hostilities ended. Movies about the war in the Pacific continued to show some Japanese soldiers acting as violent enemies, especially in films released in the decade and a half after the war, but that enemy seemed less treacherous and less given to committing atrocities than the nasty jungle-based villains portrayed in many movies during the World War II era. Several decades later, when Japan was an important U.S. ally and a major trading partner (providing a valuable market for American films), the portrayals of Japanese wartime soldiers, sailors, and aviators took a decidedly benign turn. In movies about Pearl Harbor and Iwo Jima, Japanese characters in American-made cinema seemed more like human beings in a historical drama than one-dimensional villains as they had earlier. Movies that referenced the use of atom bombs on Hiroshima and Nagasaki also reflected changing international perspectives. The facile cinematic justifications for using nuclear weapons against a large civilian population, seen in some earlier motion pictures, no longer appeared acceptable. *Fat Man and Little Boy* offered an interpretation that was relevant to the concerns of many people who were involved at the time in campaigns that opposed the nuclear arms race.

Cinematic portrayals of the Chinese also shifted substantially from generally favorable depictions in the 1930s and 1940s to images of sinister and manipulative enemies in the 1950s and 1960s. American movie audiences viewed noble Chinese peasants and farmers in films of the late 1930s and early 1940s, and they also gained exposure to Chinese appeals for freedom from the tyranny of Japan's invading armies during the war period. But after the beginning of the cold war and North Korean and Chinese invasions of South Korea, moviemakers switched rapidly toward depicting Chinese (and North Korean) characters as powerful, devious, and dangerous enemies. It is evident that Hollywood responded rapidly to new initiatives in America's foreign policy and often pivoted to new characterizations.

The influence of movies on public attitudes toward different nationalities and ethnic groups is an intriguing subject that has received extensive study. This investigation explores another dimension of the subject: To what degree can the rapidly shifting imagery in popular cinema reverse or undermine the effects of sharply negative imagery promoted in wartime? A detailed answer to that question would require extensive analysis of the reactions to those movies of both the audience and the critics. The present study can offer only tentative responses. Yet it is clear that Hollywood, acting in service to America's changing foreign policy and the movie industry's shifting opportunities at the box office, dramatically redirected its portrayals of the country's wartime enemies over several decades of filmmaking. American audiences, cognizant of their country's shifting relationships in international affairs, did not express much objection to these reversals in dramatic representations. Movie patrons enjoyed the entertainment and coincidentally received broad exposure to revised characterizations of foreign peoples and world history.

Notes

1 For wide-ranging discussions of the depiction of Asians in movies and other forms of popular culture, see, for instance, Robert G. Lee, *Orientals: Asian Americans in Popular Culture* (Philadelphia: Temple University Press, 1999); Gina Marchetti, *Romance and the "Yellow Peril": Race, Sex, and Discursive*

Strategies in Hollywood Fiction (Berkeley: University of California Press, 1994); Peter X. Feng, *Identities in Motion: Asian American Film and Video* (Durham: Duke University Press, 2002); idem, ed., *Screening Asian Americans* (New Brunswick, NJ: Rutgers University Press, 2002); Darrell Y. Hamamoto and Sandra Liu, ed., *Countervisions: Asian-American Film Criticism* (Philadelphia: Temple University Press, 2000); Dorothy B. Jones, *The Portrayal of China and India on the American Screen, 1896–1955* (Cambridge, MA: Center for International Studies, Massachusetts Institute of Technology, 1955); Jun Xing, *Asian America through the Lens: History, Representations, and Identity* (Lanham, MD: Altamira Press, 1998); Hye Seung Chung, *Hollywood Asian: Philip Ahn and the Politics of Cross-Ethnic Performance* (Philadelphia: Temple University Press, 2006).

2   Clayton R. Koppes and Gregory D. Black, *Hollywood Goes to War: How Politics, Profits, and Propaganda Shaped World War II Movies* (New York: Free Press, 1987), 75–76.

3   John Dower, *War without Mercy* (New York: Pantheon Books, 1986), 8–9. There were, of course, contrasting images of "good" Asians involved in the war effort. In *Somewhere I'll Find You,* a movie about the fighting at Corregidor, Clark Gable says, with obvious reference to U.S. allies in the Philippines, "Brown men and white men fought and died together. When they bled, their blood was the same color." See Robert L. McLaughlin and Sally F. Parry, *We'll Always Have the Movies* (Lexington: University of Kentucky Press, 2006), 75.

4   Dower, *War without Mercy*, 13.

5   Ruth Vasey, *The World According to Hollywood, 1918–1939* (Madison: University of Wisconsin Press, 1997), 154–155.

6   Koppes and Black, *Hollywood Goes to War*, 253; Dower, *War without Mercy*, 10.

7   McLaughlin and Parry, *We'll Always Have the Movies*, 129–130.

8   By the late twentieth century, American-made movies were no longer treating the subject of Japanese-American internment with approval. The nation's record of forced relocation during World War II had become an embarrassment in the age of civil rights. A 1976 made-for-television movie, *Farewell to Manzanar,* based on Jeanne Wakatsuki's memoir, showed the painful impact on a Japanese-American family. The generational divide between younger and older Japanese-Americans during the war is explored in Emiko Omori's film *Rabbit on the Moon* (1999). Omori's documentary reveals that some of the older Japanese-Americans cooperated with the American government in order to demonstrate that they were loyal citizens, but other Japanese-Americans, especially the younger ones, were less willing to accept relocation silently.

9   McLaughlin and Parry, *We'll Always Have the Movies*, 129–130.

10 Koppes and Black, *Hollywood Goes to War*, 248–251.

11 Franklin Odo recalls that, "as a third-generation sansai growing up in the 1940s and 1950s, we had . . . conflicted reactions when watching Hollywood World War II films about the treacherous "Japs" (*No Sword to Bury: Japanese Americans in Hawai'i during World War II* [Philadelphia: Temple University Press, 2004], 110).

12 The movies' representation carried messages similar to that promoted by the United States in the postwar years. During the period of the occupation, American leaders began to talk about the Japanese as good pupils for their American teachers. They projected the idea of a teacher/pupil or parent/child relationship. See Dower, *War without Mercy*, 9, 302.

13 Chung, *Hollywood Asian*, 131; Marchetti, *Romance and the "Yellow Peril,"* 161–162.

14 Jerome Shapiro, *Atomic Bomb Cinema: The Apocalyptic Imagination in Film* (New York: Routledge, 2002), 62–72.

15 Ibid., 62–71.

16 Xing, *Asian America through the Lens*, 54–57.

17 The Chinese government applied pressure on the moviemakers, demanding that the MGM crew produce a story and imagery that was acceptable to Chinese officials. See Chung, *Hollywood Asian*, 92–96.

18 Thomas Doherty, *Projections of War: Hollywood, American Culture, and World War II* (New York: Columbia University Press, 1999), 133–134; Chung, *Hollywood Asian*, 45–46.

19 David M. Kennedy, *Freedom from Fear: The American People in Depression and War, 1929–1945* (New York: Oxford University Press, 1999), 401–402.

20 McLaughlin and Parry, *We'll Always Have the Movies*, 161–162; Koppes and Black, *Hollywood Goes to War*, 235–238; Doherty, *Projections of War*, 136.

21 Koppes and Black, *Hollywood Goes to War*, 239–242; Dower, *War without Mercy*, 305.22.

PART II

READING WAR TRAUMA

CHAPTER 7

Oscillating Histories
Representations of Comfort Women from *Bamboo House of Dolls* to *Imperial Comfort Women*

Lily Wong

Over half a century has passed since the term "comfort women" came into common usage in the Pacific War, yet it remains highly contested in international politics. "Comfort women" is often interpreted as a euphemism for women of various ethnic and national backgrounds who served the Japanese military, especially those who were coerced into sexual servitude during the Pacific War. The first comfort stations documented were those set up in Shanghai for the Japanese Navy in March 1932 in the name of "preventing Japanese soldiers from raping civilians and from contracting VD [venereal disease] through contact with unauthorized prostitutes."[1] After the Japanese invasion of Nanjing (what would be later called the "Rape of Nanjing" or alternatively termed "the Nanjing Massacre") in 1937, Japanese troops increased by more than a million, leading to a rapid increase in comfort stations throughout China. After Japan's attack on Pearl Harbor in December 1941, the system of comfort women expanded beyond China, alongside the ever-expanding battlefield, to encompass the entire Asia-Pacific region under Japanese occupation. Most of the comfort women were known to be Korean, Japanese, Chinese, Taiwanese, Filipina, and Indonesian. Estimates of their total number range from 20,000 to 400,000.[2]

Official discussions for political redress over the comfort women issue didn't surface until the late 1980s, taking up a central role in international politics in the 1990s. This rise in public attention is considered to be a part of the larger post–cold war politics of human rights emerging around the world at the time. As Sarah Soh states, "the systematic rape of Bosnian women by Serb forces in the Balkan conflict beginning in the spring of 1992 . . . contributed to raising feminist consciousness about sexual violence against women during armed conflict, generating a surge of keen interest in the Korean comfort women movement and sympathetic support for the survivors by the international community."[3] The comfort women issue was thus pointed to by international feminist humanitarians as a crucial example of wartime violations of women's human rights. In response, feminist groups around East Asia formed alliances to force the issue on to the political agenda, launching an Asia-wide movement.[4]

In response to international pressure and investigations, the Japanese government issued an official report on the comfort women issue in 1992. The report was followed by an apology by the chief cabinet secretary, Kōno Yōhei, admitting the government's official involvement in the recruitment of comfort women. Many have, however, questioned the sincerity of this apology, seeing it as a political performance by the government to avoid taking legal responsibility.[5] Moreover, in the mid-1990s, controversy stirred in Japan over the way Japanese history was to be presented in textbooks. The textbook debates shed light on the rise of conservative ultranationalist voices, and the comfort women issue subsequently became a crucial fault line between what Soh calls the "self-critical progressive" and the "ethno-centric conservative" camps in Japan's political arena.[6] This debate intensified further in 2007, when Japanese Prime Minister Abe Shinzō, known for his conservative leanings, denied that the military had used any coercion in recruiting comfort women, maintaining the issue's highly controversial status.

Though struggling to have their plight politically recognized as a historical reality, the comfort women live on in the public imaginary, with a life of their own in cultural productions. In Japan, literature on comfort women can be traced back to the late 1940s. According to the Asian Women's Fund, a nongovernmental organization formed to give financial payments to former comfort women, more than two hundred Japanese documents on the issue were published after the war in various formats, from books to magazine articles, from biographies to memoirs, both fiction and nonfiction. The first documentary film about a former Korean comfort woman, Pae Pong-gi, appeared in Japan in 1979, a decade before the international redress movement. Contrary to the common conception that the issue remained a dark wartime secret uncovered only after international involvement began in the 1990s, the first media coverage of the affair in South Korea took place as early as 1964. Fictional works have been intermittently written, translated, and made into films for the general public ever since.[7] Internationally, the best known is perhaps the documentary trilogy on Korean ex-comfort women directed by Byun Young-joo and produced in the 1990s: *The Murmuring* (*Najŭn moksori,* 1995), *Habitual Sadness: Korean Comfort Women Today* (*Najŭn moksori II,* 1997), and *My Own Breathing* (*Najŭn moksori III,* 1999).[8] The trilogy spurred discussions of Korean and Japanese representations of the comfort women issue (or lack thereof) ever since. Little scholarly attention, however, has been paid to Chinese representations of comfort women, which have long featured in popular culture, appearing in historical docudramas, sexploitation films, and even television miniseries.

As one of the first representations of comfort women in Chinese popular culture, the Shaw Brothers' *Bamboo House of Dolls* (*Nü jizhongying,* 1972) straddles the fine line between sexploitation and melodrama, shouldering the historical and commercial mission of revealing Japanese war crimes for all to reproach publicly but also to savor privately. In the film, the traditional image of the comfort woman is evoked, but viewers quickly realize that it is a narrative that shifts notions of victimhood and wrestles with audience expectations. The film portrays a Chinese and American sisterhood. Through a complex staging of ethnic performance, the film curiously diverts trauma from the Chinese body onto the foreign characters. Moreover, the film's hypersexualized composition conjures sensual pleasure from the very site of historical trauma. As eroticism is smuggled in through the façade of historical exposé, similarly sensual depictions of comfort women continue in later productions such as *Military Comfort Women* (*Junji wei'anfu,* 1992), which ended up being distributed in Hong Kong as sexploitation, a genre that could be grouped under the more general title of category III films in Hong Kong's ranking system. In it, the comfort woman becomes cultural currency, performing not only Hong Kong's imaginations of a Chinese past but also the region's own cultural negotiation between ethics and economy, as well as patriotism and commerce. Because Hong Kong was not formally involved in the recruitment of comfort women, general audiences' tolerance for such sexualized representations might seem less surprising. However, in mainland China, where not only were women recruited but comfort stations were located, similarly sexploitative portrayals were allowed, even promoted, under the banner of patriotic education beginning in the early 1990s.

As Takashi Yoshida states, in the wake of the Tian'anmen Square incident in 1989, the Chinese Communist Party (CCP) deployed Pacific War history as a source of patriotic education, broadcasting the horror of Japanese aggression through mass media so to unite national sentiment behind it.[9] Docudramas on comfort women such as *Unit 731 Comfort Women* (*731 junji,* 1992) and *The 74th Comfort Women Team* (*Wei'anfu qishisi fendui,* 1994) thus can be seen as a part of this wider post-Tian'anmen media blitz focused on exposing Japanese war crimes, with the Nanjing Massacre, Japan's Unit 731 (which conducted covert biological and chemical warfare research), and comfort women as its most popular subjects. It was at this time that the first television miniseries on comfort women, *Imperial Comfort Women* (*Diguo junji,* 1995), was broadcast as part of commemorating the fiftieth anniversary of China's victory in the Anti-Japanese War. Reframed within a Chinese patriotic narrative, the comfort woman figure serves as testimony to the Chinese people's overcoming of Japanese imperialist aggression by standing united. Moreover, the comfort women's real-life struggle with the Japanese government during the textbook debates in the mid-1990s also reflects the looming threat of Japanese aggression in the miniseries' contemporary, warning the public of the rebirth of Japanese militarism and the need for the Chinese people to unite yet again. The bodies of comfort women, in other words, are evoked so to be recruited once again to negotiate between competing political desires at a time of rising nationalism in both China and Japan.

Although the often sensationalized and politicized depictions of comfort women might be precisely what prevented these Chinese-language productions from being discussed seriously, they can serve as resourceful archives not necessarily for recovering the real historical trauma from the past but for tracing how filmic projections of comfort women have become a means of negotiating the political terrain of the present. By delineating the travails and transformations of comfort women in popular culture, we see how they morph into cultural signifiers and take on lives of their own. Not to trivialize the importance of recovering the women's traumatic realities during the Pacific War, popular representations of comfort women resemble a genealogy in itself, serving different functions at disparate historical moments. In what follows, I focus on two texts, starting with a close reading of *Bamboo House of Dolls,* one of the first Chinese-language films on the subject, and ending with a discussion of the television miniseries *Imperial Comfort Women.* Oscillating between their role as historical figures and cultural symbols, these comfort women negotiate between competing imaginations of not only Pacific War history but also cross-cultural relations in the works' contemporary—projecting public affairs on the political stage and private desires on the silver screen.

Embodying the Unutterable: *Bamboo House of Dolls*

Released in Hong Kong in 1973, the Shaw Brothers' *Bamboo House of Dolls* is one of the first films to bring the issue of the comfort women into the mainstream. By this time, the Hong Kong–Singapore–based Shaw Brothers Studio had already created an extensive business network, transforming itself into a transnational film empire second only to Hollywood in the number of films produced. Many scholars, such as Poshek Fu, argue that the Shaw Brothers' success lies in the construction of a "Chinese dream"—a film fantasy that recreates an alternative "Chinese" world, which alludes to yet side-steps realities in the Chinese nation-state at a time of a large increase in Chinese diasporic communities.[10] The height of the Shaw empire, the 1950s to the 1980s, was a time of great contention in the geopolitical realm—a time of exile across the Taiwan Strait, the Pearl River, the Pacific, and beyond. It was also a time of rising global entanglement through the increasing pace and permeability of transnational information and economic exchange. As Siu Leung Li argues, the power of creating this "Chinese dream" resides in "its being a cultural sign, a semiotic commodity that could circulate and be re-imagined across boundaries quickly and with ease."[11] This is especially interesting when we consider that these fantasies were not only marketed to a diasporic Chinese community but also used to achieve global visibility.

The Shaw Brothers continually entered their films into international film festivals, enthusiastically competing with the thriving Japanese film industry in the hope of taking the prize for representing the "true Orient."[12] They were also eager to compete with mainstream markets in Europe and the United States for a share of the global market.[13] Produced in the early 1970s during the height of the Shaw Brothers' empire, *Bamboo House of Dolls* is one of the studio's first attempts to tap the global market. The film tells the story of five women, two Chinese and three American Red Cross nurses, who are abducted by Japanese troops and held at a comfort station, depicting their sisterhood and their various attempts to escape together. Not only was the story scripted around a transnational group of characters but the cast and crew came from over seven different countries.[14] The transnational nature of the issue of comfort women, as a historical trauma shared by women from various nations and ethnicities, was used as a way of attracting an international audience.

Creating some controversy, the film was marketed as part of the Shaw Brothers' growing catalog of *yanqing pian* (erotica).[15] In the early 1970s, Hong Kong experienced a large influx of European and American erotica, which had great success at the box office, a success that the Shaw Brothers were quick to emulate. As Hao Wu notes, when these films were first produced by the Shaw Brothers, many Hong Kong actresses were less willing to engage in such blatant sexual performance; therefore *yanqing* productions at the time often starred foreign actresses.[16] *Bamboo House of Dolls*, for instance, cast Birte Tove in the leading role. Tove was a Danish actress who had starred in the Shaw Brothers' early sexploitation film, *Sexy Girls of Denmark* (*Dan Ma jiaowa*, 1973). In addition to indicating the Shaw Brothers' attempt at globalization, the international staff also reflects the studio's domestic venture of introducing the *yanqing* genre to Chinese or, more precisely, sinophone audiences.[17]

This introduction of the *yanqing* genre, however, did not involve blatant displays. *Bamboo House of Dolls* was publicized as a film that would reveal a historical secret that "will not only entertain the audience but also stimulate condemning sentiments toward war."[18] The film shoulders both the historical mission of exposé and the commercial duty of sexual display. It straddles sexploitation and melodrama, mainstream commercial film and hard-core stag reel, entertainment and education, history and fiction. Like the comfort women it portrays, the film enacts, as it negotiates between, various historical and sexual desires. This gives rise to a number of questions: How is the historical issue of comfort women reimagined and transformed? What kind of historical retelling is enabled or obscured through the sensationalized lens of a sexploitation film? What kind of "Chinese dream" or, in this case, "nightmare" is the Shaw Brothers portraying? These questions drive us to take a closer look at the film.

The film opens with the heroines, mirroring the Chinese nation-state, being invaded by the Japanese and abducted from their private quarters. Hong Yulan, a Chinese revolutionary, is knocked unconscious and taken away by Japanese soldiers after witnessing her husband's murder in their house. The three Red Cross nurses meet a similarly violent fate, being kidnapped after the Japanese forcibly take over their hospital. Torn from their domestic spheres, they are in turn displaced within the spatial imaginary of a comfort station "somewhere in China." Confined within this ambiguously located camp, the women form an alternative sisterhood built not on blood or nationality but shared trauma, forging a new affiliation through a shared moment of injustice. We see a transnational sisterhood constructed amid the debris of an invaded Chinese nation-state. It is interesting, however, that at the center of the tale is a Chinese-American sisterhood. There is no historical evidence that American Red Cross nurses were abducted and sent to comfort stations, so the inclusion in the film of an American element to share and witness this historical trauma is scripted.[19] This scripted sisterhood, thus, pushes the narrative farther away from historical reality and into the realm of constructed fantasy.

Moreover, according to Tanaka, the Japanese authorities were reluctant to use Chinese comfort women due to fear of not only exacerbating anti-Japanese sentiments but also espionage, thus more than 80 percent of the women at the comfort stations were Korean.[20] The film, however, not only avoids the inclusion of Korean characters but features Korean actresses in the role of Chinese comfort women. If we read this casting of nationalities as the Shaw Brothers' publicized performance meant for an international stage, the film offers much more than mere fantasy. These Korean bodies can be seen as carrying the potential of "passing" as Chinese, yet providing the sinophone viewers with some ethnic distance between the naked Korean actresses' bodies and the historical bodies of Chinese comfort women. In addition to distancing the historical trauma from the sinophone audience, this play on nationalities can be also read as a performance of political power.

The Japanese officers in the film, for instance, are all played by male Chinese actors. The only female Chinese body is that of the actress Terry Liu (Liu Huiru), who portrays a lesbian Japanese officer named Mako, who not only oversees the heroines but even rapes one of the American nurses. Though she has a female body, Liu performs an "artificial masculinity" as she straps on her secretly kept dildo. This Chinese-impersonating-a-Japanese officer plays the penetrator, not the penetrated. As such, the violence is not only guarded from but, in turn, inflicted by the actual Chinese body. Power, in other words, is reclaimed from the Japanese through a Chinese performance. China's political power hijacked by the Japanese during the Asia-Pacific War in historical reality is thus regained, even if artificially, by a Chinese embodiment in this filmic fantasy. Negotiating between a historical event and a reconstructed fantasy, the film seemingly evokes the rape metaphor often used to describe China's victimized status in the face of the Japanese invasion, yet deflects it from the Chinese body and onto an American imaginary. This refraction of power can be read as not only reclaiming power from the Japanese from the past but claiming power over the desired powerful in the present—the white or, more specifically, American body.

This desire to penetrate the American body can be clearly seen in the way that the camera's sexual focus is predominantly the American nurses while the Chinese (in this case, Korean-impersonating-Chinese) characters receive much less attention. In the opening scene, for instance, when the heroines are abducted, not only are the nurses' uniforms ripped open, so that their bras and underpants are exposed, but the frame freezes for a few seconds to linger on their exposed breasts, legs, and buttocks.

By contrast, the Chinese heroine, Hong Yulan, is fully clothed and merely knocked unconscious. During a scene in which the women are taking a bath, a full two minutes of screen time is devoted to soft-focus shots of the three nurses playfully washing one another, while a mere two seconds are spent showing a few unknown Asian faces. With cheerful music in the background, the camera teasingly pans up and down the nurses' wet bodies, moving from one sensationalized close-up to the next.

While the American nurses perform the film's more sexual scenes, the Chinese characters are given the virtuous task to act the dual role of a revo-

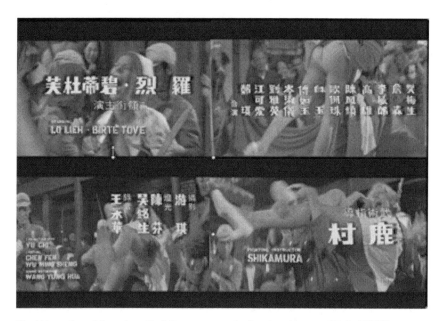

The kidnapping of American Red Cross nurses in *Bamboo House of Dolls* (1972)

lutionary victim. This double standard, between the American and Chinese characters, is portrayed most clearly in their varied rape scenes. Hong Yulan is framed as unwaveringly steadfast; even while she is being molested by a Japanese soldier, she holds her hands stiffly held to the side, with her eyes wide open as if she were a corpse. Her unbending body ultimately makes the Japanese aggressor lose interest, slapping her on the face in frustration. In this scene, the chastity of the Chinese body is maintained but its victimized status remains. Rejected by the patriotic Chinese revolutionary, this Japanese soldier displaces his desire onto a drugged American nurse laying naked, having just been sexually violated by another Japanese soldier, in the next room. Wriggling on the floor, the nurse stretches her arms open wide as the sexually frustrated Japanese soldier charges toward her, for her first aggressor's masculinity was seemingly insufficient to satisfy her. By depicting the previous Japanese aggressor as impotent, the film makes fun of Japanese masculinity even at the moment of its intended climax of abusive power.

Here, we again see sexual pleasure being stirred at the site of historical trauma, in this case the rape scene, yet it is deflected from the Chinese body only to be fulfilled by American ones. It is almost as if the Shaw Brothers are remaking their own team of comfort women, this time to serve the voyeuristic pleasures of a sinophone audience. With their filmic reframing, they recruit international bodies to satisfy the audience's desires while also secretly safeguarding the virtue of the "Chinese" body on the screen, hiding even their impersonating "double" (the Korean-impersonating-Chinese characters) from sexual projections. Through the Shaw Brothers' narrative of American characters, moreover, what is performed in its place also seems to be a desire for the American body, a desire to penetrate it, and, in turn, win over its allegiance. This is demonstrated, for instance, in the relationship between Jennifer, the head Red Cross nurse, and Cai Guodong, an undercover Chinese agent.

On a dark and stormy night, Cai secretly invites Jennifer to come to his room to tell her about Hong Yulan's true identity—she is the widow of a Chinese army officer who had recovered gold stolen by the Japanese. Just before he died, the officer managed to stash the gold and reveal its hiding place to her, yet, due to the Japanese soldiers' abuse, she is suffering from partial amnesia and needs protection in order to recover her memory. Cai ends this tale by telling Jennifer that all Chinese are patriotic and that she, too, should join their cause. His patriotic fervor is matched not only by Jennifer's political aspirations but also by personal desire. As soon as he finishes his tale, she blows out the candle and gives herself to him, showing that Chinese masculinity, along with national resilience, is strong.

Jennifer extends her newfound allegiance to the Chinese cause to her fellow Red Cross nurses, who prove their loyalty by sacrificing their lives for the sake of protecting Hong Yulan. Although Hong can be read as a stand-in for the national Chinese body, literally embodying the memory of "Chineseness" in a crisis (her amnesia being a consequence of Japanese aggression), her protection hints at a reconstructive dream of a Chinese future. In this case, what is reconstructed, rather than the actual history of these women, is perhaps an alternative vision targeted at a diasporic audience distanced from the reality of mainland China and in search of the recovery of a partially forgotten "Chineseness."

As the film puts Hong Yulan's amnesia front and center, on the one hand, it exposes the ambivalence involved in the remembering of historical atrocities, and, on the other hand, it points to the necessity of this ambivalence in articulating such a remembrance. Just as Hong is protected from her Japanese aggressors by her Chinese and American compatriots due to her amnesia, the film's own "partial reality" also retains a necessary distance to address this historical event. Like the Korean actress, who provides enough distance for the sinophone audience to revisit this historical trauma and, at the same time, displays enough ambiguity to "pass" as "authentic" (authentic in her Chinese resemblance but also in Korean women's authentic place in the real history of comfort women), the film's hypersexualized form might also be interpreted as a strategy for distancing its representation from historical reality. This foreign enactment (foreign in terms of the film's actresses as well as its form as a sexploitation production) allows for the partial recovery of public memory, which might provide enough distance for the historical event to be safely articulated.

At the same time, however, this lofty Chinese dream is tied to the pursuit of material goods, in the form of gold bars. The film's ultimate object of desire is not the heroines' bodies but gold. Here, historical justice has a material value, which hints at the economic, political, and ethical transactions involved in the Shaw Brothers' historical display. In the narrative, the gold is taken from the Chinese by the Japanese, but with the help of Hong Yulan's American compatriots, it is finally recovered by the Chinese to fund a Chinese future. This gold, thus, actualizes the Shaw Brothers' own historical project of reclaiming power from the Japanese through a reinvention of this

historical event using the historical figure of comfort women, in turn promoting a "Chinese dream" before an international audience.

Moreover, gold is a value that is physically exchanged. This physical
trading of value also works as a metaphor for the transformations of political
value physically transacted in the film's staging of nationalities. The political
power that was seemingly taken away from the Chinese by the Japanese in
historical reality is now physically recovered and re-embodied in a Chinese
performance of Japanese aggression. The site of aggression is, furthermore,
transformed into a Chinese-American alliance, displaying power dynamics
not necessarily of a historical past but of a politics of desire (desire for American allegiance, penetration of American power, and the desirable American
body) in the present.

To take this metaphor of gold a bit further *Bamboo House of Dolls*, being filmed as an erotic production, is itself also a blatant attempt to exchange
the trauma of the past for "box-office gold." It is an exchange that opens up
new ethical questions concerning the issue of comfort women. The hypersexualized framing of the film extends the historical victimization of comfort women into a new realm of media exploitation. Competing with the
Japanese film industry to reach European and American audiences at this
time, the Shaw Brothers' erotica proved one of the most profitable genres in
a Euro-American dominated marketplace. As Jasper Sharp notes, Japanese
films attained particular success in the West because of their exportation of
"Oriental allure."[21] Marketed as an erotic film that paints the Japanese as
not only undesirable but brutal, *Bamboo House of Dolls* seemingly reclaims
the profitable imagination of "Oriental allure" in the Shaw Brothers' pursuit of European and American currency.

Through the Shaw Brothers' *yanqing* reimagining of the comfort
women issue, what is consumed is a simulation of history marketed to
excite, an affective history dramatized for cultural-nationalist and economic gains. In this way, the bodies of these comfort women are recruited
once again to stimulate the consumption of the Shaw empire's "Chinese
dream," intended for a hypothetical international audience but marketed to
its loyal sinophone consumers. The film not only exposes the ambivalence
involved in, and perhaps necessary for, the remembering of historical atrocities; but also capitalizes on this very ambivalence to smuggle in political
and personal desires beyond, if not around, that of recovering historical
testimonies.

Serving Empire(s)?: Imperial Comfort Women

Moving from the first Chinese-language filmic representation to the first Chinese-language television miniseries devoted to the comfort women issue, I now turn to *Imperial Comfort Women*. The series was released in 1995, when the issue of comfort women had already been fought over fervently on the international stage. The year also marked the fiftieth anniversary of China's victory in the Second Sino-Japanese War, a perfect opportunity for the CCP to promote loyalty to a generation that never experienced Pacific War atrocities—a generation that just a few years earlier held so-called counterrevolutionary riots in Tian'anmen Square. As Yoshida shows, in the wake of the Tian'anmen Square incident, government leaders embarked on a campaign for patriotic education, teaching this restless generation that history has shown the need to move beyond domestic quarrels and point their spears at the true threat, imperialism.[22]

Perhaps to make this official rhetoric convincing, *Imperial Comfort Women* stresses the authenticity of its historical portrayal. The series was promoted as "a true exposé" of wartime secrets. Actual wartime documentary footage is sprinkled throughout, serving as a constant reminder of the story's legitimacy. Carrying the banner of historical reality, it is framed, however, within a Chinese patriotic narrative, giving rise to questions such as: what kinds of "truths" are allowed to circulate in the name of patriotic education? How are comfort women deployed in constructing these truths? And how might such a reimagining reflect the CCP's vision of itself and its place in the global community?

Imperial Comfort Women tells the story of a pan-Asian sisterhood of comfort women abducted from Japan, China, and Korea. Unlike in the Shaw Brothers' production, these transnational comfort women were all played by Chinese actresses. The spotlight, however, is on the Japanese comfort women, reframing the tale as a Chinese performance of a particularly Japanese trauma. The Japanese characters are depicted as undergoing a negotiation between personal desires and state ideologies. Kayo, a young Japanese nurse duped into becoming a comfort woman, is at first convinced by the military's official rhetoric—that she is devoting her body to serving her country, just as any soldier would. Ironically, after she contracts tuberculosis, she is denied medical treatment precisely because she is not considered, ultimately, a soldier. As she lies in quarantine in a deserted mountain cave, her most faithful customer (a soldier) storms in. Like her, he is seriously wounded and on the verge of death. As they lie shoulder to shoulder, as though comrades, they take their last moments to reflect on their loyalty to the emperor:

> *Soldier:* I'm here to see you, daughter of our holy emperor.
> *Kayo:* No, I am no imperial daughter; my name is Kayo. I've actually never even seen the emperor.
> *Soldier:* I have never seen the emperor either, yet we still fight for him. . . .
> *Kayo:* What is your name, soldier?
> *Soldier:* ggg . . .

Before he can utter his name, both fall to their death. With their last breath, the two characters aim to reclaim their individual identities from that of merely being the emperor's sons and daughters, struggling to spell out the tragedy of their perhaps blind loyalty to the throne.

While the criticism of the Japanese empire might seem ambivalent in this death scene, it is clear in the demise of the main character, Yōko. Also a Japanese nurse, Yōko goes to China to look for her brother and for her fiancé, Yagi, on the front lines. After being coerced into sexual slavery, she cries:

> I must tell my brother and Yagi what has happened to me. I must show them the true colors of the imperial army they are so proud of . . . then, I will ask them if this holy war they've embarked on is truly that holy.

Disillusioned by her nation's betrayal, she escapes from her captors and sets off on a sacred expedition to warn her family of the empire's brutality. However, she ends up being raped unwittingly by the very brother and fiancé for whom she has been searching. After they realize what has happened, the three are shocked beyond words. Yagi, therefore, takes Yōko's dagger and stabs himself to death. Almost immediately, the brother and Yōko follows his lead and commit suicide. Their tragic deaths seem to question the legitimacy of the empire for which they should supposedly be dying. By taking their lives from the imperial battlefield back into their own hands, they are choosing personal attachments over national allegiance. Here, the narrative distinguishes between the Japanese masses and the Japanese empire, indicating that the Japanese people are also victims of the empire's aggression. This theme is widely seen early in the war in anti-Japanese Chinese visual art, such as the cartoons of Zhang Ding and Cai Ruohong.[23] Yet even decades after the war, such distinctions, which place the blame on Japan's militaristic few, continued and were even further highlighted and implemented by the communist government.

As Yoshida observes, this distinction between the Japanese empire and Japan's masses has been a popular one in discussing Japanese aggression during the Pacific War, especially after 1972, when the Japanese government normalized diplomatic relations with the PRC and recognized its rulers as China's sole legitimate government. This diplomatic rhetoric can be seen, for instance, in an editorial in the state-run newspaper, *Renmin ribao* (People's Daily), published in 1972:

> Diplomatic normalization between China and Japan has finally been accomplished, as the result of long-term efforts by both the Chinese and Japanese peoples. Both the Chinese and Japanese peoples have been connected by a long history of friendship. In the past, the intrusion of Japanese militarists into China brought tremendous sufferings not only to the Chinese people, but also to the Japanese people. *The Chinese people respect the teaching of Mao Zedong, which strictly distinguishes a majority of the Japanese people from a handful of militarists and which extends deep sympathies for suffering inflicted on the Japanese people.* Since the establishment of our nation, we have cultivated friendly relations with the Japanese people, which the Japanese people have always desired friendship with the Chinese people.[24]

In this way, the government is smoothing over anti-Japanese sentiments to advance diplomatic relationships that the PRC needed for international recognition. Thus, in the surge of anti-imperialist patriotic education in the 1990s, the state had to play a delicate balancing act between maintaining diplomatic ties to secure its place in the international political arena and invoking Japanese imperialism as a threat to unify domestic public opinion.

This negotiation between diplomacy and provocation is most thoroughly played out through the Chinese comfort woman turned martyr, Liuyin. Liuyin and her little sister Liushu were abducted and sent to a comfort station after being orphaned by war. While Liushu eventually dies after being gang raped, Liuyin in turn kills Japanese soldiers in retribution. The Japanese army eventually captures her but only to find that she has gone mad. At the end, she is sentenced to be burned to death, despite the Japanese comfort women's struggle to save her. Stressing this pan-Asian sisterhood, the program shows the familiar diplomatic distinction between sympathetic Japanese masses and the brutal militaristic few. What is perhaps new is the complex depiction of martyrdom. At Liuyin's execution, the military officer proclaims:

> This Chinese woman that stands before you is the imperial army's com-
> fort woman. She embodies our Japanese soldiers' passion. Through her
> body, many soldiers who fell on the frontlines have gained the energy to
> fight on. Yet, since now she dares to point her gun at the Imperial Japa-
> nese Army, she has therefore become our enemy. . . . In order to make
> her a Chinese martyr, we will burn her to death with this fire. This fire
> will thus represent the Japanese army's respect and hatred of her.

The speech displays how competing political desires negotiate Liuyin's death. Recognizing her physical labor as a comfort woman, the narrative maintains the officer's respectability rather than setting him up as the easy villain. However, by glossing over the fact that she was coerced into service and punishing her for aggressive behavior, the program creates tension because of what is left unsaid. By granting her the title of a Chinese martyr, the Japanese officer seems dignified enough to give her a glorious end yet vicious enough to inspire protest. Her martyred body becomes a testimony to Japanese atrocities and calls for the Chinese people to sacrifice themselves, as she did, to unite and avenge such brutalities. Like the fire that makes her into a Chinese martyr, Liuyin's death embodies the Chinese state's necessary performance of respect and hatred in order to maintain diplomatic relations with Japan while stirring up nationalistic unity against it.

This nationalistic martyrdom, however, is imposed on Liuyin, rather than being claimed by her. When she killed, she killed to avenge what was done to her and her pan-Asian sisters. Not once did she mention the Chinese people. Because she has descended into madness when she is declared a Chinese martyr, what the viewers see is not her heroic declaration of patriotism but, rather, her inability, because of her madness, to have a voice. Her being called a "Chinese martyr" at her death highlights the gaps between her personal aims and the political rhetoric appropriating them. This discrepancy between personal and political desires illuminated by Liuyin's death brings up a pivotal question: As a miniseries broadcasted in the mid-1990s—a time when increasing numbers of Chinese urbanites had their own television set, and when information from various corners of the world not only clamored but are often desired by Chinese viewers—how effective would such patriotic education be?

Mayfair Yang argues that because of the growth of new media in China since the late 1980s and early 1990s, information is no longer merely given to the masses from a centralized source but allowed to flow in and from various directions.[25] Domestically produced dramas compete with programs imported from Taiwan, Hong Kong, the United States, Korea, and Japan. Not only does television broadcasting allow for the decentralization of information but such information is allowed to follow the patterns of personal and private relations, not necessarily along the politically governed boundaries of the communist state. One, thus, has the liberty to "debate, mock or reject the messages with one's family and friends . . . reducing the capacity for state media to sustain state subjects."[26] Yang suggests that the proliferation of new media, unlike state-monitored venues, allows information to be received more privately, either in the comfort of one's own living room or through personal networks.

Yang's argument shows intensifying rifts and negotiations between China's communist state ideology and personal sentiments rising alongside the escalation of new media during the post-Mao era.[27] This negotiation can be seen in the later distributions of *Imperial Comfort Women,* most commonly in the form of DVDs and online downloading. The more popular version of the DVD cover exhibits a collage of erotic images not found in the series itself, with contemporary pornographic still shots displayed over a backdrop of wartime images, provoking desires beyond patriotic sentiment. Categorized under *lunli dianying* (ethical film) on the popular online downloading site Xunlei Movies, the series has a tagline, however, describing it as an "explosive sensual depiction of beautiful women in concentration camps, [and] she is now yours."[28] Personal fulfillment, as demonstrated here, has become a central focus in this patriotic miniseries' afterlife in the virtual world. The series serves not necessarily state rhetoric but personal or, literally, physical desire. The comfort women, moreover, are not even addressed as such. They become ambiguous objects of desire. Their politically and historically marked bodies are here glossed over, being seen as "beautiful women of war" who can quench physical needs.

As the characters in the narrative leave the filmic world questioning their own relationship to the Japanese empire they serve, the miniseries' own afterlife, perpetuated by DVD sales and the Internet, questions the utility of the CCP's patriotic education. *Black Sun: The Nanjing Massacre (Hei tai-*

yang: Nanjing datusha, 1995), also released in 1995 to correspond with the fiftieth anniversary of China's victory in the Second Sino-Japanese War, had a similar fate. As Michael Berry notes, on the one hand, the film has been circulated as serious documentation on the Nanjing Massacre, as it is included in a boxed set titled *Can Japan Say No to the Truth?* distributed by the Alliance in Memory of Victims of the Nanjing Massacre (AMVNM).[29] On the other hand, it has also been widely available on the Internet, gaining an international cult following as a B-rated horror movie.[30] In other words, *Imperial Comfort Women*'s seemingly irreconcilable identities as nationalistic propaganda and transnational cult favorite are not uncommon. These films' redistribution navigates between the national and transnational, as well as the historical and the fantastic.

Thus, in *Imperial Comfort Women,* like Liuyin, who is silenced as an individual but whose death is appropriated as a symbol, the comfort women is evoked to serve political and personal ends in the present. Distributed at a post-Mao moment in Chinese history in which state ideology is constantly in tension with that of personal consumption, the image of the comfort woman negotiates not only between Sino-Japanese relations but also the tension between deterritorializing flows of mass media and the CCP's territorializing control over state allegiance.

Conclusion

This chapter focuses on two particular moments when comfort women emerged in Chinese-language cultural production, first in Hong Kong in the 1970s and then in the PRC in the 1990s.[31] Instead of recovering historical reality or reclaiming political agency for the actual wartime victims, I map out the wider political and ideological structures through which these women are represented and, in turn, re-present. The figure of the comfort woman carries historical and political weight that crosses regions (from Hong Kong to the PRC to overseas Chinese), media forms and genres (from film to television, from sexploitation to propaganda), and time periods. As such, the figure of the comfort woman and her reemergence in the cultural imaginary can be seen as constituting, in and of itself, a genealogy or what Michel Foucault calls "history of the present."[32]

The genealogy traced here, through these two popular reincarnations of the comfort women figure, oscillates between historical reality and cultural imaginary. Much like the comfort women in reality, the represented figure accommodates between public and private desires. According to official Japanese rhetoric, the comfort stations were a form of preventive state intervention, providing a clearly demarcated site for sexual activity in the hope that they would thwart cases of rape and, consequently, quell anti-Japanese sentiments in China during the war. The comfort stations were state-sponsored systems set up to publicly accommodate (and, in turn, cover up) the Japanese soldiers' most private, more specifically, sexual, desires.

Mirroring this oscillation between publicity and privacy that the issue of comfort women illuminates, the Shaw Brothers' *Bamboo House of Dolls* publicized the subject in the name of exposing historical war crimes to an international public. Behind this allegedly international mission, however, rests also this private company's task to market a shared "Chinese dream" to a particular cold war–era sinophone community outside of communist China. Moreover, by shooting the film as an internationally cast sexploitation production, the Shaw Brothers portrayed the comfort women characters as not only sexually but nationally marked, promoting a patriotic rewriting of this historical event. The film simulates the historical trauma of wartime victims, restaging it from a comfortable distance (whether via the sexploitation genre or the foreign impersonated bodies) so to serve its audiences' private desires (be it ethno-centric pride or personal sexual desires).

A similar negotiation between state-sponsored patriotic education and its private appropriation in new media plays out in *Imperial Comfort Women*. First televised as a part of the CCP's post-Tian'anmen media blitz of patriotic education, the miniseries demonstrates a balancing act between maintaining diplomatic ties with the Japanese government to secure its place in the international political arena, and invoking Japanese imperialism as a threat to unify domestic public opinion. However, the historically and politically marked comfort women in the series, after circulating in the unruly worlds of online downloading and transnational DVD distribution, are frequently consumed as sexual bodies that stimulate its viewers' personal, and often physical, desires. The comfort women represented navigate international relations and domestic governance as well as state ideology and personal fulfillment in post-Mao China. These are public and private negotiations not so different from the oscillating tensions played out with the establishment of comfort women systems in historical reality.

In this chapter I focus on the first filmic and television representations of comfort women in mainstream Chinese-language popular culture, regarding them as vanguards for discussions of the comfort woman issue in different media. Based on the limited number of works discussed here, much more is yet to be said on the topic. These two works are still popularly circulated, in their commemorative DVD re-releases, at cult film festivals, or online. Since the original release of these works, moreover, representations of comfort women have continued to emerge in the Chinese-language world in documentaries such as *Ama's Secret—Stories of Taiwanese Comfort Women* (*Ama de mimi—Taiji wei'anfu de gushi*, 1998), and feature films such as *731 Horrific Female Experiments* (*731 kongbu nüti shiyan,* 2008). This chapter thus hopes to initiate conversation on not only the need to reveal the myths behind these historical figures, but also the ongoing myth-making process in which imaginations of comfort women are evoked to accommodate desires for the past and the present.

Notes

1 Toshiyuki Tanaka, *Japan's Comfort Women: Sexual Slavery and Prostitution during World War II and the U.S. Occupation* (New York: Routledge, 2002), 3.

2 The total number of wartime comfort women has been long disputed. For more concerning the politics behind the question of numbers, see Chunghee Sarah Soh, *The Comfort Women: Sexual Violence and Postcolonial Memory in Korea and Japan* (Chicago: University of Chicago Press, 2008), 23–24.

3 Ibid., 33.

4 George Hicks notes that although these Asia-wide organizations seem to have gained support by their respective governments, due to the fact that many of these countries are dependent on Japan for aid and investment, such support can be less than wholehearted. See George Hicks, *The Comfort Women: Japan's Brutal Regime of Enforced Prostitution in the Second World War* (New York: W. W. Norton, 1995), 11.

5 For more concerning why survivors and supporters questioned the Japanese government's public apology, see Hye Jean Chung, "Reclamation of Voice: The Joint Authorship in the Murmuring Trilogy," in *Documentary Testimonies: Global Archives of Suffering,* ed. Bhaskar Sarkar and Janet Walker (New York: Routledge, 2009).

6 Soh, *The Comfort Women*, 68.

7 Popular representations include Senda Kakō', *Jūngun Ianfu* (Military Comfort Women) (Tokyo: San'ichi Shobō, 1973); Kim Il-myŏn's *Tennō no Guntai Chōsenjin Ianfu* (The Emperor's Forces and Korean Comfort Women) (Tokyo: San'ichi Shobō, 1976); and Yoshida Seiji's two confessional books—*Chōsenjin Ianfu to Nihinjin* (Korean Comfort Women and the Japanese) (Tokyo: Shinjinbutsuōraisha, 1977) and *Watashi no Sensō Hanzai* (My

War Crimes) (Tokyo: San'ichi Shobō, 1983). For more detailed discussion of popular representations of the comfort women issue, in both Japan and South Korea, see Soh, *The Comfort Women,* chap. 4.

8   The trilogy has won the Ogawa Shinsuke Award at the 1995 Yamagata International Documentary Film Festival in Japan, and the 1996 Film Critics' Special Award in Korea.

9   Takashi Yoshida, *The Making of the "Rape of Nanking": History and Memory in Japan, China, and the United States* (New York: Oxford University Press, 2006).

10 Poshek Fu, "Introduction: The Shaw Brothers Diasporic Cinema," in *China Forever: The Shaw Brothers and Diasporic Cinema*, ed. Poshek Fu (Urbana: University of Illinois Press, 2008).

11 Siu Leung Li, "Embracing Glocalization and Hong Kong-Made Musical Film," in ibid., 77.

12 As Fu states, the Shaw Brothers argued that "because the origin of Eastern civilization was in China . . . Chinese cinema should reach out to the audience as the purest and most authentic representation of 'Oriental flavor'" (*China Forever*, 9).

13 In Fu's introduction to *China Forever*, he talks about how Run Run Shaw, at a press conference in the early 1960s, stated that he would work with Western film studios on an "equal basis" as a way to "declare the entry of the Chinese cinema" into the global community of national cinemas (ibid., 9).

14 Even before the film was in theaters it was publicized as being the Shaw Brothers' most promising "international production." As in an interview in the magazine *Xianggang Yinghua* (Hong Kong Cinema), the director Kuei Chih-hun asserts that "he will try hard not to forsake the Shaw Brothers' faith in him to produce a truly 'international' film." See Wu Hao, *Disan leixing dianying* (Shaw Film Series: The Alternative Cult Films) (Hong Kong: Celestial Pictures Limited, 2004), 101.

15 For more on the Shaw Brothers' *yanqing* genre, see Lily Wong, "Sinophone Erotohistories: The Shaw Brothers' Queering of a Transforming 'Chinese Dream' in Ainu Fantasies," in *Queer Sinophone Cultures*, ed. Howard Chiang and Ari Larissa Heinrich (New York: Routledge, 2014), 84–101.

16 Wu, *Shaw Films,* 101.

17 Here, I borrow the term "sinophone" from Shih Shu-mei, as "a network of places of cultural production outside China and on the margins of China and Chineseness, where a historical process of heterogenizing and localizing of continental Chinese culture has been taking place for several centuries." See Shu-mei Shih, *Visuality and Identity: Sinophone Articulations across the Pacific* (Berkeley: University of California Press, 2007), 4.

18 Wu, *Shaw Film* Series, 101.

19 While the film's inclusion of American characters might seem to be due to its international casting, none of the actresses were in fact American but Danish, British, and Korean.

20 Tanaka, *Japan's Comfort Women.*

21 As Jasper Sharp notes, the allure of the Orient has been a crucial selling point for Western arthouse releases from *Rashomon* and *Ugetsu* onward. From as early as 1965, a whole host of Japanese erotica were being sold to territories as diverse as the United States, Canada, West Germany, Holland, Italy, Spain, and beyond. For more on this subject, see *Behind the Pink Curtain: The Complete History of Japanese Sex Cinema* (Surrey, UK: FAB Press, 2008), 177–201.

22 Yoshida, *The Making of the "Rape of Nanking."*

23 For more discussion on works that demonized the Japanese military and painted ordinary citizens as victims, see Chang-tai Hung, *War and Popular Culture: Resistance in Modern China, 1937–1945* (Berkeley: University of California Press, 1994), 93–150.

24 Yoshida, *The Making of the "Rape of Nanking,"* 103, emphasis added.

25 Mayfair Yang, "Mass Media and Transnational Subjectivity in Shanghai: Notes on (Re)cosmopolitanism in a Chinese Metropolis," in *Undergrounded Empires: The Cultural Politics of Modern Chinese Transnationalism*, ed. Aihwa Ong and Donald Nonini (New York: Routledge, 1997).

26 Ibid., 294.

27 This argument would perhaps be complicated if we take into account China's large population without access to new media and the fact that China has one of the most sophisticated and ambitious government-based censorship programs. Thus, state power, though allowing more space for decentered information to flow, is still quite present.

28 http://www.wo25.cn/movie/lunli/info-428.html, accessed June 21, 2010.

29 Michael Berry, *A History of Pain: Trauma in Modern Chinese Literature and Film* (New York: Columbia University Press, 2008), 128.

30 For more on *Black Sun's* dual life as political propaganda and cult phenomenon, see ibid, 123–126.

31 I have left out Taiwanese representations of the comfort women issue due to its relatively low visibility in popular media. Discussing the reasons for this would require a lengthy study of Taiwan's colonial past and identity politics in the present. The comfort women issue has, however, been stirred up in Taiwan again since the translation of Kobayashi Yoshinori's controversial *Taiwan lun: Xin ao gu jing shen* (On Taiwan) (Taipei: Qianwei chubanshe, 2001) hit the shelves in 2001, claiming that Taiwanese women became

comfort women voluntarily. Books have thus been appearing in reaction to the controversy, such as Sheng-mei Ma, *Chenmo de shanghen: Rijun weianfu lishi yingxiang shu* (Silent Scars: History of Sexual Slavery by the Japanese Military—A Pictorial Book) (Taipei: Shang Zhou Press, 2005); and Zhu Deilan, *Taiwan wei'anfu* (Taiwan Comfort Women) (Taipei: Wunan, 2009).

32 Foucault discusses distinctions between what he regards as mainstream historiography and what he calls "history of the present," in his *Discipline and Punish: The Death of the Prison* (New York: Vintage Books, 1995).

CHAPTER 8

Shooting the Enemy

Photographic Attachment in *The Children of Huang Shi* and *Scarlet Rose*

Michael Berry

Photography plays a looming role in contemporary atrocity cinema, the portrayal of the photojournalist Richard Boyle (portrayed by James Woods) in Oliver Stone's *Salvador* (1986) and the trio of journalists depicted in Roland Joffé's *The Killing Fields* (1984) being examples from American and British cinema. The camera often stands as a silent chronicler of history; in other cases, the camera-as-witness provides moral censure in the face of devastation and suffering; and sometimes the camera doubles for the cinematic gaze of the filmmaker in his own quest to build meaning from fractured histories and broken lives. Nowhere is the trope of photography as central as in the ever-expanding body of films and television productions depicting the Nanjing Massacre (1937). Many of the details surrounding the historical event have been strongly debated and challenged over time. The complexities of historical interpretation have inspired Takashi Yoshida's fascinating monograph *The Making of the "Rape of Nanking,"*[1] which probes the ideo logical battles waged over the event's history in China, Japan, and the United States. The tensions playing out over any number of the sensitive issues associated with the Nanjing Massacre, Japanese denial, the comfort women issue, death toll controversies, allegations of feigned "evidence," and so on have all made their way into the body of films made about the massacre. Each work, in its own way, attempts to navigate through these issues and offer its own form of cinematic testimony to that horrific page in modern Chinese history.

With some notable exceptions, the major film and television works depicting the Nanjing Massacre all emphasize the place of photography and, often, filmmaking. The camera is not simply featured as a background prop in these texts but often becomes a central device to frame narratives, drive plots, and attempt to make broader claims about the complex historical discourse surrounding the events that broke out on December 13, 1937, in the ancient capital once known as Jinling. The way in which the camera's role has been repeatedly highlighted has not escaped the notice of scholars such as Robert Chi, whose Ph.D. dissertation, "Picture Perfect: Narrating Public Memory in Twentieth-Century China,"[2] offers an illuminating exploration of this relationship. My current study borrows from and expands upon my own earlier exploration of the Nanjing Massacre in fiction, film, and popular culture,[3] isolating the trope of photography as it appears in two Nanjing Massacre visual texts, the 2008 co-production *The Children of Huang Shi* (*Huangshi de haizi*/*Huangshi renwu*) and the 2007 Chinese television miniseries *Scarlet Rose: The Goddesses of Jinling* (*Xuese meigui: Jinling nüshen*).

In the first mainland Chinese feature film that directly depicts the 1937 atrocities, *Massacre in Nanjing* (*Tucheng xuezheng*, 1987), not only was the place of photography highlighted but the central plot revolved a set of atrocity photographs taken by a Japanese soldier, developed by a Chinese photo studio, and circulated among characters who are attempting to preserve the "evidence" (*zheng*, referred to in the film's title in Chinese). Aside from the photos that serve as the chief "prop" to tie together various plotlines, the "photographic evidence" is also the underlying ideological imperative for the film to highlight historical atrocity in the face of Japanese denial. Elsewhere in the plot, *Massacre in Nanjing* employs photography and photographic tropes as an allegorical tool. One such example occurs when old photos of a Chinese prisoner and a Japanese officer from the prewar years, when they were lovers in Harbin, are suppressed, thus signaling the dissolution of Sino-Japanese friendship. Or another more disturbing example in which the owner of the Chinese photo studio who first developed the central set of atrocity photos encounters the Japanese photographer who took the photos. Concealing a blade in his sleeve, the Chinese studio owner coaxes the photographer to approach him so closely so he can slice his eyeball, rendering the "human lens" behind the disturbing atrocity photos permanently disfigured and broken.

The prominence of photography in *Massacre in Nanjing* seemed to set the tone for future films about the 1937 Nanjing atrocities. In 1995, the

Hong Kong–based filmmaker T.F. Mou (Mou Dunfei) directed the single most violent (and, in many ways, exploitative) film version, *Black Sun: The Nanjing Massacre* (*Hei taiyang: Nanjing datusha*, 1995). In this loosely structured film, a bloody chronicle of rape, torture, murder, and mass execution is strung together with a series of historically authentic black and white photos. Images of each photo appear on screen for a few seconds after narrative sections in which the moments leading up to the one in which the photos were taken are recreated in a shocking manner. Then, a decade later, in 2005 the film *Qixia Temple 1937* (*Qixia si 1937*), directed by Zhang Fangnan, featured a plot that revolved around a set of newsreels capturing Japanese atrocities in Nanjing taken by a Universal Studios filmmaker from the United States. In a storyline highly derivative of *Massacre in Nanjing*, the photographic—in this case, newsreel—evidence again circulates among several characters who preserve it for the world to see. I would even go so far as to argue that Lu Chuan's award-winning film *City of Life and Death* (*Nanjing! Nanjing!*, 2009) continued this trope less for actual plot and prop elements concerning film and photography (which were still in place albeit somewhat less central) than through the film's very cinematography, art design, and *mis-en-scène*, which adopted a black and white realism that was inspired and often mimicked actual documentary photos from the period. In *City of Life and Death*, we have a case in which a film is not so much *borrowing* photography as a prop or plot device as it is *becoming* photography as a process; in this sense the film itself performs the role of photographic evidence.[4]

These examples are not meant to represent a comprehensive history of Nanjing Massacre cinema, but they indicate that the trope of photography has loomed large in this series of films. The reasons for this "photographic attachment" is complex but can certainly be explained in part by such factors as repeated denials by Japanese politicians (from the former Tokyo mayor Ishihara Shintarō's infamous 1990 *Playboy* interview to the Nagoya mayor Kawamura Takashi's February 2012 comments to a Chinese delegation)[5], repeated visits by Japanese officials to the Yasukuni shrine, where Class-A war criminals from the Second Sino-Japanese War are interred, and ongoing controversies surrounding the narrative of the war in Japanese textbooks. At the same time, occasional acts that do not "deny" wartime atrocities but seem to "celebrate" them (e.g., manga that glorify wartime atrocities and a 2003 scandal in Zhuhai, China, in which 400 Japanese sex tourists paid for the services of hundreds of Chinese sex workers on the anniversary of the Mukden Incident) have further inflamed memories of the Nanjing Massacre, along with the general state of Sino-Japanese relations. As I have argued elsewhere,[6] this complex psychology of denial in Japan has, to a great degree, shaped and dictated China's overdetermined drive to "authenticate" and "prove" that the atrocities occurred. In the realm of Nanjing Massacre cinema, the trope of photography has emerged as the single most powerful tool used to this end. However, during China's "Olympic era," of the first decade of the twenty-first century as the nation geared up to host the 2008 Olympic Games and began to expand its use of "soft power," one can observe a shift in the role of photography in Nanjing Massacre films and other media. The remainder of this chapter is devoted to teasing out this transformation in *The Children of Huang Shi* and the popular Chinese television miniseries *Scarlet Rose: The Goddesses of Jinling,* each of which takes visual discourse of the Nanjing Massacre to unexpected new terrain.

Photographic Attachments in *The Children of Huang Shi*

In 2007 and 2008, in the months leading up to the Beijing Olympics, a new series of films and documentaries probing the Nanjing Massacre were produced, each of which pushed the cultural discourse in fascinating new directions. Thirteen years after the Fifth-Generation filmmaker Wu Ziniu directed *Don't Cry, Nanking* (*Nanjing 1937,* 2005), which drew on talent from Hong Kong, Taiwan, and the mainland, marked the first pan-Chinese film production about the event, *The Children of Huang Shi* marks the first truly transnational co-production to deal with the atrocities. Directed by Roger Spottiswoode, a Canadian with strong Hollywood ties who is perhaps best known for helming the 1997 James Bond film *Tomorrow Never Dies,* the film was billed as an Australian/Chinese/German co-production. The multinational crew included Chinese talent, such as the cinematographer Zhao Xiaoding (*House of Flying Daggers*), and the cast paired British and Australian actors such as Jonathan Rhys-Meyers (*Match Point*) and Radha Mitchell (*Silent Hill*) with the Asian superstars Chow Yun-Fat (*Crouching Tiger, Hidden Dragon*) and Michelle Yeoh (*Tomorrow Never Dies*). Produced within a year of Bill Guttentag and Dan Sturman's documentary *Nanking, Children of Huang Shi* signals a newfound interest in the Nanjing Massacre by the international filmmaking community.[7] Although the transnational origins of *Children of Huang Shi* seem to indicate a possible unburdening of the photographic attachments so implicit in Chinese representations, the camera's gaze proves difficult to escape.

The film functions as a biopic centering on the life of George Hogg (1914–1945), an Oxford graduate who went to China in 1938 and ended up remaining there for the next seven years, until his death from tetanus. He worked as a freelance journalist for the Associated Press but was best known for his work with the New Zealander communist activist Rewi Alley (1897–1987).[8] Together with Alley, Hogg ran a boys school and, when the school was threatened by the Japanese, led the boys on a 600-mile march to safety in Gansu Province. Spottiswoode's film adaptation opens in 1938 with Hogg (portrayed by Jonathan Rhys-Meyers) already in Shanghai and working as a photojournalist. Hogg's photographic attachments are highlighted from the beginning of the film, and one of the very first sequences features him photographing images of missing children posted on a street corner there.

The sequence is important for introducing not only the trope of photography but also for highlighting the plight of missing children—which foreshadows Hogg's later work running a school and saving Chinese orphans from the Japanese. But this sequence also displays a tension between the role of the photographer to objectively document and report and the tragic faces of the orphaned children, silently beckoning him to do more than simply document.

Hogg is eager to find a way into the sealed city of Nanjing to document the atrocities taking place there. Appropriating the identity of a Red Cross aid worker (another hint of the protagonist's later activist identity), Hogg, along with two fellow photographers, manage to sneak into the city. Hogg and his colleagues leap out of their truck the moment they come through the city gate and begin snapping images of the carnage and devastation that surrounds them.

After they are inside the city, the photographers split up, and Hogg soon stumbles upon a mass execution in progress, which he proceeds to capture on film. The images he shoots appear as black and white freeze frames in the narrative, much in the style of *Black Sun* (which used actual historical photos). Hogg, hiding in the shadows of a bombed-out building, takes his photos from an elevated vantage point, which seems to indicate a moral distance between his objective stance as a recorder of history and the crowds of perpetrators and victims huddled below. At this stage in the film, the photographic narrative seems to be unabashedly driven by the same politics of photographic testimony seen in films like *Massacre in Nanjing* and *Black Sun,* both of which are structured around photographic images. This, however, changes a few scenes later, when Hogg is surrounded by a battalion of Japanese troops who arrest him and confiscate his camera. The final display of Hogg's photos comes as he is being interrogated by a Japanese officer, who pursues the visual records of violence before ordering Hogg's execution. Here we are presented with a curious reversal, in which the photos meant to provide "evidence" for Japanese wartime atrocities are reappropriated by the Japanese military, which now uses them as "evidence" of Hogg's "crimes."

Hogg is dragged out of the makeshift Japanese headquarters where he was interrogated to face immediate execution. But just as he is to be decapitated, shots ring out from the periphery, we are given a close up of the executioner's samurai sword as it falls to the ground, and viewers are introduced to Jack Chen (portrayed by Chow Yun-Fat), a Chinese resister, who saves the British photographer from certain death. This moment marks a crucial turning point in the narrative, signaling the forcible end of Hogg's role as someone who is simply *documenting* history to someone who is *participating* in history. The shedding of photographic attachments is felt even more palpably a few scenes later, when Hogg and Chen witness the execution of Hogg's former colleagues, Eddie Wei (portrayed by Ping Su) and Barnes (portrayed by David Wenham)—the only other two photographers who managed to get into Nanjing to document the violence.

In the rest of the film, the imperative to *document* atrocity through photography is replaced with various strategies to *resist* atrocity. These strategies are enacted by different characters, each of which represents a different mode of resistance or activism. There is the American nurse Lee Pearson (portrayed by Radha Mitchell), who helps run a school for orphans and goes to great

Japanese office reviewing the "evidence" of George Hogg's camera and photos (left) and a close-up of one of Hogg's photos (right)

lengths to attain medicine and food to help those affected by the calamities.[9] Jack Chen turns out to be a communist guerrilla fighter who continues to carry out armed resistance even during the massacre. And then there is Hogg himself, who engages in passive resistance through education and eventually through the historic journey that leads the orphans to safety away from the Japanese. Coinciding with this transition is the end of the role of photography in the story, so central in earlier visual representations. After Hogg's camera and photos are confiscated and his fellow photographers are murdered, photographic discourse effectively drops out of the film. Replacing the image as forensic evidence of historical events is an ethical discourse in which the former photographer is compelled to participate.

In the rest of the film, the phantom of photography returns in only one sequence but in a context of reversal that forces Hogg into a renewed moral predicament. When a few Japanese soldiers isolated from their battalion come across Hogg, Chen, and the children, who are hiding in an abandoned building, they end up being taken prisoner. Hogg insists that the Japanese be spared; however, just before the group continues its journey to Gansu, a rebellious student, Shi Kai (portrayed by Guang Li), secretly kills them. Upon discovering the corpses, Hogg takes particular notice of a dead soldier clasping a photograph in his hand.

The photograph in question shows the dead soldier's family back home in Japan, probably taken just before his deployment to China. This image represents the antithesis of the photos displayed earlier. Whereas Hogg's photos of missing children and Chinese being slaughtered at the hands of Japanese swords and machine guns—all images of fractured families, violence, and pain—the image the Japanese soldier clasps in his death grip presents a complete family portrait of unity and strength. The formal components of the images also display a violent rift between the Chinese subjects caught in a natural state of distress by Hogg's camera and the highly staged Japanese studio portrait in which the subjects stare directly into the camera. Although these formal differences in staging, lighting, and engagement with the camera could be interpreted as hinting at a staged or empty quality surrounding the latter image, that is certainly not Hogg's reaction when he discovers the crinkled photo.

After Hogg finds the dead Japanese soldiers, the further discovery of this lone photograph exacerbates his shock, anger, and outrage at the perceived injustice. The image of the Japanese family seems to highlight their humanity and the loss that they, too, will suffer. As a photographer, Hogg feels an attachment to the photo that seems to momentarily redeem the power of the image, which had been lost with his confiscated camera. Instead, when an incensed Hogg confronts Shi Kai with this visual reminder of humanity, the boy simply tears the photo in two and discards it. Now that Hogg's own earlier images have been denied display, the narrative projects that same desire to deny the power of photography on to this newly discovered image. In the language of the film, Hogg's new visual attachment appears as a form of misrecognition that is ultimately overturned. This visual negation of the image is yet another reversal from earlier in the film, when the Japanese confiscated images of Chinese atrocities; now, a Chinese character similarly is negating any semblance of Japanese humanity. This second negation not only functions on a retributive level but also seems to strengthen the abandonment of the photographic image in favor of a more activist mode for coping with atrocity. Indeed, unlike earlier films in the spirit of Luo Guanqun's *Massacre in Nanjing,* this film demonstrates no further drive to preserve, display, and circulate photographic images of atrocity. Instead, Chen, who recruits the increasingly militant Shi Kai, heads to Yan'an, the early headquarters of the Chinese Communist Party, where he will deepen his struggle to resist the Japanese, and Hogg continues his journey to Gansu to establish a new school in an abandoned temple and devotes the remainder of his short life to the boys. Only at the conclusion of the film, as the credits roll, does the film reaffirm the power of historical testimony as it presents a new form of "photographic evidence" via filmed interviews with the actual students at the school, now octogenarians, who reminisce about the real Hogg.

Remaking History in *Scarlet Rose*

The implicit activism in *Children of Huang Shi* was pushed even further in the 2007 television miniseries *Scarlet Rose: The Goddesses of Jinling,* in which this revolutionary impulse is not only amplified but re-integrated, with a new twist on the photographic attachment seen in earlier films. *Scarlet Rose* hit major Chinese television markets in conjunction with the seventieth anniversary of the event and continued to run throughout 2008. It was directed by Yu Liqing, a television director active since the late 1990s, who has helmed more than a half dozen miniseries, and produced in collaboration with four media investment companies. While the series falls short in terms of production values, when looked at in conjunction with earlier visual representations of the Nanjing Massacre, *Scarlet Rose* is groundbreaking on several fronts. As a series of new films about the event, such as Zhang Yimou's *Flowers of War* (*Jinling shisan chai*) were just going into production, Yu's drama can be seen as an attempt to present the 1937 trauma in a way that both borrows from earlier tropes of representation and, at the same time, offers new possibilities for representing historical violence.

Beginning with the dedication "In Memory of the Seventieth Anniversary of the Nanjing Massacre," set against flames before segueing into vintage documentary film footage of the Japanese invasion of the city, the opening sequence of *Scarlet Rose* bears a striking resemblance to the films examined earlier, such as *Massacre in Nanjing* and *Black Sun*. Here the documentary footage is accompanied by a voiceover narrative that objectively relates details of the invasion and subsequent massacre. These documentary film methods begin the series with a detached forensic display of historical events, which help establish the validity of the narrative and historical truth behind the events depicted after the story proper begins.

In the first of the twenty-six episodes,[10] however, it quickly becomes clear that Yu's version of the story differs from that of traditional Nanjing Massacre narratives. The episode begins with a series of murders, but the victims are not the Chinese residents of Nanjing; they are the Japanese terrorizers. One after another, Japanese bodies turn up: solders, officers, and a Japanese arms dealer—each body left with the mysterious mark of a playing card with the image of a Greek-style goddess wielding a sword and the words *Jinling nüshen* (goddess of Jinling). Gradually, it is revealed to the viewer that it is actually a series of goddesses, five women vigilantes, who are responsible for the series of bloody attacks carried out against the Japanese. The women come from a variety of social groups, including a former prostitute, a Daoist nun, and the daughter of a famous martial artist. What brings them together is their common victimization (either personal or familial) at the hands of the Japanese. Also displayed through their unity is the transformative power of victimization as they overcome social and moral restrictions—a prostitute can become a martyr, a nun can commit murder—all in the name of national salvation.

The story then follows the women as they infiltrate various levels of the Japanese military in occupied Nanjing, striking fear in the hearts of the would-be-colonizers. During their nighttime assaults on the Japanese, the goddesses of Jinling display their martial arts skills, embellishing the series with dozens of highly coordinated fight sequences that employ *Crouching Tiger, Hidden Dragon*–style wirework to simulate flight and other superhuman

Fateful calling cards of the "goddess of Jinling" (left) and the Five Goddesses of Jinling taking an oath of sisterhood (right)

skills. *Scarlet Rose* is intent on displaying content and form that bend the realist conventions that dominated earlier portrayals of the Nanjing Massacre. What emerges is a reimagination of the generic limitations on Chinese-language atrocity cinema, from earlier docudramas with a strong emphasis on historical evidence to a new vision that incorporates martial arts choreography and action and spy genres. As demonstrated below, the series also incorporates more complex and elaborate plot twists that have become emblematic of contemporary mainland Chinese television drama, even borrowing tropes from the socialist realist tradition and revolutionary model operas.

The girls not only rely on incredible physical prowess as they leap from rooftop to rooftop but also often wear a variety of costumes and disguises à la *Charlie's Angels,* alternately dressing (or cross-dressing) as Japanese soldiers, police officers, housewives, high-society men, and prostitutes to carry out their missions of revenge. It is the guise of the prostitute that deserves a closer look, not only because it is among their most frequently used disguises while exacting revenge but also because of the inversion of their codename *nüshen* (goddess) to *shennü,* a common term for a prostitute during the Republican era (1911–1949). It is precisely this dual identity as goddess/prostitute that enables the team to carry out their revenge.

The women chose their targets carefully, getting them drunk with alcohol before finally slaughtering them. Whereas Chinese historiography (along with earlier representations) of the Nanjing Massacre highlights the widespread murders and rapes committed by the Japanese during their six-week siege of the city, here we are presented with a curious reversal. Not only

The *shennü* seducing the enemy in *Scarlet Rose* (2007)

are the vast majority of murders and deaths depicted in the series those of Japanese soldiers and officers but even the widespread violation of women that earned the event the name as the "Rape of Nanjing" is inverted, with the goddesses of Jinling visually simulating a rape of the Japanese. One sequence even shows one of the girls straddling the half-naked body of a Japanese officer as she repeatedly "penetrates" him with her dagger.

When coupled with the startling number of murders carried out by the group, the series of symbolic rapes they commit seem to be a direct challenge to the massive numbers of actual rapes committed by the Japanese military. The often cited (but also disputed) numbers—six weeks, 20,000 rapes, 300,000 murders—which have become such an iconic component of national memory, are never mentioned in this production; rather, the producers seem intent on using their goddesses of Jinling to reverse the long-standing notion of Chinese victimization, which haunted so many earlier representations. Not content with simply inverting the rapes and murders, the series even introduces its own new numbers game. In one sequence, the leader of the goddesses, Ximen Piaoxue, is at her desk diligently writing. When one of the other girls asks what she is doing, Ximen replies, "I'm doing the bookkeeping. . . . The Japs killed twenty-eight in my family, six in your family, that comes to thirty-four. We must make them pay with their blood; we make them pay ten times over, a hundred times over!" Thus, the numbers of Chinese victims are referenced only to illustrate the much higher Japanese death toll to come, further inverting the trope of victimization. Even the name of the city is inverted, with "Nanjing" almost never spoken in the miniseries; instead the city is consistently referred to as Jinling, its poetic classical name. Thus, the miniseries wipes clean the myriad associations with the "city of massacre," replacing them with a new romanticized vision of the city's past.

The murder and "rape" of Japanese soldiers by the goddesses of Jinling disguised as prostitutes

The politics of historical reversal are perhaps best demonstrated by one of the major plotlines stretching over several episodes, which reintroduce the notion of photographic attachment. One of the most infamous and frequently cited incidents that occurred in the days leading up to the Nanjing Massacre involves a killing contest between Mukai Toshiaki and Noda Tsuyoshi. The competition, which played out as their battalions marched toward Nanjing, was initially to decide who would be the first to cut down a hundred Chinese using a samurai sword. The contest was reported in the mainstream Japanese press as if it were a sporting event, allegedly to increase excitement and patriotic support over the war effort. The newspapers *Osaka Mainichi Shimbun* and *Tokyo Nichi Nichi Shimbun* ran four articles on the contest between November 30, 1937, and December 13, 1937, with the target numbers of deaths eventually increased to 150 after the two soldiers could not determine who had reached 100 first. The horrific nature of the contest was surpassed after December 13, when the army arrived in Nanjing and atrocities commenced on a much larger scale. However, because of the media attention generated by the contest, it was cited in the International Military Tribunal for the Far East (Tokyo War Crimes Trial), held after the war, from 1946 to 1948. Having been convicted of committing war crimes, Mukai and Noda were extradited to China, where they were executed in Nanjing on January 28, 1948.[11]

But *Scarlet Rose* presents an alternate ending to the killing contest between Mukai Toshiaki and Noda Tsuyoshi. In what becomes one of the most significant subplots in the series, the goddesses read about the killing contest in a Japanese newspaper and decide to take it upon themselves to kill the killers. They first disguise themselves as Japanese troops to infiltrate a military compound one night. Then they murder more than a dozen Japa-

The historical Mukai Toshiaki and Noda Tsuyoshi in history (left) and in fiction (right)

nese, but the two men whom they believed were Mukai and Noda were, in fact, decoys. The two are under special protection as Japanese national heroes, so getting to them proves increasingly difficult. Eventually, the goddesses don their prostitute garb in a second attempt to assassinate the Japanese soldiers; however, just as they are on the point of doing in the unsuspecting victims, they are interrupted, when their superior officer summons them. It eventually becomes clear that the real contest is not between the two Japanese soldiers (who are never seen killing Chinese) but between the goddesses of Jinling as they track their subjects down. The game of decapitating Chinese civilians has been reframed, with Mukai and Noda as the prey.

On their third attempt, the goddesses finally succeed in finding the elusive Japanese soldiers and they accomplish this through an unlikely method. The Japanese photojournalist Kojima Kawao is sent by the *Kochi Shinbun* to cover the killing contest. The goddesses kidnap Kojima and, using the knowledge that his wife has been kidnapped by the Japanese army to serve as a comfort woman to ensure his loyalty, eventually convince him to lead them to Mukai and Noda. With the photographer's help, the girls lure the two soldiers into the open and spray them with bullets. In the immediate aftermath of the execution, Kojima takes his own life for having betrayed his country. The fascinating and sometimes self-contradictory layers of meaning projected onto photography and how it ties into the revisionist interpretation of this historical contest drives us to reconsider the function of photography in Nanjing Massacre texts. Whereas in earlier films about the event the photograph was almost always equated with evidence of historical victimization, bringing history into the realm of chronicle, *Scarlet Rose* uses a much bolder strategy of considering photos as a means of *remaking history*.

By taking a historical event with a known outcome (the soldiers were executed in 1948), *Scarlet Rose* uses photography as an entry point to revisit the incident and rewrite the outcome, exacting a more severe and more immediate judgment upon the perpetrators. At the same time, the narrative displaces the violence the Japanese participants in the killing contest committed with an extended campaign of violence and punishment against the Japanese. In the process, the photographer, the creator of the original image of violence, is transformed into the instrument the girls use to exact their revenge. The very Japanese photographer who produced one of the most inflammatory press images of Nanjing Massacre—an image that has gone on to wield great symbolic power in the Chinese nation's collective memory of Japanese wartime atrocities—here proves instrumental in aiding the goddesses to carry out their (fictional) execution of Mukai and Noda. Along the way, the goddesses of Jinling produce their own trail of photographic evidence to counter the Japanese discourse that relegates the Chinese to victimhood.

If we compare the newspaper report and photo reporting the goddesses of Jinling's assassination of a Japanese arms dealer to the original image of the Japanese soldiers' killing contest, we can see the politics of reversal at play. This reversal is perhaps demonstrated most clearly by the relative absence of depictions of Japanese crimes in the series, which are inferred but

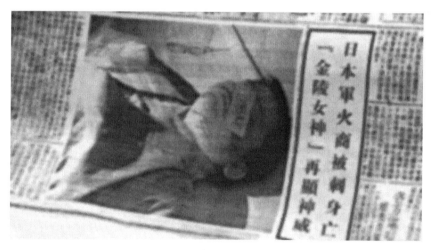

Newspaper report covering the goddesses of Jinling's assassination of a Japanese arms dealer

often not displayed, in favor of extended sequences in which the goddesses take revenge on the enemy.[12] In *Scarlet Rose,* historical figures and incidents are cited and "photographic evidence" is employed collectively not to substantiate history but to produce a new historical reimagination that topples notions of Chinese victimization and passivity.

Over the course of the series, the goddesses of Jinling carry out a series of secret missions, most of which are intricately tied to key aspects of wartime atrocities, including an assignment to find and destroy a secret stockpile of biological weapons. But most relevant for the current study is a mission to recover three reels of film shot by an American cameraman documenting atrocities committed by the Japanese. Like the killing contest subplot, this is inspired by the true story of the American missionary John Magee (1884–1953), who shot six reels of film. The film was smuggled out of China in 1938 by his fellow missionary George Fitch (1883–1979), who eventually showed the films to the media in the United States at a series of public lectures as well as for the House Foreign Affairs Committee. Variations of this story have inspired similar plot lines in several Nanjing Massacre films, including *Massacre in Nanjing* and *Qixia Temple 1937,* but here the story is embellished even further, as it falls to the goddesses of Jinling to find the lost film and deliver it to another American in Shanghai.

This segment, which proves to be the single most substantial subplot in the series, includes four separate screenings of the film reels, first in flashback, as a priest views the footage with a mixture of shock and sadness. Later, as the Japanese try to confiscate the film, we are privy to a "pseudo-screening" in which the original reels are switched with reels from old Hollywood films, so the Japanese end up watching musicals and romances. The switch not only protects the "evidence" from falling into Japanese hands but effectively denies the Japanese access to this archive of victimization. Only after much sacrifice do the goddesses of Jinling finally view the film, providing further justification for their larger mission of revenge. By the time the reels are finally handed over to the American representative in Shanghai, the screening is replaced with a detached documentary-style voiceover, identical to the voice that began the series, and the footage shown is that of the Tokyo War Crimes Trial. The narration declares:

> After the victory of the Second World War against fascism, these three reels of film were sent to the International War Tribunal, where Japanese war criminals were being tried. There [the film] provided the most

tangible and powerful proof in condemning Japan's militarists who had
created this horrific tragedy known as the Nanjing Massacre. And with
the help of this film, the leaders of the Japanese armed forces were sent
to the gallows.

In reality, even Magee's six reels of film, which were the inspiration for this
portion of the film, though submitted, were never actually shown at the trial.
Like the depiction of the killing contest, we are once again presented with
a tension between actual historical film footage and documentary film techniques used within a pseudo-historical narrative that embellishes reality with
techniques borrowed from spy thrillers and martial arts fantasies and, even
more remarkable, "red classics," those iconic socialist texts from the golden
age of Chinese communism.

Yu Liqing's production of *Scarlet Rose* proves revolutionary in more ways
than one. The series not only conjures up photographic memories of the massacre but also taps into another series of memories of iconic images from
socialist China, many of which might seem irreconcilable with the history
of the Nanjing Massacre. Early in the series, as the goddesses begin to attract media coverage for their exploits against the Japanese, their activities
also gain the attention of secret agents working in Nanjing for both the Nationalists and the communists. After several successful missions working
alone, the goddesses of Jinling eventually decide to join the Chinese Communist Party's (CCP's) underground guerrilla movement. The goddesses are
recruited into the ranks of the CCP by Ji Hongtao, a character introduced
early in the series who turns out to be a high-ranking underground communist officer. The visual and narrative modes chosen to relate the history
of the girls' integration into the CCP borrows heavily from the story of Wu
Qinghua in the classic revolutionary ballet and, later, film *The Red Detachment of Women* (*Hongse niangzi jun,* 1961), from the presence of the good
communist officer masquerading as the enemy who "liberates" the girls (in
Scarlet Rose, there are two such officers) to the participation at a rural training camp in an idyllic setting and ultimately the trope of revolutionary martyrdom. In one key speech to the girls, comrade Ji Hongtao explains:

> Today I'm going to explain what it means to "do battle for the nation's
> people." . . . All of you are aware [of what hatred is]. The five of you all
> carry deep personal hatred. And so why did we save you? What did we
> bring you together for? . . . Each of you has hatred, but your hatred is

individual hatred—we must transform this individual hatred into national hatred. Bringing you together is so that you can "do battle for the nation's people" and defeat the Japanese!

The speech is almost identical to one that Hong Changqing delivers in *The Red Detachment of Women,* in which he urges Wu to let go of her personal vendetta against the landlord who exploited her in favor of a broad national vision in which the collective comes first. These tropes not only run throughout the narrative but also can be seen in the visual strategies employed in the transformation of the goddesses of Jinling from a vindictive group of individuals to good communist soldiers.

The series of stills indicate that even in terms of art design, costumes, and framing of various scenes, *The Red Detachment of Women* is very much

Bound in chains: *Scarlet Rose* (2007) (left) and *The Red Detachment of Women* (1961) (right)

Educating the women soldiers: *Scarlet Rose* (2007) (left) and *The Red Detachment of Women* (1961) (right)

Cadre instruction: *Scarlet Rose* (2007) (left) and *The Red Detachment of Women* (1961) (right)

the urtext for the large narrative arc in *Scarlet Rose* that traces the ideological development of this new group of female soldiers. The numerous references to stances, poses, and images from *The Red Detachment of Women* represent a different mode of "photographic memory," tapping into collective visual memories from the socialist realist tradition and model operas. Although the intertextual relationship between these works is certainly interesting, even more fascinating is the added layer of historical tension this intertextual intervention introduces when we juxtapose this communist enlightenment story with the history of the Nanjing Massacre. The event is traditionally regarded in mainland Chinese historiography as a distinctly Nationalist failure, and very little communist activity took place in Nanjing after the fall of the city. *The Red Detachment of Women,* by contrast, not only tells the tale of one woman's journey from slave to member of the CCP but often is read as a chronicle of revolutionary history. By borrowing the rhetoric, narrative structure, and iconography from this communist classic, *Scarlet Rose* effectively attempts to reintegrate this great (fictional) struggle against the Japanese that took place during the Nanjing Massacre into Chinese communist history.

More than any previous visual text depicting the Nanjing Massacre, *Scarlet Rose* is a hybrid, combining historical docudrama with martial arts fantasy, spy thriller, and, of course, communist history as recounted in the canonical "red classics." As obscene as the textual and generic interbreeding may be, *Scarlet Rose* marks a true breakthrough in terms of visual representations of the Nanjing Massacre, which for the first time is unburdened from the generic limitations present in so many earlier works. But does this signal a fundamental change in the cultural policies dictating such representations in China? On the one hand, the shedding of the image of China as the passive victim as seen in earlier Nanjing Massacre films can be taken as a sign of the confident, and perhaps even aggressive, China in 2008. This is the "China that can say no," the China of skyscraper skylines, and an Olympian metropolis. But that bold new nation is not content merely to recreate its future but also wishes to rewrite its past. Perhaps in the twenty-first century, China's national identity is contingent upon a renegotiation of those stained pages in its inglorious history. This China is reinventing its past in order to help forge a bold new vision for its future. But we should bear in mind that this obsession with a painful past (since *Scarlet Rose* premiered in 2007, there have been two additional feature length narrative films, a major television miniseries about the massacre adapted from the same source material as *Flowers of War*, and even a 2012 follow-up series also directed by Yu Liqing entitled *Scarlet Rose: Special Female Commando Unit* [*Xuese meigui zhi nüzi biedongdui*], in addition to numerous documentary films and television specials) is an ironic reminder of the extent to which historical trauma and memories of national victimization still weigh on the collective soul of the country. And while certain aspects of the official party line are still being toed, seventy years after the massacre and a full twenty years after the first feature film representation, the forces in control of the politics of representation have dramatically shifted. Unlike 1987's *Massacre in Nanjing,* which was produced by a single state-run film studio, *Scarlet Rose* was produced by a conglomerate of four privately held companies whose primary loyalty is not to the party line but to profit margins. The new market economy dictates that historical drama "entertain the people," marrying martial arts sequences borrowed from *Crouching Tiger* with Shanghai political intrigue reminiscent of *Lust, Caution,*[13] within a fascinating amalgamation that straddles competing entertainment genres while never letting go of the historical obsessions of earlier Nanjing Massacre films. The contradictions that arise in this textual Frankenstein, which internally touts lofty visions of socialist sacrifice while unabashedly drawing on popular commercial genres to please audiences and consumers, opens a new chapter in visual representations of the Nanjing Massacre. At the same time, we should not forget the traumatic ghosts lurking behind a narrative that is detached from the realistic tradition. Often a literal representation of traumatic events is simply too difficult to face, requiring a distance between the event and the version that can be narrated, or what Wendy Hesford has called "bodily pain and trauma tellable."[14] In *Scarlet Rose* the murders and the rapes so deeply embedded in the memory of the Nanjing Massacre have been thoroughly inverted, reversed, and reimagined within a matrix of martial arts and socialist realist fantasy. Perhaps the very vehicle for this radical restaging—that is the form itself, which seems far removed from our "historical understanding" of the Nanjing Massacre—is in fact the lingering specter of a traumatic past too horrific to face.

Notes

1 Takashi Yoshida, *The Making of the "Rape of Nanking": History and Memory in Japan, China, and the United States* (New York: Oxford University Press, 2006).

2 Robert Yee-sin Chi, "Picture Perfect: Narrating Public Memory in Twentieth-Century China" (Ph.D. diss., Harvard University, 2001).

3 Michael Berry, *A History of Pain: Trauma in Modern Chinese Literature and Film* (New York: Columbia University Press, 2008).

4 For more on this topic, see my article, "Scorched Earth: Why *City of Life and Death*'s Treatment of the Nanking Massacre Ignited Controversy in China," *Film Comment* (May/June 2011).

5 In a 1990 interview with *Playboy* magazine, Tokyo mayor Ishihara Shintarō made a series of highly controversial comments that questioned the legitimacy of the Nanjing Massacre and incited widespread anger and protests among Chinese citizens. Among his comments, Ishihara stated: "People say that the Japanese made a holocaust but that is not true. It is a story made up by the Chinese. It has tarnished the image of Japan, but it is a lie." On February 20, 2012, the Nagoya mayor Kawamura Takashi expressed doubt that Japanese troops had massacred civilians in Nanjing to a visiting delegation of officials from China. These are but two of the higher profile instances of denial on the part of Japanese politicians.

6 Berry, *History of Pain*.

7 It should be noted that these are but the first wave in a series of multinational film productions on the massacre, which include a German biopic *John Rabe* (2009, directed by Florian Gallenberger) and a Hollywood production titled *Iris Chang: The Rape of Nanjing* (2007, directed by Anne Pick and William Spahic).

8 Rewi Alley was written out of the film, a decision that elicited much criticism from critics and historians; see, for instance, Paul Byrnes, "Children of the Silk Road," *Sydney Morning Herald*, July 3, 2008, http://www.smh.com.au/news/film-reviews/children-of-the-silk-road/2008/07/03/1214950902051.html.

9   The character of Lee Pearson is actually based loosely on the historical figure
     Kathleen Hall, a New Zealander nurse who worked closely with Rewi Alley
     to aid Chinese children during this period.

10   In some Chinese markets, the series was apparently edited into thirty-four
     shorter episodes.

11   Since their death, there has been lingering controversy surrounding the
     Mukai and Noda's killing contest. In recent years, Bob Wakabayashi has
     claimed the contest was fabricated, and a defamation suit was brought to
     court in 2003 by the soldiers' families further claiming the entire incident
     was a fabrication. The case was thrown out in 2005 after a judge ruled the
     statute of limitations had expired and, further, there was no way to prove for
     certain whether the incident occurred. On the fabrication claim, see Bob
     Tadashi Wakabayashi, "The Nanking 100-Man Killing Contest Debate:
     War Guilt amid Fabricated Illusions, 1971–75," Journal of Japanese Studies
     26, no. 2 (2000): 307–340.

12   There are, of course, numerous murders and rapes that the Japanese
     committed over the course of the twenty-six episodes; these sequences,
     however, still pale in comparison to the violence committed by the
     goddesses. Even when two of the goddesses die, it is not as a "victim" of the
     Japanese but in a grand act of revolutionary martyrdom—they strap
     dynamite to their own bodies in the spirit of communist heroes like Dong
     Cunrui and Ji Guanglei to blow up the enemy and destroy the secret
     stockpile of biological weapons.

13   During one sequence, when the girls go to Shanghai to deliver the three reels
     of film, the tone of the series shifts to a spy thriller with costumes, sets, and
     scenarios highly reminiscent of Ang Lee's 2006 film.

14   Wendy S. Hesford, "Reading Rape Stories: Material Rhetoric and the
     Trauma of Representation," *College English* 62, no. 2 (November 1999): 194.

CHAPTER 9

War and Nationalism in Recent Japanese Cinema
Yamato, Kamikaze, Trauma, and Forgetting the Postwar

Aaron Gerow

New Films about War

The recent spate of Japanese films dealing with World War II or with Japan
fighting modern wars raises questions about what kind of histories are
being narrated, both wartime and postwar, what they say about Japanese
responsibility for World War II, and how they relate to current trends in nationalism.[1] The fear is that such movies resonate with other phenomena, from
the comments of Japanese officials, recently exemplified by the speeches and
writings of General Tamogami Toshio, Japan's Air Self-Defense Force
(ASDF) chief of staff, to popular manga like Kobayashi Yoshinori's work,
that seem to legitimize Japan's pursuit of war in East Asia and deny that it
committed any atrocities.[2] I have already argued elsewhere—with regard to
two cinematic imaginations of Japan at war, the alternative World War II
history *Lorelei: The Witch of the Pacific Ocean* (*Rōrerai,* 2005) and the Maritime Self-Defense Forces mutiny movie, *Aegis* (*Bōkoku no ijisu,* 2005)—
that such fears of rising revisionist nationalism in cinema are not always
justified.[3] Both works attempt to revive a Japanese cinema long under the
shadow of Hollywood by rendering the spectacle of war entertaining. They
present a "victorious" Japan, populated by young people willing to sacrifice
themselves for their community, and thus a more "healthy nationalism" (*ken-
zenna nashonarizumu*) founding a "normal country" (*futsūna kuni*) led by
father figures returned to authority. That healthiness is, however, in entertainment films aimed at mass consumption, predicated upon an often con-

flicted effort to avoid offense, projecting strong nationalism on problematic characters, hiding obvious symbols of the nation such as the flag or the emperor, openly advocating "living," not dying for the nation, and making the aim of battle more the defense of specific individuals (in *Lorelei,* a German girl) than of the abstract nation. It is as if the filmmakers are so conscious of a consumer base with conflicting opinions about the war and nationalism that they attempt to construct a hegemonic vision of the nation that appeals to all sides, only to end up writing about a Japan that is an empty sign that can mean anything to anyone.

One could claim that this emptiness is due to these two films' fictional status and may be less evident in works that must struggle with real historical events, such as the fraught narrative of World War II and its aftermath. Other films released around the same time took up actual historical moments and figures, particularly ones centered on kamikaze pilots or other suicidal missions. *Yamato* (*Otokotachi no Yamato,* 2005), for instance, about the final days of the famed battleship, was a significant box-office success, grossing 5.1 billion yen in ticket sales (approximately $46 million at the 2005 exchange rate), the sixth-best-selling Japanese film in a year when Japanese movies outgrossed foreign films for the first time since 1985 (it was also the most successful Japanese war film in decades). *For Those We Love* (*Ore wa, kimi no tame ni koso shini ni iku,* 2007), focusing on the real-life woman who ran an eatery frequented by kamikaze pilots and became popularly known as the "mother of the kamikaze," was the result of the right-wing Tokyo governor Ishihara Shintarō's effort to document and celebrate the sacrifices of those young men.[4] Ishihara supervised the production, wrote the script, and his associate, the Okinawan director Shinjō Taku, directed. Such films have been the focus of greater attention and controversy because of their connection to real historical events and the tendency among critics, scholars, and many viewers alike to privilege codes of realism. Because the question of Japan's responsibility for World War II has been the subject of such extended controversy, it has also served as the primary hermeneutic framework for interpreting myriad cinematic texts, including those not directly portraying the war. Such focal points threaten to obscure the emptiness of these films, which is found less in what they depict than in what they work to elide—an emptiness they create precisely to avoid another contentious if not traumatic history.

Yoshikuni Igarashi has noted that post-2000 kamikaze films such as *The Firefly* (*Hotaru,* 2001), responding to the end of the period of history called the Shōwa era and the cold war, are increasingly moving away from previous narrative patterns that marked division between the war and the postwar period—and the significance of the war—by depicting the heroic deaths of the kamikaze, as if their demise signified the end of the war and its problems.[5] Newer films are considering the lingering traumatic effects of the war on postwar Japan in the form of surviving kamikaze. The focus is thus shifting from the war to the postwar, but even then, the effect of many of these films is to engage not what they are obviously depicting, the post-1989 present or even the wartime, but the problematic history in between. Igarashi argues that *The Firefly* ultimately avoids dealing with the trauma of the war by narrating a second set of deaths in the present, which cleanly concludes the postwar and divides it from today. *Yamato* and similar films, by contrast, which offer no such second deaths, re-enact wartime trauma in a vicarious fashion, using its disruptive effects so as to enable forgetting of what for the majority of the audience, born after the war ended, might be the greater trauma: the postwar era and its history of economic up-heaval, U.S. military bases, cultural neocolonialism, student protest, and "democracy." That these films are also appearing at the time of the "Shōwa 30s" boom, featuring nostalgic narratives of Japan between 1955 and 1965 (Shōwa 30–40), such as the successful film series *Always—Sunset on Third Street,* is no coincidence. Some films ignore the war and the long history of postwar conflict to construct an idyllic postwar, while others "remember" wartime trauma in order to skip to a present when that trauma has been alleviated. Both, however, construct an empty postwar in order to avoid deal-ing with its traumatic and divisive history, primarily in order to establish the illusion of a more unified present.

The Battleship *Yamato*, Cinema, and Postwar History

Yamato was produced by Takaiwa Tan, the chairman of the movie studio Tōei, and Kadokawa Haruki, a maverick producer who in the 1970s and 1980s introduced new marketing strategies for big-budget spectaculars to the Japanese film industry. The film was Kadokawa's return to success after his cocaine bust in 1993 and reunited him with the director Satō Jun'ya, a regular of blockbuster movies who had helmed such early Kadokawa suc-cesses as *Proof of the Man* (*Ningen no shōmei*, 1976) after establishing himself with yakuza films and a kamikaze film titled *The Last Kamikaze* (*Saigo no tokkōtai,* 1970). Reportedly budgeted at 2.5 billion yen (approximately $23 million), quite high by Japanese standards, *Yamato* featured an all-star cast, including Nakadai Tatsuya, Sorimachi Takashi, Nakamura Shidō, Matsuyama Ken'ichi, Okuda Eiji, Suzuki Kyōka, Aoi Yū, Terajima Shinobu, and Watari Tetsuya, and a colossal set: a life-size reproduction of the front half of the battleship *Yamato,* the largest battleship ever constructed.

Yamato narrates the last days of the famous ship, which was sunk off Japan on April 7, 1945, with a loss of 2,740 lives during a suicidal mission to defend Okinawa. It does this using two structuring devices. The first focuses on several young recruits who board the ship at age fifteen, experience the problems of military life and, at age seventeen, willingly take part in the final battle. The second is a framing narrative in which one of those recruits, Kamio Katsumi, is asked sixty years later by Makiko, the daughter of a former shipmate named Uchida Mamoru, to take her to the site of the sinking. Both devices are central to articulating the film's ambiguous, if not contradictory, politics. By concentrating on the young men, the film, which was based on an award-winning book by Henmi Jun (Kadokawa Haruki's sister), is able to narrate a tale of innocent, promising spirits needlessly sent to a grisly death by a naval command to which even the fleet commander, Itō Seiichi, registered objections.[6] Although the older, adult trio of Uchida, Moriwaki Shōhachi, and Karaki Masao, who are directly in charge of these young recruits, can convincingly voice their desire to sail to their deaths because of their love for *Yamato* (and, correspondingly, the nation its name also refers to) and their hope of defending their families at home, the greenhorns' similar statements lack such force and are even questioned by Moriwaki. Quite a number of voices, including that of the director, claimed this was an antiwar film, one revealing the horrible waste of life caused by reckless leaders.[7] Yet right-wing commentators could also point to the same chaste sailors or related texts like the lyrics to Nagabuchi Tsuyoshi's honorific ending song, and claim that the film offered an example of selfless patriotism for all Japan to follow.[8]

The framing structure only reinforces these possible contradictory readings. Kamio's narration of what happened after *Yamato*'s loss, especially the deaths of his girlfriend Taeko and Uchida's lover Fumiko in the atom bomb attack on Hiroshima, prompts him to declare that even the hope of dying to save their families came to naught. Wakakuwa Midori has noted a change in kamikaze films from wartime works showing young men dying for the emperor, in which women are only an obstacle to that goal, to films like *Yamato,* in which the women are what the men die for.[9] But these men fail to do that. Kamio, in particular, is presented as a victim of trauma after the war, unproductive (without wife or children) and reclusive (he did not even know that Uchida had survived the *Yamato* sinking), whose problematic relation to memory is exemplified by both his refusal to take part in *Yamato* memorials and a physical debilitation (a heart ailment) that worsens as the site of his traumatic experience nears. Coupled with Uchida, who was presumably rendered sterile by the war (his children are all adopted), Kamio represents the loss of the masculine bravura that Moriwaki and Uchida exemplified with almost violent physicality during the war.

The inclusion of scenes from the present is a significant difference between *Yamato* and previous cinematic accounts of the sinking and thus proves central to its orchestration of trauma. The first postwar film version was *The Battleship Yamato* (*Senkan Yamato*), a 1953 movie directed by Abe Yutaka, who is famous for being trained in Hollywood in the 1920s but also for his wartime propaganda film *Dawn of Freedom* (*Ano hata o ute*, 1944) and his 1954 memorial to the officers who resisted Japan's surrender in August 1945, *Japan Undefeated* (*Nihon yaburezu*). Another major cinematic adaptation was the 1981 blockbuster *The Imperial Navy* (*Rengō kantai*), which covered the history of the imperial fleet from before the attack on Pearl Harbor but focused especially on the carrier *Zuikaku* and the *Yamato*. It was directed by Matsubayashi Shūe, a naval officer during World War II who ended up specializing in *salaryman* comedies and war films, including the influential *The Human Torpedoes* (*Ningen gyorai kaiten*, 1955), about the pilots on suicidal submarine missions.[10] Although *The Battleship Yamato* was narrated from the perspective of an intellectual junior officer, Yoshimura, who survived the sinking, his voiceover emerges from the present, abstract and bodiless, and thus is not too different from the anonymous, third-person, omniscient narration found in the voiceover and explanatory titles of *The Imperial Navy*. In both, the point of narration is from a present secure not only in the knowledge of a history defined by a basic break between war and postwar but also in a subjectivity that is unaffected by the violent past.

Their differences inform their divergent worldviews, not unrelated to their varying historical contexts. *The Battleship Yamato* personalizes narration in a figure who is the most liberal and humanistic on board (Yoshimura does not even slap his underperforming charges but lets them slap him) and thus offers the audiences assurances that present-day authority is more enlightened. The concluding thrust of the film is thus relatively future oriented in that, while it laments the loss of individual lives during the war and shows conflicts between the junior officers (one is in fact an American Nisei who is subject to discrimination), its emphasis is on the technical skill of the crew, abilities clearly needed for the economic revival begun with the Korean War. As Isolde Standish notes of many kamikaze films, divisions between the men are ultimately dissolved when all subsume their individual desires to the collective,[11] but their reasons for doing so here stem less from the desire to protect family or the homeland than from, in the words of a senior officer, their orders and the fact that their "training will not die."[12]

The Imperial Navy could be said to express that managerial Japan, in which individuals are shaped and defined by institutional practices, is on the eve of its decline. Characters are of two types: officers at the top echelons of the Navy who make the decisions, and a select set of junior officers and their families who must carry them out. If the latter are melodramatic subjects, with the men doing their duty and the women suffering the consequences, the former are ostensibly political subjects, debating and then deciding the course of the war. If the film has an antiwar stance, it is in presenting the views of commanders like Admiral Yamamoto Isoroku, who questioned the wisdom of forming the Three-Power Alliance between Japan, Germany, and Italy, or pursuing war with the United States. Yet just as the cinematic narration tends to cut away before a decision is made on a matter, leaving the spectators to deal with the results in the next scene as if they were faits accomplis, so the film narrates the history of war as inevitable. Some officers, such as Ozawa Jisaburō, express displeasure at this overwhelming sense of inevitability, but in the end even he goes along with what has been decided. Matsubayashi is frequently described as bringing a Buddhist worldview to his films, but *The Imperial Navy* shares as much with his *salaryman* movies in celebrating the dedication and skill of mid- to upper-level management whose lot is to perform to their utmost the tasks determined elsewhere. Although this may locate the failure to assume responsibility for the war in Japan's institutional (and perhaps also cinematic) structures, the film offers little critique of this situation. In fact, in contrast to the still hopeful *The Battleship Yamato, The Imperial Navy*, with all its battles and special effects, or even its brief postwar scene showing the small son of one of the dead officers, is a claustrophobic film, suffocating under its own inevitability.

Both films take pains to separate the time of narration from the problems of war, but this is not so as to dig an impassible barrier between the war and the postwar. Rather, the effects of the war are elided precisely to enable the postwar to assume a superior position, capable of reconstructing wartime events like the sinking of the *Yamato* in accordance with postwar needs. Thus, although neither film takes on the myriad problems of postwar Japan, they are as much about that era as the wartime. Yet by not depicting the postwar other than as an authoritative purveyor of knowledge, project-ing various visions of the stages of postwar institutional competency on past communities, such as that of the *Yamato,* these works assume a better post-war by default. Paradoxically, by evading the postwar and dwelling in the military past, such war films create a more perfect image of the postwar.

Yamato and Trauma Cinema

Yamato, in contrast, by framing its narration using present-day episodes, fo-cuses more on the effects of the war on what came afterward. Yet we must focus on how temporalities are related and negotiated through cinematic nar-ration. The original script for *Yamato,* for instance, which was penned by No-gami Tatsuo,[13] also begins with Kamio in the present, but instead of being a reclusive victim of trauma, he is a silent veteran taking part in a special expedi-tion with other *Yamato* survivors to view the wreck on television via a remote-controlled submersible. What triggers a vision of the past is not his troubled memory but, rather, first his assertion that today's youth cannot understand what war was like and then the dredging up of some relics by the submers-ible. In fact, unlike the film, the flashback is not motivated by any one character's memory. Nogami's script is more conventional historiography, not only filling its pages with obscure details about the structure and daily routine of the *Yamato* but also presenting itself as an objective narration in-stigated by the unearthing of historical traces. Nogami's film was, then, to presuppose a temporal gap between past and present that can be bridged only by cinematic historiography. The narration itself is never questioned; in fact, cinema is subject to praise because the representative of ignorant youth at the beginning is a television reporter. What she and her crew learn by the end is not just the actual history of the *Yamato* but also the inade-quacy of television practice: the inferiority of words obtained in interviews compared to a more cinematic long take of Kamio's back as he stares out to sea. The original script's direct depiction of the postwar period may thus problematize the postwar as a space in which history has been lost, but it does so only to the extent that it celebrates its own (postwar) ability to reconstruct history as a series of periods in which the distinctions between past and pres-ent, war and peace, memory and actuality, trace and presence are clear.

　　Yamato ostensibly transforms these dynamics by having the war seep into the postwar through presenting subjects suffering from trauma. The

postwar is no longer the unseen source of authoritative knowledge, as Kamio, the film's main on-screen narrator, is severely debilitated. One can initially hypothesize that, just as the previous two films utilized the *Yamato* to
express a postwar moment, this is an indication of yet another historical
stage, one that follows *The Imperial Navy*'s evocation of the managed society (*kanri shakai*) of the high-growth era at its saturated limit. The narration is, in fact, split: Kamio's narration is often personal, triggered by his
gaze and not by his words, and thus presumably occurring more in his head
than expressed to others; in parallel, however, is the depersonalized narration of the explanatory titles and voiceover. Thus, although the film, in a
continuation from Nogami's script, still attempts to maintain authority over
history, it also frames a narrative problem to be investigated. The way in
which this problem is defined as trauma, as well as the way in which the film
frames and "alleviates" this trauma, is central to the way in which the film
depicts both the war and the postwar.

The present-day narrative is supposed to show how Kamio overcomes
his trauma and, like films in a similar vein, such as *Titanic* and *Saving Private Ryan,* makes *Yamato* a film that combines ostensibly accurate spectacles of past events with the work of processing memory for contemporary
purposes. Perhaps it belongs to the category of "trauma cinema" that E. Ann
Kaplan, Joshua Hirsch, Janet Walker, and others have discussed.[14] Initially,
however, one might not think so. Given that mental trauma is usually theo-
rized as coming from an experience so shocking and forceful that normal
psychological structures are unable to process it, thus leaving the traumatic
memory in the mind unprocessed and occasionally able to wreak havoc,
many have regarded trauma cinema as films that deal with experiences so
overwhelming that normal modes of cinema, particularly the classical realism of Hollywood, cannot properly deal with it. Trauma in film is essentially
a problem of representation, with the symptoms of that experience being
manifested in the body of the film, especially in its form. Prominent examples of trauma cinema include Alain Resnais's *Night and Fog* (*Nuit et brouillard,* 1955)—films that are modernist in form, evincing in their disjunctive
cinematic structures both the rupturing effects of trauma and innovative
methods of representing experiences that are inherently difficult to represent.

Yamato, however, as many critics noted, even when judging it favorably, uses a style that is largely conventional, if not cliché. The form on which
it relies is not just the war film but the television history program, since it
features both the familiar voice of the TV Asahi announcer Watanabe

Noritsugu as the narrator and the explanatory titles common to Japanese television documentaries and historical dramas. Actually it begins with documentary footage and images of the Yamato Museum in Kure (though eventually tied to the perspective of Makiko, who is visiting there in the first scene). *Yamato* depicts a loss that is not hard to represent and that has already been memorialized in conventional ways. In some ways, it is simply a reminder for those who have not gone to the museum.

That, however, does not account for either the film's pretensions or its effects and popularity. Uchida's daughter goes to the Yamato Museum at the beginning but must go farther, to the spot where the *Yamato* sank. Yet this is a place where there is nothing, no trace of either the ship or the event. The film must fill in these blanks. Nakamura Hideyuki has argued, with regard to both kamikaze films in general and *Yamato* in particular, that such works function as ceremonial courtesy, representing those on such suicide missions as essentially divine.[15] Makiko, Kamio, and even the fifteen-year-old deckhand Atsushi thus must travel to this place of nothingness because the journey itself ceremoniously honors the dead. The fishing boat's journey certainly has such a ritual dimension, yet it is also ostensibly therapeutic, because it is directed not just at the honored dead but also at the troubled living—not just at a heroic past but at a crippled present.

In order to grasp the crucial difference between recent films, such as *Yamato* and *For Those We Love,* and many past kamikaze films, we must detail how the trip is represented and the functions that film is supposed to play, both temporally and cinematically. Narratively, the voyage to this location is the occasion for Kamio's remembrances, with the authentic geography working to double their veracity. Like Nogami's script, it is an occasion for historiography. What specifically triggers his recollections, however, is not the lack of knowledge that Nogami specified but the presence of photography (a portrait of Moriwaki, Uchida, and Karaki that Makiko shows him).

And just as the photo sparks his voyage into the past, so *Yamato* the film similarly offers itself to the audience as a privileged means of not only accompanying them on this authentic journey but also obtaining unique access to the truth of the traumatic event. A homology between Kamio and the audience is being established, one that structurally emphasizes the photographic/cinematic narration of history (many of Kamio's flashbacks commence with his internal visions—not his recounting of events to others—and thus it is not entirely clear whether the past is being viewed by anyone but the audi-

Yamato (2005):A photograph of Karaki, Uchida, and Moriwaki summons the past

ence). Yet if the trip helps to cure Kamio, so should it—and the movie—presumably help Japanese audiences manage a problematic history.

Before considering how it does that, we must ask of what the film ostensibly cures them. One can debate whether the trauma of World War II and Japan's defeat is still felt, over sixty years after the fact, by an audience that mostly had not yet been born at the time and, we are repeatedly told, has not been fully educated about those events. What is more important is that the film itself cites no such problem for the average Japanese. Even their representatives on the boat, Makiko and the deckhand Atsushi, fail to speak of haunting memories that need to be addressed. World War II as trauma is definitely constructed as a generational issue within the film. Unlike Kamio, perhaps theirs is not a narrative of trauma but of coming of age: through Atsushi, the adolescents who boarded the *Yamato* (and were the same age as Atsushi) but who could not grow up, due to war and the loss of a masculine father figure, can finally become adults, largely, like Makiko, by discovering the identity of their absent father.

Nakamura, however, tries to bring this narrative back to the issue of World War II by reading Atsushi's determined steering of the boat in the last scene, complete with a towel wrapped around his forehead, as a resurrection of the kamikaze in modern times. Wakakuwa Midori more strongly declares that Atsushi is the generation of the future that the film, as a "film for revising the constitution and remilitarizing" Japan, is recommending go to war.[16] These are certainly possible interpretations, ones that firmly place *Yamato* in an ideological position that affirms Japan's actions in World

War II and call for a present that relives the past. The problem with these assured readings, however, is that they not only assume that the past is the best framework for reading the present (when the opposite might be the case) but also valorize a dominant reading; however, the problem the young face in this film—and in the audience—lies largely in the absence of a dominant or even common reading, an issue that the coming-of-age narrative must face. Even if some do read the film—either positively or critically—in the way that Nakamura or Wakakuwa outline, how can we argue that these interpretations are in fact shared by a national audience? My own view is that a film like *Yamato* attempts to resurrect a common reading by utilizing trauma to render the postwar void and envelop spectators in a self-confirming, circular, but ultimately empty mode of historical interpretation.

The Malaise of Interpretation

Discussing *Yamato* as a whole, Fukuma Yoshiaki argues that its realism is a result less of its ability to truly evoke the absurdity and meaningless of death in war than of its effect in containing that within such safe narratives as "the bonds of male camaraderie," which give them meaning.[17] Although this is definitely a factor in the film, it presumes that audiences can safely read the film in terms of those narratives. Observers, however, have recognized the problem of interpretation even since World War II. As I have written elsewhere,[18] the issue of audience reception was of great concern to wartime commentators. They recognized that spectators, both at home and in the occupied territories, help make the film and thus could bolster or undermine any national film production. That was why there was talk of training spectators to read films properly as well as of exemplary audiences, who managed their movie interpretations as they did their behavior when waiting in lines to obtain rationed goods. This task became more difficult in the postwar, when there was less certainty over what the films were supposed to mean in the first place. When the first spate of war movies was released around 1953—after the San Francisco Treaty, which formally concluded the Pacific War and realigned relations between Japan and the United States, had been signed in 1951 and the end of Occupation-era film censorship in 1952—the film magazine *Kinema junpō* (Movie Times) expressed enough concern over the potential meaning of these films, for instance, noting audiences cheering a Japanese attack in an American war movie, that it conducted audience surveys. Realizing that some who saw *The Battleship Yamato* were nostalgic for wartime despite the producer's intention to "pray for world peace," the magazine's editors gave the last word in the article to the critic Ishigaki Ayako, who argued that "it makes you realize, regardless of the intentions of the producers of war films, how difficult and dangerous it is in this sense to make war films in today's Japanese society."[19] Reception, it seemed, could not be trusted to provide consistent readings either for or against war, so some believed that the occasion for reception—the film itself—should not be produced.

Some of this confusion over the cinematic textuality and reception of war films may relate to the nature of genre, which, as Rick Altman argues,[20] is much more divided and mixed than most would have it. The majority of popular film genres are produced by studios that have a vested interest in increasing their potential audiences (e.g., by appealing to those on both the left and right with regard to war). Yet there also exists an argument, evident in some of the films, that the inability to properly read narratives of the war is a particularly postwar malaise, one linked to censorship. The film *For Those We Love* is, in many ways, a film less about the kamikaze fighters themselves than about the obstacles faced by their narratives in being told. One of the major subplots of the movie relates the efforts of the heroine, Torihama Tome, the "mother of the kamikaze," to send letters composed by the men directly to their families in contravention of censorship regulations. She is stopped and even abused by the Kempeitai (the military police). Although, on the surface, this moment in the film is critical of wartime Japan, Tome's inability to transmit the voices of the kamikaze must also be read in conjunction with the film's advertising, which both quotes Ishihara declaring the movie to represent "the true voices of the kamikaze that [Torihama Tome] heard" and proclaims that "the shocking truth of the kamikaze that has been covered up [*fūin*] will now be revealed."[21] The movie thus equates itself with the censored letters of the kamikaze, texts that supposedly are a better form of communication because they were not self-censored and were addressed only to a familiar (familial) audience, which should have no problem in understanding the message.

For Those We Love proposes such an audience for itself, with the nation replacing the family while still being familiar. The censorship to which its promotional materials refer, however, is no longer by the Kempeitai but a postwar phenomena—presumably including the political left, Ishihara's opponents, who, instead of seeing the supposed "truth" of these brave young men sacrificing their lives for "those they love," offer according to neo-nationalists, only a self-defeating (*jigyakuteki*) history of Japan. But there is a sense here that a larger discursive illness has plagued the country, making it difficult for even surviving kamikaze pilots to tell the "truth" about their bravery.[22] *For Those We Love* also has its suffering survivor, Lieutenant Na-kanishi, who, like Kamio, is riddled with guilt over living on after all his buddies died. Ishihara's film, however, makes the argument that the aphasia of such men is caused by trauma that occurred not during the war—since Ishihara, wanting "to leave behind [for posterity] the figure of beautiful Japanese who lived through such hard times,"[23] declares that their wartime behavior is nothing to be ashamed of—but after it, as the postwar climate would not allow them to proudly narrate the actions of their buddies. Instead, both Kamio and Nakanishi are essentially reduced to being spectators in the postwar, with *Yamato* essentially being the film of the vision that Kamio, beginning with his point-of-view shot looking into the past at the bow of the *Yamato,* sees while on his fishing boat in the present.

What is supposed to cure this malaise is the realization that there is no reason for suppressing these stories, that they should be told and then consumed with a reverence that, like Tome's letters of the kamikaze, sees them only as intimate and truthful—and thus impossible to misinterpret. In the narratives, this is often accomplished by utilizing a circular temporality to alleviate the trauma, justify the narration of wartime stories, and effectively insulate that narrative's reception from the problem of consensus and mediation. One common element in *Yamato, For Those We Love,* and *Sea without Exit* (*Deguchi no nai umi,* 2006)—Sasabe Kiyoshi's film about the human torpedo squadron (Kaiten)—is a declaration that the story of the kamikaze is so meaningful that it should be repeatedly read or viewed by future generations.[24] Such a realization, in fact, is what ostensibly cures Kamio and Nishitani of their survivor's guilt: their reason for living, it is argued, is precisely to relate to others the truth about those who died. This truth could be ideologically variable, showing either the cruelty of war or the heroism of the young men, but it often, under the rationale of refusing to make their deaths meaningless, could function as a foundation for contemporary Japan. Thus, the well-known actress Kishi Keiko, who plays Torihama Tome, could proclaim in an ad for the film her "anger at a war that killed the young kamikaze pilots who were under orders that were disguised as volunteering" and yet, at the same time, declare, "I would like to see even a few more people think about how the peace we have today is founded on their sacrificing their precious lives."[25] This may appear to be a post-facto attempt to overcome the trauma of defeat, but these narratives can go so far as to claim the existence of such ideas before the deaths occur. This involves not just

For Those We Love, in which Vice Admiral Ōnishi Takijirō, as he is helping to formulate the kamikaze policy, declares that if Japan is to lose, it must do so by showing the true spirit of the nation (*kokutai*) beforehand but also in *Yamato,* in the now-legendary statement by Lieutenant Usubuchi Iwao[26] on the ship the day before its final battle: that Japan can progress only through defeat and that the *Yamato*'s demise was necessary for the rebirth or awakening of Japan.[27] The need for the narration of death is projected back in time, before even the deaths occur.

This can appear to be a postwar reconstruction of wartime events for postwar needs. Yoshikuni Igarashi has interpreted stories that rewrite the war defeat as a sacrifice necessary for the betterment of Japan as a part of what he terms the foundational narrative for postwar Japan.[28] However, although narratives like *The Battleship Yamato* are mostly linear, the circularity and self-referentiality of this logic in recent films is crucial. This is most evident in the case of Namiki Kōji, the talented college baseball pitcher in *Sea without Exit* who volunteers for the human torpedo squad. His reasons for volunteering remain unclear for much of the film until he is asked by one of his mechanics, an admirer who also played baseball. Namiki's response is essentially that he is going to die simply to show that the human torpedoes existed.[29] This kind of almost tautological explanation for kamikaze actions is also the most inoffensive, because it largely isolates the dead from history. However, it also depends on the narration, as if kamikaze existed in order to be narrated as existing. As in *For Those We Love,* this effectively functions as self-justification for these movies themselves, reducing the kamikaze to a textual operation, as if their suicidal missions were essentially themselves acts of narration but only about themselves. Perhaps this makes these films "ceremonious" in Nakamura's sense, holy texts owed the same reverence as the last letters and poems of the kamikaze. Yet the fact that these narratives aim to imbricate the act of narration (the films, the internal storytellers), the subject of narration (the kamikaze sailors or pilots), and the reception of narration (the film audience or the survivors of the war) all in the same circular, unmediated textual process, purports to circumvent alternative interpretations. Note that this does not attempt to enforce certain readings by relying on a dominant interpretive context (e.g., a consensus of opinion about war and the nation) but, rather, attempts to avoid the problem of consensus by divorcing the text from the larger context and narrowing the textual operation to essentially one of self-reference: we can all agree on the importance of the kamikaze because they were important for this text. The media text need not be mediated through acts of reading or other texts because it purportedly exists in unmediated relation to itself.

Yamato and Vicarious Trauma

Yet as if acknowledging that such narrative strategies are insufficient to ensure a national unity of spectatorship, these films pursue in parallel other approaches to bring the viewer into the purview of the text. *For Those We Love,* for instance, attempts to utilize pronouns to place the spectator in the subject position of the pilots (e.g., *ore* [I] in the Japanese title; the English-language title unabashedly joins the two in a communal "we"). This is epitomized in the film's official home page, which is designed as the cockpit of a kamikaze fighter, literally placing the viewer in the position of a man seeking to die for his country. There are problems in these efforts, not least of which is the question of gender. Women in the audience are left behind in *For Those We Love,* as *ore* in the Japanese title refers to men; women are relegated at best to the pronoun *kimi,* the general group that includes girlfriends, mothers, siblings, and even possibly the emperor for whom they are fighting. An equally vexing problem is the difficulty of linking the individual narratives presented in these films to the collective nation. Most American war films attempt to do this by providing a variety of grunts of different backgrounds and ethnicities, ostensibly representing the melting pot of the United States as a whole. These Japanese films do that to some extent as well, with even *For Those We Love* throwing in one pilot who seemingly commits suicide rather than go ahead with a meaningless strategy as well as a Korean pilot.

   Yet one problem in attempting to link the present to wartime by skipping the postwar is the huge gap created for structures of identification to cross. How are today's youth in their teens and twenties supposed to identify with figures long since dead who lived in utterly different circumstances? Some fantasy narratives, such as the versions of "The Winds of God," have tried to do that by literally sending representative contemporary youth back in time to 1945.[30] *Yamato* attempts to place a delegate of today's young people in the narrative in the person of Atsushi, who can also be said to exemplify the audience within the film. But *For Those We Love* exhibits particular difficulty in linking through filmic form the individual and the collective. On the one hand, much of the film is shot in medium-long to long shots, a peculiar choice if the film is attempting to encourage audience identification. Perhaps the movie is attempting to resurrect the kind of "monumental style" that

Darrell Davis has identified in wartime cinema, which attempted to represent the nation not just through propagandistic content but also in reconstructing an inherent Japanese aesthetic in a film style that is overly staid and pictorial.[31] But in order to work, a monumental style, as I have argued elsewhere, requires both a clear aesthetic context and an engaged audience, neither of which is always evident in *For Those We Love*.[32] The film at last has an emotional close-up two-thirds of the way through and includes more in an attempt to build up to the melodramatic climax of Nishitani's spiritual reunion with his dead buddies, but the movie remains fissured and divided over how to represent the nation.

Yamato also has this problem but attempts to overcome it—as well as solve the problem of postwar history—through vicarious trauma. *Yamato* was in some ways a traumatic film for spectators, too. In comments on Yahoo Japan and other sites, viewers often describe feeling speechless after seeing the film. What tends to be so shocking is less the general narrative of the loss of the *Yamato* than the way in which the innocent young recruits are killed in such a graphic mode of cinematic representation.

The gore exceeds narrative necessity, and while it might be somewhat justified thematically if the film is antiwar, it is a brutal form of filmmaking that can be cruel to both its characters and its audience.

Perhaps that filmic barbarity is a symptom of another repressed loss, but it is important to understand that simply showing violence does not guarantee a particular meaning, antiwar or not. What is important is how it is manifested in this film at this juncture. First, the violence toward multiple characters can function to collectivize Kamio's individual trauma, to

Yamato (2005): A vicariously traumatic depiction of young deaths

form a national experience that is epitomized within the narrative by the salute of three generations to the honored dead at the end of the film.

As a disruptive phenomenon, however, trauma helps to disguise the inherent differences between these experiences. Although Kamio's trauma is rooted not just in the meaningless loss of young lives but also in his survivor's guilt and powerlessness to alter this history—his problem is linear, based in an inability to turn back the clock—the spectator's trauma is circular because it refers to itself and allows for revisiting. Because the film touts its ability to represent the violent source of Kamio's trauma, the audience's own trauma can refer as much to the film they have watched as to the loss of young lives. This form of vicarious trauma is different from the one described by Joshua Hirsch, who valorizes some cinema as "a traumatic relay," actually transmitting, sometimes in analogous form, aspects of the original traumatic experience.[33] There might be an element of this in *Yamato,* but here the vicariousness functions more as an indirect substitute than as an empathic identification—one that allows spectators to experience trauma in a safe, detached circularity. This is confirmed at the end of the film, which, after giving audiences a strong emotional experience, allows them to remember and memorialize it only minutes later through slow-motion flashbacks of the same brutal battle scenes under the credits—shots that are appropriately coupled with images of Makiko laying flowers at a *Yamato* memorial—and a circular return to some of the underwater footage of the *Yamato* that began the film. Just as trauma reflects back on the film itself, the process of remembering that experience is itself directed toward the movie. It is thus

Yamato (2005): Makiko, Kamio, and Atsushi salute the nation's dead

fitting that when *Yamato* became a hit, the set of the movie became a tourist attraction in the six months after the film's release for over one million people interested in reliving their movie or *Yamato* experience.[34]

Kamio's problem is solved by becoming similarly circular: the assertion that he has survived in order to remember and memorialize the dead. That, however, does not answer the traumatic question of why these young men died in a film that minutes before questioned the meaning of their sacrifice. If Kamio survived so that he could memorialize the dead, did they die only so that they could be memorialized? How this cause is supposed to bring about the effect is uncertain, but the paradoxical victory of Japan through defeat clearly depends on the constant reiteration of that defeat. This may be the justification for the film *Yamato* at a time of political and economic stagnation in Japan, but it writes a peculiar history, because linear progress can be based only on a repeated return to the past if part of that history is ruptured, dismembered, and forgotten.

In *Yamato,* it is again the history of postwar Japan that is forgotten. That is practically stated by Kamio, who, at his moment of resolution, declares that for him the Shōwa era is finally over. He has overcome his problem with history by recalling what happened sixty years before, as if that alone is sufficient to deal with the entire problem of the Shōwa era, which continued until 1989. Gone is the long-standing narrative of the postwar as a return to prewar democracy, as the formation of a new international economic power. The historical break between wartime and postwar is now seemingly less important because the linearity of Nogami's story has been replaced by a circularity in which the postwar itself has been elided, in which the past is now easily accessible because the ravages of postwar time have healed. This does not necessarily create a historical equation between wartime and contemporary Japan, because the two are operationally unified less by positive characteristics than by their both *not* being the postwar. One can postulate that this became possible only through the process of trauma—which by definition is often an unprocessed and unmediated experience.

The erasure of the postwar is evident in how *Yamato* rewrites one of the emblematic moments in postwar Japanese cinema: the scene in Kurosawa Akira's 1947 film *No Regrets for Our Youth* (*Waga seishun ni kui nashi*) in which Yukie, played by Hara Setsuko, sets out during the war to tend the rice paddies belonging to her mother-in-law, despite the public approbation sparked by her husband's execution as a political traitor. It shows her moral determination, the democratic core that will help Japan change after the war. *Yamato* shifts this into the immediate postwar, as Kamio tends the paddies of his dead buddy Nishi's mother not out of determination to maintain his values or to change society but out of guilt that he survived, not Nishi. Memorable postwar transformations morph into forgettable postwar paralysis that supposedly lasts for the rest of the Shōwa era and becomes the focus of male melodrama—until they are forgotten. Next to shock, tears were the most common response reported by *Yamato*'s audiences, and, as Mitsuhiro Yoshimoto has argued, melodrama was also a crucial narrative in immediate postwar cinema.[35] But whereas cinema in the 1950s used the melodrama of postwar suffering as a means of forgetting wartime atrocities, *Yamato,* if not other recent kamikaze films as well, uses wartime suffering to forget not only Japanese war responsibility but also a postwar increasingly defined, especially in contemporary popular culture, by emasculation and hypocrisy or ahistorical idealization. The latter is evident in the rise of cultural nostalgia for the "Shōwa 30s," which peaked around 2005. In cinema, this was exemplified by the two successful "Always" films, both tales set in the late 1950s of a *gemeinschaft* community in a lower-class section of Tokyo, apparently free of the political or cultural strife that helped define those years.[36] Such nostalgia for the postwar, however, should be seen as the other side of the coin of an attempt to forget or bypass the postwar, since both forgetting the postwar and celebrating the Shōwa 30s reveal a fundamental aversion to confronting the historical transformations and sociopolitical divisions that occurred in that era.

If *Yamato* deals with or reflects historical trauma, it is less that of the war than that of the postwar; this is the history that its audience had really experienced and desired to see erased through the shock of defeat and the tearful eyes of Japanese masculinity. This is the trauma that the film cannot really face except through displacement, and so the postwar can directly appear in the film only through plot inconsistencies (how could Kamio not know that Uchida had survived?) and the inability to acknowledge contemporary political reality (i.e., showing Maritime Self-Defense Force ships returning from a "refueling mission in the Indian Ocean" without daring to mention that this is part of Japan's support for the Iraq War). This displacement, at least in *Yamato,* is made possible through the use of vicarious trauma. Trauma, an experience that has not been properly processed, repeatedly returns (because it remains undigested) in ways that can seem as direct as the original experience, even if they do not necessarily truly reflect that event. Vicarious trauma in *Yamato* allows spectators to share in the experience presented in the story while also enabling the movie to jump between the past and the present, in the story and in Japanese history, while avoiding the mediations and digestive processes of linear narration and linear postwar history.

War films like *Yamato* certainly seek a consensus by positing a direct link between wartime and present-day Japan that skips the postwar, but in the end that consensus differs little from the empty national one on which their more fantastic brethren rely. Postwar trauma should be avoided—or displaced using such techniques as vicarious trauma—precisely because of the intense divisions and turmoil created during that period; these films can imagine a unified audience only if they render the disputes of the postwar null and void, creating an imagined community only if such an empty postwar is equally imagined.[37] The danger of these films lies in their doing precisely that, but accomplishing it can also be said to be a symptom of the very postwar trauma and turmoil that the films try to elide. A new history that severs and skips the postwar (just as previous histories skipped the wartime) and re-members a cycle of return between the present and the memorialized wartime is problematic, especially for a film like *Yamato* that has at least some antiwar pretensions. This is part of the source of its contradictory nationalism: hoping to recover a lost masculinity in war while also fearing its excesses;[38] celebrating life and survival like many other contemporary war films, yet also depending on death and defeat for its reworking of postwar history; imagining an adult Japan in the new millennium, but without being able to narrate either a linear history of Japan's economic recovery and growth (its becoming adult?) or its geopolitical dependency on the United States (or its lingering infantile capitalism, to borrow Asada Akira's term).[39] *Yamato* strategically uses the ruptures of trauma to try to efface these aporia, all the while reassuring its shocked audiences with a familiar, conventional film style. Remembering is here re-membering, but with the dismembered parts of the nation, cinema, and history still poorly connected after their rearrangement.[40]

Notes

1   The first version of this paper was originally presented at a conference at Stanford in 2008. I would like to thank the organizers and other participants for their helpful comments and questions.

2   In October 2008, in a contest sponsored by a construction company whose CEO has espoused right-wing views, General Toshio Tamogami won a lucrative prize for an essay titled "Was Japan an Aggressor Nation?" His main arguments were that Japan was manipulated into participating in World War II by China and the United States under the influence of the Communist International (Comintern) and that Japan's reliance on the United States for military defense is destroying its national culture. In the ensuing controversy, he was eventually relieved of his post and pressed into retirement. Kobayashi's manga, beginning with the notorious *Sensōron* (On War) (Tokyo: Gentōsha, 1998), have aggressively attempted to rewrite Japan's history of war and colonization and advocate a nationalism that abandons the selfishness of today's youth and emulates the sacrifices of the *kamikaze* pilots.

3   Aaron Gerow, "Fantasies of War and Nation in Recent Japanese Cinema," *Japan Focus,* February 20, 2006, http://www.japanfocus.org/products/details /1707/.

4   Ishihara's film was not that successful. It came in twenty-ninth on a list of best-grossing Japanese films in 2007, with 1.08 billion yen (about $9.2 million in 2007) in total box office receipts, but with a budget of 1.8 billion yen (about $15 million), and with producers normally only getting a fraction of each yen paid at the ticket window, the movie probably lost money. It, however, was the third highest grossing film of the year for Tōei, one of the major studios.

5   Igarashi Yoshikuni, "Kamikaze Today: The Search for National Heroes in Contemporary Japan," in *Ruptured Histories: War, Memory, and the Post-Cold War in Asia,* ed. Sheila Miyoshi Jager and Rana Mitter (Cambridge, MA: Harvard University Press, 2007), 99–121.

6   As if emphasizing this innocence, the concept that these young recruits became more adult was expunged from the film. The earlier script had them not only visiting bordellos and rising in rank but also doling out the same violence on younger sailors that they had experienced when they first boarded the ship.

7   See the discussion between the activist reporter and film director Mori Tatsuya and Satō Jun'ya, in Satō Jun'ya and Mori Tatsuya, "*Otokotachi no Yamato* wa hansen eiga ka!?" (Is *Yamato* an Anti-war Film?) *Shūkan kinyōbi* 588 (January 6, 2006). See also comments by Kadokawa and Satō in Julian Ryall, "Raising the Yamato," *Number One Shimbun* 38, no. 2 (February 2006).

8   See, for instance, the rightwing blog http://red.ap.teacup.com/sunvister/134 .html, accessed December 15, 2013.

9   Wakakuwa Midori, "Jendā no shiten de yomitoku sengo eiga: *Otokotachi no Yamato* o chūshin ni" (Reading Postwar War Films from a Gender Perspective, Focusing on *Yamato*), *Tōzai nanboku* (2007).

10   While I emphasize the historical differences between many of these films,
      their continuities should not be ignored. Most of these films were made at
      Tōhō, Tōei, and earlier Shintōhō (a Tōhō spin-off), studios for which war
      films were a profitable proprietary genre. That helps explain the connections
      in terms of personnel. Matsubayashi was a "supporting director" on *The
      Battleship Yamato* (a Shintōhō film), which starred actors such as Fujita
      Susumu (famous for Tōhō's war films during the war), who later appeared in
      The Imperial Navy (Tōhō). That film also featured actors such as Nagashima
      Toshiyuki and Kotegawa Yūko, who appeared in *Sea without Exit* (a
      Shōchiku film); Naraoka Tomoko, who played the "kamikaze mother" in
      The Firefly (Tōei); and Nagato Hiroyuki, who joined the cast of *For Those We
      Love* (which was distributed by Tōei). The assistant director on *The Firefly*,
      Sasabe Kiyoshi, ended up becoming the director of *Sea without Exit,* and
      the producer of the former, Takaiwa Tan, also produced *Yamato* (again
      distributed by Tōei). Some overlaps are inevitable given the limited size of
      Japan's actor pool, but they also show that war cinema in Japan was shaped
      not just by personal ideology but also by studio identities, genre, and star
      personas.

11   Isolde Standish, *Myth and Masculinity in the Japanese Cinema* (Richmond,
      UK: Curzon, 2000).

12   This is actually spoken by Lieutenant Usubuchi, during the same narrative
      situation—a fight between junior officers questioning their suicidal mission
      and those praising it—that *Yamato* uses to present a different but now more
      famous Usubuchi speech about Japan's need to lose in order to progress.
      The Battleship Yamato's version is more befitting a moment one decade
      before the start of high-economic growth.

13   Nogami has said that he was originally asked to write the script before
      Kadokawa or Satō came on board. His version was later rewritten without
      his knowledge by Satō, while still keeping much of what Nogami introduced,
      such as the focus on the young sailors and characters such as Kamio. After
      fighting with the producers, he eventually asked for his name to be removed
      from the credits. See Nogami Tatsuo, "Watashi ga *Otokotachi no Yamato* no
      kyakuhonka o orita riyū," (The Reasons I Withdrew My Name as the
      Screenwriter of *Yamato*) *Shinario* 62, no. 1 (2006).

14   E. Ann Kaplan, *Trauma Culture: The Politics of Terror and Loss in Media and
      Literature* (New Brunswick, NJ: Rutgers University Press, 2005); Joshua
      Hirsch, *Afterimage: Film, Trauma, and the Holocaust* (Philadelphia: Temple
      University Press, 2004); Janet Walker, *Trauma Cinema: Documenting Incest
      and the Holocaust* (Berkeley: University of California Press, 2005).

15   Nakamura Hideyuki, "Tokkōtai hyōshōron," (Representing the Kamikaze)
      in *Iwanami kōza: Ajia, Taiheiyō sensō,* vol. 5: *Senjō no shosō* (Iwanami Lecture

Series: The Asian Pacific War, vol. 5: Various Aspects of the Battlefield), ed. Kurasawa Aiko, et al. (Tokyo: Iwanami Shoten, 2006); idem, "Girei toshite no tokkō eiga: *Otokotachi no Yamato/Yamato* no baai," (Kamikaze Films as Ceremonial Courtesy: The Case of *Yamato*) *Zen'ya* 7 (Spring 2006).

16 Nakamura, "Girei toshite no tokkō eiga"; Wakakuwa, "Jendā no shiten de yomitoku sengo eiga," 12.

17 Fukuma Yoshiaki, "*Otokotachi no Yamato* to 'kandō' no poritikusu," (Yamato and the Politics of Emotion) in *Media bunka o shakaigaku suru,* (Sociologically Analyzing Media Culture) ed. Takai Masashi and Tanimoto Naho (Kyoto: Shakai Shisōsha, 2009).

18 Aaron Gerow, "Narrating the Nationality of a Cinema: The Case of Japanese Prewar Film," in *The Culture of Japanese Fascism,* ed. Alan Tansman (Durham, NC: Duke University Press, 2009); idem, "*Miyamoto Musashi* to senjichū no kankyaku," (Miyamoto Musashi and Wartime Spectators) in *Eiga kantoku Mizoguchi Kenji,* (Film Director Mizoguchi Kenji) ed. Yomota Inuhiko (Tokyo: Shinyōsha, 1999).

19 "Hansen ka hanBei ka?—Senki eiga no tadotte iru michi," (Anti-war or Anti-American? The Road War Films Have Taken) *Kinema junpō* 39 (August 1, 1953), reprinted in *Besuto obu Kinema junpō,* vol. 1 (Tokyo: Kinema Junpōsha, 1994): 225–229.

20 Rick Altman, *Film/Genre* (London: BFI, 1999).

21 *Ore wa, kimi no tame ni koso shini ni iku,* at www.chiran1945.jp.

22 The former kamikaze Itazu Tadamasa was part of the film's publicity efforts, and he stressed his long inability to tell others, even his family, of his wartime experiences. See Itazu Tadamasa, "Itazu Tadamasa ni tōji o kiku," (Asking Itazu Tadamasa about the Times Then) *Kinema junpō* 1483 (May 15, 2007).

23 See note 20.

24 Yoshikuni Igarashi has interpreted stories that reimagine the war defeat as a necessary sacrifice for the betterment of Japan as an element in what he terms the foundational narrative for postwar Japan. See Igarashi Yoshikuni, *Bodies of Memory: Narratives of War in Postwar Japanese Culture, 1945–1970* (Princeton, NJ: Princeton University Press, 2000). I argue that more recent films, while echoing such a function, deviate from it by being more self-referential and creating a more circular history.

25 From an ad in the evening edition of *Asahi shinbun,* April 25, 2007, cited in Amano Keiichi, " 'Utsukushii kuni' no 'utsukushii shi,' " (The "Beautiful Death" of a "Beautiful Country") *Inpakushon* 158 (July 2007).

26 Played by Nagashima Kazushige, son of the baseball legend Nagashima Shigeo.

27 While there are doubts about the authenticity of this statement, it was popularized by Yoshida Mitsuru's *Requiem for Battleship Yamato.* The same sentiment is expressed in *Lorelei* as well.

28 Igarashi, *Bodies of Memory.*

29 His ultimate death may then be ironic, since he dies not in an attack but from suffocation after his sub gets stuck in a rock formation underwater during practice.

30 Originally a stage play written by the actor Imai Masayuki (the English title was used in Japan), this story has been made into a theatrical film twice, in 1995 and in 2006, and as a television movie in 2005. It has also been novelized.

31 Darrell William Davis, *Picturing Japaneseness: Monumental Style, National Identity, Japanese Film* (New York: Columbia University Press, 1996).

32 Gerow, "*Miyamoto Musashi* to senjichū no kankyaku."

33 Hirsch, *Afterimage.*

34 "Onomichi fan kakutoku ni kōken," (Contributing to Acquiring Fans of Onomichi) *Chūgoku shinbun,* May 8, 2006.

35 Yoshimoto Mitsuhiro, "Melodrama, Postmodernism, and Japanese Cinema," *East West Film Journal* 5, no. 1 (1991).

36 *Always—Sunset on Third Street* (*Always—sanchōme no yūhi*) was released in 2005, and *Always—Sunset on Third Street 2* (*Always—zoku sanchōme no yūhi*) hit theaters in 2007. Both were based on the manga by Saigan Ryōhei and directed by Yamazaki Takashi. The first film was the seventh-highest-grossing Japanese film of 2005, and its sequel the third highest of 2007.

37 One could interpret the efforts of the second Abe cabinet to "escape the postwar regime" by working to change Japan's constitution and security apparatus as the political equivalent of the project of forgetting the postwar.

38 Represented in the film by the corporal punishment onboard ship, which are shown to be quite brutal but never fully problematized as it was in older Japanese war films.

39 Asada Akira, "Infantile Capitalism and Japan's Postmodernism," in *Postmodernism and Japan,* eds. Masao Miyoshi and H.D. Harootunian (Durham, NC: Duke University Press, 1989).

40 This article was completed before the kamikaze film *The Eternal Zero* (*Eien no 0,* 2013) became a major hit. Further analysis is needed to judge whether it functions in the way *Yamato* does, or how conditions of reception for war films may have changed under the second Abe cabinet, but the movie does share much with previous kamikaze films: a narration that begins in the present with young people ignorant of the wartime past; important roles given to those who value life over death; and a critical attitude toward the postwar. In fact, one can hypothesize that the film does not only work to forget the postwar, it urges that forgetting by depicting a present—the product of that postwar—that features not only morally lax and ignorant young people, but also fundamentally incorrect information about wartime heroes.

CHAPTER 10

The Promise and Limits of "Pop Culture Diplomacy" in East Asia

Contexts-Texts-Reception

Chiho Sawada

In 2004 a summit meeting between the leaders of the Republic of Korea
(ROK, South Korea) and Japan began with a conversation on pop culture
and its impact on relations between the two countries.[1] The Japanese prime
minister mentioned that the Korean television drama *Winter Sonata* (*Kyŏul
yŏn'ga,* 2002) had gained a tremendous following in Japan, becoming "something of a social phenomenon" and sparking wider interest about Korea. The
South Korean president responded that Japanese pop culture was increasingly accepted in his country in tandem with the lifting of import restrictions
on cultural products, such as music and animation (anime). They went on to
declare that official efforts to resolve "issues of the past" and fashion a "future-
oriented relationship" in Asia ultimately rely on a foundation of mutual
understanding and shared values built through people-to-people interactions
in cultural and economic realms.[2]

This apparently light exchange about television dramas and anime
actually captured very weighty issues for the Asia-Pacific region. First, it
acknowledged that "squarely facing history"—facing, that is, injustices committed amid colonialism, war, and dictatorship as well as ongoing disputes
about this dark past—is imperative for improving regional relations. In this
instance, the burden of confronting historical legacies and responsibilities
necessarily falls more heavily on Japan, since it had not only militarily occupied Korea for almost four decades, starting in the early twentieth century

but also waged aggressive wars throughout the Asia-Pacific region from the 1930s until its defeat in 1945. Second, the conversation underscored the limits of state power in addressing historical injustices and advancing reconciliation. In other words, state-to-state negotiation may be sufficient for restoring normalized relations between former antagonists, and thereby arriving at what has been called *thin* reconciliation, but diverse and sustained intersocietal interactions are crucial for realizing an enduring *thick* reconciliation (which entails forgiveness, empathy, and shared visions of the past and future).[3] Third, the two leaders identified the present—the beginning of the twenty-first century—as an opportune moment for attaining thick reconciliation, given the erosion of cold war–era barriers to trade and travel as well as the emergence of new (or renewed) facilitating factors to cross-border interactions.[4] Their words, as we shall see below, echoed great hopes for popular diplomacy—and, in particular, a new "pop culture diplomacy"— that was often articulated by pundits and politicians in the Asia-Pacific region at the dawn of the new millennium.[5]

The question remains as to whether transnational flows of pop culture can significantly affect historical consciousness across two or more national communities and contribute to a regional reconciliation. It may be helpful to begin by considering the words of prominent thinkers on the relationship between popular culture and history. In the stimulating book *Silencing the Past: Power and the Production of History,* Michel-Rolph Trouillot points to a disjuncture between academic historiography and the formation of collective historical consciousness or public memory. He observes, in this connection, that the people-at-large most often access their communal senses of the past not by reading scholarly works but by partaking in "celebrations, site and museum visits, movies, national holidays."[6] Other scholars, such as Andreas Huyssen and Arjun Appadurai, have also acknowledged the importance of such forms of informal education in shaping collective historical consciousness. Among informal modes of history education, Huyssen and Appadurai place special emphasis on what the former calls "the new media" and the latter "electronic capitalism." Pointing to a global "memory boom" or a shift "from present futures to present pasts," Huyssen goes so far as to declare that we "cannot discuss personal, generational, or public memory separate from the enormous influence of the new media as carriers of all forms of memory."[7]

> [I]t is no longer possible, for instance, to think of the Holocaust or of any other historical traumas as a serious ethical and political issue apart

from the multiple ways it is now linked to commodification and spectacu-
larization in films, museums, docudramas, Internet sites, photography
books, comics, fiction, even fairy tales (Roberto Benigni's *La vita è bella*)
and pop songs.[8]

Similarly, Appadurai has argued that manifestations of "electronic
capitalism"—cinema, television, and now Internet videos—are central to the
formation of new collective identities and memories in an era marked by
accelerating global flows of migrants, capital, information, and products.[9]
Huyssen and Appadurai are by no means alone in their views. In recent decades, scholarly interest in the historicizing potential of film, television, and
other forms of electronic media has grown.[10]

These observations clearly apply to the Asia-Pacific region. In many
parts of this region, entertainment and leisure activities are increasingly en-
twined with the construction of popular memories and collective identities
as state controls on cultural production are relaxed and new media platforms
proliferate. People are routinely exposed to "issues of the past" as they watch
history-based television dramas and films, browse and chat on websites and
social media, and play computer games. Informal education in these forms
is accessible and appealing because it entertains—and usually involves lower
costs (in terms of time, effort, expense) than, say, attending a semester-long
class, traveling to a historic site, or visiting a national museum. It is also freed
from geographic or spatial constraints.[11]

Thinking seriously and critically about pop culture—especially in connection to informal education—can help us better discern potential ave-
nues and obstacles to resolving historical disputes between Japan and its
Asian neighbors. For example, "pop culture diplomacy" complicates the
widely held notion of the "textbook controversy" as central to this dispute.
I certainly do not disavow the importance of the textbook issue, particularly because it has inspired debates on a transnational level extending well
beyond the classroom and into courts of law, newspapers, and everyday conversations.[12] Yet we should also consider the possibility that people in the
Asia-Pacific region engage public memory via mass-mediated entertainment
as well as directly from history textbooks. Scholars have begun to take notice. Several studies in recent decades explore, for instance, how wars in modern Asia are remembered as well as forgotten in literature, film, and other
popular art forms. This chapter seeks to build on this emerging literature.[13]

The next section, "Contextualizing Pop Culture Diplomacy," briefly surveys factors that account for the rise of pop culture as a prominent component of Korean-Japanese relations, situating this phenomenon within a matrix of global, regional, and nation-specific developments. The first half of the survey emphasizes key state actions and the second private-sector initiatives that have brought pop culture to the forefront of efforts to bring Japan and Korea closer together.[14] Then two sections, on "Textual Analysis of TV Drama and Film" and "Media Effects, Audience Reception, and Critical Interventions," respectively, analyze as well as problematize the notion that transnational flows of pop culture lead to mutual understanding about the past and shared goals in the present.

Contextualizing Pop Culture Diplomacy

In 1993, Federico Mayor, the then–director-general of the United Nations Educational, Scientific, and Cultural Organization (UNESCO), observed that the potential for cultural exchange had grown substantially in the aftermath of the cold war:

> New factors are working to bring different cultures into ever closer contact. Global upheavals have broken down old political barriers to movement. People can travel freely. Information can flow where it is needed. At the same time, tremendous advances in communications technology have created a planet-wide network capable of relaying information, sound and images from any one point on the globe to any other, instantaneously.[15]

He expressed the hope that cultural interactions facilitated by these "new factors" would, in turn, beckon a "multicultural springtime" of tolerance and reconciliation. A UNESCO leader obviously had an organizational interest in speaking this way. Nonetheless, subsequent developments in the Asia-Pacific region suggested that his optimistic vision might not be so far from the truth.

State-Led Initiatives toward Pop Culture Diplomacy between Korea and Japan

In October 1998, Kim Dae Jung, then the president of South Korea, visited Tokyo to confer with the then–Japanese prime minister Obuchi Keizō, which resulted in a "Joint Declaration of Partnership toward the Twenty-First Century."[16] Obuchi offered "deep remorse and heartfelt apology"—marking the first explicit apology by the Japanese government for its colonial past in Korea. There was much to apologize for. Countless people were killed in Japan's conquest of the Korean Peninsula and subsequent suppression of anticolonial uprisings. Even in relatively peaceful times, Koreans endured life as second-class citizens—suffering, on the one hand, all kinds of formal and informal discrimination and, on the other hand, assimilation policies that some have equated with cultural genocide. The final decade of Japanese rule was especially tragic. Hundreds of thousands of Korean individuals were wrenched from their homes and mobilized to support the expanding Japanese empire as soldiers, prison guards, laborers in mines and munitions factories, and—in the most infamous instances of historical injustice—as "sex slaves" for the Imperial Japanese Army. Kim expressed appreciation for this acknowledgment of history, which he deemed a prerequisite for "a future-oriented relationship based on reconciliation . . . and cooperation."[17] Although this exchange was largely symbolic (skirting the knotty issue of colonial reparations) and has subsequently been refuted by some Japanese leaders, it was heralded at the time as an important step forward in Korean-Japanese reconciliation.

To provide "concrete form to this partnership," the declaration enumerated priorities for future cooperation. This shortlist was not restricted to the cultural realm per se. Starting with recommendations for enhanced state-to-state consultation on security issues, it advocated new agreements on fishing rights, customs taxes, technology transfers, and other issues pertaining to cross-border commerce, travel, and communications. Significantly, however, the declaration culminated in a call for people-to-people interactions based on cultural exchange as a necessary ingredient for thick reconciliation. That is, to realize "mutual understanding" between the peoples of the two countries and "raise to a higher dimension the cooperative relations . . . which have been built since the normalization of relations in 1965."[18]

According to the Joint Declaration, the state would maintain a key role in promoting cultural exchange and thick reconciliation, but its actions were to be carefully calibrated, enhancing those that facilitated intersocietal interactions and curtailing those that did not. Thus, on the one hand, the two leaders advocated greater state activism to support "exchanges among various groups and regions at various levels in the two societies—*inter alia*, [students], teachers, researchers, journalists, civic associations." On the other hand, they acknowledged that state-administered barriers to Korean-Japanese interactions must be rolled back. This entailed, for instance, easing visa requirements for Korean citizens wishing to visit Japan. It was also in this context that President Kim pledged that his country would begin lifting in several stages the half-century-old ban on the importation of Japanese pop culture. Such steps, Obuchi and Kim concluded, would allow "peoples of both countries to share the spirit of this Joint Declaration and participate in joint efforts to build and develop a new partnership."

In parallel with the 1998 Joint Declaration and dismantling of Korean import bans on Japanese pop culture, the 2002 FIFA (Fédération Internationale de Football Association) World Cup propelled pop culture diplomacy. The 2002 rendition of this huge international sports event was unusual in that it was co-hosted by two countries: South Korea and Japan. To build on the spirit of cooperation and unity symbolized by the joint hosting of the World Cup, in late 1999 the Japanese and Korean governments designated 2002 as "The Year of National Exchange" and began to sponsor a series of initiatives foregrounding pop culture, aimed especially at young audiences. The actresses Fujiwara Noriko (a former Miss Japan, who regularly appeared in television dramas) and Kim Yun-jin (who starred in the Korean blockbuster film *Shiri* [*Swiri*, 1999]) were appointed goodwill ambassadors to promote the year of cultural exchange. Musical artists from the two countries were commissioned to compose an official theme song for the 2002 World Cup. The song—titled "Let's Get Together Now" and sung in a mixture of Japanese, Korean, and English—offered the following message:

> Don't you think it's time we all let go of the fear inside
> Open up our minds, understand each other
> If we just decide to be as one, we'll set our spirits free
> Let this be a time, we can always keep within our hearts
> Far beyond today, till the end of time
> No longer a dream, peace and love becomes reality
> . . .
>
> *Let's Get Together Now*[19]

Aided by enthusiastic press coverage in both countries (which lavished attention on everything from the arrival of a Korean youth soccer team in Tokyo to the release of a Japanese film in Seoul), the message spread that cultural exchange promised a new future of peace and unity.

Pop culture diplomacy continued to unfold after the final round of the 2002 World Cup. On January 1, 2004, the Korean government implemented the fourth stage in the lifting of import bans on cultural products from Japan. Earlier stages in this process—enacted in October 1998, September 1999, and June 2000, respectively—sanctioned importation of books and magazines, instrumental music, award-winning feature films, and a small number of animated programs. As Lee Chang-dong, the minister of culture and tourism (and famed filmmaker), explained at a December 2003 press conference, the fourth stage removed bans on computer game software as well as music with Japanese-language vocals and permitted broadcasting of television programs. In the first months of 2004, Korea hosted concerts by popular Japanese bands, such as TUBE (which was featured on the *2002 FIFA World Cup Official Album*), and a sumo-wrestling tournament that was also carried on television. Moreover, the Japanese and Korean governments launched yet another "Year of National Exchange" to commemorate the 2005 World Exposition in Aichi, Japan.

Societal Agency in the Pop Diplomacy Phenomenon

By 2003 announcements about opening South Korea to Japanese cultural imports elicited only muted protests, whereas just a few years earlier there had been widespread concerns about "cultural imperialism" and the corrosive effects of Japanese pop culture on Korean economy and society. Exploring the underlying causes of this shift suggests that the state has often been a supporting rather than leading actor in cultural exchange.

Various overlapping factors account for reduced Korean anxieties about transnational cultural flows. The first crucial factor was a growing awareness in Korea of how regulatory changes conform to social realities. Furtive importation of Japanese pop culture (in particular by comics and anime aficionados) had been going on for decades prior to the 1998 Joint Declaration and consequent policy changes. By 1998 satellite television, the Internet, and broadband technology had made Japanese pop culture accessible at the click of a button—rendering futile attempts at blocking such access. It was only a matter of time before the people-at-large recognized that the official opening to Japanese pop culture was a belated effort by the state to assert a modicum of influence over transnational cultural flows. Second, entertainment and media companies generally welcomed the regulatory changes. To be sure, some Korean business interests lobbied to prolong import restrictions on Japanese anime and television programs to protect emerging domestic firms in these sectors from "excessive competition." Many companies nonetheless perceived the changes as a great opportunity: to combat online piracy (thereby maximizing profits from sales of compact disks and digital video disks [CDs/DVDs] and fee-based file sharing), gain new sources of capital and content, and tap emerging markets.[20] A third important factor was the rising confidence among Koreans about the quality and appeal of domestically produced pop culture. Dire warnings about a Japanese cultural juggernaut and the weakness of Korean culture industries proved exaggerated. Japanese films, to cite a key example, captured only about 3 percent of the Korean domestic market between 2001 and 2003. Meanwhile, the Korean film industry experienced a veritable renaissance, reversing a dominance by American films to regain a robust 40 percent share of the domestic market in these years—and even reaching 60 percent in 2006.

Anxieties about Japanese cultural imperialism have been displaced by hopeful visions of a Korean cultural wave that flows across national and ethnic borders to win a following throughout Asia and beyond. This wave was born of numerous transformations in South Korea since the late 1980s. Among them, the following were perhaps most significant. Democratic consolidation brought a moderation of government censorship over cultural production. A shift from heavy industries to the "new economy" and from capital scarcity to surplus promoted greater investment in information technology and entertainment ventures. Although the major industrial conglomerates (*chaebŏl*) withdrew from investing in films in the aftermath of the 1997–1998 financial crisis, venture capital firms like Mirae Esset and film distribution companies such as CJ Entertainment turned to financing big-budget films and other pop culture productions. The general public, which was finally enjoying increased purchasing power and access to all sorts of products from abroad, demanded greater diversity of domestic pop culture. Thousands of people, many of them young and with modest means, eagerly bought up "Netizen funds" and became film investors themselves. All these changes allowed for a new generation of creative spirits—less encumbered than their predecessors by censorship, funding shortages, or the imperative of expressing political dissent—to channel their energies in myriad directions.

Building on indigenous influences as well as formats and content from overseas, this new generation has sought to fashion pop culture products that can compete with those from Hollywood and other global centers of cultural production. Whereas Korean films of the early 1980s consisted primarily of low-budget "quota quickies," by the end of the decade a critical "new wave" cinema had emerged. And by the late 1990s blockbuster movies began to span a range of internationally popular genres, such as the spy thriller, buddy film, romantic drama, and gangster comedy. Similar trends marked other entertainment sectors, with the appearance of highly polished Korean variations on the television soap opera, hip hop music, and so on. Thus was born a Korean-produced pop culture that is winning over audiences in Korea, the Asia-Pacific region, and far beyond.

By 2000 the imagery of a "Korean wave" (K: *hallyu*; C.: *hanliu*; J: *kanryū*) appeared in Chinese-language media, referencing the sudden craze for South Korean pop culture among residents of Hong Kong, Taiwan, Vietnam, and other parts of Southeast Asia. The term was soon picked up by media sources throughout Asia, making it an integral part of everyday conversation. Today—when "Gangnam Style" has become one of the most popular YouTube videos of all time and the performer in it, Psy, can hobnob with U.S. president Barack Obama—*hallyu* is accepted as a commonplace.

Toward Intersocietal Cultural Exchange and Reconciliation?

Japan did not escape the "Korean wave." Small ripples reached the islands by 2000, as evidenced by the successful theatrical release of the spy thriller *Shiri* and popularity of musical acts such as S.E.S. and BoA. *Hallyu* finally hit Japan at full force with the national broadcast of *Winter Sonata* on the NHK satellite television channel in 2003. *Fuyusona* (as the hit series is affectionately known in Japan) became undeniably "something of a social phenomenon." Bae Young-joon, the actor who plays the male lead role in *Winter Sonata,* quickly gained a legion of adoring Japanese fans. By mid-2004 NHK's publishing arm had sold over a million copies combined of the DVD/videocassette boxed set and spin-off novel. More significantly, the program has inspired viewers to sample other manifestations of Korean culture. *Fuyusona* fans subscribed to digital television services offering Korean programming, purchasing a variety of Korean novels and films, and, in quite a few cases, visiting the peninsula. This wave continues to flow strongly throughout Japan.

Hallyu heightens the potential for genuine cultural exchange between the two countries. During the thirty-five years that Japan occupied Korea (1910–1945), the official policy was to assimilate, or Japan-ize, Koreans. While it was sometimes acknowledged that Japan benefited in past centuries from cultural interactions with the peninsula, contemporary Korean cultural forms were denigrated as derivative and degenerate. Following Japan's defeat in World War II and the dissolution of the Japanese empire, the Japanese media and public typically ignored Korean culture—except, it seemed, to point out instances in which a Korean pop song or television series had allegedly copied a Japanese original. This dismissive, indeed neocolonialist, attitude may have appeared justifiable to some so long as Korea maintained a ban on Japanese pop culture. (Of course, it should be noted again that the import ban was neither effectively nor consistently enforced. During the five decades prior to the 1998 Joint Declaration, in addition to furtive importation of Japanese comics, anime, fashion magazines, and so on, about 2,000 popular Japanese books deemed sufficiently "literary" were translated into Korean and sold legally.) Japan, in any case, no longer has a convenient excuse for ignoring Korean cultural products. Korea's official "opening" to Japanese pop culture, bilateral promotional activities leading up to the 2002 FIFA World Cup, and private-sector initiatives (e.g., the Avex-SM Entertainment partnership) have combined to prod the Japanese people-at-large toward the *hallyu* phenomenon. Having done so, many appear to be awed by what they have found—and pleasantly surprised at discovering their own long-suppressed capacity for appreciating Korean cultural forms.

Japan's rediscovery of Korea, together with the latter's more receptive stance toward Japanese cultural products, heralded the flowering of pop culture diplomacy. There are undeniable signs of growing transnational linkages through pop culture, involving state as well as societal initiatives, and extending across stages of production, distribution, and consumption of cultural products. Not only political leaders but also many media pundits and scholars have expressed optimism that such linkages will translate into shared visions of the past and present—and thereby relieve ethnic tensions. A journalist for *Japan Times,* for example, expressed his hope that the impact of *hallyu* in Japan would gradually reduce discrimination against Japanese residents of Korean descent: "Now the Korean culture is hip, perhaps they will be appreciated for their difference."[21] A scholar at Kyoto University sounded even more confident:

> Culture can have tremendous significance in international relations. For example, the South Korean drama series *Kyŏul yŏn'ga* (Winter Sonata) became a major hit when it was broadcast in Japan . . . and it is now widely credited with helping many Japanese feel a sense of closeness to South Korea, which up to now has often been described as "near but far"—geographically close to Japan, but psychologically distant. Also, a

survey of public opinion in South Korea has found that university students who are fans of Japanese pop music tend to be more lenient than non-fans on the issue of Japan's past colonization of the Korean Peninsula.[22]

Furthermore, a survey of over 1,700 Japanese people conducted jointly by the newspapers *Dong-A Ilbo* (South Korea)—*Asahi Shimbun* (Japan) in 2005 suggests a strongly positive relationship between watching Korean movies and television dramas and "becom[ing] friendlier toward Korea."[23] Pop culture diplomacy, in other words, offered heady visions of transforming Japanese-Korean relations from "thin" to "thick" reconciliation. Unfortunately for advocates of pop culture diplomacy, the reality has proven more complicated—a point illustrated by shifting from a broad discussion of context to critical analysis of the content of specific pop culture texts.

Textual Analysis of Television Drama and Film

Through textual analysis of two media sources released with much hoopla in the run-up to the 2002 FIFA World Cup—the four-episode TV "miniseries" *Friends* and the blockbuster film *2009 Lost Memories,* this section explores the extent to which commercial pop culture captures the complexities of historical injustice and persisting interethnic conflict. It also asks whether pop texts like *Friends* and *2009* contain messages that can help promote reconciliation in a manner that transcends ethnic nationalism. In the remainder of this section, I provide brief descriptions of these contrasting texts—one promoting comforting visions of ethnic harmony and the other emphasizing insuperable conflict—and then consider their potentials and limitations with respect to helping resolve contentious issues of the past and present.[24]

Love Conquers All?

Born of a partnership between TBS (Tokyo Broadcasting System) and MBC (Munhwa Broadcasting Company, Seoul), *Friends* proposes that the Japanese and Korean peoples can get along after all. TBS offers the following synopsis of the drama:

> Left alone on a trip to Hong Kong, Tomoko finds herself the victim of a purse snatching. The police arrest the man she points out, but it turns out to be the wrong person: a young Korean man named Chi-hun. Despite his anger and humiliation he takes her out to dinner since she has

lost all her money, and in return she agrees to model for his amateur film. What follows is a magical and romantic two days. Upon returning to their respective countries, Tomoko must return to her nine-to-five job and Chi-hun must resume studying to join the family business rather than pursuing his dream of becoming a film director.

All is not lost, however, as "the two begin to email each other and rekindle their relationship despite the distance and obstacles between them." The synopsis triumphantly concludes—"Marking the very first time in television history that a drama has been co-produced between Japan and South Korea, the story show us that love has no borders."[25]

Framing Chi-hun's and Tomoko's union as Korean-Japanese relations writ small, *Friends* represents the bridging of cultural distance. Starting in the liminal, transnational spaces of Hong Kong (signified by shots of store signs in Japanese, Korean, Chinese, and English) and the Internet, the protagonists gradually learn about each other and their respective countries. Tomoko (played by the then-rising Japanese "idol" Fukuda Kyōko) initially thinks Chi-hun (played by the Korean heartthrob Wǒn Bin) is a Chinese

"Friends" with the culturally hybrid Hong Kong as backdrop

resident of Hong Kong. When Chi-hun corrects her, she enthusiastically lists all the things she knows about Korea: "kimuchee, yakiniku, karubi, bibinba . . ." That is, not much beyond Japanese renditions of iconic Korean dishes. Chi-hun, in turn, presumes that Tomoko embodies the unflattering stereotype of young Japanese women as spoiled consumers, flitting about traveling and shopping. In Hong Kong, they meet by chance and find they have little in common—other than an undercurrent of sexual attraction and the fact their given names share a Chinese character (智, knowledge). But mutual understanding gradually develops through their email exchanges (which are facilitated by a friend of Chi-hun's who has studied Japanese). Tomoko and Chi-hun reveal to each other their hopes and fears. Both, it turns out, are struggling to negotiate an almost universal rite of passage: to find a place in the world while balancing individual desires, family expectations, and social norms. Inspired, Tomoko decides to take night classes to learn Korean and eventually lands a job with a travel agency in Seoul catering to Japanese tourists. She also encourages Chi-hun to pursue his dreams, which leads first to an apprenticeship as a production assistant in Seoul and later to an internship in northern Japan. Although a series of obstacles conspires to separate them, the two "friends" never give up hope.

Ethnicity Trumps Friendship?

2009 Lost Memories borrows a compelling, counterfactual scenario from a novel by the South Korean writer Pok Kŏ-il: What if imperial Japan had fought alongside the Allies in World War II and Korea had remained its colony?[26] A bricolage of familiar cinematic genres—history-based epic, futuristic science fiction, buddy film—*2009* begins with an attempt by Korea's national hero An Chung-gŭn in 1909 to gun down the Japanese statesman Itō Hirobumi. In reality, An mortally wounded Itō (who headed Japan's "protectorate" regime in Korea, 1905–1909); but in the film a descendant of a colonial governor travels back in time to foil the assassination attempt. This intervention disrupts the flow of "history" and triggers a series of distortions, which are pithily presented in the film's second shot: Japan's victory in World War II, emergence as a nuclear power, and continued appropriation and effacement of all things Korean. After this arresting opening sequence, the film cuts to a shot of Seoul in 2009—depicted as the third city, behind Tokyo and Osaka, of the "Great Japanese Empire." A century of Japanese rule has reduced the Korean resistance to a small, beleaguered underground movement, which calls itself a "Liberation Army" but is dismissed

A (post)colonial buddy film?

by officials and the Japanese-controlled media as "terrorists" or "lawless gooks." The group carries out an attack on a Japanese exhibition of ancient Korean artifacts to reclaim a "Lunar Stone" that can unlock a portal in time and allow them to put history right. Enter the Japanese Bureau of Investigation (JBI), which is charged with stopping the underground separatist movement.

The narrative is driven by competing relationships, which parallel as well as cut across the battle between Japanese colonizers and Korean Liberation Army. Viewers are first introduced to the quasi-brotherly bond linking two JBI officers, Sakamoto Masayuki (played by the Korean actor Chang Tong-gŏn) and Saigō Shōjirō (played by the Japanese actor Nakamura Tōru). Sakamoto and Saigō are not only partners on the job but also best friends, having supported each other in college and at the JBI Academy. Though they are united by friendship and occupational prerogative, a fault line runs through their relationship: Saigō belongs to the ruling ethnic group, whereas Sakamoto is ethnically Korean. Sakamoto does his best to deny this source of tension. He appears to epitomize the assimilated colonial subject, who has mastered the Japanese language, has adopted a Japanese name, prefers sushi over kimchi, and voluntarily demonstrates his loyalty to the empire by leading efforts to crush Korean separatists.

But Freudian trouble lurks beneath the surface. We soon learn that Sakamoto's assimilationist zeal is symptomatic of his ambivalent struggle

Ethnic nationalism over friendship

with the memory of his father, who was rumored to have been a corrupt official who accepted bribes from Korean "terrorists." Ashamed of both his ethnic and family background, he tries to forget by throwing himself into his work—to no avail. What he consciously denies seeps into dreams (Sakamoto is haunted by fragmented images of the Lunar Stone and a mysterious Korean woman who, viewers later learn, is one of the resistance leaders), which propel him toward his destiny.

As the story unfolds, the tensions in these relationships (and in Sakamoto's psyche) become untenable. Fearing that Sakomoto is close to deciphering the secrets behind Japan's manipulation of history, his bosses at the JBI move to stop him by framing him for murder. Saigō, albeit reluctantly, aids the conspiracy when he learns that his family's welfare is at stake. On the run, Sakamoto is drawn to the underground. Once there, he not only encounters the woman from his dreams but also discovers the glorious history of the Korean nation (which has been suppressed by Japanese-controlled media and education), his father's true role as a secret agent for the resistance, and, ultimately, his ethnic identity. Thus enlightened, Sakamoto chooses ethnicity over friendship, turning his guns on his former colleagues—including his best friend, Saigō.

Toward Mutual Understanding and Shared Values?

Friends and *2009 Lost Memories* were launched in no small part by the desire to cash in on new opportunities afforded by the aforementioned regulatory changes and the hype surrounding the joint hosting of the 2002 World Cup. Many in the entertainment industry seized on joint ventures, seeking lower production costs, new creative synergies, and larger markets. For Japanese filmmakers, shifting location shots to Korea and other parts of Asia makes good business sense given the high costs and onerous regulatory restrictions that accompany shooting in Japan. Korean filmmakers welcome added sources of funding and a new pool of stars to enhance the regional exportability of their films. Performers, both Korean and Japanese, are attracted by the prospect of expanding their fan base beyond the border of their own country. Overall, industry insiders throughout Asia are angling to increase profits by sharing production skills, formats, and content, while pooling promotional and distribution power.

These less-than-altruistic motivations notwithstanding, the people behind the two works also professed the spirit of the 1998 Joint Declaration: that is, to nurture a new Korean-Japanese partnership, founded on mutual understanding and shared values. Kijima Seiichirō, the executive producer of *Friends,* has spoken of "the possibilities and responsibilities" of the televised drama:

> There is still a great gap between Korea and Japan. However, if we *understand our differences,* we will realize that the passion for drama-making is [the] same for both countries. We hope that you will see in this drama *the possibilities and responsibilities of the TV media,* and the dreams and delight it creates.[27]

Members of the joint writing team for *Friends* reportedly labored for many months on the script in an effort to bring serious issues affecting regional relations into the story line. In fact, the drama references, inter alia, persistent discrimination facing residents in Japan of Korean ancestry; the comparatively tight visa restrictions Japan maintains against visitors from Korea; and tensions on the peninsula that have continued compulsory military training for Korean men.

Similar good intentions were involved in the making of *2009 Lost Memories.* Its co-producer, Kim Yun-yŏng, has claimed, for example, that the joint production team attempted to put on screen Korean historical concerns in a manner that engages young Japanese audiences.[28] Imamura Shōhei, one of Japan's most renowned directors, whose films have consistently evinced antiestablishment views and critiqued prewar Japanese militarism, found the screenplay of *2009* compelling enough to serve as a consultant and make a cameo appearance. The actor Nakamura Tōru has been attracted to roles in works that consider serious aspects of Japanese-Korean and Sino-Japanese interactions. Amid the entertaining action sequences and special effects, *2009* does in fact introduce real Korean grievances against Japan regarding "issues of the past." The exhibition attack and Lunar Stone theme reference the contentious issue of reparations: in this case, repatriating Korean cultural treasures removed to Japan during the colonial period. Sakamoto poignantly represents the tragedy of colonial-era assimilation policies that forced Koreans to suppress their ethnicity while denying them genuine inclusion.[29] His character is also innovative, portraying a Korean member of the colonial police force in sympathetic ways and thereby injecting an element of complexity into the still highly controversial issue of colonial collaboration. And, of course, the time-travel/alternate history theme both references colonial-era experiences and indicts renewed postcolonial attempts among reactionary elements in Japan to promote history textbooks that whitewash the country's imperial past in Asia.

Numerous factors nonetheless undermine the progressive potential of these two pop culture texts. Though *Friends* introduces many important issues, they are not developed or treated in a nuanced manner. The issue of discrimination against ethnic Koreans in Japan is brought into the story by way of a third-generation Korean-Japanese (*zainichi*) character named Kaneda Midori (played by Toda Naho) that Tomoko befriends at night school—but this promising thread is quickly dropped.[30] *Friends* can also be criticized for reifying ethnic and gender stereotypes. Korean cultural patterns are simplistically contrasted with those of Japan. For example, Korean families are depicted as "traditional" *qua* patriarchal; Japanese families are presumably the polar opposite, characterized by weak family life. Predictably, it is Chi-hun who exercises agency by achieving acclaim as a director, which gives him the confidence to challenge his father's authority and reclaim Tomoko, the object of his affections. (Meanwhile, Tomoko, having given up a bid at an overseas career and returned to her old life, pines away for her man.) To put matters another way, Chi-hun masters cinematic language and controls visual representation; Tomoko is the object of the gaze.[31]

All these shortcomings—lack of depth, reliance on dichotomous stereotypes, and problematic gender construction—arguably characterize popular movies and television dramas in general, which are, first and foremost, vehicles for entertaining and selling. *Friends* projects a fantasy world in which complex issues of the past and the present are reduced to the ups-and-downs of an imagined relationship between two media-generated "idols"—a world in which our eyes are guided by a camera that lingers on not only their tight embrace but also boutique windows and fashionable accessories (e.g., a baseball cap with a New York Yankees logo). In other words, to the extent that

Friends promotes shared values that transcend ethnic fault lines, it may most effectively reinforce the desire for a consumption-oriented, corporate-driven modernity. Some thinkers, notably Arjun Appadurai, suggest that even modernity of this sort can be liberating. He discerns spaces for transnational agency in the interstices of "electronic capitalism" and hyperconsumption—spaces for imagining myriad "diasporic public spheres" rather than only dominant "imagined communities" of nation-states. But other theorists who hew closer to the Frankfurt school of cultural interpretation might wonder whether the world depicted in *Friends* is actually an "open-air prison."[32]

The promising threads found in *2009* are intertwined with hypermasculine and ethnic nationalist excess. By the second half of the film, the critique of Japanese militarism and imperialism becomes muted—a syncopated accompaniment to a dominant theme celebrating "Greater Korea." Sakamoto, upon meeting the spiritual leader of the resistance, is told that the Lunar Stone and the portal it unlocks, a giant stele, were originally located in Manchuria because that territory was and shall again be a part of Korea. (Such a claim hardly helps ameliorate present-day conflicts between Korea and China over the cultural heritage of Manchuria!) He also learns that the Japanese resorted to historical distortion not only to wash away the humiliation of defeat in World War II but also in a desperate attempt to prevent the emergence of a reunified Korea that will rightly be the "new light of Asia." Rather than disavow irredentist ethnic nationalism, the film invokes one strain as more legitimate than another version.

2009 exploits cinematic techniques—notably, cross cutting and non-diegetic music—to drive home this problematic message to mind-numbing and ear-splitting effect. Consider the agonizingly drawn-out sequence (just after Sakamoto learns the truth about his father and fatherland) when the JBI attacks the rebels' underground base. Sakamoto reaches out to try to protect a young boy, who runs toward him trailed by a hail of bullets. This action is repeatedly intercut with parallel action occurring aboveground. Saigō, enjoying a festival with his family, holds out his arms to catch his young daughter, who scampers toward him as fireworks dance in the background. The boy stumbles, shot in the back just before reaching Sakamoto; the girl lands happily in her father's arms. The message is unmistakable. Japanese-Korean relations are framed in zero-sum terms: the luxury and levity enjoyed by ethnic Japanese derived from oppressing Koreans—and, when push comes to shove, mercilessly killing them.

As if this ethnic nationalist narrative were not already clear enough, the filmmakers have amplified it with a melodramatic score, excessive use of slow motion, and yet another layer on the theme of hallowed paternity. As the boy stumbles, he drops a box that had been clutched against his chest, causing cherished belongings to spill on to the ground—including a photograph of his father. At this moment, multiple paternal narratives converge. Sakamoto, to his dismay, realizes that he had cut down the boy's father, who was the leader of the exhibition attack. His authentic (read: ethnic) self finally awakened, he stands up (literally and metaphorically) and seizes a hefty machine gun. Emerging from his collaborationist nightmare, Sakamoto vows to atone for his past sins by turning his gun on the Japanese and vindicating all the fathers who had died for the Korean nation.

Mixed Motivations and Mixed Messages

The very attributes that make film and television highly effective media for shaping public memory also complicate their potential for promoting interethnic understanding and resolving "issues of the past." As vehicles for entertainment and profit, didactic appeals to universal harmony—as expressed in the 2002 World Cup theme song "Let's Get Together Now"—are often overshadowed by other elements (action, sex, fantasy, violence, chauvinism) that appeal to less noble instincts and desires. Furthermore, by seeking to facilitate historical reconciliation between Japan and Korea as well as achieve commercial success, the makers of *Friends* and *2009 Lost Memories* produced pop texts that inevitably project mixed messages. Both begin strong with respect to the first objective, but commercial imperatives and genre limitations undermine their critical, progressive potential. *Friends,* as explained above, does touch on important issues of ethnic discrimination and cultural difference. But framing Japanese-Korean relations as a charming love story— and adhering to the conventions of romantic comedy and the television family drama *qua* product-placement vehicle—derails an exploration of historical and structural factors that inhibit interethnic reconciliation. *2009,* as a "history-based film," outdoes *Friends* in projecting instances of historical injustice and lingering ethnic animosities on screen. Yet *2009* is also hampered by reliance on generic formulae: most notably, the crowd-pleasing story of the heroic underdog beating a well-armed band of bad guys. As *2009* unfolds, it grapples less and less with complex issues such as cultural assimilation, gives way to gunplay and special effects, and begins to resemble other

Korean-produced films, television dramas, and other pop media that have portrayed Japan as evil incarnate.[33]

Friends and *2009* represent two basic templates for representing Korean-Japanese relations on big and small screens. Since the early 2000s there has been a steady trickle of television dramas depicting contemporary interethnic romances and feature films set in the colonial Korea. Examples of the former include *Star's Echo* (K: *Pyŏl ŭi soli* / J: *Anata ni aitakute*, 2004) and *Tokyo Shower* (*Tok'yo yŏubi*, 2008); the latter *YMCA Baseball Team* (*YMCA yagudan*, 2002), *Rikidōzan: A Hero Extraordinary* (*Yŏkdosan*, 2004), *Blue Swallow* (*Ch'ŏng-yŏn*, 2005), *Virgin Snow* (*Ch'ŏtun*, 2007), and *Once Upon a Time* (2008). Although interesting twists have appeared on the two templates—such as the horror film *Epitaph* (*Kidam*, 2007) and an Asian re-interpretation of the Spaghetti Western, *The Good, the Bad, the Weird* (*Choŭn nom, nappŭn nom, isanghan nom*, 2008), both set in the colonial period—all these works arguably have failed to transcend the genre limitations and commercial imperatives mentioned earlier.[34]

One might be tempted to dismiss such critiques, saying that *2009* is "just a movie" and *Friends* "only a TV show." Doing so may not be prudent, however, as movies and television can cloak politicized, tendentious historical views by calling them innocuous entertainment—something not to be taken too seriously, while subtly embedding such interpretations in the minds of viewers as historical knowledge. Fortunately, audience members are not mere dupes. Cultural texts like *Friends* and *2009 Lost Memories* not only are imbued with multiple messages at various stages of production but also take on new meanings as they are received and interpreted by viewers. In the final section, I turn briefly to issues of media effects and audience reception, which further complicate the pop culture diplomacy thesis.

Media Effects, Audience Reception, and Critical Interventions

As Korea opened its cultural market, a news segment on KBS (Korea Broadcasting System) decried that "computer games imported from Japan and China have been found to present distorted explanations of Korean history." The segment called for state action to curtail such phenomena, noting: "the government takes extra care about the issue of Japan's distortion of history in textbooks and China's move to limit access to ancient Korean historic sites in northeast China. But the government has failed to show any response to the problem of computer games."[35] This suggestion, however well intentioned, is misguided. The paradigm of state regulation to root out "distorted" history and enforce "correct" history is difficult to apply to pop culture. (Although it is reasonable to expect compilers of official textbooks to be mindful of personal and ethnic-cultural biases in their works—despite the elusiveness of what Peter Novick has called "that noble dream" of historical objectivity—creators of historical fiction are usually not bound by such an obligation.) Rather than demand that art and entertainment conform to strict content requirements and represent historical narratives that government-commissioned bodies deem appropriate, a more fruitful approach might be not only to study the polysemous content of pop culture but also to explore how individuals and social groups engage cultural texts. This brings us to another layer of complications: questions of media effects and audience reception.

Acknowledging the polysemy of pop culture discourages the adoption of any simple notion of direct media effects. Sometimes called the "hypodermic needle model" or "bullet theory," the concept of direct effects posits that the media (including, *inter alia,* common forms of mass media, those controlling media production and distribution, specific media texts) inject weak unsuspecting audiences directly with their potent effects.[36] If, for example, *hallyu* pop products circulating throughout Asia contain multiple and even contradictory meanings, we must at the very least ask which messages leave impressions on audiences. Asking such a question may lead, in turn, away from a view of audiences as passive receptacles and toward a more nuanced approach that seeks to understand how people selectively consume and interpret the many meanings embedded in pop culture.

In contrast to the hypodermic needle model, theories of "minimal or limited effects" hold that "we selectively expose ourselves to media messages that are most familiar to us, and . . . retain messages that confirm values and attitudes we already hold."[37] Korean consumption of Japanese pop culture demonstrates such minimal effects in some ways. Although formal studies (especially in English) on the spread of Japanese pop culture to other Asian countries often emphasize putatively favorable qualities to explain its appeal, my conversations in Korea and with Korean exchange students in the United States reveal a more complex picture. To be sure, Korean aficionados of Japanese pop culture often admit to seeing their favorite idols or products as synecdoche for desirable attributes that presumably characterize Japanese culture and society as a whole—for instance, diversity (relative to Korea in decades past) and technical sophistication. Yet compliments of this sort are typically accompanied by another opinion. Unbeknownst perhaps to champions of pop culture diplomacy, Korea's "opening" to cultural imports from its island neighbor did little to diminish stereotyping of Japanese society as excessively permissive and its pop culture as fetishizing violence and "deviant" sexuality.[38]

These examples also point to other ways of understanding media effects: variants of the familiar "uses and gratifications model" and more recent cultural studies approaches that, in a sense, turn the question of media effects on its head. These approaches do not so much ask what mass media do to us as explore "how people make meanings, understand reality, and order experience through their use of cultural symbols in print and visual media."[39] On the side of studies foregrounding positive reasons for the wide appeal of Japanese pop culture, the cultural analyst Aoyagi Hiroshi speaks of the emotional power of its signature "cute" (*kawaii*) style and further hypothesizes that consumers use it to create a unifying regional consciousness. He suggests, for instance, that Japanese pop idols (as representatives of the first Asian country to experience industrialization) have served to help young people in Korea, Taiwan, Hong Kong, and mainland China "mak[e] sense of the changing social and workplace conditions that accompany economic growth and 'modernization' in Asia."[40] At the same time, selective attention by Koreans to somewhat unorthodox manifestations of Japanese pop culture can be interpreted as more than vicarious enjoyment of the exotic and passive reinforcement of existing stereotypes about a morally bankrupt Japan. It may also represent efforts to map out (ethnic-nationalist) claims of enduring difference (and superiority), rather than growing similarity or unity. In other words, this rhetorical distancing maneuver might be read as an active, albeit defensive, response to the specter of neocolonial assimilation to a Japanese-centered modernity and the reality of increasing regional integration in cultural production, distribution, and consumption.

These complications about media effects and audience reception also apply to Japanese consumption of cultural products from various Asian countries. Although celebrants of pop culture diplomacy invoke the promise of a "multicultural springtime" bringing interethnic tolerance, shared values, and historical reconciliation, cautious observers like Iwabuchi Kōichi point to persistent cultural stereotyping and ethnic-nationalist inflections in the Japanese reception to other Asian pop cultures.

> As [regional] economic development stirred Japanese media and indus-
> try attention and broadened Japanese interest in Asian popular culture
> in the 1990s . . . a reflexive posture [to engage Asia on equal terms] was
> gradually swallowed up by Japan's historically constituted conception
> of a culturally and racially similar, but always "backward" Asia.[41]

That many Asian nations are "modernizing" is not denied. But the majority
of Japanese people, according to Iwabuchi, "refus[e] to accept that [Japan]
shares the same temporality as other Asian nations." This refusal inhibits,
he says, a conscious or emotional sense of "coevalness" with other groups
that might be expected to emerge from partaking in a common set of cultural products. Ironically, it also strengthens a narcissistic impulse while
looking outward to other societies. Regarding Japan's "Asia boom" of the
1990s, which began with a focus on cultures to "the south" (i.e., Okinawa,
Hong Kong, and Singapore), Iwabuchi emphasizes that people have tended
to "nostalgically see Asia as embody[ing] a social vigor and optimism for
the future that Japan allegedly is losing or has lost."[42] This stream of critique
can be applied to the more recent "Korean wave" in Japan. Part and parcel
of the craze for Korean pop culture is the championing of supposedly
essential Korean qualities (i.e., filial piety, simplicity)—a discourse that
feeds a nostalgic and narcissistic fixation on what postbubble, "postmodern"
Japan has supposedly lost. Japanese fans of Korean pop culture claiming a
new appreciation for Korea may be gazing at an imagined version of
"Korea" and possibly hoping that this imaginary will serve as a magical
mirror to reflect and restore their former selves.

Fortunately, there is also evidence to the contrary. For example, an
Asahi Shimbun–Dong-A Ilbo opinion poll in 2010 revealed that 47 percent
of Japanese respondents considered Korea "on par" with Japan in terms of
technology (which even exceeded the proportion of Korean respondents who
saw their country as having caught up with Japan).[43] Moreover, a qualita-
tive study based on interviews of Japanese "middle-aged female" viewers of
Korean television dramas reveals more self-awareness and critical insights
among fans than the aforementioned warnings imply. The viewers acknowledge that their "fandom" is steeped in nostalgia and at the same time claim
to have learned that Korea is not behind or inferior to Japan.

> Korea was very far from me. I thought that they just copied us. I was
> only thinking what we could give to them, but I thought there was noth-

ing I could receive from them. After watching *Winter Sonata,* Korea got closer, but a strong gap still exists: it is our history. We can easily say that we love *Yon-sama,* we love Korea, but they cannot. I have Korean-Japanese friends and Korean-American ones, but not real Korean friends. I was confronted when I saw, during my tour, what the Japanese military authority did in Korea. But now I believe that women like me can be a good breakthrough, by loving Korean dramas and actors, even if Korean people may be surprised at us.[44]

The point I wish to emphasize here is that transnational flows and consumption of pop culture—various obstacles and complications notwithstanding—can encourage deep reflection on complex issues of history and injustice.

Conclusion

The full effects of the latest "Korean wave" and the (re)emergence of a regional cultural market in Asia remain to be seen, and carefully analyzed, as both are relatively recent phenomena that continue to unfold. At this point, we must proceed with the hypothesis that while pop culture and public memory are undeniably linked—as Trouillot, Huyssen, Appadurai, and many other thinkers have emphasized, transnational flows of pop culture do not necessarily lead directly to conscious and conscientious reflections on history. A report on *hallyu* compiled by the Ministry of Culture and Tourism of the Republic of Korea is revealing. In a sample of just over 2,000 people in Hong Kong, Taiwan, and China surveyed about their "desired purpose for visiting Korea," more than two-fifths chose "visit[ing] TV drama/movie locations" as their first priority. But less than one in ten respondents mentioned "want[ing] to know more about Korea," such as its culture and history.[45] In another study, after interviewing numerous Japanese fans of Hong Kong pop culture, the lead researcher could claim no more than that transnational cultural consumption had encouraged *"at least some* [to become] more critically aware of Japan's modern experiences and imperialist history."[46] To offer a comparative perspective, a survey in the United States by Roy Rosenzweig—an influential figure in the development of the public history movement and the founder of the Center for History and New Media—revealed that among 653 people "who reported watching a history film or television program, only 11 wanted to immediately discuss what they had seen."[47] These examples offer only rough indicators of the frequency at which transnational flows of pop culture prompt an individual or a community to reflect on questions of historical injustice and reconciliation. They illustrate, nevertheless, that the former does not perforce lead to the latter.

Furthermore, whereas evidence abounds of increasing linkages between Japanese and Korean societies facilitated by pop culture, we must acknowledge uncertainty as to whether such interactions do more to break down or reinforce ethnic nationalism. The lack of systematic study on such questions is problematic, especially considering that as economic liberalism and "electronic capitalism" spread across the Asia-Pacific region, the forms of informal history education discussed in this chapter are correspondingly increasing. Many governments in the region have also bolstered their cultural diplomacy efforts, not only within the Asia-Pacific region but also other key places in the world, including the Middle East and Africa. Amid this activity are troubling signs extending beyond government circles. In discussions of pop culture and international relations/global politics, notions of "soft power" and unilateral benefits deriving from cultural exports are increasingly inflected, rather than multilateral cultural exchange and genuine dialogue. The "Korean wave" has even triggered occasional nativist reactions in Japan and China, which deploy virulently ethnic-nationalist comics and web pages. (Such tendencies have been strengthened by rising tensions over maritime territorial disputes.) In short, pop culture diplomacy remains largely uncharted territory that presents at least as much peril as promise.

It is my hope that more and more scholars, from a variety of disciplinary and cultural backgrounds, will grapple with open questions about the relationships between pop culture, public memory, and interethnic relations, rather than retreat in the face of these uncertainties. In this connection, I turn again to Trouillot, who counsels that the historical lessons that people acquire from movies, holiday celebrations, and other sources of informal education can be "sustained, modified, or challenged by scholars"—particularly if the latter "become increasingly quick at modifying their targets and refining their tools for investigation."[48] Rosenzweig similarly has emphasized that "history professionals" are uniquely equipped to facilitate critical, transformative dialogue in partnership with "popular historymakers."

> [P]roviding context and comparisons and offering structural explanations, history professionals can turn the differences between themselves and popular historymakers into assets rather than barriers. History professionals can help to enrich popular uses of the past by introducing

people to different voices and experiences. They can help to counter false
nostalgia about earlier eras . . . and make people aware of possibilities
for transforming the status quo.[49]

By acknowledging pop culture as a site of important historical and political
dynamics, and by serving as public intellectuals who engage discourses on
pop culture reaching far beyond the academy, scholars can intervene in the
complex processes of informal education—and, I hope, in a manner that
enhances the edifying potential of pop culture in the global quest for peace
and justice.

Notes

1   This chapter is the product of many rewarding conversations with colleagues
and mentors as well as valuable feedback following presentations at Stanford
University, the International Studies Association Annual Convention,
University of San Francisco, University of North Carolina at Charlotte, Holy
Names University, University of Washington, and the Carnegie Endowment
for International Peace. An earlier version of this chapter appeared in Soon-
Won Park, Gi-Wook Shin, and Daqing Yang, ed., *Rethinking Historical
Injustice and Reconciliation in Northeast Asia* (New York: Routledge, 2007).
I am also grateful to the anonymous readers for their helpful editorial
suggestions. Finally, I thank Dr. Gi-Wook Shin, director of the Walter H.
Shorenstein Asia Pacific Research Center at Stanford, and Dr. Barbara
Bundy, founding executive director of the Center for the Pacific Rim at the
University of San Francisco and former president of Dominican University,
for their insightful advice and generous sponsorship for this research project.

2   Ministry of Foreign Affairs of Japan, Summary Transcript of "Japan-Korea
Summit Meeting" (in Korea), July 21–22, 2004. This meeting brought
together with then–President Roh Moo Hyun of the Republic of Korea and
then–Prime Minister Junichirō Koizumi of Japan.

3   On "thin" and "thick" reconciliation, see David Crocker, "Reckoning with
Past Wrongs: A Normative Framework," *Ethics and International Affairs* 13
(1999).

4   President Roh and Prime Minister Koizumi noted, for example, that whereas
"the annual number of tourists between Japan and the ROK stood at 10,000
people" back in 1965 (when formal diplomatic ties were established), "the
same number of people now travel between the two countries in a single day."

5   Since the 1990s, the term "pop culture diplomacy" has appeared in mass
media and occasionally even academic writing and government statements.
See, for example, Ministry of Foreign Affairs of Japan, "Pop-Culture

Diplomacy," August 14, 2014, http://www.mofa.go.jp/policy/culture /exchange/pop/, accessed October 27, 2014. However, the term is usually not precisely defined. Instead, advocates of pop culture diplomacy seem to associate it with more familiar concepts such "public diplomacy," "cultural diplomacy," and, of course, "soft power." Public diplomacy most commonly "refers to government-sponsored programs intended to inform or influence public opinion in other countries; its chief instruments are publications, motion pictures, cultural exchanges, radio and television" (U.S. Department of State, *Dictionary of International Relations Terms,* 1987). According to the Center for Public Diplomacy at University of Southern California, public diplomacy also encompasses "private activities—from popular culture to fashion to sports to news to the Internet—that inevitably, if not purposefully, have an impact on foreign policy and national security as well as on trade, tourism and other national interests." In this chapter, I use the term "pop culture diplomacy" in a straightforward way to signify cultural diplomacy relying centrally on pop culture. Generally speaking, "pop culture" can be understood to include popular books and magazines (i.e., novels, comics, self-help manuals), murals, poster art, movies, television programs, music, and computer/Internet games.

6   Michel-Rolph Trouillot, *Silencing the Past: Power and the Production of History* (Boston: Beacon Press, 1995), 20.

7   Andreas Huyssen, "Present Pasts: Media, Politics, Amnesia," *Public Culture* 12, no. 1 (2000).

8   Ibid., 29.

9   Arjun Appadurai, *Modernity at Large: Cultural Dimensions of Globalization* (Minneapolis: University of Minneapolis Press, 1996).

10   See, for example, Marcia Landy, ed., *The Historical Film: History and Memory in Media* (New Brunswick, NJ: Rutgers University Press, 2001); Steven Mintz and Randy W. Roberts, ed., *Hollywood's America: Twentieth-Century American through Film,* 4th ed. (Hoboken, NJ: Wiley-Blackwell, 2010); Robert A. Rosenstone, *History on Film/Film on History,* 2nd ed. (New York: Routledge, 2012).

11   One does not, for instance, need to be in Japan (or near its largest cities, where the best museums tend to be located) to interact with discourses on "Japanese" memories. Conversely, a person in Japan can access pop culture texts from other communities near and far.

12   The "textbook controversy" refers to an ongoing battle over the content of official Japanese textbooks—most notably with respect to the representation of Japan's role in World War II. For analysis of the textbook controversy, see Laura Elizabeth Hein and Mark Selden, ed., *Censoring History: Citizenship and Memory in Japan, Germany, and the United States* (Armonk, NY: M.E.

Sharpe, 2000); Yoshiko Nozaki, *War Memory, Nationalism and Education in Postwar Japan, 1945–2007: The Japanese History Textbook Controversy and Ienaga Saburo's Court Challenges* (New York: Routledge, 2008); Gi-Wook Shin and Daniel C. Sneider, ed., *History Textbooks and the Wars in Asia: Divided Memories,* reprint edition (New York: Routledge, 2013).

13 See, for instance, T. Fujitani, Geoffrey M. White, and Lisa Yoneyama, ed., *Perilous Memories: The Asia-Pacific War(s)* (Durham, NC: Duke University Press, 2001); Tessa Morris-Suzuki and Peter Rimmer, "Virtual Memories: Japanese History and Debates in *Manga* and Cyberspace," *Asian Studies Review* 26, no. 2 (June 2002). For additional sources, see Chapter 1 in this book.

14 In this chapter, unless otherwise stated, "Korea" refers to South Korea (the Republic of Korea).

15 Federico Mayor, *The Multi-Cultural Planet,* ed. Ervin Laszlo (London: Oneworld, 1993), ix.

16 Kim Dae Jung's visit to Japan was part of a broader diplomatic program throughout the 1990s. South Korea not only made significant steps toward democratic consolidation but also undertook *Nordpolitik* diplomacy—in which relations were normalized with erstwhile antagonists Russia (1990) and the People's Republic of China (1992), and an agreement struck for South Korea and North Korea to become members of the United Nations (1991). Granted, efforts at inter-Korean reconciliation hit an impasse with the emergence of the first Korean nuclear crisis in 1993–1994 and remains strained today. South Korean cultural and educational exchanges with Russia and China nonetheless grew dramatically in the 1990s, pushing a transition from "thin" to "thick" reconciliation. Kim Dae Jung staked his administration (1998–2002) on democratic consolidation domestically and removing obstacles to reconciliation in the Asia-Pacific region. Kim gained worldwide renown for the "Sunshine Policy" of rapprochement with North Korea, which—despite its shifting fortunes—would garner him a Nobel Peace Prize. Less dramatic but no less significant was his role in improving bilateral relations with Japan.

17 For a transcript of the joint statement, see, for instance, the Ministry of Foreign Affairs of Japan, "Joint Declaration: A New Partnership towards the Twenty-first Century," October 8, 1998 (www.mofa.go.jp).

18 This phrase might be read as an admission that "cooperative relations" since normalization had not extended to the people at large. In fact, scholars have noted that bilateral relations during the era of military rule in South Korea (1961–1987/1992) were shaped "primarily through backroom deals between elites in late-night parlors in Seoul and Tokyo." See Victor D. Cha, "Hypotheses on History and Hate in Asia: Japan and the Korean Peninsula,"

in *Reconciliation in the Asia-Pacific,* ed. Yoichi Funabashi (Washington, DC: U.S. Institute of Peace Press, 2003).

19   Vocals for "Let's Get Together Now" were provided by Brown Eyes (Korea), CHEMISTRY (Japan), Lena Park (Korean-American), and Sowelu (Japan), with lyrics written by Sawamoto Yoshimitsu, Matsuo Kiyoshi, Lena Park, and Kim Hyung-suk, and music composed by Kim Hyung-suk and Kawaguchi Daisuke. See *2002 FIFA World Cup Official Album: Songs of Korea/Japan* (Sony Music Asia, 2000).

20   For example, in November 2000, SM Entertainment (Korea) and Avex (Japan) signed a mutual licensing agreement in which the former would market Avex's music compact disks (CDs) in Korea, and the latter would market SM Entertainment's CDs in Japan. Then, in February 2004 Avex announced that it had agreed to purchase nearly 2 billion wŏn worth of shares in SM Entertainment: "to bolster the strategic relationship between our two companies in order to better compete in Southeast Asian (particularly Chinese) music markets." See AVEX, Inc., press release (February 4, 2004).

21   Philip Brasor, "Korean Wave May Help Erode Discrimination," *Japan Times* (June 27, 2004).

22   Shiraishi Takashi, "Introduction," *Japan Echo* 31, no. 6 (December 2004).

23   "Opinion Poll on Japanese Attitudes: Face-to-Face Interviews with 1,781 Persons," *Dong-A Ilbo—Asahi Shimbun,* March 27–28, 2005.

24   In the spirit of the 2002 World Cup, *Friends* and *2009 Lost Memories* were Korean-Japanese joint productions: a type of pop culture text born of regulatory changes. Several points should be made about these Korean-Japanese joint productions. First, they contain input from peoples of both countries, and works in this genre often address contentious issues affecting bilateral relations. Second, these two hybrid or transnational texts have circulated widely, crossing many national borders. *Friends* was broadcast nationwide in both Japan and Korea in February 2002, then exported to Southeast Asia and beyond as digital video disks (DVDs). *2009* had a successful theatrical run in Korea in 2002, ranking seventh in box-office receipts among domestic releases. Though it did not fare quite as well in Japan, it was promoted at film festivals throughout the country. The film was, moreover, a hot seller as DVDs and video compact disks, reaching not only Korean and Japanese diasporic communities outside East Asia but also many other Asian communities globally. Its enduring appeal prompted theatrical re-releases in the United States and other national markets. Third, the two texts represent the two most common genres of subsequent pan-Asian joint venture films and television: the romantic melodrama and action thriller. For all these reasons, *Friends* and *2009 Lost Memories* present good

case studies to test the proposition that pop culture provides key resources for helping societies work through historical disputes and contemporary tensions. For more information on co-produced films, see, for example, Usui Chizuru et al., eds., *The Guide to Japanese Film Industry and Co-Production 2009,* trans. Ben Dimagmaliw (Tokyo: UNIJAPAN International Promotion Department, 2009).

25 See TBS online catalogue for *Friends* (www.tbs.co.jp).

26 Pok Kŏ-il, *Pimyŏng ŭl ch'ajasŏ: Kyŏngsŏng, syouwa 62-yŏn* (In search of an epitaph: Keijō, Shōwa Year 62) (Seoul: Munhak kwa Chisŏngsa, 1987). The book created a sensation because of its provocative scenario—which is retained in the film *2009 Lost Memories.* But Pok's novel also evinced a belief in science and a critical spirit (manifested at times as black humor) to address historical and contemporary problems. In this connection, he took issue with the way his novel was adapted for the screen and sued to have his name removed from the film credits.

27 See note 26. Emphasis added.

28 For example, the screenplay was tested in Japan on college students, who were asked to read it and offer their opinions.

29 Sakamoto embodies bitter memories of Japanese colonial policies that promoted distorted forms of inclusion, denying Koreans equal opportunity in most arenas of public life while channeling them to join the police force.

30 "Kaneda" (金 田) is a common Japanese version of the familiar Korean surname Kim (金). This example of "name change" recalls painful memories of forced assimilation during the last decade of the Japanese empire.

31 For foundational writings on gendered aspects of cinematic representation, see Laura Mulvey, *Visual and Other Pleasures* (London: Palgrave Macmillan, 1989).

32 Appadurai, *Modernity at Large.* For a sampling of works by an iconic figure of the Frankfurt School, see Theodore W. Adorno, *The Culture Industry: Selected Essays on Mass Culture,* ed. J. M. Bernstein (London: Routledge, 1991).

33 Ultimately, *2009 Lost Memories* might be accused of deviating entirely from the humanistic spirit and encouraging rather cavalier attitudes toward suffering in that the bombings of Hiroshima and Nagasaki are uncritically framed as imperatives for restoring justice and the Korean nation.

34 A partial list of South Korean, Japanese, and joint production films since 2002 set against the backdrop of Korean-Japanese relations includes *YMCA Baseball Team* [*YMCA yagudan*] (Kim Hyeon-suk, South Korea, 2002); *Rikidōzan* [*Yŏkdosan*] (Song Hae-sung, South Korea/Japan, 2004); *Blue Swallow* [*ch'ŏngyŏn*] (Yoon Jong-chan, South Korea, 2005); *Breaking Through* [*Pacchigi!*] (Izutsu Kazuyuki, Japan, 2005); *Virgin Snow* [*Ch'ŏtun*]

(Han Sang-hye, South Korea/Japan, 2007); *Once Upon a Time* (Kang Hyun-woo, South Korea, 2008); *The Good, the Bad, the Weird* [*Choŭn nom, nappŭn nom, isanghan nom*] (Kim Ji-Woon, South Korea, 2008); *Boat* [K: *Bot'ŭ* / J: *No Boizu, No Kurai*] (Kim Young-nam, South Korea/Japan, 2009).

35   The news segment aired on KBS News on October 1, 2004.

36   Richard Campbell, *Media and Culture: An Introduction to Mass Communication* (London: St. Martin's Press, 1998), 420.

37   Ibid., 421.

38   Many Korean people were aware of a subset of pop phenomena in Japan (i.e., *Toruko* baths, *hentai anime, ko gyaru*) that confirm an image of decadence. This stereotype was so prevalent in Korea that, as the fourth-stage opening to Japanese pop culture approached (see the section "Contextualizing Pop Culture Diplomacy"), officials there were forced to announce that a strict ban would remain in place against products from the Japanese adult entertainment industry.

39   Ibid., 426.

40   Aoyagi Hiroshi, "Pop Idols and the Asian Identity," in *Japan Pop! Inside the World of Japanese Popular Culture,* ed. Timothy J. Craig (Armonk, NY: M.E. Sharpe, 2000), 323; Aoyagi Hiroshi, *Islands of Eight Million Smiles: Idol Performance and Symbolic Production in Contemporary Japan* (Cambridge, MA: Harvard University Asia Center, 2005).

41   Iwabuchi Kōichi, *Recentering Globalization: Popular Culture and Japanese Transnationalism* (Durham, NC: Duke University Press, 2002), 158.

42   Ibid., 158.

43   "*Asahi Shimbun/Dong-A Ilbo* Joint Public Opinion Poll." June 10, 2010, archived in The Maureen and Mike Mansfield Foundation "Asian Opinion Poll Database," http://mansfieldfdn.org/program/research-education-and -communication/asian-opinion-poll-database/asahi-shimbundong-a-ilbo -june-2010-joint-public-opinion-poll-10-21/, accessed August 27, 2014.

44   Yoshitaka Mōri, "*Winter Sonata* and Cultural Practices of Active Fans in Japan: Considered Middle-Aged Women as Cultural Agents," in *East Asian Pop Culture: Analyzing the Korean Wave,* ed. Chua Beng Huat and Koichi Iwabuchi (Hong Kong: Hong Kong University Press, 2008).

45   "Survey Report Outline on Actual Conditions of Hallyu (Korean Fever) Tourism" (Korean National Tourism Organization [KNTO], ROK Ministry of Culture and Tourism, 2004). The survey was conducted by KNTO overseas branches in Beijing, Hong Kong, and Taibei, between September 20, 2003, and October 14, 2003. It yielded a total of 2,004 "valid samples": Beijing (399), Shanghai (402), Guangzhou (207), Hong Kong (398), and Taiwan (398).

46 Iwabuchi, *Recentering Globalization,* 179.

47 Roy Rosenzweig and David Thelen, "The Presence of the Past: Popular Uses of History in American Life," in *The Public History Reader,* ed. Hilda Kean and Paul Martin (New York: Routledge, 2013), 37.

48 Trouillot, *Silencing the Past,* 20.

49 Rosenzweig and Thelen, "The Presence of the Past," 51.

CHAPTER 11

History and Its Alternatives
War Games as Social Form

Eric Hayot

In the latter part of 1908, three years after the conclusion of the Russo-Japanese War, *Cosmopolitan* magazine published a series of three articles written by Richmond Pearson Hobson under the collective title "If War Should Come!" The then-clause completing that opening was fulfilled at elaborate and illustrated length in the pages of *Cosmopolitan* (26 pages, including maps and photos) by Hobson's predictions regarding a three-front war opened by a Japanese-led, pan-Asian attack in the Pacific, accompanied by British invasions over land (through Canada) and sea, and eventually, after much expenditure of lives and treasure, a victory secured by the irrepressible strength of the American industrial economy.

Lest such a scenario seem overly fantastic to *Cosmopolitan*'s readers, the editor's notes that accompanied the articles cautioned their readers against taking Hobson's doomsday scenarios too lightly: "This is no work purely of the imagination," they noted, "but the result of "careful study"; these are "facts" marshaled by an "expert," one whose naval experience and muscular heroism (Hobson volunteered for an exceptionally dangerous mission during the Spanish-American War, was captured and released, and became a national celebrity) guaranteed the authenticity and relevance of his speculations.[1]

What does it mean to imagine a history that has not happened yet? In what follows, I describe essays like Hobson's as "histories of the future," and suggest that in the case of war in the Pacific such histories have had a long and interesting, well, history of their own—a history that makes the concept of a "Pacific war" a relatively unusual one. As I suggest in what follows, thinking about the history of Pacific wars means thinking partly about its *imaginary* prehistories, as well as, of course, the various kinds of postwar representations that have followed Pacific wars over the last several hundred years. (In case no one else has pointed it out, perhaps now is a good place to note the irony of an ocean named for peace being the site of such activity and such speculation; but if we let such ironies in human history detain us too long, we would never get anywhere, as history is full of them.)

This chapter asks you to think about the prehistorical representations of Pacific war as a kind of "play," a kind of imaginative game that writers play with the future, though a game with quite serious stakes. We will consider a number of "alternative" forms of fictional representation of historical wars in the Pacific, from essays like Hobson's to alt-history novels by John Birmingham and Newt Gingrich, to video games. And though the concept of historical "play" might be most obvious when it comes to the video games, I will suggest throughout that in fact the play in future histories may be more broad, and more interesting, than the historical play in video games. This is because, as I will show, video games are a relatively strange kind of representational form; by focusing on the ways in which they do *not* resemble novels, we will come to understand new things about both video games themselves, and about the ways in which historical play has functioned in the Pacific imaginary in the last few decades.

I.

But back to Hobson. The contrast between the editor's sobering note and the exclamation point that concludes the title of his essay recalls how intimately the imaginaries of fiction ravel histories of the future. Histories of the future? That will be my name for a mode of writing that includes among its genres prophecy, speculative fiction (including some science fiction), and the type of predictive prose characterized by Hobson's report, whose most important feature lies in its straddling the abyss that separates the imaginary and the historical, the unreal and the real. Hence the history of the future's paradoxical name, for what this mode attempts is to write the future *as* history, to transform the realm of the imaginary into the field of the highly probable, tying an imaginary *not yet* so firmly into the causal chains of an existing present that it becomes, in effect, as inevitable as the present.

Histories of the future orient themselves toward the potential future's relentless passage into the actionable present, and particularly toward the *manners* in which that passage occurs.[2] This is why histories of the future occur in the relatively near term: futures ten thousand years from now may well allegorize some aspects of contemporary life, but they cannot make their relationship to the contemporary historical as such, since the process of getting from here to there involves too many contingencies to register as an effect of the kinds of causal or developmental changes that we associate with historical action.[3] Historical causation and development, intimately linked to the present of the text's production, form the core of the history of the future as a genre.

With their relentless focus on the transformation or maintenance of the future through action in the present, historians of the future thus mark for their cultural moment the felt shape of history as such. In this shaping, we witness the transformation of historical content into historical form, whereby a feature of the diegesis—the relations between story and historical time—reveals itself as a law of genre. That law has to do with the representation of what one might call the *means of historical production:* how history itself is *made,* or understood to be made. (Ask yourself: what kind of event will create history? For Adam and Eve, it was the eating of an apple; but in, for instance, books of twentieth-century history, you will not find many apples being eaten. Our theory of how history gets made—about what kinds of events create historical activity—differs from that of the authors of the Book of Genesis). These differ from society to society and genre to genre: religious prophecy in the Judeo-Christian tradition locates those means in the self-transformation of the individual and his or her community, while for modern secular histories like Hobson's (or its fictional equivalents) the motive forces of history stem almost entirely from state action revolving around warfare.[4] We can therefore immediately note that the diegetic subjects of the conflicts at stake in any given history of the future—the conflict between the people of Israel and God, between the Soviet Union and the United States, between the terrorists and the democratizers—can, from a certain perspective, be seen as an epiphenomenon. An epiphenomenon of what? Of the far more formal and, from the perspective of the *longue durée,* central, debate over how history itself is controlled, produced, and made. That is: the debate about what might happen in history is always a debate as well about what kinds of things make history happen.

From this perspective, the entire point of a history of the future is not only to imagine the future but to assure you of the predictable unfolding of the future that it imagines. The mode's ambition is thus also the site of its greatest anxiety: the genres that unify the imaginary and the historical must go to great lengths to insist that they have not *merely* unified the imaginary and the historical but that through this unification they have transformed the former into the latter.

We can observe the popularity of this mode as it applies to the American Pacific if we remember that by the late 1800s readers in the United States were already well acquainted with fiction and nonfiction treatments of alien invasions, many of them from Asia. The nonfiction sort featured in many short stories of the impending Yellow Peril, novels like Ignatius Donnelly's wildly popular *Caesar's Column: A Story of the Twentieth Century*, Arthur Vinton's substantially less successful *Looking Further Backward* (both 1890), or Jack London's *The Iron Heel*, a heavily footnoted pseudo-historical edition of an imaginary manuscript whose diegetic geopolitical system features a Japanese empire in East Asia.[5] London's novel appeared in 1908, the same year *Cosmopolitan* published Hobson's essays on the imminent threat Japan posed to the United States, which testifies to the intense cross-pollination of these two genres of the future historical mode—the fictional and the essayistic—and to the necessity for those writing explicitly in non-fictional prose to warn their readers that the futures they presented were not, despite being products of the imagination, "purely" imaginary. In Hobson's case, the fact that *Cosmopolitan* in those years routinely published pieces of short fiction surely exacerbated the potential confusions.

The *Cosmopolitan* editor's attempt to draw a clear line between Hobson's work and fictional histories of the future was thus doomed from the start, largely because the context in which drawing such lines became necessary was one in which the lines had already been crossed over, blurred, and otherwise violated or ignored. Indeed such violations are the very stuff of realistic fiction. Hence the enormous efforts of novels and short stories to attribute the realism of their imaginaries to personal experience or academic expertise, or to place markers in the diegetic space that would label the fiction as a form of historical discourse (the presence of Napoleon in Balzac, for example). Still today, the legitimacy of the frequently preposterous futures imagined by such writers as Michael Crichton or Tom Clancy is secured by their well-known intellectual bona fides, their nonfictional prefaces, their use of scientific detail, and their inclusion of newspaper articles, scientific reports, and other forms of nonfiction inside their fictional frames.[6] Rob van Kranenburg has attributed a growing critical interest in Clancy's work to "the dawning of the idea that the novel as a textual form is slowly attempting to replace that which we conventionally labeled 'history,' " a claim that, though it fails to recognize the crucial importance of historical writing (and history more broadly) to the long-term development of the modern novel in English (consider Walter Scott) nonetheless captures the contemporary importance of speculative fiction as a site for the reworking of the relationship between history and the imagination.[7]

In recent years the conjunction between science or speculative fiction and the U.S. government has drawn even tighter: the former Speaker of the House Newt Gingrich suggested in 2009 on a Fox News website that President Barack Obama base his national security policy on the futures laid out in two recent novels that imagine nuclear attacks on the United States— only one year after Gingrich had co-written two novels that imagine what would have happened if Admiral Yamamoto Isoroku had personally led the attack on Pearl Harbor in 1941.[8] Meanwhile, the U.S. Department of Homeland Security now regularly consults with science fiction writers in order to obtain ideas on how to combat future terror attacks.[9] The almost delightful, crazy quality of these facts is, as the kids say, a (historical) feature, not a bug: it registers the cultural importance of this mode of thinking and the relationships it generates, which—despite being from one perspective mockable and even ridiculous—are nonetheless undertaken by people whose seriousness the media and political establishments takes as given. From Hobson's essays in *Cosmopolitan* to Gingrich's novels requires only a short trip through mediatic history, especially when one remembers that Hobson served, from 1907 to 1915, as one of Alabama's representatives to the U.S. Congress.

II.

The story so far: there is a mode of cultural production, a sort of super-genre, that I am calling "history of the future." It is characterized most importantly by the desire to turn the imaginary into the historical, a task whose near-impossibility produces a great deal of self-reflexive anxiety. That anxiety is managed at least partly by the division of the *mode* into *genres,* each of which stabilizes and authorizes the transformation of the future into history by tying it to an epistemological justification particular to it: prophecy to revelation, fiction, and the essay to a culturally appropriate balancing of the imaginary force of narrative (which dominates in fiction) against the force of knowledge, research, and expertise (which dominates in the essay). Finally, we are assuming that the history of the future is a kind of serious "play" with history, and that playing with history, in turn, is one of the ways in which a culture thinks about what counts as or makes history happen.

All this matters to cultural representations of Pacific wars because the transpacific war fought between 1941 and 1945 appears in the historical reality in a field of U.S. cultural production and play that established its possibility, its outcomes, and indeed its position in a longer national- and world-historical perspective, long before such a war *ever took place.* At least in the United States, no representation of the 1941–1945 war with Japan was not already a re-representation and remediation (of fiction into journalism, e.g.) of the war that had been such an active subject of the U.S. historical imaginary for six or seven decades prior to its occurrence. In the years since World War II, that conflict—that is, the *future* conflict, whose lessons differ significantly from those of the historical one—has remained a crucial part of the U.S. national imaginary, as we can see from the anxieties over Japanese industrial and economic production in the 1980s, concerns regarding potential invasions from China in the 1990s, and the degree to which Asia has figured so relentlessly for American writers, from Ernest Fenollosa to Neil Stephenson, as some version of the *future as such,* a role which has as much to do with East Asia's geographic closure of the expansionist Euro-American circle as with the largely repressed memory of its dominance of the world economy in the ten centuries that preceded industrialization and imperialism.[10]

All of this reminds us that to focus exclusively on any single genre or medium within the pantheon of representations will, if one does not register the larger formal structures that shape such representations—these having to do not only with the formal laws of genre or mode, but also with the particular interactions of those laws with the putatively independent "content" to which they have referred—produce a series of local insights that mistake text for context, or emphasize local differentiation at the expense of understanding differentiation's function in a system. This is as true for representations of Pacific wars as anything else. As I have suggested above, in this context the history of representations involves the early appearance and indeed dominance of the history of the future as a mode, and the interaction of that mode with larger cultural trends that pair East Asia so consistently with the idea of the future—two facts that must be accounted for if we are to grasp the nature and function of the Pacific here. To them we can add a recognition of the Pacific's geographic, biohistorical, and cultural features, which include the oceanic vastness of its territory, the political and conceptual roles played by its "rim," its chains of islands, its weather, its native flora, fauna, and people—all of which make Pacific wars quite different from Atlantic wars, never mind continental ones.

Now all these general statements will still apply as we shift our focus to video games. What's more, I want to insist that my understanding of how these general principles work actually comes *from* my thinking about video games. That is because thinking about video games has taught me to be very suspicious of the kinds of reading that literature professors normally do, in which they focus in on very small, poetic units of a novel or a film, and use those to build up a big picture analysis of the total activity of that object. For some objects, and in some situations, the macro matters more than the micro—and this is the case for both histories of the future and, I am about to suggest, for video games. That is because in video games the major features that determine how a game works or what it does operate at the level of *genre* or *form,* rather than content. Those levels, which are in some sense both "higher" and more abstract, or structural, than the content—just as the form of a novel is more abstract than a sentence in a novel—tend in video games to be more determinative of the game's final meaning than would the same structures in a novel. To put it another way, in video games the form/content balance is more heavily weighted toward form than it is in novels.

What this means, paradoxically, is that there can be no such thing as an essay on "video-game representations of Pacific wars," since the study of video games shows how the very habits that govern our understanding of the relationships between medium, form, and content—habits that allow scholars to write essays of the type "study of [name of medium]-based representations of [type of content]"—belong to the critical language that governs the media and genres from whose study they initially emerged, namely, the printed page and the work of highbrow literature. This is not simply a question of saying that a study on video-game representations of something ought to be contextualized inside a longer, trans-mediatic representational history, but, rather, of saying that we need to ask whether the content that video games represent is the same content that novels represent, or indeed whether video games represent content at all.

III.

Again: in video games the balance between form and content differs significantly from the balance that obtains in literary fiction.[11] In video games, form dominates content. This is true to such an extent that video games are not "about" things in the way that novels are "about" things; the whole concept of being "about" that governs the general discussion of novels (or films) has very little traction in video games at all. That is because video games are, more or less, "about" things their consumers *do,* and not about the content that makes that doing visible. To say that the content of a video game has to do with the Pacific theater in World War II communicates very little information at all to an experienced player of games, who will want to know, instead, what *genre of doing* the game belongs to: turn-based or real-time strategy (RTS), first-person shooter (FPS), adventure, simulation, massively multiplayer online role-playing game (MMORPG), and so on. The player's experience of the game will be governed almost entirely by the answer to that question, since from those generic differences will flow the game's organization of time, player activity, characterization, point of view, speed, density, type of action, and so on.[12] Similarities among FPS games—and indeed the formal force of the FPS genre—come largely from features that determine doing, not from whether the player happens to be shooting aliens, Japanese soldiers, demons, or zombies.[13]

Two implications stem from these facts: first, that the analysis of any given video game genre should focus largely on the formal rules that govern it. The most important context for those rules is the social sphere within which the game emerges: the degree to which the games *as form* coalesce and organize social experience, and represent (or fail to represent) social structures of action or knowledge that can be aligned with other interests operating in a given society. Second, that if we wish to say something about the content of games, we will have to consider the content of a single game within the structural framework that determines the range of types of content appropriate to the genre to which it belongs, a range whose social meaning is as determined by its gaps and absences as by its most obvious commitments.

In the case of FPS games, for instance, one might read their most salient formal features—the enactment of solitary, focused violence whose point of view encourages profound identification with a subject position but not a character, the use of maze- or object-based puzzles, the establishment of a narrative arc organized around contained spaces and progressive increases in ludic (gameplay) difficulty—as expressions of broader social forces involving the technologization of violence or the relentless expression of the idea that military success occurs most properly through singular heroes whose success depends entirely on talent, not luck or forms of social preference.[14] (Again, here, the easiest way to think about this is to ask: what creates historical activity in an FPS game? That is, what kinds of action "cause" events to change or to move? Can players change all of history? Or only small parts of it? And so on.) One might also observe that the total range of content of FPS games, which for obvious reasons focus on shooting people, inevitably involves the wide variety of war scenarios appropriate to the culture or subculture in which they appear. In the U.S. market, the preponderance of such games based on World War II, and the relative paucity of games based on World War I, and the total absence of such games set in Vietnam, results from the fact that historical FPS games invariably map the series of individualized, first-person "missions" that constitutes their gameplay alongside a series of cut-scenes and voiceovers that locate those missions along a realistic historical trajectory (cut-scenes are the little cinematic intervals between gameplay; they move the story forward and usually take place with no input from the player). The player's victory at the ludic level thus tracks the victory of the player's side at the historical and representational level—with the result that a game in which the player's side loses the war in general (imagine an FPS whose final mission involved escaping to a helicopter on a Saigon rooftop) would violate the conventions of the genre (and probably be unpopular, though I can imagine such a game being quite popular in Vietnam).[15]

Beyond this, one must also recognize that the generic conventions of different types of video games powerfully shape the kinds of historical representation that the games generate. Because FPS games involve a characterized first-person point of view, they necessarily narrate historical events through the relationship between the single individual and the larger events (movements of armies, navies, and so on) that determine that individual's location in the historical fabric. Whether the game frames the player's avatar as simply a generic soldier who happens to participate in the major combat missions of a war, or whether it makes the player's avatar occupy a unique position within the war's history, depends on its designers, who sometimes choose both at once: in *Call of Duty: World at War,* which alternates between missions set in the Pacific theater and the Soviet one, the American soldier remains more or less anonymous, whereas the Soviet soldier (though he remains a private) eventually raises the hammer and sickle over the Berlin Reichstag. Though we can make something of these differences, we must also remark on the generic freedoms and constraints within which these choices take place. Though the particular route (and indeed the layout of individual buildings, the names of his companions, the speed, demograph-

Call of Duty: World at War (2008): A classic first-person shooter

ics, or timing of the battle) the player's avatar takes through a given mission may be entirely "free" of historical constraint, what is not free is that progress in the game from a mission-by-mission perspective coincides with a total fidelity to the large-scale linear progress of historical events (as conventionally understood). FPS players can win the battle for Berlin or Okinawa *differently* than the way it was actually won, but they cannot choose not to win the battle at all.

In this respect, historical war FPS games resemble historical war simulation games, which put the player in control of technologies that do not make sense as effects of a purely first-person interface, mostly naval vessels and aircraft. Some such games may tie the player's progress to one or more characters in the historical diegesis, as is the case in *Battlestations: Midway,* which aligns the characters' progress in military rank with ludic success and ludic challenge (a captain has more difficult missions and controls more ships than a lieutenant, and so on). Other, simpler games may leave the people out of things entirely, as does *Pacific Gunner,* an arcade-like gunnery simulation in which the player's point of view, resolutely first person, nonetheless occurs from such a wide variety of ships and bunkers as to suggest that the player has no characterological presence in the game world at all. Both

Battlestations: Midway (1976): though you get to see your character in cut-scenes (little movie clips that advance the story), in the actual game play "you" are a battleship, not a person

games nonetheless orient general ludic progress toward the historical victory of the U.S. forces as a whole, so that winning the game means winning the war.

The approaches to history privileged by FPS and simulation games diverge sharply from those preferred by real-time or turn-based strategy titles. Whereas, as Campbell has argued, the remediations of FPS games are most often cinematic, strategy games remediate the older pen-and-paper board games, in terms of both their top-down, impersonal point of view and the relation between diegetic narrative and historical reality.[16] Whereas FPS games present the player with a diachronic historical constraint—one that frames the player's experience throughout the entirety of game play—the turn-based strategy game begins with an *opening* constraint but does not extend that constraint forward. A game like *People's General,* whose debt to the older board game model can be seen in its use of hexagonal map squares, opens its scenarios with a state of affairs and arrangement of forces: a Chinese invasion of Taiwan, a coup in Cambodia, trouble on the Korean Peninsula. Though the scenarios themselves are historical (in the case of *People's General,* they are histories of the future), the outcomes are not. One of the plea-

Pacific Gunner (2002): The "player" is just a set of guns labeled 1–10; there are no people involved

sures of such games involves replaying historical scenarios—as players could do in the important World War II board game, *Axis & Allies,* or as they can today in the *Hearts of Iron* series—in order to see whether one can produce outcomes other than those that occurred in the real world. For such games, the problem of historical representationality thus occurs at quite a different level than for FPS games, and this in two ways. First, by virtue of their focus on an entire war, the historical means of production highlighted by such games tend to involve factors operating at national or economic scales, including such issues as the availability of soldiers, problems of supply and the management of war matériel, and the industrial capacity necessary to produce them. Second, the actual history of the planet in such games emerges as but one privileged outcome of a set of starting conditions, a position perhaps most clearly visible in the fact that in these games the player can play the war scenario *on more than one side,* leading both the Chinese and the Americans to victory in *People's General,* or turning Switzerland into a major international power in the World War II setting of *Hearts*

People's General (1998): the classic hexagonal board game (note hexagons on right, as units explore new territory)

of Iron. Such games therefore represent not a historical *narrative* (inside which individual narratives can occur), but historical *situations* (out of which historical narratives can appear). That such games imagine the forces capable of altering those situations as armies, nations, or economies registers the widespread contemporary belief that only actors operating at those scales are capable of changing modern history. We can contrast the complete obviousness of this theory for the modern period—where a game or a novel in which a single soldier changed the outcome of a major war would be understood as at least partly "fantastical" or ideological—with the opposed position taken by the Tolkein-influenced fantasy genre, in which remarkable single individuals routinely function as the engines of historical transformation.[17]

The difficulty of reconciling individual heroic action with real-world historical action may explain the relative paucity of MMORPGs focused on historical topics, because those games necessarily direct the player toward the development of individual characters whose role in the historical diegesis can never exceed a certain threshold of influence.[18] That is why most MMORPGs take place in science fictional or fantasy worlds, where the rules governing the individual's relation to history are looser and why the few such games that advertise themselves as historical tend to be set far enough back in time—in ancient Rome or Egypt, the Three Kingdoms period in China, or the age of Caribbean piracy—as to essentially be fantasy worlds, especially since players cannot substantially affect what one might think of as the game-world's historical "nature," the set of rules governing not only its physical laws but its patterns of development and transformation.[19] Among historical MMORPGs set in the twentieth century, two focus heavily on arcade action, making them in effect massively multiplayer simulations or FPSs with mild role-playing elements.[20] A third is *Kangzhan yingxiong zhuan,* known in English as *Anti-Japan War Online (AJWO)*.[21] Set during the Second Sino-Japanese War (1937–1945), *AJWO* allows the player to take on and develop a young revolutionary from his or her earliest missions (killing guards hired by evil landlords, stealing maps from Japanese encampments) to membership in the Eighth Route Army of the Chinese Communist Party (CCP). Like all MMORPGs, the game encourages heavy identification with a character-avatar, which the player names, clothes, trains, and otherwise cares for over the course of gameplay, even as the nonplayer characters (NPCs) with whom the character interacts (usually higher-ups in the communist hierarchy) frame their training and their orders in the language of national resistance and communist thought—hardly surprising, given the historical context, or the fact that the game is partially sponsored by the China Communist Youth League.

At the level of gameplay, not much distinguishes *AJWO* from most other games of its type. Its action appears in a top-down, three-quarter view that is popular in East Asian MMORPGs; its graphics are conventional; its character development tree and experiential structures are likewise ordinary. But its relation to history is technically and formally unique in the MMORPG genre, since the real-world historical events to which it refers not only establish the general look of the game's diegetic space (including its objects and its population of NPCs) but also establish the general trajectory of the game's historical progress.

And what can we learn from their choice of the latter strategy, which though far less interesting from a historical perspective, is from a commercial one surely the smarter move? That since the war effectively cannot end without the game ending, no player can at any time be allowed to engage in activities that would "complete" any portion of the historical trajectory to which the game refers.

The game must therefore allow for individual players to experience a *form* of historical progress without actually allowing historical progress to

Anti-Japan War Online (2006): A classic three-quarter view East Asian online role-playing game. What decision faced the AJWO designers as they sought to reconcile the formal imperatives of the MMORPG genre with the historical ground of the game's diegetic world?

influence the game world. Accordingly, though every single player who be-gins the game as a soldier in the CCP stronghold of Yan'an will be given a mission to obtain a map from the Japanese commander of a nearby base (and will have to kill the commander and his guards to do so), and though the vast majority of players will complete that mission, the mission must none-theless remain active and available for subsequent players to complete as well. At no moment will that Japanese camp be eliminated or removed from the game world; though its soldiers and the commander can be killed, they (and the crucial map) will reappear a few minutes after their deaths, in order to allow the next player to complete his mission. The diegetic, historical effects of the player's activities thus inevitably take place "off stage": the recruiter tells the player that his stolen map has helped the CCP win an important victory in some other town, somewhere the player can never visit or see. What happens, in effect, is that the historical trajectory of the war as a whole is remapped from the diegesis onto the player-character's development: though that particular Japanese commander lives on, the player will progress from the completion of that mission to another, more complicated one, and the sequence of these missions—killing ever-more important Japanese commanders, coming ever closer to the large-scale, named events and personages of real history—articulates from the point of view *of the player* the historical passage of time in the real-world Sino-Japanese War. Even as, in the diegetic game world, time stands forever still.[22]

The MMORPG's "representation" of historical experience thus combines two features that make up what we commonly recognize as history: the population of a space with objects, NPCs, and a set of physical or natural laws that represent mimetically a recognizable historical context in which the individual character "lives,"[23] and a causal structure that demonstrates the character's interactions with changes occurring at a recognizably "historical" scale. In this case, quite different from the historical novels of Scott or even Balzac, in which the process and nature of history is revealed through a close attention to the actions of individuals who in some sense typify it as an *age,* in the MMORPG the process and nature of history are not so much revealed as re-enacted, and their field of effect is not the world itself but simply the character who re-enacts them. This relation to history differs importantly from the FPS genre insofar as the MMORPG locates the effect of history directly in the diegesis (where it is encoded in the player-character), whereas the FPS simply maps historical time onto the extradiegetic progress of the game narrative itself.

In these different approaches to history, we begin to discern a historical typology of the video-game medium, which we can map along two major formal lines.

First, we need to remark for any game the way in which its genre determines a mode of *diegetic characterization,* which establishes the relation between the player's presence in the game and the kinds of historical effect that presence can create, whether these be characterized but undevelopable first person (the FPS, *Battlestations: Midway*); characterized and developable first or third person (the RPG or MMORPG); noncharacterized first person (squad combat games, simulations like *Pacific Gunner*); or noncharacterized third person (the turn-based or real-time strategy game).

Second, we must understand the game's *alignment of history and story,* which will determine whether the player faces synchronic (situational) or diachronic constraints, and how the effects of history on the game world translate (or do not translate) into the game's ludic structure (the FPS) or diegetic process (the MMORPG). What do I mean? That the way the player plays the *game* is connected to the way the game *plays* history. In other words, the form and structure of the game will determine not only the player's own practice of game-playing—whether s/he runs through three-dimensional space and shoots a gun in an FPS, or plans a battle from a top-down view in a simulation game—but also the relationship that the player has to history itself. What you might say is that in the vast majority of historical video games, the player (or, in some games, two or three players) aims simply to *recreate* history, to experience it from the inside, as it were, as a single cog in a vast machine of historical activity (the war itself, controlled by nations, presidents, generals, and so on). The only exceptions are the simulation games, in which the very freedom to act as a general means acquiring access to the means of historical production, and thus to the power to change history, and not just live it.

IV.

With these formal structures in mind, we can begin to talk about representation in historically oriented video games by asking what they show us about actual history.[24] Let us turn, therefore, to the most interesting representational problem for historical games set in the Pacific theater of World War II: the atomic bombings of Hiroshima and Nagasaki in August 1945. The first thing to say is that no game I know of represents those events within its ludic structure, which would require (in a first-person game) that the player play the role of *Enola Gay* pilot Paul Tibbets or (in a strategy game) that the U.S. player have access to a weapon whose diegetic effects would, if they were realistic, essentially end game-play.[25] For some games, this representational lack makes ludic sense—in an FPS like *Call of Duty: World at War,* for instance, there is no room for a ludic representation of the bombings, because they were not undertaken by a single soldier in a land combat mission. But this does not mean that such a game cannot represent Hiroshima at all: the dropping of the atomic bomb appears in grainy stock footage, with voiceover narration, in the scenes that conclude the American campaign of the game. As a conclusion, it can be paired with the Soviet flag raising over Berlin, though the former can appear inside the diegesis, while the latter is limited to a cinematic representation of an event that it cannot capture in FPS terms.

But even a game that could ludically represent the actual bombing from a first-person point of view, like *Battlestations: Midway,* does not do so, choosing instead to end its campaign with the Battle of Midway (in 1942, when the naval war effectively ended). The closest any of these World War II games comes to putting Hiroshima into the ludic picture is, strangely, *Pacific Gunner,* where a secret cheat code can be activated by going to the page for August 6, 1945, in the game's "History" screen. This is not exactly "representation," though the fact that the cheat code makes it possible for the player to win the game quite easily can be seen as a "translation" of the meaning of the Hiroshima bombing into the sphere of ludic control.[26]

That it would be more shocking to represent Hiroshima than to avoid it—and that for me at least the *Pacific Gunner* cheat code feels creepy and inappropriate—is not, perhaps, surprising. It reminds us that video games are, after all, games, and that their major formal constraint is, finally, winning. From such a perspective, the Hiroshima event cannot exactly be enjoyable, both because the *Enola Gay's* mission was historically fairly simple, and because the games follow the conventional American judgment on the bomb itself, which tends to view it as an unstoppable and effectively omnipotent instrument of the war's conclusion—as, in effect, a kind of "cheat code" that allows the United States automatically to "win" the war. There may also be, frankly, a modicum of historical sensitivity here; though games have not shied away from representing nuclear warfare in general, and though in all these games the death of enemy soldiers is the subject of both diegetic and ludic celebration, a game that celebrated the bombings in such a manner would be hard to imagine.[27] As for what it feels like to be German or Japanese and play these games, which require benefiting from the deaths of hundreds of Japanese or Germans infantrymen, well, the pleasures of identification are complicated—though, as Rafael Miguel Montes has noted, the games themselves seem to find the idea of such players inconceivable.[28]

More to the point, however, we may remark that the closure of historically "accurate" FPS and simulation games with the U.S. victory suggests how closely history in such games must cleave to the macro-level events that make it up, even as it allows room for individual variations that, in the long run, makes no difference. Pearl Harbor will be attacked; the United States will win the Battle of Midway; the *Enola Gay* will fly its mission: these pillars of actuality are in fact what make these games historical as such, what locate and frame their narrative realism. We might therefore be tempted to revise our initial reading of Hiroshima as a form of content, at least when it comes to such games, since its necessity as a diegetic event is as much a representation of the formal necessities created by these games as medium and genre.

V.

Let us consider some of the recent alterative histories of the Pacific front in World War II: Harry Turtledove's two novels on the Pacific War, John Birmingham's Axis of Time series, and the two novels by Gingrich with his coauthor William Forstchen. The first imagines a Japanese land invasion of the Hawai'ian Islands; the second that a quantum loophole in the year 2021 catapults a number of modern warships backward in time to 1942; the third that Admiral Yamamoto takes command of Japan's Pacific fleet. We can put these novels into the general representational framework that includes the material I've discussed above, as well as the other alternative historical novels that imagine different outcomes for World War II (most notably, when it comes to the Pacific, Philip K. Dick's *The Man in the High Castle*). And we can locate them in relation to the history of the future as a mode by noting that alternative histories, though they work through many of the same problems as the history of the future (the relationship between the imaginary and the possible, the theorization of the historical means of production), have a radically different relationship to their contemporary moment. Whereas the history of the future emphasizes the profound historical possibility located in the present, and constitutes therefore a call to some kind of political action that will alter the future it imagines as almost inevitable, the alternative history emphasizes the contingency of the present moment, the degree to which it might not have turned out this way (whatever this way is) and thus the degree to which the very normalcy of history can or should be understood as a matter of luck or of, as we shall see, profound inevitability.

The inclusion of alternative histories brings to three the number of general types of historical fiction under consideration here: the history of the future (Hobson, London, Clancy); the history of the past, also known simply as "historical fiction," the most neutral of these genres (novels like Leon Uris's Mila 18; the FPS, simulation, and historical MMORPG); and alternative history (Turtledove, Dick; the strategy game). Each of these types names a set of relationships that the aesthetic object (fictional or nonfictional) establishes with history. Those relationships are in turn cross-cut with a number of other generic or mediatic considerations that help determine how they ramify in the object as such, and which is, formally speaking, the *function* (in the mathematical sense) of those relationships and those considerations.

In alternative history, any of the following premises constitutes a legitimate diegetic ground for change that the novel recognizes as substantially historical: a Japanese land invasion of Hawai'i (Turtledove); Admiral Yamamoto's taking command of Japan's Pacific fleet (Gingrich and Forstchen); a quantum anomaly sends warships back in time to 1942 (Birmingham). Each of these changes—even the last one—relies on significant alteration to a *single* factor in the known historical record; each of them interfaces with the recognized means of historical production of war outcomes (which are themselves highly "historical"). The novels' other alterations of the historical record are neither singular nor oriented toward the means of production: individual characters caught up in the novel's events, whether fictional (a police detective in the Birmingham novels; a surfer in the Turtledove series) or historical (the various admirals and other figures on either side of the war), can do and say all kinds of things that do not change history but illustrate it.[29] Note, finally, that some forms of content cannot be substantially altered without destroying the status of the fiction as an alternative history—if all the U.S. soldiers were 20 feet tall or shot lasers out of their eyes, we would have a historically oriented fiction that was not, or not exactly, historical.[30]

All this suggests that the changed, unchanging, and fictionalizable aspects of a recognizably "historical" text (i.e., a text that declares itself to have a relation to history) constitute a system of historical meaning through which its theory of history and the historical means of production appears. And it suggests, also, that the relation between historicity and the imagination that such texts articulate relies as heavily on the *stability* of certain diegetic facts as it does on the *alterability* of others.

Consider for instance the apparent necessity, in alternative and realistic histories of the 1941–1945 war in the Pacific, of representing cultural differences through the differential treatment of civilians and prisoners of war (POWs). In the realistic historical record established by such video games as *Call of Duty: World at War* or *Medal of Honor: Pacific Assault,* both of which include cinematic cut-scenes of Japanese soldiers violently abusing American prisoners, one observes how the Japanese character circa 1942 justifies the eventual loss of the war and the violence done to Japanese soldiers and (however regrettably) Japanese civilians along the way.

Likewise for the alternative histories, which despite their willingness to alter any number of historical facts never alter the fact that Japanese culture circa 1941 leads inevitably to war crimes against military and civilian populations.[31] No matter what Admiral Yamamoto does, or how many quantum anomalies appear, the Americans in these (American) representations remain resolutely American, and the Japanese resolutely Japanese. The features that define them as such involve both the normal trappings of cultural difference (food, language, habit) but also those markers of cultural or even anthropological necessity that determine, in the long run, the emotional and historical valence of their actions.

Thinking about why or how such facts might be altered in an "alternative" history reveals culture's strange relationship to historical production. What would an alternative history look like if it imagined that the Japanese had never kept women as sex slaves or if the Americans had routinely worked POWs to death (instead of just keeping them, as they did with Japanese Americans, in isolated camps)? In the logic of the alternative history, such a change is not singular enough: insofar as the treatment of POWs expresses culture, it belongs to a field of historical production whose causes stretch back far enough into the past, and connect to so many different axes of social, cultural, or political causality, as to be immune to the logic of historical alternativity itself. These novels thus express a general sense of the relation between culture and history, and indeed between culture and historical production, which simultaneously treats culture as an overwhelmingly powerful engine of history—it is in some sense *immune* to historical change and determines its very valences—even as they dismiss it as irrelevant to the question of historical outcomes—since these latter depend on the kind of singular, malleable factors whose alteration the novels recognize as historically relevant and culturally legitimate.[32] From this perspective, we can observe that the very appearance of culture (in all its manifestations) in these historical novels is not a matter of content but, once again, of generic form: that is, that what looks like "extra" or "background" material, namely knowledge/information about culture, turns out to have a central, formative, and structural role in determining how history, and the novels, unfold. Again, what is at stake here is the nature of historical play. I am speaking not just of how to play at history, but of the ways in which these games imagine the "play" that is in history (the way there might be "play" in the tightness of a bolt or screw): how much wiggle room do they imagine there to be in what actually happened?

VI.

That culture becomes, in historical fictions of the speculative type, a formal feature of genre should not come as a surprise to the reader of this chapter. For my argument has been all along that the entire question of mimetic representation is meaningless without an intense and ongoing awareness of the ways in which mimesis emerges through and as an effect of aesthetic structure, most especially those formal structures that govern the laws of medium and genre. I am inclined to make this a general argument, but that would take this discussion too far afield. Let me say, therefore, that at least in the case of genres oriented toward the question of history, the rule of form applies strongly and exerts a determinative effect on the vast majority of content. This does not mean that content is unfree or that the text cannot surprise or undermine its context: rather it means that its freedoms, its surprises, and its underminings will come in relation to the laws of form that govern its genre—and that the first form of freedom a text has involves the decision to align itself with one or another of the available genres, or to attempt to refuse genre entirely.[33]

In such a context, anything one says about Pacific wars, about the Pacific as a site of international tension and conflict, violence and history, will oscillate between large-scale questions involving the prominence of certain forms of content in a given genre—the prevalence of histories of the future focused on China in the late nineteenth century, and of ones focused on Japan in the early twentieth—and observations regarding the ways in which different genres express, or are allowed to express, relations between those imaginary wars, the historical wars held in and around World War II, and the new imaginary wars currently being written into being in speculative and science fiction, or in nonfiction prose of the Hobson type (in such books as *America's Coming War with China*).[34]

More broadly, it ought to be possible to observe the degree to which the very question of representing history in this case intersects with a history of representation that precedes, surrounds, and succeeds it. Pacific war has since the late 1800s always been included in the American political and cultural record. The addition of video games to that record does not, from my perspective, tell us much more about the nature of that record, its motivations, or its likely cultural effects. What games do tell us, however, is that the forms of history, and indeed the very historicity of history, can be transformed by the game medium and its genres into sites for intense and compelling *play*, and that such play articulates history in relationships that differ substantially from those present in literature and film. Play's formal articulation of possible relationships to history offers gamers the opportunity to participate in, re-enact, or imagine in advance not only history's events but the *forms* in which it is experienced and made (first person, characterized, synchronically constrained, and so on). This suggests that what we have to learn from Pacific war video games has far more to do with the history of history than with the history of the Pacific.

Any such conclusion—though well in keeping with the interest this chapter displays in form—would have to consider to what degree the apparent disappearance or irrelevance of Pacific war content in the video-game medium might be reconceived, either through a careful consideration of the continued relevance of the irrelevant (and thus an argument that the Pacific matters precisely by virtue of its not appearing to matter),[35] or, more compellingly to me at this moment, by recognizing the degree to which the representational system that defines "form" in relation to "content" can be reframed within a larger media ecosystem that includes video games. That these latter teach us, or remind us, to see "Pacific war" itself as a *form* of historical apprehension (in both senses) is, to my mind, one of the major advantages of their inclusion here. This reminds us that the formal patterns of historical play will always have less to say about their putative subject—whether that subject is war in the Pacific, Atlantic, or elsewhere—than they do about their formal adherence to a logic of history, within which whatever play they imagine (FPS, simulation, historical novel) takes place.

Notes

1   Richmond Pearson Hobson, "If War Should Come! First Article—The Question of Preparedness," *Cosmopolitan* (June 1908): 584; idem, "If War Should Come! Second Article—The Conflict," *Cosmopolitan* (July 1908): 38.

2   They are not to be confused with science fiction, since not every science fiction relies on a causal historical logic to indicate the relation between its diegetic future and the present, or establishes the if-this, then-that structure that typifies the calls to immediate and substantive action made by prophets, political commentators, and other writers of future histories.

3   It is also why most such histories are dystopian. Utopias are most often reached through a metaphysical aperture (the storm, the wormhole, the time machine) or a social transformation whose process cannot be narrated (everyone realized something had to be done, and it has been done, but no one describes it, as in Edward Bellamy's *Looking Backward* 2000–1887 (published in 1887), which means that their possible futures rarely belong to conventional history. The political force of utopia lies not in the process whereby one arrives there, but in the ethical obligation that is created, in the present, by the possibility of imagining a perfected world.

4   The combined weight of the thousands of novels written in this genre
     teaches us that the fact of military conflict and the modalities of action and
     actor particular to it lie at the heart of what those novels imagine as the
     means (of production) through which the future can be leveraged into being.
     Consider in this context the historical changes in the American science
     fiction novel, which moves from a stage in the 1950s and 1960s focused
     largely on industrial technology involving space travel, to a more cybernetic
     phase (beginning with Isaac Asimov's robot novels and extending through
     cyberpunk), to a biologistic orientation largely derived from a new sense of
     the vital importance of genetics, to, only in recent years, imaginations of the
     future as largely constructed out of the activities of unfettered finance
     capitalism.

5   London's Japanese invasion story, "The Unparalleled Invasion," which first
     appeared in *McClure's* magazine in 1910, purports to be an excerpt from
     "Walt Mervin's *Certain Essays in History.*" Vinton's *Looking Further
     Backward,* a Chinese invasion story, was set in 2023 and narrated by a
     Chinese history professor. See Jack London, "The Unparalleled Invasion,"
     in *The Strength of the Strong and Other Stories* (Sandy, UT: Quiet Vision,
     2003); Arthur Vinton, *Looking Further Backward, Being a Series of Lectures
     Delivered to the Freshman Class at Shawmut College by Professor Won Lung
     Li* (Albany, NY: Albany Book Company, 1890). Later in the twentieth
     century, no one made a more rigorous attempt to illustrate and think
     through the resemblances of fiction and nonfiction than Jorge Luis Borges,
     with the result that first-time readers of his often do not know whether they
     are reading works "purely of the imagination" or not. Among contemporary
     American authors the documentary impulse driving the work of William
     Vollman, or the stylistic registers of David Foster Wallace, illustrate the
     continued fecundity of this register. For a fuller treatment of the Vinton
     novel, see Eric Hayot, *The Hypothetical Mandarin: Sympathy, Modernity,
     and Chinese Pain* (New York: Oxford University Press, 2009).

6   That the September 11, 2001, attackers flew planes into the World Trade
     Center was taken by many people at the time as a confirmation of Clancy's
     prescience, since he had imagined a *Japanese* commercial airliner being
     deliberately flown into the U.S. Capitol in his 1994 novel *Debt of Honor*
     (New York: G. P. Putnam's Sons, 1994).

7   Rob van Kranenburg, "Tom Clancy" in *St. James Encyclopedia of Popular
     Culture,* ed. Tom Pendergast and Sara Pendergast (Farmington Hills, MI: St
     James Press, 2000), vol 1., p 524.

8   Newt Gingrich, "America at Risk: Two Novels President Obama Should
     Read," *Fox Forum,* June 15, 2009; Newt Gingrich and William R.

Forstchen, *Pearl Harbor: A Novel of December 8* (London: St. Martin's Griffin, 2008).

9   David Montgomery, "U.S. Mission for Sci Fi Writers: Imagine That," *Washington Post,* May 22, 2009; Stuart Winter, "Can Science Fiction Beat Bin Laden?" *Daily Express,* June 3, 2007, http://www.express.co.uk/posts /view/8730/Can+science+fiction+beat+Bin+Laden/, accessed June 15, 2009.

10   For an overview of contemporary research on these topics, see *MELUS* 33, no. 4 (Winter 2008), a special issue titled "Alien/Asian." I have written elsewhere about the degree to which such histories of the future during the presidency of Bill Clinton articulated a more general anxiety about the geopolitics of the post–cold war era and indeed about the historical relationships between those futures and the ones laid out by writers on the American West Coast a century earlier. See Eric Hayot, "Chineseness: A Prehistory of Its Future," in *Sinographies: Writing China,* ed. Eric Hayot, Haun Saussy, and Steven G. Yao (Minneapolis: University of Minnesota Press, 2007).

11   By "literary fiction," I mean novels that differentiate themselves from the standard subgenres of their era, whether romance, science fiction, or *Bildungsroman.* Literary fiction is also a genre, but its convention operates partly through a negative relation to generic plots, as well as through certain stylistic features, some of which appear exclusively at the level of the sentence. See Mark McGurl, *The Program Era: Postwar Fiction and the Rise of Creative Writing* (Cambridge, MA: Harvard University Press, 2009).

12   This difference is perhaps best illustrated by a thought experiment: imagine that someone had set out to write an essay on historical representations of the Napoleonic wars in the English sonnet. And imagine that such a person concluded that for the writers of English sonnets such wars were inevitably conceived of as happening in three brief and equally sized movements, followed by a concluding gesture that either summarized that history or gave it an ironic twist. Whatever theory of the apprehension of history of *content* such a person would develop would, in effect, turn out to an unconscious theory of the sonnet as form, since the 4–4–4–2 structure of·English sonnets determines in a structural way the becoming-visible of their content.

13   From this we learn that "video games" is not, structurally, a category of the same type as the category "novel." Video games are a type of software, in the same way that codex books are a type of printed matter. They differ from novels (as do books) in being media, not genres. Novels (along with romances, picaresques, *monogatari* [Japanese works of extended prose fiction], or the *xiaoshuo* [Chinese works of extended prose fiction]) are in turn a subgenre of prose fiction, and are one possible textual form of the book.

14 James Campbell has in fact made just such an argument about World War II–based FPS games, noting that "heroic behavior" in such games "becomes relatively common because it is relatively risk-free," since avatar death carries no significant cost to the player. But Campbell mistakes a feature of *all* FPS games for a feature of World War II–based games in particular and is thus led to argue that this feature of the games he discusses tells us something about what the United States thinks about World War II. Maybe, but it seems curious that the United States thinks exactly the same thing about heroism when it comes to demons (in the *Doom* series), aliens (in *Half Life*), and drug-crazed inhabitants of an abandoned underwater city (in *BioShock*).

15 There are games not in the FPS genre set in Vietnam, including *Battlefield Vietnam,* which is a squad combat game, as well as a number of board-based strategy games. But neither of these genres (the turn-based strategic war game, the squad combat game) require the presence of a long-term historical arc that tracks the progress of the actual war in general against the player's progress through a number of missions. Hence the question of winning, so crucial in the FPS, simply has a different valence in other genres.

16 To describe the point of view as "impersonal" means largely that it is not *characterized:* though the player may be encouraged to think of him- or herself as a "general" or a "commander," those names represent the historical role and diegetic control the player has, and not a character whose diegetic development has anything to do with the game narrative.

17 The book that grasps the full implications of the ongoing appeal of that genre and that places its historical perspective in a transgeneric, transmediatic context has yet to be written. Fredric Jameson remarks on fantasy in the first few chapters of *Archaeologies of the Future: The Desire Called Utopia and Other Science Fictions* (New York: Verso, 2005) point in one useful direction.

18 Eric Hayot and Edward Wesp, "Reading Game/Text: *EverQuest,* Alienation, and Digital Communities," *Postmodern Culture* 14, no. 2 (January 2004).

19 Note that this does not have to be so for fantasy worlds. Both *Dark Ages of Camelot* and *Star Wars: Galaxies* offered players the opportunity to play significant roles in the "historical" development of those worlds, allowing them to affect state boundaries or planetary growth in ways that registered player effects as more than simply quotidian. But, of course, in those cases no relation to actual history need be maintained.

20 *Battleground Europe: WWII Online,* for instance, actually refers to itself as an MMOFPS.

21 A translation that, sadly, fails to take account of 传 (*zhuan*) which in Chinese classical literature marks a narrative as the story of a (usually

biographical) process, whose use captures perfectly the individualized, developmentally oriented arc of the MMORPG character.

22 This is true, to some extent, of all MMORPGs, in which any number of quests given to players (or victories garnered over particularly important foes) are treated by the nonplayer characters as though they were unique, even though players know quite well that they are not. In the case of the historical MMORPG, this situation acquires a certain poignancy: a game designed to illustrate the winning of a war cannot, finally, allow that war to be won.

23 The first feature of which is the formal or philosophical context that constitutes its world as a totality.

24 Though this discussion focuses on Pacific war games, historically oriented games come in a number of shapes and sizes, including city- or civilization-builder games (*Rome; Civilization*), economic or political management games (*Patrician; Machiavelli*); turn-based or real-time strategy games (*Diplomacy; Age of Kings*) and so on.

25 In *Hearts of Iron II: Doomsday,* which begins in 1945, the U.S. player has atomic weapons, and other nations can research and use them. But since *Hearts of Iron* is a real-time strategy game, the bombing of Hiroshima is not inevitable (and only the starting position is constrained); indeed the 1945–1953 period of that game has been described by Brett Todd as a shift away from the series' realism and into speculative fiction. See Brett Todd, "*Hearts of Iron II: Doomsday* Review," *GameSpot,* April 11, 2006, http://www .gamespot.com/pc/strategy/heartsofironiidoomsday/review.html, accessed June 15, 2009.

26 Note that the cheat code in *Pacific Gunner* allows the player to win the game automatically by pressing w in each mission, but such a victory is neither ludic (since the w key has no other function) nor diegetic (since the game provides no explanation for why the player has won).

27 Nuclear warfare is a major feature of many contemporary games, though its results are almost inevitably represented without individuals (thus forestalling identification). The most striking exception to that rule occurs in the recent *Call of Duty 4,* in which one of the two major characters controlled by the player dies a slow death as a result of a nuclear explosion, while remaining under the player's control the entire time (the player is thus helpless against circumstance, a very unusual situation for a game).

28 The obvious exception here is the U.S. Army–funded squad combat title, *America's Army,* in which all players see themselves and their teammates as U.S. soldiers and the other team as "terrorists."

29 For some alternative histories, the singular historical character *is* the means of production, as is Charles Lindbergh in Philip Roth's *The Plot to*

Save America (New York: Vintage, 2005). In other cases the alternative history reveals a minor historical figure as the unrecognized means of historical production, as in *Forrest Gump*—though such films tend to be comedies, and generate much of their comedy from the pairing of the unrecognized means of production (Gump himself) with various important events.

30 From this perspective Birmingham's quantum anomaly, though realistically generated in the fictional world set in 2021, produces something like "fantastic" history, a subgenre of alternative history in which we might also place David Drake and Eric Flint's Belisarius novels, whose premise is that benevolent aliens choose the Byzantine general Flavius Belisarius (an actual historical figure) as their avatar, and help him win battles against an Indian force aided by evil aliens.

31 Another context: that as games have over the past few years pursued far more "realistic" (that is, grimmer) approaches to the representation of violence than had been permissible through the 1980s and even the 1990s, war crimes have become a crucial part of game play. The recent expansion pack for the immensely popular MMORPG *World of Warcraft* includes a quest, "The Art of Persuasion," that requires the player to torture a prisoner, which set off vigorous online debate. Clive Thompson has written that because "games are excellent vehicles for helping people inhabit complex, difficult situations," we need more rather than less torture in video games, that is, more and more complex versions of what torture is, and its effects on the individuals and societies that practice it. See note 28 for more on this topic. I leave aside any discussion of the notorious and contemptible *KZ Manager* games, which involve managing a Nazi concentration camp.

32 All of this can be thought in relation to the fact that *Call of Duty: World at War* forces the player to participate in a war crime. As a member of the Soviet army, the character comes across a group of German soldiers being held captive. In a cut-scene in which the player has no control over the action, the soldier's comrades threaten to burn the Germans alive. The character's sergeant tells him to shoot the Germans, as that would be more merciful, and control returns to the player, who has approximately five seconds to shoot the Germans, after which the other soldiers will set them on fire. The player therefore has two choices: to murder the German soldiers or to passively collaborate in their immolation. The Japanese war crimes (false surrender and the torture of prisoners) appear by contrast entirely in cut-scenes in which the player has no control.

33 Successful attempts of this type are hard to imagine, perhaps because when they are truly successful, they create their own genre—consider *Don Quixote*.

34   Ted Galen Carpenter, *America's Coming War with China: A Collision Course over Taiwan* (London: Palgrave Macmillan, 2006).

35   An argument I have made at length about the place of China in European philosophy and literature, in the introduction to Hayot, *The Hypothetical Mandarin*.

Films, Television, and Videogames

1941. Spielberg, Steven. USA. 1979.

2009 Lost Memories. Lee Si-myung (Yi Simyŏng). South Korea/Japan. 2002.

731 Horrific Female Experiments (*731 kongbu nüti shiyan*). Zhang Jiabei. China. 2008.

The 74ᵗʰ Comfort Women Team (*Weianfu qishisi fendui*). Chen Guijun. China. 1994.

Above and Beyond. Frank, Melvin, and Norman Panama. USA. 1953.

Across the Pacific. Huston, John. USA. 1942.

Adada (*Adada*). Im Kwŏnt'aek. South Korea. 1987.

Address Unknown (*Such'wiin pulmyŏng*). Kim Kiduk. 2001.

Advancing upon French Indo-China (*Futsuin shinchū*). 1941.

Aegis (*Bōkoku no Ījisu*). Sakamoto Junji. Japan. 2005.

Agent Peony (*Qingbaoyuan baimudan*). Jin Cheng'en. Taiwan. 1966.

Ah, Special Attack Corps (*Aa tokubetsu kōgekitai*). Inoue Yoshio. Japan. 1960.

Always—Sunset on Third Street (*Always: Sanchōme no yūhi*). Yamazaki Takashi. Japan. 2005.

Always—Sunset on Third Street 2 (*Always: Zoku sanchōme no yūhi*). Yamazaki Takashi. Japan. 2007.

Ama's Secret—Stories of Taiwanese Comfort Women (*Ama de mimi—Taiji wei'anfu de gushi*). Xie Zhunliang. Taiwan. 1998.

An Unseen Triggerman (*Leibao fengyun*). Li Jia. Taiwan. 1965.

Anti-Japan War Online (*Kangzhan yingxiong zhuan*). Software. Zhongqing Quanwang. China. 2006.

The Assault (*Xuezhan*). Tien Shun. Taiwan. 1958.

Assembly (*Jijie hao*). Feng Xiaogang. China. 2007.

Baatan. Garnett, Tay. USA. 1943.

Bamboo House of Dolls (*Nü jizhongyin*). Gui Zhihong (Kuei Chi-hung). Hong Kong. 1972.

Barefoot Gen (*Hadashi no Gen*). Mori Masaki. Japan. 1983.

The Battle of Okinawa (*Gekido no shōwashi: Okinawa kessen*). Okamoto Kihachi. Japan. 1971.

The Battle of Tai'erzhuang (*Xuezhan Tai'erzhuang*). Yang Guangyuan and Zai Junjie. China. 1987.

Battle under Orion (*Manatsu no Orion*). Shinohara Tetsuo. Japan. 2009.

The Battleship Yamato (*Senkan Yamato*). Abe Yutaka. Japan. 1953.

Battlestations: Midway. Software. Eidos Interactive. United Kingdom. 2007.

The Beginning or the End. Taurog, Norman. USA. 1947.

Behind the Rising Sun. Dmytryk, Edward. USA. 1943.

The Bell of Nagasaki (*Nagasaki no kane*). Oba Hideo. 1950.

The Best Years of Our Lives. Wyler, William. USA. 1946.

Between Life and Death (*Yingyang jie*). Wu Ziniu. China. 1988.

Beyond the Clouds (*Kumo nagaruru hateni*). Ieki Miyoji. Japan. 1953.

The Big Mill (*Da mofang*). Wu Ziniu. China. 1990.

Black Rain (*Kuroi ame*). Imamura Shōhei. Japan. 1989.

Black Sun: The Nanjing Massacre (*Heitaiyang Nanjing datusha*). Tun Fei Mou (Mou Dunfei). Hong Kong. 1995.

Blood on the Sun. Lloyd, Frank. USA. 1943.

Blood on Wolf Mountain (*Langshan diexueji*). Fei Mu. China. 1936.

Bloodshed on the Green Mountains (*Qingshan bixue*). He Jiming. Taiwan. 1957.

Bloody Battle of Ta-pa-ni (*Xuezhan jiaobanian*). He Jiming. Taiwan. 1958.

Blue Sky (*Ch'anggong-ŭro . . .*). Lee In-su (Yi Insu). South Korea. 2006.

Blue Swallow (*Ch'ŏng-yŏn*). Yoon Jong-chan (Yun Chŏngch'an). South Korea. 2005.

Boat (K: *Bot'ŭ* / J: *No Boizu, No Kurai*). Kim Yŏngnam. South Korea/Japan. 2009.

Breaking Through (*Pacchigi!*). Izutsu Kazuyuki. Japan. 2005.

The Bridge Over the River Kwai. Lean, David. USA. 1957.

Broken Arrow. Daves, Delmer. USA. 1950.

Brotherhood of War, aka *Tae Guk Gi: The Brotherhood of War* (*T'aegŭkki hwinallimyŏ*). Kang Je-gyu. South Korea. 2004.

Call of Duty: World at War. Software. Activision. USA. 2008.

The Call of the Front (*Guixin sijian*). Li Jun. China. 1978.

Cape No. 7 (*Haijiao qihao*). Wei Te-sheng (Wei Desheng). Taiwan. 2008.

Capture Mount Hua by Stratagem (*Zhiqu Huashan*). Guo Wei. China. 1953.

Cease Fire. Crump, Owen. USA. 1953.

The Children of Huang Shi (*Huangshi de haizi/Huangshi renwu*). Spottiswoode, Roger. Australia/China/Germany. 2008.

Ch'oe Hakshin's Family (*Ch'oe Hakshin-ŭi ilga*). O Pyongcho. North Korea. 1966.

Children of the Atom Bomb (*Gembaku no ko*). Shindō Kaneto. Japan. 1952.

China. Farrow, John. USA. 1943.

Chocolate and Soldiers (*Chokoreto to heitai*). Satō Takeshi. Japan. 1938.

City of Life and Death (*Nanjing! Nanjing!*). Lu Chuan. China. 2009.

The Cockpit. Imanishi Takashi. Japan. 1993.

Code Name Heaven No. 1. Zhang Ying. Taiwan. 1964.

Come, Come, Come Upward (*Aje aje para aje*). Im Kwŏnt'aek. South Korea. 1989.

Comfort Women Team 74 (*Wei'anfu qishisi fendui*). Chen Guijun. China. 2003.

Corporal Norakuro (*Norakuro Gunsō*). Murata Yasuji. Japan. 1934.

Coup d'Etat (*Kaigenrei*). Yoshida Yoshishige. Japan. 1973.

The Critical Moment (*Zuihou guantou*). Su Yi et al. Hong Kong. 1937.

Crossroads (*Shizi jietou*). Shen Xiling. China. 1937.

Cruel Story of War (*Rikugun zangyaku monogatari*). Satō Jun'ya. Japan. 1963.

Daughters of China (*Zhonghua ernü*). Ling Zifeng and Zhai Qiang. China. 1949.

Dawn of Freedom (*Ano hata o ute*). Abe Yutaka. Japan. 1944.

Devils at the Doorstep (*Guizi laile*). Jiang Wen. China. 2000.

Disturbance (*Dōran*). Moritani Shirō. Japan. 1980.

Doctor No. Young, Terence. USA. 1962.

Dong Cunrui (*Dong Cunrui*). Guo Wei. China. 1955.

Don't Cry, Nanking (*Nanjing 1937*). Wu Ziniu. China. 2005.

Dove Tree (*Gezi shu*). Wu Ziniu. China. 1985 (banned).

Downfall (*Der Untergang*). Hirschbiegel, Oliver. Germany. 2004.

Dr. Strangelove or: How I Learned to Stop Worrying and Love the Bomb. Kubrick,
   Stanley. United Kingdom/USA. 1964.

Dragon Seed. Bucquet, Harold S., and Jack Conway. USA. 1944.

Eight Hundred Heroes (*Babai zhuangshi*). Ting Shan-hsi (Ding Shanxi). Taiwan.
   1975.

Eight Hundred Heroic Soldiers (*Babai zhuangshi*). Ying Yunwei. China. 1938.

Electric-Lightning Squadron Mobilized (*Dengekitai shutsudō*). Japan. 1944.

Elegy to Violence (*Kenka ereji*). Suzuki Seijun. Japan. 1966.

Emperor. Webber, Peter. USA. 2013.

The Emperor's Naked Army Marches On (*Yuki yukite shingun*). Hara Kazuo. Japan.
   1987.

Epitaph (*Kidam*). Jung Sik (Chŏng Sik) and Jung Beom-sik (Chŏng Bŏmsik).
   South Korea. 2007.

Escape at Dawn (*Akatsuki no dassō*). Taniguchi Senkichi. Japan. 1950.

The Eternal Wave (*Yong bu xiaoshi de dianpo*). Wang Ping. China. 1958.

Evening Bell (*Wanzhong*). Wu Ziniu. China. 1988.

The Everlasting Glory (*Yinglie qianqiu*). Ding Shanxi. Taiwan. 1974.

Fantasia. Disney, Walt. USA. 1940.

Farewell My Love (*Songjun xin mianmian*). Liang Zhefu. Taiwan. 1965.

Farewell to Manzanar. Korty, John. USA. 1976.

Fat Man and Little Boy. Joffé, Roland. USA. 1989.

Female Agent No. 7 (*Di qi hao nüjiandie*). Jin Long. Taiwan. 1964.

The Fighting Acrobats (*Dihou zhuangshi xie*). Wang Yin. Taiwan. 1963.

The Firefly (*Hotaru*). Furuhata Yasuo. Japan. 2001.

Fires on the Plain (*Nobi*). Ichikawa Kon. Japan. 1959.

Five Scouts (*Gonin no sekkōhei*). Tasaka Tomotaka. Japan. 1938.

Flag of Honor (*Qi zheng piaopiao*). Ting Shan-si (Ding Shanxi). Hong Kong. 1987.

Flags of Our Fathers. Eastwood, Clint. USA. 2006.

Flower Street (*Huajie*). Yue Feng. China. 1950.

The Flowers of War (*Jinling shisanchai*). Zhang Yimou. China. 2011.

For Those We Love (*Ore wa, kimi no tame ni koso shini ni iku*). Shinjō Taku. Japan. 2007.

Friends. Tokyo Broadcasting System. Japan/South Korea. 2002.

From Victory to Victory (*Nanzheng beizhan*). Cheng Yin and Tang Xiaodan. China. 1952.

From Victory to Victory (*Nanzheng beizhan*). Cheng Yin and Wang Yan. China. 1974.

Gada Meilin (*Gada Meilin*). Feng Xiaoning. China. 2002.

Gandhi. Attenborough, Richard. USA. 1982.

Garlands at the Foot of the Mountain (*Gaoshan xiade huahuan*). Xie Jin. China. 1984.

Gate of Flesh (*Nikutai no mon*). Suzuku Seijun. Japan. 1964.

The Go Masters (*Mikan no taikyoku*). Satō Jun'ya and Duan Jishun. Japan. 1982.

God of Peace (*Heping zhi shen*). Hou Yao. China. 1926.

Godzilla (*Gojira*). Honda Ishirō. Japan. 1954.

Godzilla Raids Again (*Gojira no gyakushū*). Oda Motoyoshi. Japan. 1955.

Golden Chicken Heart (*Jinjixin*). Zhang Ying. Taiwan. 1965.

Gone with Honor (*Xianghuo*). Xu Jinliang (Hsu Chin-Liang). Taiwan. 1979.

The Good Earth. Franklin, Sidney. USA. 1937.

The Good, The Bad, The Weird (*Choŭn nom, nappŭn nom, isanghan nom*). Kim Jee-woon (Kim Chiun). South Korea. 2008.

Gran Torino. Eastwood, Clint. USA. 2008.

The Great Empire of Japan (*Dai-Nippon teikoku*). Masuda Toshio. Japan. 1982.

Grief Over the Yellow River (*Huanghe juelian*). Feng Xiaoning. China. 1999.

Guadalcanal Diary. Seiler, Lewis. USA. 1943.

The Guard Post (*GP506*). Kong Suchang. South Korea. 2008.

Guerrillas along the Railroad (*Tiedao youjidui*). Zhao Ming. China. 1956.

Guerrillas on the Plain (*Pingyuan youjidui*). Su Li and Wu Zhaodi. China. 1955.

Guerrillas on the Plain (*Pingyuan youjidui*). Wu Zhaodi and Chang Zhenhua. China. 1974.

Guess Who's Coming to Dinner. Kramer, Stanley. USA. 1967.

Gung Ho! Enright, Ray. USA. 1943.

Habitual Sadness: Korean Comfort Women Today (*Najŭn moksori II*). Byun Young-Joo. South Korea. 1997.

Harp of Burma (*Biruma no tategoto*). Ichikawa Kon. Japan. 1956.

Hearts of Iron. Strategy First. Sweden/Canada. 2002.

Hearts of Iron II. Paradox Interactive. Sweden. 2005.

Hero Zheng Chenggong (*Yingxiong Zheng Chenggong*). Wu Ziniu. China. 2000.

Heroes from Lüliang Mountains (*Lüliang yingxiong*). Lü Ban and Yi Lin. China. 1950.

Heroes of the Eastern Skies (*Jianqiao yinglie zhuan*). Zhang Zengze. Taiwan. 1977.

Heroes on the Island (Taiwan yinglie zhuan). Cai Qiulin. Taiwan. 1965.

Heroic Sons and Daughters (Yingxiong ernü). Wu Zhaodi. China. 1964.

The Highway (Dalu). Sun Yu. China. 1935.

Holy War (Seisen). Japan. 1939.

Hoodlum Soldier (Heitai Yakuza). Masumura Yasuzō. Japan. 1965.

Hooray for the Black Cat (Kuroneko Banzai). Nakano Takao. Japan. 1933.

The Human Bullet (Manga no nikudan). Kiyohara Hitoshi. Japan. 1932.

The Human Bullet (Nikudan). Okamoto Kihachi. Japan. 1968.

The Human Condition (Ningen no jōken). Kobayashi Masaki. Japan. 1959–1961.

The Human Torpedoes (Ningen gyorai kaiten). Matsubayashi Shue. Japan. 1955.

The Illusion of "the Nanjing Massacre" (Nankin gyakusatsu no kyoko). Tanaka
    Masaki. Japan. 1984.

Imperial Comfort Women (Diguo junji). Qiu Litao. China. 1995.

The Imperial Navy (Rengō kantai). Matsubayashi Shūe. Japan. 1981.

In Their Prime (Tamen zheng nianqing). Zhou Xiaowen. China. 1986 (banned).

Into the Fire aka *71: Into the Fire (Pohwa sŏkŭro)*. Lee Jae-han (Yi Chaehan).
    South Korea. 2010.

Iris Chang: The Rape of Nanjing, television documentary. Spahic, Bill, and Anne
    Pick. Canada. 2007.

Japan Has Not Lost (Nihon yaburezu). Abe Yutaka. Japan. 1954.

Japan's Longest Day (Nihon no ichiban nagai hi). Okamoto Kihachi. Japan.
    1967.

Japanese War Bride. Vidor, King. USA. 1952.

Joint Security Area (Kongdong kyŏngbi kuyŏk). Park Chan-wook (Pak Ch'anuk).
    South Korea. 2000.

Joyous Heroes (Huanle yingxiong). Wu Ziniu. China. 1988.

The Killing Fields. Joffé, Roland. USA. 1984.

Lady from Chungking. Nigh, William. USA. 1942.

Landmine Warfare (Dilei zhan). Tang Yingqi, Xu Du, and Wu Jianhai. China.
    1962.

The Last Kamikaze (Saigo no tokkōtai). Satō Jun'ya. Japan. 1970.

Lay Down Your Arms If You Want to Live (Jiaoqiang busha). Tsang, Eric (Zeng
    Zhiwei). China. 2007.

Legend of Bagua Mountain (Baguashan chuanqi). China. 1965.

Letter with Feather (Jimao xin). Shi Hui. China. 1954.

Letters from Iwo Jima. Eastwood, Clint. USA. 2006.

Life Line (Shengming xian). Kwan Moon (Guan Wenqing). Hong Kong. 1935.

Little Tokyo, U.S.A. Brower, Otto. USA. 1942.

Little Toys (Xiao wanyi). Sun Yu. China. 1933.

Lorelei: The Witch of the Pacific Ocean (Rōrerai). Higuchi Shinji. Japan. 2005.

Love in a Chilly Spring (Chunhan). Chen Junliang. Taiwan. 1979.

Love Is a Many-Splendored Thing. King, Henry. USA. 1955.

Love You Until Death (Ai ni dao si). Xu Shouren. Taiwan. 1967.

Lust, Caution. Lee, Ang. USA. 2006.

A Man Who Lost His Fatherland (Meiyou zuguo de ren). Xin Qi. Taiwan.

The Manchurian Candidate. Frankenheimer, John. USA. 1962.

The Marco Polo Bridge Incident (Lugouqiao shibian). China. 1937.

The Marines Who Never Return (Tolaoji annŭn haebyŏng). Yi Manhŭi (Lee Man-hee). South Korea. 1963.

Massacre in Nanjing (Tucheng xuezheng). Luo Guanqun. China. 1987.

May and August (Wuyue Bayue). Du Guowei. China. 2002.

Medal of Honor: Pacific Assault. Software. Electronic Arts. USA. 2004.

Meiji Emperor and Russo-Japanese War (Meiji tennō to Nichi-ro sensō). Watanabe Kunio. Japan. 1957.

Memoirs of a Geisha. Marshall, Rob. USA. 2005.

The Men. Zinnemann, Fred. USA. 1950.

Merdeka 17805 (Murudeka 17805). Fuji Yukio. Japan. 2001.

The Meridian of War (Zhanzheng ziwu xian). Feng Xiaoning. China. 1990.

Midway. Smight, Jack. USA. 1976.

Military Comfort Women (Junji weianfu). Lu Xiaolong. Hong Kong. 1992.

Military Prize (Zhangong). Lu Jie and Xu Xingfu. China. 1925.

The Mission. Joffé, Roland. USA. 1986.

Momotaro of the Sky (Sora no Momotarō). Murata Yasuji. Japan. 1931.

Momotaro's Divine Navy (Momotarō umi no shinpei). Seo Mitsuyo. Japan. 1945.

Momotaro's Sea Eagles (Momotarō no umiwashi). Seo Mitsuyo. Japan. 1943.

Mud and Soldiers (Tsuchi to heitai). Tasaka Tomotaka. Japan. 1939.

The Murmuring (Najŭn moksori). Byun Young-Joo (Pyŏn Yŏngju). South Korea. 1995.

My Own Breathing (Najŭn moksori III). Byun Young-Joo (Pyŏn Yŏngju). South Korea. 1999.

My Sweet Memory (Mimi xiangsilin). Zhang Peicheng. Taiwan. 1976.

Nakano Spy School (Rikugun Nakano gakkō). Masumura Yasuzō. Japan. 1966.

Nanjing 1937 (Nanjing datusha). Wu Ziniu. China. 1995.

Nanking. Guttentag, Bill, and Dan Sturman. USA. 2007.

The National Anthem (Guoge). Wu Ziniu. China. 1999.

The Naval Brigade at Shanghai (Shanhai rikusentai). Kumagai Hisatora. Japan. 1939.

New Story of Heroic Sons and Daughters (Xin ernü yingxiong zhuan). Lü Ban and Shi Dongshan. China. 1950.

Night and Fog (Nuit et brouillard). Resnais, Alain. France. 1955.

Night Fragrance aka Miss Evening Sweet (Yelaixiang). Bu Wancang. Taiwan. 1957.

No Regrets for Our Youth (Waga seishun ni kui nashi). Kurosawa Akira. Japan. 1947.

Oba: The Last Samurai aka *Codename: Fox* (*Taiheiyō no kiseki: Fokkusu to yobareta otoko*). Hirayama Hideyuki. Japan. 2011.
Once Upon a Time (*Wŏnsŭ ŏp'on ŏ t'a'imu*). Jeong Yong-ki (Chŏng Yŏngki). South Korea. 2008.
One and Eight (*Yige he bage*). Zhang Junzhao. China. 1984.
The Operations of Spring Winds (*Wang chunfeng*). Xu Jinliang. Taiwan. 1977.
Pacific Gunner. Atari. USA. 2002.
Pearl Harbor. Bay, Michael. USA. 2001.
People's General. Strategic Simulations, Inc. USA. 1998.
The Place Promised in Our Early Days (*Kumo no mukō, Yakusoku no basho*). Shinkai Makoto. Japan. 2003.
Pork Chop Hill. Milestone, Lewis. USA. 1959.
Pride: The Fateful Moment (*Puraido—unmei no toki*). Itō Shunya. Japan. 1998.
Proof of the Man (*Ningen no shōmei*). Satō Jun'ya. Japan. 1976.
Purple Heart. Milestone, Lewis. USA. 1944.
Purple Sunset (*Ziri*). Feng Xiaoning. China. 2001.
Put Your Hands Up (*Juqi shoulai*). Feng Xiaoning. China. 2003.
Qixia Temple 1937 (*Qixia si*). Zheng Fangnan. China. 2005.
Rabbit on the Moon. Omori Emiko. USA. 1999.
Rape of Nanjing. Joseph, Rhawn. USA. 2006.
Rashōmon. Kurosawa Akira. Japan. 1950.
Recapturing Tai'erzhuang (*Kefu Tai'erzhuang*). China. 1939.
Reconnaissance across the Yangtze (*Dujiang zhenchaji*). Tang Huada and Tang Xiaodan. China. 1974.
Reconnaissance across the Yangtze (*Dujiang zhenchaji*). Tang Xiaodan. China. 1954.
Record of a Living Being (*Ikimono no kiroku*). Kurosawa Akira. Japan. 1956.
Red Angel (*Akai Tenshi*). Masumura Yasuzō. Japan. 1966.
The Red Detachment of Women (*Hongse niangzi jun*). Xie Jin. China. 1961.
Red Light District (*Akasen chitai*). Mizoguchi Kenji. Japan. 1956.
Red River Valley (*Honghe gu*). Feng Xiaoning. China. 1997.
Red Rose, Real and False (*Zhenjia hongmeiguei*). Liang Zhefu. Taiwan. 1966.
Red Scarf (*Ppalgan mahura*). Shin Sang-ok (Sin Sangok). South Korea. 1964.
Red Sorghum (*Hong gaoliang*). Zhang Yimou. China. 1987.
Return from Hainan Island (*Hainandao zhanhou guilai*). Wei Zhongmin. Taiwan. 1958.
Return My Land (*Huangwo shanhe*). Wang Cilong. China. 1934.
Rhapsody in August (*Hachi-gatsu no kyōshikyoku*). Kurosawa Akira. Japan. 1991.
Rikidōzan: A Hero Extraordinary (*Yŏkdosan*). Song Hae-seong (Song Haesŏng). South Korea/Japan. 2004.
Salvador. Stone, Oliver. USA. 1986.

Sands of Iwo Jima. Dwan, Alan. USA. 1949.

Saving Private Ryan. Spielberg, Steven. USA. 1998.

Sayon's Bell (Sayon no kane). Hiroshi Shimizu. Japan. 1943.

Sayonara. Logan, Joshua. USA. 1957.

Scarlet Rose: The Goddesses of Jinling (Xuese meigui: Jinling nüshen). Yu Liqing. China. 2007.

Sea without Exit (Deguchi no nai umi). Sasabe Kiyoshi. Japan. 2006.

Secret Agent Chungking No. 1 (Chongqing yihao). Liang Zhefu. Taiwan. 1970.

Secret Agent Queen (Tewu nüjiandie wang). Wu Wenchao. Taiwan. 1965.

Secret Agent Yangtze River No. 1 (Changjiang yihao). Liang Zhefu. Taiwan. 1970.

The Secret Reunion (Ŭi-hyŏngje). Jang Hun (Chang Hun). South Korea. 2010.

Seven Women Prisoners (Ch'il-in ŭi yŏp'oro). Yi Manhŭi (Lee Man-hee). South Korea. 1965.

Sexy Girls of Denmark (Dan Ma jiaowa). Chi Lu. Hong Kong. 1973.

Shanggan Ridge (Shangganling). Sha Meng and Lin Shan. China. 1956.

Shanghai Rhapsody (Shanhai bansu kingu). Fukasaku Kinji. Japan. 1984.

Shining Light. Yamagami Tatsuhiko. Japan. 1970.

Shiri (Swiri). Kang Je-gyu (Kang Chegyu). South Korea. 1999.

Sights of the Eight Provinces (P'aldogangsan). Pae Sokin. South Korea. 1967.

Silmido. Kang Woo-suk. South Korea. 2003.

The Slut and the Saint (Dangfu yu shengnnü). Chen Tian. Taiwan. 1959.

Songs of Southern Island (Hun duan nanhai). Bai Ke. Taiwan. 1958.

South Pacific. Logan, Joshua. USA. 1958.

Southern Cross (Minami jūjisei). Maruyama Seiji and Peter Maxwell. Japan. 1982.

Southern Guerrilla Forces (Nambugun). Chŏng Chiyŏng. South Korea. 1990.

Space Battleship Yamato (Uchū senkan Yamato). Masuda Toshio. Japan. 1977.

The Spider and the Tulip (Kumo to chūrippu). Seo Mitsuyo. Japan. 1944.

Spring Dream (Chungui mengli ren). Hou Yao. China. 1925.

Spring in a Small Town (Xiaocheng zhi chun). Fei Mu. China. 1948.

Spring in My Hometown (Arŭmdaun sijŏl). Yi Kwangmo. South Korea. 1998.

Spring River Flows East (Yijiang chunshui xiangdong liu). Cai Chusheng and Zheng Junli. China. 1947.

Spy Number One (Tianzi diyihao). Chen Liting. China. 1946.

Spy Red Rose (Jiandie hongmeigui). Liang Zhefu. Taiwan. 1966.

Star's Echo (K: Pyŏl ŭi soli / J: Anata ni aitakute). MBC/Fuji TV. South Korea/Japan. 2004.

Steel Helmut. Fuller, Samuel. USA. 1951.

Storm over the Yangtze River (Yangzijiang fengyun). Li Hanxiang. China. 1969.

Story of a Prostitute (Shunpuden). Suzuki Seijun. Japan. 1965.

Story of Liubao Village (Liubao de gushi). Wang Ping. China. 1957.

Stray Dog (Nora Inu). Kurosawa Akira. Japan. 1949.

Street Angel (*Malu tianshi*). Yuan Muzhi. China. 1937.

Summer of the Moonlight Sonata (*Gekkō no natsu*). Koyama Seijirō. Japan. 1993.

Surrogate Mother (*Ssibaji*). Im Kwŏnt'aek. South Korea. 1986.

Taegukgi: The Brotherhood of War (*T'aegŭkki hwinallimyŏ*). Kang Je-Gyu. Korea. 2004.

Tarzan and the Treasure (*Taishan yu baozang*). Liang Zhefu. Taiwan. 1966.

Teahouse of the August Moon. Mann, Daniel. USA. 1956.

Titanic. Cameron, James. USA. 1997.

Tokyo Shower (*Tok'yo yŏubi*). SBS. South Korea/Japan. 2008.

Tokyo Trial (*Tōkyō saiban*). Kobayashi Masaki. Japan. 1983.

Tokyo Tribunal (*Dongjing shenpan*). Gao Qunshu. China. 2006.

The Tombstone of the Fireflies (*Hotaru no haka*). Takahata Isao. Japan. 2008.

Tomorrow (*Ashita*). Kuroki Kazuo. Japan. 1988.

Tora! Tora! Tora! Fleischer, Richard, and Fukasaku Kinji. USA/Japan. 1970.

Transformers. Bay, Michael. USA. 2007.

The Truth of Nanking (*Nankin no shinjitsu*). Mizushima Satoru. Japan. 2008.

Tunnel Warfare (*Didao zhan*). Ren Xudong. China. 1965.

Turbulance at Musha (*Wushe fengyun*). Hong Xinde. Taiwan. 1965.

Under the Flag of the Rising Sun (*Gunki hatameku motoni*). Fukasaku Kinji. Japan. 1972.

Unit 731 Comfort Women (*731 junji*). China. 1992.

Unknown Heroes I–IIX (*Irŭmŏpnŭn yŏngungdŭl I–IIX, 1979–1981*). Ryu Hosun. North Korea. 1979–1981.

Victory (*Meihua*). Liu Jiachang. Taiwan. 1976.

Virgin Snow (*Ch'ŏtun*). Han Sang-hye. South Korea/Japan. 2007.

Waiting for You Year after Year (*Deng ni yinian guo yinian*). Liang Zhefu. Taiwan. 1964.

Wake Island. Farrow, John. USA. 1942.

War and Humanity (*Sensō to ningen*). Yamamoto Satsuo. Japan. 1970–1973.

War and Love (*Zhanhuo zhong de qingchun*). Wang Yan. China. 1959.

The War at Sea from Hawai'i to Malaya (*Hawai'i Mare oki kaisen*). Yamamoto Kajirō. Japan. 1942.

Warriors of the Rainbow: Seediq Bale (*Saideke bului*). Wei Te-sheng. Taiwan. 2011.

Welcome to Dongmakgol (*Welk'ŏm t'u tongmakgol*). Park Kwang-hyun (Pak Kwanghyŏn). South Korea. 2005.

White Badge (*Hayan chŏnjaeng*). Chŏng Chiyŏng. South Korea. 1992.

White Jasmine (*Molihua*). Chen Junliang. Taiwan. 1980.

Wings of a Man (*Ningen no tsubasa*). Okamoto Akihisa. Japan. 1995.

Wings of the Pacific (*Taiheiyō no tsubasa*). Matsubayashi Shue. Japan. 1963.

Winter Sonata (*Kyŏul yŏn'ga*). Yoon Seok-ho (Yun Sŏkho). Korea. 2002.

Wŏlmi Island (*Wŏlmi-do*). Cho Kyŏngsun. North Korea. 1982.

World of Warcraft. Software. Blizzard Entertainment. USA. 2004.

Yamato (Otokotachi no Yamato). Satō Jun'ya. Japan. 2005.

Yasukuni. Li Ying. Japan. 2007.

YMCA Baseball Team (YMCA yagudan). Kim Hyun-seok (Kim Hyŏnsŏk). South Korea. 2002.

Zero Fighter Burns (Zerosen moyu). Masuda Toshio. Japan. 1984.

Zhang Ga, a Boy Soldier (Xiaobing Zhang Ga). Cui Wei and Ouyang Hongying. China. 1963.

Zhao Yiman (Zhao Yiman). Sha Meng. China. 1950.

Bibliography

Adorno, Theodore W. *The Culture Industry: Selected Essays on Mass Culture,* ed. J. M. Bernstein. London: Routledge, 1991.

Akiyama Masami. *Maboroshi no sensō manga no sekai* (The world of illusory war comics). Tokyo: Natsume shobō, 1998.

Altman, Rick. *Film/Genre.* London: BFI, 1999.

Amano Keiichi. "'Utsukushii kuni' no 'utsukushii shi'" (A "beautiful history" for a "beautiful country"). *Inpakushon* 158 (July 2007): 169–171.

Amano, Masanao. *Manga Design,* ed. Julius Miedemann. Cologne: Taschen, 2004.

Aoyagi, Hiroshi. *Islands of Eight Million Smiles: Idol Performance and Symbolic Production in Contemporary Japan.* Cambridge, MA: Harvard University Asia Center, 2005.

Aoyagi, Hiroshi. "Pop Idols and the Asian Identity." In *Japan Pop! Inside the World of Japanese Popular Culture,* ed. Timothy J. Craig, 309–326. Armonk, NY: M.E. Sharpe, 2000.

Appadurai, Arjun. *Modernity at Large: Cultural Dimensions of Globalization.* Minneapolis: University of Minnesota Press, 1996.

"Aramata Hiroshi Interviews Matsumoto Leiji, Part 1." *Aramata Hiroshi no denshi manga nabigētā, ebookjapan,* October 7, 2011, http://www.ebookjapan .jp/ebj/special/manganavi/manganavi_11-1a.asp.

Asada, Akira. "Infantile Capitalism and Japan's Postmodernism." In *Postmodernism and Japan,* ed. Masao Miyoshi and H.D. Harootunian, 273–278. Durham, NC: Duke University Press, 1989.

Bailey, James. "War Films Depict Japan as Misunderstood Victim." *New York Times,* November 10, 1985.

Barkawi, Tarak, and Keith Stanski. *Orientalism and War.* New York: Columbia University Press, 2013.

Basinger, Jeanine. *The World War II Combat Film: Anatomy of a Genre.* Middletown, CT: Wesleyan University Press, 2003.

Benjamin, Walter. *Illuminations: Essays and Reflections,* ed. Hannah Arendt and trans. Harry Zohn. New York: Schocken, 1969.

Berry, Michael. *A History of Pain: Trauma in Modern Chinese Literature and Film.* New York: Columbia University Press, 2008.

Berry, Michael. "Scorched Earth: Why *City of Life and Death*'s Treatment of the Nanking Massacre Ignited Controversy in China." *Film Comment* 47, no. 3 (May/June 2011).

Braester, Yomi. *Witness against History: Literature, Film, and Public Discourse in Twentieth-Century China.* Stanford, CA: Stanford University Press, 2003.

Brasor, Philip. "Confusion Reigns after 'Yasukuni' Doesn't Tell Us How to Feel." *Japan Times,* April 13, 2008.

Brasor, Philip. "Korean Wave May Help Erode Discrimination." *Japan Times,* June 27, 2004.

Breen, John. "Yasukuni Shrine: Ritual and Memory." *Asia-Pacific Journal: Japan Focus,* June 3, 2005, http://www.japanfocus.org/-John-Breen/2060/.

Broderick, Mick, ed. *Hibakusha Cinema: Hiroshima, Nagasaki, and the Nuclear Image in Japanese Film.* London: Kegan Paul, 1996.

Buruma, Ian. *The Wages of Guilt: Memories of War in Germany and Japan.* New York: Farrar, Straus & Giroux, 1994.

Campbell, Richard. *Media and Culture: An Introduction to Mass Communication.* London: St. Martin's Press, 1998.

Carpenter, Ted Galen. *America's Coming War with China: A Collision Course over Taiwan.* London: Palgrave Macmillan, 2006.

Cha, Victor D. "Hypotheses on History and Hate in Asia: Japan and the Korean Peninsula." In *Reconciliation in the Asia-Pacific,* ed. Yoichi Funabashi, 37–59. Washington, DC: U.S. Institute of Peace Press, 2003.

Chang, Iris. *The Rape of Nanking.* New York: Basic Books, 1997.

Chapman, James. *War and Film.* London: Reaktion, 2008.

Chen Kehua. "Huangminhua de yueguang." *Lianhebao* August 17, 2011, D3.

Chen Ying. "Yi wushe shijian weizhu de taiwan dianying zuopin" (Taiwan films about the Musha Incident). *OttoCat bangqiu xinwen zaji,* June 27, 2011.

Chi, Robert Yee-sin. "Picture Perfect: Narrating Public Memory in Twentieth-Century China." Ph.D. diss., Harvard University, 2001.

Chou, Wan-yao (Zhou Wanyao). "'Shayong zhi zhong' de gushi ji qi zhoubian polan" (The story of "Sayon's Bell" and its subsequent development). In *Hai xin xi de niandai: Riben zhimin tongzhi moqi Taiwan shilun ji,* (Collected historical essays on the final years of Taiwan's colonial period under Japan) 13–31. Taibei: Yunchen wenhua, 2003.

Chung, Hye Jean. "Reclamation of Voice: The Joint Authorship in the Murmuring Trilogy." In *Documentary Testimonies: Global Archives of Suffering,* ed. Bhaskar Sarkar and Janet Walker, 135–154. New York: Routledge, 2009.

Chung, Hye Seung. *Hollywood Asian: Philip Ahn and the Politics of Cross-Ethnic Performance.* Philadelphia: Temple University Press, 2006.

Clancy, Tom. *Debt of Honor.* New York: G. P. Putnam's Sons, 1994.

Craig, Timothy J., ed. *Japan Pop! Inside the World of Japanese Popular Culture.* Armonk, NY: M.E. Sharpe, 2000.

Crocker, David. "Reckoning with Past Wrongs: A Normative Framework." *Ethics and International Affairs* 13 (1999): 43–64.

Dai Jinhua. *Dianying lilun yu piping shouce* (Handbook on film theory and criticism). Beijing: Kexue jishu wenxian chubanshe, 1993.

Davis, Darrell William. *Picturing Japaneseness: Monumental Style, National Identity, Japanese Film.* New York: Columbia University Press, 1996.

Dick, Philip K. *The Man in the High Castle.* New York: Vintage, 1992.

Doherty, Thomas. *Projections of War: Hollywood, American Culture, and World War II.* New York: Columbia University Press, 1999.

Donnelly, Ignatius. *Caesar's Column: A Story of the Twentieth Century.* Teddington, UK: Echo Library, 2007.

Dower, John. *War without Mercy.* New York: Pantheon Books, 1986.

Ebert, Roger. "Reviews: *Rhapsody in August.*" *Chicago Sun-Times,* February 21, 1992.

Edwards, Paul W. *A Guide to Films on the Korean War.* Westport, CT: Greenwood, 1997.

Erni, John Nguyet, and Siew Keng Chua. *Asian Media Studies.* Malden, MA: Blackwell, 2005.

Feng, Peter X. *Identities in Motion: Asian American Film and Video.* Durham, NC: Duke University Press, 2002.

Feng, Peter X., ed. *Screening Asian Americans.* New Brunswick, NJ: Rutgers University Press, 2002.

Foucault, Michel. *Discipline and Punish: The Birth of the Prison.* New York: Vintage Books, 1995.

Fu, Poshek. "Introduction: The Shaw Brothers Diasporic Cinema." In *China Forever: The Shaw Brothers and Diasporic Cinema,* ed. Poshek Fu, 1–26. Urbana: University of Illinois Press, 2008.

Fu, Poshek. "Japanese Occupation, Shanghai Exiles, and Postwar Hong Kong Cinema." *China Quarterly,* no. 194 (2008): 380–394.

Fujitani, Takashi, Geoffrey M. White, and Lisa Yoneyama, ed. *Perilous Memories: The Asia-Pacific War(s).* Durham, NC: Duke University Press, 2001.

Fukuma Yoshiaki. "*Otokotachi no Yamato* to 'kandō' no poritikusu" (*Yamato* and the politics of emotion). In *Media bunka o shakaigaku suru* (Sociologically analyzing media culture), ed. Takai Masashi and Tanimoto Naho, 244–265. Kyoto: Shakai shisōsha, 2009.

Gateward, Frances. "Waiting to Exhale: The Colonial Experience and the Trouble with *My Own Breathing.*" In *Seoul Searching: Culture and Identity in Contemporary Korean Cinema,* ed. Frances Gateward, 191–218. Albany: SUNY Press, 2007.

Gerow, Aaron. "Fantasies of War and Nation in Recent Japanese Cinema." *Japan Focus,* February 20, 2006, http://www.japanfocus.org/products/details/1707/.

Gerow, Aaron. *"Miyamoto Musashi* to senjichū no kankyaku" (Miyamoto Musashi and wartime spectators). In *Eiga kantoku Mizoguchi Kenji* (Film director Mizoguchi Kenji), ed. Yomota Inuhiko, 226–250. Tokyo: Shinyōsha, 1999.

Gerow, Aaron. "Narrating the Nationality of a Cinema: The Case of Japanese Prewar Film." In *The Culture of Japanese Fascism,* ed. Alan Tansman, 185–211. Durham, NC: Duke University Press, 2009.

Gerow, Aaron. "What Are Japanese Fantasy Films Telling Us?" *History New Network,* February 26, 2006.

Gildenhard, Bettina. " 'Tasha' to shite no hittorā" (Hitler as "The Other"). In *Manga no naka no 'tasha'* ("The Other" in comics), ed. Itō Kimio, 196–221. Kyoto: Rinsen shoten, 2008.

Gingrich, Newt. "America at Risk: Two Novels President Obama Should Read." *Fox Forum,* June 15, 2009.

Gottlieb, Nanette, and Mark McLelland, ed. *Japanese Cybercultures.* New York: Routledge, 2003.

Green, Michael J. "Can Tojo Inspire Modern Japan?" *SAIS Review* 19, no. 2 (1999): 243–250.

Gritten, David. "Memoirs of a Very Controversial Geisha." *The Telegraph,* December 2, 2005.

Hamamoto, Darrell Y., and Sandra Liu, ed. *Countervisions: Asian-American Film Criticism.* Philadelphia: Temple University Press, 2000.

"Hansen ka hanBei ka?—Senki eiga no tadotte iru michi" (Anti-war or anti-American? the road war films have taken). *Kinema junpō* 39 (August 1, 1953), reprinted in *Besuto obu Kinema junpō,* vol. 1, 225–229. Tokyo: Kinema Junpōsha, 1994.

Harootunian, Harry. "Japan's Long Postwar: The Trick of Memory and the Ruse of History." *South Atlantic Quarterly* 99, no. 4 (fall 2000): 715–739.

Hayot, Eric. "Chineseness: A Prehistory of Its Future." In *Sinographies: Writing China,* ed. Eric Hayot, Haun Saussy, and Steven G. Yao. Minneapolis: University of Minnesota Press, 2007.

Hayot, Eric. *The Hypothetical Mandarin: Sympathy, Modernity, and Chinese Pain.* New York: Oxford University Press, 2009.

Hayot, Eric, and Edward Wesp. "Reading Game/Text: *EverQuest,* Alienation, and Digital Communities." *Postmodern Culture* 14, no. 2 (January 2004).

Hein, Laura Elizabeth, and Mark Selden, ed. *Censoring History: Citizenship and Memory in Japan, Germany, and the United States.* Armonk, NY: M.E. Sharpe, 2000.

Hesford, Wendy S. "Reading Rape Stories: Material Rhetoric and the Trauma of Representation." *College English* 62, no. 2 (November 1999).

Hicks, George. *The Comfort Women: Japan's Brutal Regime of Enforced Prostitution in the Second World War.* New York: W.W. Norton, 1995.

High, Peter B. *The Imperial Screen: Japanese Film Culture in the Fifteen Years' War, 1931–1945.* Madison: University of Wisconsin Press, 2003.

Hirano, Kyoko. *Mr. Smith Goes to Tokyo: Japanese Cinema under the American Occupation, 1945–1952.* Washington, DC: Smithsonian Institution Press, 1992.

Hirsch, Joshua. *Afterimage: Film, Trauma, and the Holocaust.* Philadelphia: Temple University Press, 2004.

Hobson, Richmond Pearson. "If War Should Come! First Article—The Question of Preparedness." *Cosmopolitan* (June 1908): 584–593.

Hobson, Richmond Pearson. "If War Should Come! Second Article—The Conflict." *Cosmopolitan* (July 1908): 28–47.

Hong, Junhao. "The Evolution of China's War Movie in Five Decades: Factors Contributing to Changes, Limits, and Implications." *Asian Cinema* 10, no. 1 (1998): 93–106, http://web.archive.org/web/20061209130115/http://online.sfsu.edu/~soh/comfortwomen.html.

Huang Ren. *Beiqing taiyu pian* (Taiwanese-language films of sadness). Taibei: Wanxiang tushu, 1994.

Huang Ren, ed. *Hu Jinquan de shijie* (The world of Hu Jinquan). Taibei: Yatai tushu, 1999.

Huang Ren. *Xin Qi de chuanqi* (Legend of Xin Qi). Taibei: Yatai tushu, 2005.

Huang Ren. "Yangzijiang fengyun guanhougan" (After watching *Storm over the Yangtze River*). In *Yangzijiang fengyun yingpingji* (Essays on *Storm over the Yangtze*), ed. Zhongguo dianying zhipianchang 47–49. Taibei: Zhongguo dianying zhipianchang, 1969.

Huangfu Yichuan. *Zhongguo zhanzheng dianying shi* (History of Chinese war films). Beijing: Zhongguo dianying chubanshe, 2005.

Hung, Chang-tai. *War and Popular Culture: Resistance in Modern China, 1937–1945.* Berkeley: University of California Press, 1994.

Huyssen, Andreas. "Present Pasts: Media, Politics, Amnesia." *Public Culture* 12, no. 1 (2000): 21–38.

Igarashi, Yoshikuni. *Bodies of Memory: Narratives of War in Postwar Japanese Culture, 1945–1970.* Princeton, NJ: Princeton University Press, 2000.

Igarashi, Yoshikuni. "Kamikaze Today. The Search for National Heroes in Contemporary Japan." In *Ruptured Histories: War, Memory, and the Post–Cold War in Asia,* ed. Sheila Miyoshi Jager and Rana Mitter, 99–121. Cambridge, MA: Harvard University Press, 2007.

Irokawa Daikichi. *Aru Shōwashi* (A certain history of Shōwa Japan). Tokyo: Chūō kōronsha, 1975.

Ishihara Shintarō and Morita Akio. *"NO" to ieru Nihon: shin Nichi-Bei kankei no kādo* (A Japan that can say "no": a new card for Japan-U.S. relations). Tokyo: Kobunsha, 1989.

Ishiko Jun. *Manga ni miru sensō to heiwa 90-nen.* Tokyo: Horupu shuppan, 1983.

Itazu Tadamasa. "Itazu Tadamasa ni tōji o kiku." *Kinema junpō* 1483 (May 15, 2007): 150–152.

Itō Kimio. "Sengo Nihon otoko no ko bunka no naka no sensō." In *Sengo Nihon no naka no sensō,* ed. Naka Hisao. Tokyo: Sekai shisōsha, 2004.

Iwabuchi, Kōichi. *Recentering Globalization: Popular Culture and Japanese Transnationalism.* Durham, NC: Duke University Press, 2002.

Jameson, Fredric. *Archaeologies of the Future.* London: Verso, 2005.

Jameson, Fredric. *Japanese Film.* London: Kegan Paul International, 1996.

"Japan's PM Apologizes to WW II Era Sex Slaves." Associated Press, March 26, 2007, http://www.msnbc.msn.com/id/17795448/.

Jia Leilei. "Shijian dianying: *Jijie hao*" (*Assembly:* an event film). *Dangdai dianying* (Contemporary cinema) 3 (2008): 4–7.

Jiao Xiongping (Peggy Chiao). *Shidai xianying: Zhongxi dianying lunshu* (Images for the age: essays on Chinese and western cinema). Taibei: Yuanliu, 1998.

Jones, Dorothy B. *The Portrayal of China and India on the American Screen, 1896–1955.* Cambridge, MA: Center for International Studies, Massachusetts Institute of Technology, 1955.

Kaplan, E. Ann. *Trauma Culture: The Politics of Terror and Loss in Media and Literature.* New Brunswick, NJ: Rutgers University Press, 2005.

Kawamura Minato. "Popular Orientalism and the Japanese Views of Asia." In *Reading Colonial Japan: Text, Context and Critique,* ed. Michelle M. Mason and Helen J. S. Lee, 271–298. Stanford, CA: Stanford University Press, 2002.

Kean, Hilda, and Paul Martin, ed. *The Public History Reader.* New York: Routledge, 2013.

Kelts, Roland. *Japanamerica: How Japanese Pop Culture Has Invaded the U.S.* New York: Palgrave Macmillan, 2006.

Kennedy, David M. *Freedom from Fear: The American People in Depression and War, 1929–1945.* New York: Oxford University Press, 1999.

Kim, Dongchun. *War and Society: What Was the Korean War to Us?* Seoul: Tolbegae, 2000.

Kim, Il-myŏn. *Tennō no Guntai Chōsenjin Ianfu* (The emperor's forces and Korean comfort women). Tokyo: San'ichi Shobō, 1976.

Kim, Kyunghak, et al. *Korean War, Community, and Residents' Memories.* Seoul: Hanul Academy, 2005.

Kim, Kyung Hyun. *Virtual Hallyu: Korean Cinema of the Global Era.* Durham, NC: Duke University Press, 2011.

Kim, Suk-Young. *DMZ Crossing: Performing Emotional Citizenship along the Korean Border.* New York: Columbia University Press, 2014.

Kim, Suk-Young. *Illusive Utopia: Theater, Film, and Everyday Performance in North Korea.* Ann Arbor: University of Michigan Press, 2010.

Kitamura, Hiroshi. *Screening Enlightenment: Hollywood and the Cultural Reconstruction of Defeated Japan.* Ithaca, NY: Cornell University Press, 2010.

Kitamura, Masayuki. "War Flick Touting Japan's Role in Indonesia's Birth Irks Jakarta." *Japan Times,* March 27, 2001.

Kobayashi, Yoshinori. *Sensōron* (On war). Tokyo: Gentōsha, 1998.

Kobayashi, Yoshinori. *Taiwan lun* (On Taiwan). Taibei: Qianwei Chubanshe, 2001.

Koppes, Clayton R., and Gregory D. Black. *Hollywood Goes to War: How Politics, Profits, and Propaganda Shaped World War II Movies.* New York: Free Press, 1987.

Korean National Tourism Organization. "Survey Report Outline on Actual Conditions of Hallyu (Korean Fever) Tourism." Republic of Korea Ministry of Culture and Tourism, Seoul, 2004.

Landy, Marcia, ed. *The Historical Film: History and Memory in Media.* New Brunswick, NJ: Rutgers University Press, 2001.

Lee, Hyangjin. *Contemporary Korean Cinema: Identity, Culture, Politics.* Manchester, UK: Manchester University Press, 2000.

Lee, Robert G. *Orientals: Asian Americans in Popular Culture.* Philadelphia: Temple University Press, 1999.

Lentz, Robert J. *Korean War Filmography: 91 English Languages Features through 2000.* Jefferson, NC: McFarland, 2008.

Li, Siu Leung. "Embracing Glocalization and Hong Kong-Made Musical Film." In *China Forever: The Shaw Brothers and Diasporic Cinema,* ed. Poshek Fu, 74–94. Urbana: University of Illinois Press, 2008.

Li Zhongdao. "Zhang Zizhong jingshen yongchui buxiu: Guanshang 'Yinglie qianqiu' you gan" (Long live the undying spirit of Zhang Zizhong: my thoughts on *The Everlasting Glory*). In *Yinglie qianqiu yingping ji* (Collection of reviews of *The Everlasting Glory*). Zhongyang dianying shiye gongsi, 96–99.

Liang Liang. "Taiwan shezhi de kangri dianying." *Dianying biji,* August 22, 2005.

Liang Liang. "Xianggang kangri dianying" (Hong Kong anti-Japanese films). *Dianying biji,* August 23, 2005.

Liu Weihong. "Yu Wu Ziniu tan Wu Ziniu" (An interview with Wu Ziniu). *Dangdai dianying,* no. 4 (1988): 104–113.

London, Jack. *The Iron Heel.* New York: Penguin, 2006.

London, Jack. "The Unparalleled Invasion." In *The Strength of the Strong and Other Stories.* Sandy, UT: Quiet Vision, 2003.

Long Baoshan. "Guojia jingshen jiaoyu" (National spirit education). In *Zhonghua baike quanshu diancangban* (Chinese encyclopedia online). http://ap6.pccu.edu.tw/Encyclopedia/data.asp?id=1620.

Ma Sheng-mei. *Chenmo de shanghen: Rijun weianfu lishi yingxiang shu* (Silent scars: history of sexual slavery by the Japanese military—a pictorial book). Taibei: Shang Zhou Press, 2005.

Marchetti, Gina. *Romance and the "Yellow Peril": Race, Sex, and Discursive Strategies in Hollywood Fiction.* Berkeley: University of California Press, 1994.

Mayor, Federico. *The Multi-Cultural Planet,* ed. Ervin Laszlo. London: Oneworld, 1993.

McLaughlin, Robert L., and Sally F. Parry. *We'll Always Have the Movies.* Lexington: University Press of Kentucky, 2006.

Ministry of Foreign Affairs of Japan. "Joint Declaration: A New Partnership towards the Twenty-First Century." October 8, 1998, www.mofa.go.jp.

Ministry of Foreign Affairs of Japan. "Pop-Culture Diplomacy." August 14, 2014, http://www.mofa.go.jp/policy/culture/exchange/pop/.

Ministry of Foreign Affairs of Japan. "Summary Transcript of 'Japan-Korea Summit Meeting' (in Korea)." July 21–22, 2004.

Mintz, Steven, and Randy W. Roberts, ed. *Hollywood's America: Twentieth-Century American through Film,* 4th ed. Hoboken, NJ: Wiley-Blackwell, 2010.

Miyadai Shinji et al., ed. *Sensōron bōsōron* (Delusions of *On War*). Tokyo: Kyōiku shiryō shuppansha, 1999.

Mizuki Shigeru. *Komikku Shōwashi* (A comic history of Showa Japan)*,* vol. 3: *Nitchū zenmen sensō-taiheiyō sensō kaishi* (The Sino-Japanese War and the Pacific War start). Tokyo: Kōdansha, 2008.

Mizuki Shigeru. *Shiroi hata* (White flag). Tokyo: Kōdansha, 2010.

Mizuki Shigeru. *Sōin gyokusai seyo!* (All toward glorious deaths!). Tokyo: Kōdansha, 1995.

Montes, Rafael Miguel. "*Ghost Recon: Island Thunder:* Cuba in the Virtual Battlescape." In *The Players' Realm: Studies on the Culture of Video Games and Gaming,* ed. J. Patrick Williams and Jonas Heide Smith. Jefferson, NC: McFarland, 2007.

Montgomery, David. "U.S. Mission for Sci Fi Writers: Imagine That." *Washington Post,* May 22, 2009.

Mori, Yoshitaka. "*Winter Sonata* and Cultural Practices of Active Fans in Japan: Considered Middle-Aged Women as Cultural Agents." In *East Asian Pop Culture: Analyzing the Korean Wave,* ed. Chua Beng Huat and Koichi Iwabuchi, 127–141. Hong Kong: Hong Kong University Press, 2008.

Morris-Suzuki, Tessa, and Peter Rimmer. "Virtual Memories: Japanese History and Debates in *Manga* and Cyberspace." *Asian Studies Review* 26, no. 2 (June 2002): 147–164.

Mulvey, Laura. *Visual and Other Pleasures*. London: Palgrave Macmillan, 1989.

Nakamura Hideyuki. "Girei toshite no tokkō eiga: *Otokotachi no Yamato/Yamato no baai*" (Kamikaze Films as Ceremonial Courtesy: The Case of *Yamato*). *Zen'ya* 7 (Spring 2006): 134–137.

Nakamura Hideyuki. "Tokkōtai hyōshōron" (Representing the kamikaze). In *Iwanami kōza: Ajia, Taiheiyō sensō*, vol. 5: *Senjō no shosō* (Iwanami lecture series: the Asian Pacific War, vol. 5: various aspects of the battlefield), 301–330. 2006.

Nakazawa, Keiji. *Barefoot Gen: A Cartoon Story of Hiroshima*. Philadelphia: New Society, 1986.

Napier, Susan. *Anime: From Akira to Princess Mononoke*. New York: Palgrave, 2000.

Neale, Steve. *Genre and Hollywood*. London: Routledge, 2000.

Niizeki Seika. "Aikoku manga kesshitai" (Patriotic comic commandos). In *Maboroshi no sensō manga no jidai*, ed. Akiyama Masami, 162–173. Tokyo: Natsume shobō, 1998.

Nishiyama, George. "Abe Risks Ire by Meeting Son of Indian Judge." Reuters, August 23, 2007.

Nogami Tatsuo. "Watashi ga *Otokotachi no Yamato* no kyakuhonka o orita riyū" (The reasons I withdrew my name as the screenwriter of *Yamato*). *Shinario* 62, no. 1 (2006): 72–75.

Nornes, Abé Markus. "The Body at the Center: The Effects of the Atomic Bomb on Hiroshima and Nagasaki." In *Hibakusha Cinema: Hiroshima, Nagasaki, and the Nuclear Image in Japanese Film*, ed. Mick Broderick, 120–159. London: Keegan Paul, 1996.

Nozaki, Yoshiko. *War Memory, Nationalism and Education in Postwar Japan, 1945–2007: The Japanese History Textbook Controversy and Ienaga Saburo's Court Challenges*. New York: Routledge, 2008.

Obinata Sumio. "Sensōron wa nani wo dō katatte iruka" (What does "On War" talk about, and how does it do so?). In *Kimitachi wa sensō de shineruka: Kobayashi Yoshinori 'sensōron' hihan* (Are you willing to die in a war? critiques of Kobayashi Yoshinori's "On War"), ed. Obinata Sumio, Yamada Akira, and Yamashina Saburō, 28–33. Tokyo: Ōtsuki shoten, 1999.

Odo, Franklin. *No Sword to Bury: Japanese Americans in Hawai'i during World War II*. Philadelphia: Temple University Press, 2004.

Onishi, Norimitsu. "Decades after War Trials, Japan Still Honors a Dissenting Judge." *New York Times*, August 31, 2007.

"Onomichi fan kakutoku ni kōken" (Contributing to acquiring fans of Onomichi). *Chūgoku shinbun*, May 8, 2006.

Pickowicz, Paul G. "Victory as Defeat: Postwar Visualizations of China's War of Resistance." In *Becoming Chinese: Passages to Modernity and Beyond,* ed. Wen-hsin Yeh, 365–398. Berkeley: University of California Press, 2000.

Pok, Kŏ-il. *Pimyŏng ŭl ch'ajasŏ: Kyŏngsŏng, syouwa 62-yŏn* (In search of an epitaph: Keijō, Shōwa Year 62). Seoul: Munhak kwa Chisŏngsa, 1987.

Qu Liping. "Zhanzhengpian xushi moshi jiqi yanbian" (Transformation of narrative patterns in war films). In *Zhongguo dianying zhuanye shi yanjiu: dianying wenhua juan* (Studies in the history of Chinese cinema: The volume on film culture), ed. Yang Yuanying, 195–241. Beijing: Zhongguo dianying chubanshe, 2006.

Rao Shuguang. "*Jijie hao* zai sikao" (Thoughts on *Assembly*). *Dangdai dianying* 3 (2008): 18–21.

Reinhardt, Mark, Holly Edwards, and Erina Duganne, ed. *Beautiful Suffering: Photography and the Traffic of Pain.* Chicago: University of Chicago Press, 2007.

Robertson, Roland. *Globalization: Social Theory and Global Culture.* London: Sage, 1992.

Rosenstone, Robert A. *History on Film/Film on History,* 2nd ed. New York: Routledge, 2012.

Rosenstone, Robert A., ed. *Revisioning History: Film and the Construction of a New Past.* Princeton, NJ: Princeton University Press, 1995.

Rosenzweig, Roy, and David Thelen. "The Presence of the Past: Popular Uses of History in American Life." In *The Public History Reader,* ed. Hilda Kean and Paul Martin, 30–55. New York: Routledge, 2013.

Roth, Philip. *The Plot against America.* New York: Vintage, 2005.

Ryall, Julian. "Raising the Yamato." *Number One Shimbun* 38, no. 2 (February 2006).

Satō Jun'ya and Mori Tatsuya. "*Otokotachi no Yamato* wa hansen eiga ka?" (Is *Yamato* a self-reflective film?). *Shūkan kinyōbi* 588 (January 6, 2006): 8–15.

Satō Kōji. "*Otokotachi no Yamato* o megutte: rekishigaku no shiza kara" (Exploring *Yamato*: from a historiographical perspective). *Kikan sensō sekinin kenkyū* 56 (Summer 2007): 74–80.

Schilling, Mark. *Contemporary Japanese Film.* New York: Weatherhill, 1999.

Schodt, Frederik L. *Manga! Manga! The World of Japanese Comics.* New York: Kodansha International, 1986.

Senda, Kakō. *Jūgun Ianfu* (Military comfort women). Tokyo: San'ichi Shobō, 1973.

Shapiro, Jerome. *Atomic Bomb Cinema: The Apocalyptic Imagination in Film.* New York: Routledge, 2002.

Sharp, Jasper. *Behind the Pink Curtain: The Complete History of Japanese Sex Cinema.* Surrey, UK: Fab Press, 2008.

Shi, Bogong. "The Anti-Japanese Movies from 1932 to 2005." *Contemporary Cinema* 5 (2005): 80–86.

Shih, Shu-mei. *Visuality and Identity: Sinophone Articulations across the Pacific.* Berkeley: University of California Press, 2007.

Shimada Keizō. "The Adventures of Dankichi." In *Reading Colonial Japan: Text, Context and Critique,* ed. Michelle M. Mason and Helen J. S. Lee, 263–270. Stanford, CA: Stanford University Press, 2002.

Shin, Chi-Yun, and Julian Stringer, eds. *New Korean Cinema.* New York: NYU Press, 2005.

Shin, Gi-Wook, and Daniel C. Sneider, ed. *History Textbooks and the Wars in Asia: Divided Memories,* reprint edition. New York: Routledge, 2013.

Shirado Sanpei. *Nanatsu-oke no iwa: Shirado Sanpei ishoku sakuhinshū* (The rock of seven pails: a collection of Shirado Sanpei's unusual works). Tokyo: Shōgakkan, 2000.

Shiu Ruei-mei (Xu Ruimei). *Zhizuo "youda": zhanhou Taiwan dianying zhong de Riben* (A constructed "friend": Japan in postwar Taiwan cinema). New Taibei City: Daw Shiang, 2012.

Silbergeld, Jerome. *Body in Question: Image and Illusion in Two Chinese Films by Director Jiang Wen.* Princeton, NJ: P.Y. and Kinmay W. Tang Center for East Asian Art, Princeton University, 2008.

Soh, Chunghee Sarah. *The Comfort Women: Sexual Violence and Postcolonial Memory in Korea and Japan.* Chicago: University of Chicago Press, 2008.

Standish, Isolde. *Myth and Masculinity in the Japanese Cinema.* Richmond, UK: Curzon, 2000.

Standish, Isolde. *A New History of Japanese Cinema: A Century of Narrative Film.* New York: Continuum, 2005.

Takamura, Kōtarō. *A Brief History of Imbecility: Poetry and Prose of Takamura Kōtarō,* trans. Hiroaki Sato. Honolulu: University of Hawai'i Press, 1992.

Tam, King-fai, Timothy Y. Tsu, and Sandra Wilson, ed. *Chinese and Japanese Films of the Second World War.* London: Routledge, 2014.

Tanaka, Toshiyuki. *Japan's Comfort Women: Sexual Slavery and Prostitution during World War II and the U.S. Occupation.* London: Routledge, 1997.

Tezuka, Osamu. *Adolf.* 5 vols. San Francisco: Viz Media, 1995–1997.

Tezuka, Osamu. "Kanon" (Proper name). In *Sensō manga kessakusen* (The Great War comics selection), 2:19–20. Tokyo: Yōdensha, 2007.

Tezuka, Osamu. "Sukippara no burūsu" (Sukippara blues). In *Sensō manga kessakusen* (The Great War comics selection), 224–231. Tokyo: Yōdensha, 2007.

Thompson, Clive. "Why We Need More Torture in Video Games." *Wired,* December 15, 2008.

Tian, Benxiang, and Shi Bogong. *Kangzhan dianying* (War of Resistance films). Kaifeng: Henan daxue chubanshe, 2005.

Tierney, Robert. *Tropics of Savagery: The Culture of Japanese Empire in Comparative Frame*. Berkeley: University of California Press, 2010.

Todd, Brett. "*Hearts of Iron II: Doomsday* Review." *GameSpot*. April 11, 2006, http://www.gamespot.com/pc/strategy/heartsofironiidoomsday/review.html, accessed June 15, 2009.

Treat, John Whittier. *Writing Ground Zero: Japanese Literature and the Atomic Bomb*. Chicago: University of Chicago Press, 1995.

Trouillot, Michel-Rolph. *Silencing the Past: Power and the Production of History*. Boston: Beacon Press, 1995.

Tsutsui, William M., and Michiko Ito, ed. *In Godzilla's Footsteps: Japanese Pop Culture Icons on the Global Stage*. New York: Palgrave Macmillan, 2006.

Turtledove, Harry. *Days of Infamy*. New York: Roc Books, 2005.

Turtledove, Harry. *End of the Beginning*. New York: Roc Books, 2006.

Usui, Chizuru, et al., ed. *The Guide to Japanese Film Industry and Co-Production 2009*, trans. Ben Dimagmaliw. Tokyo: UNIJAPAN, 2009.

Van Kranenburg, Rob. "Tom Clancy." In *St. James Encyclopedia of Pop Culture*. Farmington Hills, MI: Gale Group, 1999.

Vasey, Ruth. *The World According to Hollywood, 1918–1939*. Madison: University of Wisconsin Press, 1997.

Vinton, Arthur. *Looking Further Backward, Being a Series of Lectures Delivered to the Freshman Class at Shawmut College by Professor Won Lung Li*. Albany, NY: Albany Book Company, 1890.

Virilio, Paul. *War and Cinema*. New York: Verso, 1986.

Wakabayashi, Bob Tadashi. "The Nanking 100-Man Killing Contest Debate: War Guilt amid Fabricated Illusions, 1971–75." *Journal of Japanese Studies* 26, no. 2 (2000): 307–340.

Wakakuwa Midori. "Jendā no shiten de yomitoku sengo eiga: *Otokotachi no Yamato* o chūshin ni" (Reading postwar war films from a gender perspective: focusing on *Yamato*). *Tōzai nanboku* (2007): 6–17.

Walker, Janet. *Trauma Cinema: Documenting Incest and the Holocaust*. Berkeley: University of California Press, 2005.

Wang, Ban. *Illuminations from the Past: Trauma, Memory, and History in Modern China*. Stanford, CA: Stanford University Press, 2004.

Wang Chaoguang. "Kangri zhanzheng lishi de yingxiang jiyi: yi zhanhou Zhongguo dianying wei zhongxin" (Visual memories of the history of the War of Resistance Against Japan: with a focus on postwar Chinese films). *Xueshu yanjiu* 6 (2005): 91–100.

Wang Dao. "Yangzijiang fengyun." *Zhongguo dianying zhipianchang*, 102–106.

Wang Yan. "*Nanjing:* lishi jiyi yu zhenshi zaixian" (*Nanjing:* historical memory and truthful representation). *Waiguo wenxue* 2008, no. 1: 79–83.

Williams, Kevin. *Understanding Media Theory.* New York: Oxford University Press, 2003.

Winter, Jay. *Remembering War: The Great War Between Memory and History in the Twentieth Century.* New Haven, CT: Yale University Press, 2006.

Winter, Stuart. "Can Science Fiction Beat Bin Laden?" *Daily Express,* June 3, 2007, http://www.express.co.uk/posts/view/8730/Can+science+fiction+beat +Bin+Laden/, accessed June 15, 2009.

Wong, Lily. "Sinophone Erotohistories: The Shaw Brothers' Queering of a Transforming 'Chinese Dream' in Ainu Fantasies." In *Queer Sinophone Cultures*, ed. Howard Chiang and Ari Larissa Heinrich, 84-101. New York: Routledge, 2014.

Wu Hao. *Disan leixing dianying* (Shaw films: alternative cult films). Hong Kong: Celestial Pictures Limited, 2004.

Wu Junhui. "Xin Qi fantalu: lishi, ziwo, xiju, dianying" (Interview with Xin Qi: history, my life, theatre and film). In *Taiyupian shidai* (The age of Taiwanese-language cinema), ed. Dianying ziliaoguan koshu dianyingshi xiaozu, 109–145. Taibei: Taibei Film Archive, 1994.

Wu Ziniu. "Pai *Guoge* de chuzhong" (My original intention in shooting *The National Anthem*). *Dangdai dianying* 5 (1999): 5–6.

Xing, Jun. *Asian America through the Lens: History, Representations, and Identity.* Lanham, MD: Altamira Press, 1998.

Xue Huiling and Wu Junhui, ed. "Taiyu pian pianmu" (Taiwanese-language filmography). In *Taiyu pian shidai* (The age of Taiwanese-language cinema), ed. Dianying ziliaoguan koshu dianyingshi xiaozu, 309–384. Taibei: Taibei Film Archive, 1994.

Yamagami Tatsuhiko. *Hikari no kaze* (The shining wind). Tokyo: Shōgakkan, Creative Imprint, 2008.

Yang, Daqing. "The Malleable and the Contested: The Nanjing Massacre in Postwar China and Japan." In *Perilous Memories: The Asia-Pacific War(s)*, ed. Takashi Fujitani, Geoffrey White, and Lisa Yoneyama, 50–86. Durham, NC: Duke University Press, 2001.

Yang, Mayfair. "Mass Media and Transnational Subjectivity in Shanghai: Notes on (Re)cosmopolitanism in a Chinese Metropolis." In *Undergrounded Empires: The Cultural Politics of Modern Chinese Transnationalism*, ed. Aihwa Ong and Donald Nonini, 287–319. New York: Routledge, 1997.

Yeh, Emilie Yueh-yu. *Gesheng moying: Gequ xushi yu zhongwendianying* (Phantom of the music: song narration and Chinese-language cinema). Taibei: Yuanliu, 2000.

Yoshida, Mitsuru. *Requiem for Battleship Yamato*. Seattle: University of Washington Press, 1985.

Yoshida, Seiji. *Chōsenjin Ianfu to Nihinjin* (Korean comfort women and the Japanese). Tokyo: Shinjinbutsuōraisha, 1977.

Yoshida, Seiji. *Watashi no Sensō Hanzai* (My war crimes). Tokyo: San'ichi Shobō, 1983.

Yoshida, Takashi. *The Making of the "Rape of Nanking": History and Memory in Japan, China, and the United States*. New York: Oxford University Press, 2006.

Yoshimoto, Mitsuhiro. "Melodrama, Postmodernism, and Japanese Cinema." *East West Film Journal* 5, no. 1 (1991): 28–55.

Yu, Mo-wan (Yu Muyun). "The Relationship between Chinese Films and Hong Kong Films." In *Huayu dianying lishi yantaohui lunwenji* (Symposium on Chinese film history), 1–19. Taibei: Taibei Film Archive, 2003.

Yu Yeying. *Cuican guangying suiyue: Zhongyang dianying gongsi jishi* (The glorious age of cinema: a historical record of Central Motion Picture Corporation). Taibei: Zhongyang dianying shiye gufen youxian gongsi, 2002.

Zhang Junxiang and Cheng Jihua, ed. *Zhongguo dianying da cidian* (Encyclopedia of Chinese cinema). Shanghai: Shanghai cishu chubanshe, 1995.

Zhang, Rui. *The Cinema of Feng Xiaogang: Commercialization and Censorship in Chinese Cinema after 1989*. Hong Kong: Hong Kong University Press, 2008.

Zhang, Yingjin. *Chinese National Cinema*. London: Routledge, 2004.

Zhang, Yingjin. *Cinema, Space, and Polylocality in a Globalizing China*. Honolulu: University of Hawai'i, 2009.

Zhang, Yingjin. *"Evening Bell:* Wu Ziniu's Visions of History, War and Humanity." In *Chinese Films in Focus: 25 New Takes,* ed. Chris Berry, 81–88. London: British Film Institute, 2003.

Zhang, Yingjin. *Screening China: Critical Interventions, Cinematic Reconfigurations, and the Transnational Imaginary in Contemporary Chinese Cinema*. Ann Arbor: Center for Chinese Studies, University of Michigan, 2002.

Zhang, Yingjin. "Zhao Dan: Spectrality of Martyrdom and Stardom." *Journal of Chinese Cinema* 2, no. 2 (2008): 103–111.

Zhang, Yingjin, and Zhiwei Xiao. *Encyclopedia of Chinese Film*. London: Routledge, 1998.

Zhao Min and Lu Ye. "Wenhua shenfen de shengcheng yu zaizao: cong 'Shayang zhizhong' dao 'Yueguang xiaoyuqu'" (The creation and reconstruction of cultural identity: From "Sayon's Bell" to "Moonlight Serenade"). *Xinwen daxue* 1 (2007): 75, 116–121.

Zhongyang dianying shiye gongsi, ed. *Yinglie qianqiu yinping ji* (Collection of reviews of *The Everlasting Glory*). Taibei: Zhongyang dianying shiye gongsi, 1973.

Zhongguo dianying zhipianchang, ed. *Yangzijiang fengyun yingpingji*. Taibei: Zhongguo dianying zhipianchang, 1969.

Zhongguo dianying ziliaoguan, ed. *Zhongguo wusheng dianying juben* (Screenplays of Chinese silent films), vol. 1. Beijing: Zhongguo dianying chubanshe, 1996.

Zhou Zhengbao and Zhang Dong. "Zhanzheng pian yu Zhongguo kangzhan ticai gushi pian" (War films and Chinese feature films dealing with the anti-Japanese war). *Wenyi yanjiu* 5 (1995): 13–20.

Zhu Deilan. *Taiwan wei'anfu* (Taiwanese comfort women). Taibei: Wunan, 2009.

Contributors

Michael Berry is professor of contemporary Chinese cultural studies at the University of California, Santa Barbara. He is the author of *Boiling the Sea: Cinematic Memories of Hou Hsiao-hsien; Speaking in Images: Interviews with Contemporary Chinese Filmmakers; A History of Pain: Trauma in Modern Chinese Literature and Film;* and *Jia Zhangke's Hometown Trilogy.* He is also the translator of several novels, including *The Song of Everlasting Sorrow* (with Susan Chan Egan); *To Live, Nanjing 1937: A Love Story;* and *Wild Kids: Two Novels about Growing Up.*

David Desser is professor emeritus of cinema studies, University of Illinois. He is the author of *The Samurai Films of Akira Kurosawa* and *Eros Plus Massacre: An Introduction to the Japanese New Wave Cinema;* the co-author of *American Jewish Filmmakers;* the editor of *Ozu's Tokyo Story;* and co-editor of numerous other books, including *Reframing Japanese Cinema: Authorship, Genre, History; Cinematic Landscapes: Observations on the Visual Arts of China and Japan; Hollywood Goes Shopping; The Cinema of Hong Kong: History, Arts, Identity.*

Aaron Gerow is professor of Japanese cinema in the Film Studies Program and the Department of East Asian Languages and Cultures at Yale University. He is the author of *Kitano Takeshi, A Page of Madness;* and *Visions of Japanese Modernity: Articulations of Cinema, Nation, and Spectatorship, 1895–1925.* He is also co-author (with Abe Mark Nornes) of the *Research Guide to Japanese Film Studies.*

Eric Hayot is professor of comparative literature and director of the Asian Studies Program at Penn State University. He is the author of *On Literary Worlds, Chinese Dreams,* and *The Hypothetical Mandarin: Sympathy, Modernity, and Chinese Pain.* He is also the co-editor of *Sinographies: Writing China* and general editor for the "Global Asias" book series at Oxford University Press.

Kyu Hyun Kim is associate professor of Japanese and Korean history at the University of California, Davis. He is the author of *The Age of Visions and Arguments: Parliamentarianism and the National Public Sphere in Early Meiji Japan.* Kim also serves as the academic adviser and resident film reviewer for www.koreanfilm.org.

Hyangjin Lee is professor of sociology in the College of Intercultural Communication at Rikkyo University, Japan, and an honorary researcher in East Asian culture at the

University of Sheffield. She is the author of *Contemporary Korean Cinema: Identity, Culture and Politics.* She has worked as the director of the UK Korean Film Festival since 2001.

Wenchi Lin is professor and the chair of the English Department at Central University, Taiwan. He is the author of *Exploring the Nation of Cinema: Wenchi Lin's Film Writings* and *Allegory and National Identity in Chinese Cinema* and the co-editor of *Passionate Detachment: The Films of Hou Hsiao-hsien, The Voice of Taiwan Cinema,* along with several other collections on film and visual culture. Lin is also the author of numerous articles and the translator of several books. He is also active in the Taiwan film community as an editor, juror, and consultant and has provided audio commentary for several important contemporary Taiwan films. Since 2013 he has served as director of the Chinese Taipei Film Archive.

Chiho Sawada is executive director of the Asia Pacific Peace Studies Institute and associate professor of history and peace studies at Holy Names University. The author or editor of numerous articles, he has served as associate editor of the *Journal of Korean Studies* and is currently editor-in-chief of the Japan Policy Research Institute and the *Asia Pacific Peace Studies* journal. He has also helped launch and served as consultant to Asian film festivals in Austin and San Francisco.

Robert Brent Toplin is professor emeritus of history at the University of North Carolina at Wilmington. Toplin has published a dozen books, including *Michael Moore's Fahrenheit 9/11: How One Film Divided a Nation; Reel History: In Defense of Hollywood; History by Hollywood: The Use and Abuse of the American Past; Ken Burns's The Civil War: Historians Respond;* and *Oliver Stone's USA: Film, History, and Controversy.* Toplin has been a principal creator of historical dramas that appeared nationally on PBS Television and the Disney Channel, including *Denmark Vesey's Rebellion, Solomon Northup's Odyssey,* and *Charlotte Forten's Mission.*

Lily Wong is an assistant professor in the Department of Literature at American University. She has published articles in journals including *Asian Cinema, Pacific Affairs,* and *China Review International,* and book chapters in *World Cinema and the Visual Arts* (Anthem Press, 2012) and *Queer Sinophone Cultures* (Routledge, forthcoming). She is currently completing a book manuscript on cultural representations of prostitution in Chinese, Sinophone, and Asian-American communities.

Yingjin Zhang is director of the Chinese Studies Program and professor of Chinese literature and film, comparative literature, and cultural studies at the University of California, San Diego. He is the author of *The City in Modern Chinese Literature and Film: Configurations of Space; Time, and Gender; Screening China: Critical Interventions, Cinematic Reconfigurations, and the Transnational Imaginary* *in Contemporary Chinese Cinema;* and *Chinese National Cinema;* co-author of *Encyclopedia of Chinese Film;* editor of *A Companion to Chinese Cinema, China in a Polycentric World: Essays in Chinese Comparative Literature,* and *Cinema and Urban Culture in Shanghai, 1922–1943;* and co-editor of *From Underground to Independent: Alternative Film Culture in Contemporary China.*

Index

Note: Page numbers in **boldface** type refer to illustrations.